HERK: *Hero of the Skies*

Larlin Corporation
Marietta, Georgia
1986

Joseph E. Dabney

HERK: *Hero of the Skies*

THE STORY OF THE LOCKHEED C-130 AND ITS ADVENTURES AROUND THE WORLD . . . FROM ASHIYA TO XINGU AND A FEW THOUSAND SPOTS IN BETWEEN . . . TIMBUCTU . . . YELLOWKNIFE . . . RODRIQUEZ DE MENDOZA . . . KATMANDU . . . SUCUA . . . DEADHORSE . . . LEH . . . ADANA . . . UMIAT . . . DOME CHARLIE . . . PLEIKU . . . EN-TEBBE . . . TARAPOTO . . . STANLEYVILLE . . . N'DOLA . . . ANTA . . . BOAVISTA . . . CHING CHUAN KANG . . .

Library of Congress Cataloging-in-Publication Data

Dabney, Joseph Earl.
  Herk: hero of the skies.

  Includes index.
  1. Hercules (Turboprop transports)   I. Title.
[UG1242.T7D3   1986]   358.4'4   84-14330
ISBN 0-89783-039-3
ISBN 0-89783-028-8 (pbk.)

Manufactured in the United States of America

ISBN: 0-89783-028-8 (Paper)
ISBN: 0-89783-039-3 (Hardback)
(Previously ISBN: 0-932298-16-8)

Printing History
    First Printing – June 1979 – 9000 copies
    Second Printing – September 1979 – 5000 copies
    Third Printing – August 1980 – 2000 copies
    Fourth Printing (Paperback) – September 1981 – 2000 copies
    Fifth Printing (Paperback) – June 1982 – 2000 copies
    Sixth Printing (Paperback) – April 1983 – 2000 copies
    Revised Edition (Paperback) – December 1986 – 2000 copies

Published by arrangement with
Copple House Books, Inc., Lakemont, GA

Larlin Corporation
P.O. Box 1523, Marietta, GA 30061

To the people of
Lockheed - Georgia:
Airplane Builders Supreme

ACKNOWLEDGEMENTS

When I launched the research for this Hercules biography as a spare time project, I realized that the task was formidable. After all, how can one adequately tell the worldwide story of an airplane so peripatetic and multitalented as the C-130?

Indeed, it was a massive undertaking. But the task was made much easier, thanks to the help of scores of people around the world, who responded so generously to my written and phoned appeals for help.

First of all, I wish to express deep thanks for the tremendous cooperation and assistance I have received from C-130 crewmen, past and present, in the U.S. Air Force and other services and nations which operate the Hercules.

Next, I must express my gratitude to Lockheed, its engineers, flight crewmen, technical support people and other experts who willingly shared their expertise, their records and photographs.

To my bosses over the past 21 years, Everett Hayes and Lee Rogers, I am particularly grateful. Their counsel and support during the various stages of the book's development were very helpful.

To the publisher of Copple House Books, Ed O'Neal, I am particularly appreciative. He showed confidence and enthusiasm for *Herk* from the time he saw the first few chapters and his enthusiasm is reflected in the care and attention he has devoted to its production. And to my new publisher, Ken Boyd of Larlin Corporation, my sincere thanks for giving *Herk* new life with this new edition.

Lastly, my appreciation is extended to Hercules operators worldwide who indeed have made the *Herk* an international instrument of humanitarian good will.

J.E.D.

July 1, 1986

The author acknowledges with appreciation permission to quote from the following books and magazines: Chapter 2, The Sunday Telegraph, *by permission of the author, Duff Hart-Davis, and* AIRMAN *magazine; Chapter 3,* LONG ARM OF AMERICA, *by permission of the author, Martin Caidin; Chapter 7, from* AIR CLASSICS *magazine, by permission of the author, H.G. Maxwell, and the* Redlands, Calif., Daily Facts; *Chapter 8,* AIRMAN *magazine; Chapter 10,* National Geographic; *Chapter 11,* TIME *magazine, Bantam Books, Inc.,* 90 Minutes at Entebbe; *Chapter 12, Canadian Aviation magazine; Chapter 13,* TIME *magazine,* The Atlanta Journal, The Armed Forces Journal *and* The Atlanta Constitution; *Chapter 14,* TAC ATTACK, *and* Philadelphia Inquirer.

The author also acknowledges several articles and books which provided background for two of the chapters in this history. The book, "111 Days at Stanleyville," by Reader's Digest *Roving Editor David Reed and published in 1965 by Harper and Row, New York, was particularly helpful in developing the chapter, "Rescue Mission to Stanleyville." In the chapter, "Thunderball: Miracle at Entebbe," helpful background source material was contained in several publications: "90 Minutes at Entebbe," by William Stevenson, published in 1976 by Bantam Books, Inc., New York; "Entebbe Rescue," by Yeshayahu Ben-Porat, Eitan Haber and Zeev Schiff, published in 1976 by Dell Publishing Co., Inc., New York, and copyrighted 1976 by Zmora, Bitan, Modan Publishers, Tel Aviv, and articles on the Entebbe rescue published in* The London Observer, New York *magazine,* Newsweek *magazine and* TIME *magazine.*

FOREWORD

It was February of 1963 and icy Himalayan winds whipped down the narrow valleys at Leh, in India's Ladakh province.

Nestled between barren mountains sat Leh's two-mile high "uphill" runway—the aerial staging area for India's forces then fighting to defend their northern borders against the Chinese. The tide of battle was turning, thanks to a dozen intrepid C-130 transports and their crews which were put to New Delhi's disposal by President John F. Kennedy.

At a shack beside Leh's windswept runway, U.S. Air Force Second Lieutenant James P. Morgan, taking a break from his airlift chores, chugalugged his cup of hot tea and goat's milk, zipped up his flight jacket and turned to go to his airplane.

The pilot stopped in his tracks when he noticed an aged, weathered Tibetan standing reverently ahead of him, five feet from the airplane. The old man was staring intently at the winged aluminum behemoth, an odd-looking machine with a black pinocchio nose and three-story high scorpion tail.

In respect to the elderly visitor, Lieutenant Morgan himself stood in silence, savoring the moment. Obviously the old man never before in his life had seen an airplane up close.

"He was dressed in native clothing, a heavy fur coat with a fur collar, baggy pants tucked into crude leather boots and that strange pointy hat that dropped sharply from the peak to the up-curl about ear level.

"As I watched, he took a few steps forward, reached out his hand and touched the skin of the C-130 before quickly withdraw-

9

ing it. Satisfied no harm had come to him, he drew closer and once more placed his hand on the aircraft, this time leaving it there as he measured the texture and feel with a small rotary motion.

"About that time, he noticed me watching and drew back with a shy smile on his face."

Jim Morgan, now a U.S. Air Force lieutenant colonel, often imagines what happened to the old man and wonders what stories

he has told of the shiny big bird that landed in Leh and that he encountered in his travels.

On Alaska's North Slope, oilfield roustabouts call her the "flying dump truck."

In Antarctica, she is "a huge bobsled with wings."

South Americans have dubbed her "the flying jeep."

People in the Middle East refer to her as "air camel."

In Southeast Asia, the affectionate title she has received is "Klong Bird," a reference to the network of canals that connect countries.

U.S. Air Force pilots call her a lot of things . . . "Hercules Hilton" and "Herky Bird" among others and, when outsiders are not listening, "the screaming green and brown trash hauler."

Over the world, the clichés are endless. . ."jet age workhorse" . . ."Herky the hefty". . . "bulldozer with wings". . . and "angel of mercy." To airlines and governments, "tramp steamer of the sky" is a designation often used.

But the name she received at her christening — *Hercules,* Herk for short — perhaps sums up better than any other what she is about. . . a rugged aerial weightlifter of men and material whose labors are legendary and whose versatility seems endless.

The Lockhead C-130 Hercules is, indeed, an airplane for all seasons that in a brief 25 years has become a legend in her own time and probably the most versatile air machine ever to take to the skies.

And yet the superlatives do not stop there. This is the airplane that has blossomed into more than thirty *known* versions. . . that is being flown by operators in over 57 countries representing every continent on earth. . . that has performed so many unusual missions in so many places that it would be virtually impossible to catalogue them all. . . a plane that holds the world record for continuous production of a four-engine cargo/personnel transport (with a total of now more than 1,540 produced). . . a plane the world-wide fleet of which is accumulating flight hours at the impressive rate of 63,000 hours per month (with total flight time already exceeding seventeen million hours).

How can one adequately salute such an airplane?

Perhaps it is best that we leave this job to the Hercules, herself, who has brought and continues to bring cheer and hope to people around the world, swooping out of the skies as a graceful angel of mercy. Hercules has played this role well — saving lives of earthquake victims in Iran, Italy, Morocco, Peru and Turkey; flying UN troops to maintain peace in Africa, the Middle East, Cyprus and Bangladesh; aiding famine and cholera victims in sub-Sahara Africa, Bangladesh, Ethiopia, Nepal and Pakistan; airdropping food and supplies to snow-bound regions of Japan; bringing food, shelter and doctors to victims of tidal waves in the Bay of Bengal and Chile, and typhoons in the Philippines, Australia, Guam and Japan; and, more recently, giving aid to victims of disastrous floods and snow and ice storms in the United States. Her work has been honored with stamps issued by Indonesia, Ascension Island, and the Ross Dependency. An inlet and névé have been named in her honor in Antarctica and a mountain in Morocco, where she rushed in to help victims of the Agadir earthquake.

Perhaps the aircraft to be saluted should be the first operational C-130, Air Force tail number 5023, which, amazingly is still on duty, flying with the Air Force Reserve at O'Hare International Airport, Chicago, as a transport and training aircraft. Number 5023, the "City of Ardmore," was delivered to the Air Force's Tactical Air Command (463rd Troop Carrier Wing) at Ardmore AFB, Oklahoma, on December 9, 1956. In the intervening 29 years, the airplane has seen action in Europe, Japan, Africa and Okinawa and was in the thick of the Vietnam war effort as a hefty hauler of troops and cargo.

The story of the first operational C-130 reflects the theme that recurs throughout this book — that of endurance and self-renewal. It is only now that many of the "A" model C-130s are being considered for retirement. Subsequent C-130 models, longer lived even than the first, will be with us for many years to come. Current "H" models likely will be flying well into the 21st century. (Lockheed's production line, meanwhile, continues to hum, turning out Herk's at the rate of three per month!)

That's the story that I have tried to capture and tell in this expanded and updated volume — a virtually never-ending saga of humanitarian performance and endurance. When the story of the Herk will end is impossible to forecast or even speculate. But now, while her many heroic deeds are still hot and fresh on the memory, let us get them down in print, to preserve for generations yet to come.

Joseph Earl Dabney
Atlanta, Georgia
July 1, 1986

CONTENTS

I

THE 'CAN-DO' AIRLIFTER

She's a real draft horse.

—Jim Hunt,
Lockheed Tech Rep

RESCUE MISSION TO STANLEYVILLE

> I salute with gratitude the crews
> of the United States Air Force.
>
> — King Baudouin

> It was a new milestone in the
> precision employment of tactical air-
> power.
>
> — General John P. McConnell
> Chief of Staff, U.S. Air Force

Tuesday morning, November 24, 1964:

Twelve silver C-130E Lockheed Hercules, bearing U.S. Air Force star emblems on their wings, sliced silently through the moonlit, predawn skies four miles high over central Africa. Their immediate destination: Basoko, where the Congo and Aruwimi Rivers converge.

Seventy miles to the north, another Hercules was in the air—a "talking bird" bearing Colonel Clayton Isaacson of the U.S. Strike Command, overall commander of the top secret mission, "DRAGON ROUGE."* Thus began one of the most dramatic mercy missions of modern times—the rescue of over 1,600 civilians being held hostage by outlaw rebel forces in the northern Congo.

The first five aircraft, "Chalk One" through "Chalk Five," carried 320 Red Berets of Belgium's elite First Paracommando Reg-

*i.e., "Red Dragon"

17

iment. Among the 64 paratroopers in the lead plane was their commander, Colonel Charles Laurent, 51, a scrappy, battle tough soldier with 1,000 jumps to his credit. He would be one of the first to jump.

Also aboard Chalk One was the airlift chief, U.S. Air Force Colonel Burgess Gradwell, 45, commander of Detachment 1 of the famed 322nd Air Division at Evreux AFB, France. No stranger to the Congo, Gradwell was a can-do airlift expert whose C-124 "Old Shaky" survived 21 hits from ground fire in a 1961 UN supply flight to Elizabethville, Katanga.

Armada of C-130Es pictured on Ascension Island on Thursday, November 18, 1964, the day after they reached the rocky island in the Atlantic on a long flight from Belgium via Spain. On Ascension, the Belgian Red Berets had a few days to relax on the ground before flying to the Congo. But much of their time was spent in practicing jumping from the C-130. (All photos in this chapter courtesy of USAF).

After the Red Berets cleared the field of automobile bodies and steel drums filled with water, (top photo), the first C-130s were able to land.

Seven other C-130s flew 30 minutes behind, in 30-second intervals, bearing more troops and equipment. Chalk Six and Seven bore four radio jeeps and four armored jeeps. Aircraft eight and nine carried 64 paratroopers each. Number 10 had aboard two dozen three-wheel "weasels," fast, light personnel carriers. Chalk 12 was a flying hospital, carrying 600 pounds of medicines, plus equipment, stretchers and a flight surgeon, Dr. Robert O. May.

At 5:30 a.m., the radar scopes in the Herk flight stations picked up the two big rivers converging at Basoko. The four-engine propjets, following Capt. Warren "Huey" Long in Chalk One, banked to the left in a wide, sweeping circle. They were tightening up for a closer formation.

To the northeast, Colonel Isaacson looked out from his "talking bird" and liked what he saw. Except for a few isolated thunderclouds, the sky was relatively clear. The moon painted the skies with a luminous, golden glow. Below, endless miles of rain forests stretched to the horizon.

"Press on," Isaacson radioed Gradwell.

The first five C-130s, flying at 21,000 feet, pointed toward Stanleyville 100 miles upriver, and began diving to 5,000 feet. For the last 25 miles, they would be down to 700 feet for a "close look" skim at 280 miles per hour on a course that would take them right over the runway of Stanleyville's old Sabena Airport, hard by the Congo River.

*　　*　　*

The violence against the Americans in Stanleyville began on Tuesday, August 11, 1964, at the American Consulate, a red-roofed white villa overlooking the white rapids of the Congo River's Stanley Falls.

Michael Hoyt, a tall, black-haired Chicagoan who had come into Stanleyville two weeks earlier as temporary U.S. Consul, was standing outside, directing a Belgian carpenter who was repairing the flagpole.

A carload of rebel Simbas, outlaws to the legitimate government, roared into the driveway, jumped out with automatic weapons and ordered the Americans to sit on the consulate steps. In addition to Hoyt, they were the Vice Consul, David Grinwis, and three radio operators, Ernest Houle, Donald Parkes and James Stauffer. All the other consular people had been evacuated by air the night before, less than an hour before the rebels marched into Stanleyville single file, chanting "Mai, Mai," and swinging palm branches from side to side.

Two of the Simbas drove off, returning with Lambert Nasor, a tough-talking major whose pride and joy was the black mane of a lion that dangled from his hat.

The Simbas poked the backs of the Americans with their rifle butts and ran Hoyt into the building, forcing him to open a safe. Outside, Hoyt's aides were ordered to stand rigidly at attention with two U.S. flags. A Simba dashed out with small American flags meant for consular cars and stuffed them into the mouths of the foursome. "Mangez, Mangez" (eat, eat), the Simbas yelled. (Chew as they might, the Americans made only slight dents in the tough fabric.)

After pushing the five captives around inside the consulate, the rebels loaded them into a truck and hauled them to Camp Ketele, on the southern edge of the city.

There, more than a thousand Simba soldiers and dependents—many high on hemp and primed with anti-American propaganda—swarmed around the truck, screaming for blood.

"Dance for us!" they yelled. The Americans climbed down and jumped and skipped around. Their feet were clubbed all the while by the screaming onlookers. During the uproar, the major with the black lion mane shouted angrily, "American troops are fighting us in the Congo!"

The Americans were ushered into the courtroom. The rebel dictator, General Nicolas Olenga, tall and mustachioed and wearing the uniform of a Belgian Army officer, was seated at the rostrum.

He apologized to the Americans for the bruises they had received. "You've been beaten?" he asked sheepishly, as if unaware of what had happened. He then declared:

"I have decided that I do not want to break diplomatic relations with America. You won't be expelled. We want you to remain in Stanleyville and operate normally. We'll give you whatever protection you need."

* * *

For 111 days, the beautiful little city of Stanleyville, carved out of the dark jungle and straddling the Congo River, was in the grip of the Simbas. Simba means "lion" in Swahili, and the rebels had taken this as their symbol. Many wore lion manes on their caps and hats.

The reign of terror was intense. The former mayor was strung up at the Lumumba monument, his heart and liver ripped out. He died an agonizing death while Simbas laughingly ate his flesh. Every day, the steps to "the monument"—a life-size portrait of the late Patrice Lumumba on a small bandstand in the city park—absorbed fresh blood of loyal Congolese citizens who had worked for or cooperated even slightly with the central government of the newly-independent nation. The daily executions did not stop there. Even those citizens with something of an education were put to cruel deaths. Before the bloodshed ceased, thousands of the Congo's most educated citizens were executed by the upstarts.

At first Stanleyville's 1,600 foreigners—including 29 Americans, 500 Belgians, 400 other Europeans and 400 Indians and Pakistanis—thought they were safe. But soon they found their situation precarious. The beatings of the American diplomats on August 11th was only the prelude. Suddenly, all of the foreigners had become hostages—pawns.

On September 5th, the American consul and his four aides were thrown into Stanleyville's Central Prison. For the foreigners, it was the beginning of three months of terror, including beatings, rapes and humiliations.

*   *   *

In Addis Ababa, Premier Tshombe appealed to his African neighbors to send him support to put down the rebellion that was savagely destroying the chosen leaders of the fledgling nation. No help was offered. When he returned to his capital city of Leopoldville, he told intimates he had reached the end of his options. To save his nation from anarchy, he was thinking of calling on mercenaries who perhaps could help his loyal troops retake those regions of his nation seized by the Simbas.

*   *   *

Throughout September and October, all across Stanleyville and northeast Congo, foreigners of more than 20 nationalities were beaten by the rebels and put under house arrest in hotels, military bases and at the Stanleyville airport. On October 9th, the five American consulate officials were seized in their rooms at the Congo Palace Hotel (where they were under house arrest) and were taken by truck to the Central Prison. It was their third time to be incarcerated in the prison, a dark, dank building which also served as an insane asylum. Wild Lingala cries reverberated across the courtyard at night. "Kill the Americans . . . Kill the Americans," the lunatics chanted. Shrill anti-American statements were issued daily over Radio Stanleyville, much of it by the rebel "president," Christopher Gbenye, who declared all Americans and Belgians were "prisoners of war."

On October 23, the jailed Americans received a compatriot cellmate—Paul E. Carlson, 36, a physician missionary from Redondo Beach, California. Carlson was destined to become an international figure before the Congo drama ended. He was arrested by Simbas for owning a radio, was accused of spying and was taken by Gbenye to Stanleyville where he was put on public display as a captured "U.S. Army major." But to the 100,000 Congolese around Wasolo, "the lost corner" of northern Congo, he was "Monganga Paul"—Doctor Paul. The people came to him from over the province, seeking his aid, walking along jungle paths or paddling down the rivers in dugout canoes. Carlson took his family to safety across the border in the Central Africa Republic but he himself returned to Wasolo, refusing to turn his back on the lepers and other people whom he knew needed his help.

As the escalation against foreigners continued, General Olenga bloodied the nose of the Belgian Consul, Baron Patrick Nothcomb, and forced him to tape a message over Stanleyville Radio. The Belgians and Americans were being held hostage, Nothcomb said in the broadcast, under duress, and would be freed only if the U.S. and Belgium stopped their support of the Tshombe government.

*   *   *

In Washington, Belgian Premier Paul Henri Spaak personally appealed to Averell Harriman and Secretary of State Rusk. Belgium wanted to rescue the hostages, whose situation was daily becoming more desperate, and they needed help. The plea went immediately to President Johnson, who on November 3rd had won election to a four-year term.

* * *

On Sunday evening, November 15, Colonel Burgess Gradwell arrived at Chateauroux, France, headquarters of the 322nd Air Division, after a harried drive from Evreux. He had been summoned for an emergency, top secret meeting with his boss, the commander of the 322nd, Brig. General Robert D. Forman.

The general handed Gradwell a large, brown envelope marked DRAGON ROUGE.

"Better pack your bags, boy," General Forman told him, "It looks like you're going."

As Gradwell peeked inside, his eyes bulged. It was a contingency plan calling for a joint Belgian-American military rescue mission deep into the Congo. The Tshombe Government in Leopoldville had given the green light for the project. The U.S. Air

It was "first light" when the C-130s swooped in over Stanleyville's old Sabena airport. The first five aircraft dropped 320 Belgian paras. Colonel Burgess Gradwell, the airlift commander, circled overhead at 2,000 feet in "Chalk One." Later in the day, the plane, piloted by Capt. "Huey" Long, was struck by ground fire and had to head back to Kamina with fuel streaming from a fuel tank.

The first Red Beret to parachute onto Stanleyville airport was the paras' commander, Col. Charles Laurent, pictured (top photo) in the middle on one of the Belgian's three-wheeled "weasels." A number of the unique little "Army Goat" vehicles were brought in with the C-130s which subsequently landed. Lower photo, Belgian paras fan out into Stanleyville in the lightning humanitarian rescue mission.

Force, with its new C-130E Hercules, would handle the airlift part of the humanitarian operation. Belgium's First Parachutist Battalion of the Paracommando Regiment would carry out the para-drop and rescue strike into Stanleyville. The action was contingent on final approval by the Belgian and American Governments—and their approval awaited final appeals to the Congolese Rebels to free the hostages.

Under the plans drawn up in Brussels by Belgian and American officials, the U.S. would put 12 C-130Es into the operation to transport the Belgian paratroopers and their equipment. There would be three additional Hercules—a communications aircraft, a spare airplane, and a maintenance plane. The armada would depart Europe on Tuesday, November 17. Target date for the rescue— assuming the operation got a "go" signal— was Monday, November 23. The first five C-130s would fly in over the Stanleyville airport at the break of dawn, dropping 320 Belgian paras from 700 feet. Once they secured the field and cleared the debris, the other seven aircraft would come in and land with 225 additional paratroopers and equipment. The troops would then move quickly into Stanleyville to bring out the hostages.

Grad Gradwell, a veteran of 24 years with the Air Force, all of it flying transport aircraft, well knew the perils of the mission. During World War II, he had flown airlift support in Sicily, Italy, France and North Africa. He flew supplies to Tito's forces in Yugoslavia and to Polish patriots fighting the Battle of Warsaw. Then, in 1960 and 1961, he piloted UN troops and supplies to the Congo in C-124s. While transporting Irish UN troops to Elizabethville, his "Old Shaky" was peppered with ground fire and he had to take off with only three engines and fly to Kamina for repairs.

DRAGON ROUGE, though, was just about the most ambitious airlift of its type ever attempted. It was a military mission with a humanitarian objective. The lives of the civilian hostages were at stake. "It was a short-notice launch," Gradwell recalled. "I got word on Sunday night, and we were to leave the following Tuesday."

Rushing back to Evreux, Gradwell quickly began putting together his airlift fleet. Neither he nor Laurent were absolutely sure that DRAGON ROUGE would go off—political considerations being of high importance—but he knew he had to have the very best in the way of airlift equipment. He was delighted that he had at his disposal the new long range C-130E.

"The Lockheed C-130E was just what we needed for DRAGON ROUGE. It was and is a most versatile, capable aircraft. It has a great deal of power and is reliable—especially the E model. It carries a big load a long way. It's an airplane that paratroopers really enjoy jumping out of because it was built that way. It is fast, has good range and is a comfortable airplane—especially for crews."

Gradwell also knew that the C-130E was capable of making high altitude, long distance flights at 320 mph, and then drop to a low altitude and go over a drop zone at a reduced speed of only 145 mph.

Colonel Gradwell had all of the C-130Es then on rotation duty with NATO all across Europe to come back to Evreux. Some had to fly back from as far away as Athens. At the time, there was a squadron of C-130Es then on three-month "rotation" duty from the Tactical Air Command's 464th Troop Carrier Wing based at Pope AFB, North Carolina, and a squadron of "A" models from Lockbourne AFB, Ohio.

Gradwell called in the commander of the 777 squadron, Lt. Colonel Bob Lindsay and the 322nd Air Division's Tactical Air Command liaison officer, Colonel Gene Adams, and launched detail planning. Nine C-124s flew on directly to Kamina in the Southern Congo, carrying two tank trucks that would refuel the C-130s on the ground. Ten tons of C-rations were put aboard the Hercules to feed the hostages being evacuated. Then there were the bull horns needed to call out the hostages. The Air Force rounded up a dozen and put them aboard.

*   *   *

In the squad rooms at Evreux AFB, tension was rising. Air Force crewmen were mystified and curious as to what was in the wind. Lt. Colonel Mack Secord (Ret.) of Atlanta—who was to win a DFC on the mission—recalled the mood.

"Our squadron commanders called us in and didn't tell us much. They said, 'Some of you will be going on a very special, max effort, simulated mission involving the highest levels of diplomacy. It might be tonight. So go to your barracks and get some rest.'

"All we did," Secord recalled, "was to go back to our rooms and stew."

About 5 o'clock on the afternoon of Monday, November 16, the armada of Hercules took off from Evreux, at 10-minute intervals.

"We weren't even told the destination," said Secord, a captain and a command pilot. "They filed our flight plans and gave our navigators sealed envelopes, to be opened after we got airborne."

Climbing through 2,000 feet, Secord pulled off his head set and turned to his navigator, 2nd Lt. John F. Knetchtges.

"Where we goin', John?"

"Klinebrogel."

"Klinebrogel? WHERE's that?"

"Belgium."

Klinebrogel was the start of an 18-hour "open corridor" flight —by way of Moron, Spain—that would take the armada of C-130s and 545 paratroopers 4,298 nautical miles to Ascension Island, a British-owned volcanic rock in the South Atlantic.

*   *   *

In Stanleyville, the rebel newspaper, *Le Martyr*, published a front page statement from renegade "president" Gbenye.

> "We hold in our claws more than 300 [sic] Americans and more than 800 Belgians . . . . At the slightest bombardment of our regions or of our revolutionary capital, we shall be forced to massacre them . . . ."

The same day, Stanleyville Radio announced that a war council tribunal had sentenced Dr. Paul Carlson to death. But there was a clincher: The Stanleyville government, it was said, had agreed to an offer by U.S. Consul Michael Hoyt to negotiate Carlson's fate.

Carlson and Hoyt—languishing in Cell 8 of the Stanleyville Central Prison—had never heard of the "sentencing," much less the "negotiations."

*   *   *

In Alhambra, California, Mrs. Ruth Carlson—under strain of worrying about her son, Paul—collapsed with a heart attack.

Secretary of State Dean Rusk wired Jomo Kenyatta, Prime Minister of Kenya, urging him to intervene in the case.

". . . Dr. Carlson is not in any way connected with the U.S. Military," the cable read. "Dr. Carlson is a man of peace who has served the Congolese people with dedication and faith for three and a half years, taking care of the sick and wounded, including members of the rebel force. His execution on charges which are patently false would be an outrageous violation of international law. . . ."

*　　*　　*

At 1 p.m. Wednesday, November 18, the C-130s landed at Ascension and the Belgian paratroopers and American flight crews got a much needed period of rest and relaxation.

But for the Americans in Stanleyville's Central Prison, November 18 was a day they would never forget. They awoke to the noise of a huge crowd in downtown Stanleyville. Five thousand shouting and screaming people thronged Lumumba Square. Simba guards pulled the Americans, five diplomats and three missionaries, from their jail cell, and threw them into a jeep and a VW bug.

"Where are you taking us?" Hoyt asked.

"To the Lumumba Monument," a Simba replied, ". . . to be killed."

A grim David Grinwis turned to Michael Hoyt. "This is the end," he said.

At the monument, the crowd taunted the "convicted" Americans. Simba guards formed a protective ring around them. Even so, angry people kept breaking through, scratching the Americans, burning them with cigarette lighters and punching them with knives and pins.

"We're going to eat you," some of the Simbas yelled, indicating which parts of their bodies they would consume.

Just as the eight men were lined up in front of the Lumumba monument, General Olenga, the dictator, broke through the mob and announced he was cancelling the executions. To the disappointment of the throng, he ordered the guards to haul the prisoners to the Presidential Palace.

Another crowd awaited them there, along with "President" Gbenye. Speaking from the balcony, he told them, "Major Carlson has been tried and condemned to death . . . . We have postponed the execution because of an appeal from Jomo Kenyatta." Carlson was to be executed the following Monday, Gbenye decreed, unless "negotiations" with the United States bore fruit.

It was the first time Carlson had heard of the death sentence. After Gbenye's long harangue, Carlson was shaken and pale. He swallowed a barbiturate to settle his nerves.

"Don't worry," Hoyt declared, trying to comfort him. "We'll all get out alive. You're their trump card. They won't play it."

*   *   *

Wednesday, November 18, was also a day of great import at Kindu, 250 miles south of Stanleyville. At dawn, the 70-vehicle force of Congolese Government troops and mercenaries—code named "Lima 1"—crossed the Lualuba River for their final big push northward into rebel territory. After a string of victories, they had paused 13 days at Kindu, repairing their vehicles and weapons and resting up for the next big leg of their offensive. Right behind them was "Lima 2"—a force of 300 Africans and 50 white mercenaries—which had caught up with the first force the day before. Two days later, the combined forces, packing murderous firepower, captured Punia and moved north toward Stanleyville.

*   *   *

In Washington, the Stanleyville situation was being watched with increasing apprehension. Officials knew that if the government troops and mercenaries pushed into Stanleyville, the hostages could be the victims of a mass murder. The State Department learned that Gbenye had postponed Paul Carlson's execution at the request of Kenyatta, but that he would be killed November 23 unless Washington began "negotiations" with the Stanleyville rebels. The State Department sent a radio message to Gbenye:

"We stand ready at any time for discussions to insure the safety of United States nationals now in the Stanleyville area . . . ."

*   *   *

In Stanleyville, Michael Hoyt was summoned from his jail cell for an audience with the rebel president. It was Friday, the 20th of November.

"Come in, Monsieur Hoyt," Christophe Gbenye declared.

"Your ambassador in Leopoldville has offered to begin negotiations with my government over the American citizens in Stanleyville." He said talks might be held in Nairobi.

That night, on orders of Gbenye, Hoyt and the other Americans were moved from prison into the Victoria Residence, an apartment hotel. As they arrived, the Victoria was in a state of uproar. The rebels had just received word that the Congolese regulars and mercenaries had captured Punia that day, only 210 miles from Stanleyville. A Simba colonel harangued the crowd, threatening to kill all of the foreigners. The tension left many of the whites upset. Huddling in one corner of the lobby, a Belgian and his wife shook with fear. Carlson walked over and examined the man. "Here, take these pills," he said with a reassuring voice. "You've got nothing more than a case of jitters."

The Belgian thanked him and said, "Are you Dr. Carlson, the American missionary?"

"Yes," Carlson said calmly. "They say I'm a mercenary. I'm due to be shot on Monday."

*   *   *

On Saturday, Stanleyville Radio resorted to desperate statements. "The whole population (of the city) is decided to devour all of the prisoners in case of bombardments of our region," the commentator said. He warned that drums of gasoline had been stationed around houses holding the hostages and that if the U.S. refused to negotiate by the following Tuesday, the rebels would "burn the prisoners alive."

Throughout Stanleyville, meanwhile, the Simbas braced themselves on the word that the loyal government forces were moving north. The rebels stationed themselves behind trees over the city, each man armed with a spear.

*　　*　　*

On Ascension Island, the Belgian paras and American airmen went through three practice alerts and the Belgians practiced jumping from the C-130.

At 6:30 p.m. that Saturday, Colonel Gradwell received the message everyone had anticipated. The operation was ON . . . but only as far as Kamina in the Southern Congo, three hours' flying distance from Stanleyville. At 7:30 p.m., the first Hercules took off and headed almost due east.* The other C-130s followed in open trail formation. Nine hours and 2,490 nautical miles later, they reached their destination. Even though dense fog covered the airfield, a highly experienced control tower operator with a clipped British accent confidently talked them in one at a time with direction finding (DF) steers, a non-radar type approach using transmissions from the aircraft to get them positioned. "He was just as good as the tower at Chicago's O'Hare," said Mack Secord. "We landed into that soup right at daylight. That was our introduction to Katanga."

*　　*　　*

In Washington, President Johnson stayed on the phone constantly with the Pentagon and the State Department, inquiring about the Congo drama. He knew that the armada of C-130s and their passengers—a highly experienced Belgian paracommando strike force—were now on Congo soil, with the express permission of the Congo government in Leopoldville. The Hercules armada included 13 C-130s from Evreux, and two C-130E "talking birds" that came in from Leopoldville.

But the big attention that Saturday was focused on Nairobi, the mile-high capital of Kenya, where the U.S. was making a last ditch, all-out diplomatic effort to get the hostages freed. The U.S. Ambassador, William Attwood, drove up at noon at Jomo

---

*No flight plans were filed as the fleet wished to arrive with as little attention as possible.

Kenyatta's home, but the rebel representative, Thomas Kanza, never appeared. He finally reached the city on Sunday and Kenyatta arranged the meeting for Monday.

In Stanleyville, "President" Gbenye became more strident. He announced over Stanleyville Radio that he had postponed Carlson's execution until Tuesday, but urged his rebels to remain on the alert. "If the Americans bomb the capital," he said, "take your machetes and cut up foreigners in pieces."

* * *

On the Kamina ramp, the 14 C-130s were fueled and poised for takeoff, and the DRAGON ROUGE crewmen—who turned on the gas turbine auxiliary power units (APUs) in their Hercules so they could listen in to the BBC—knew action was imminent.

The Hercules "talking bird," which came from Leopoldville, was the center of activity. A tall antenna had been erected next to the airplane, along with an APU. Inside, the Hercules was packed with the latest in powerful, sophisticated communications gear. The radio kept in constant touch with "Fireman"—Washington.

* * *

An impasse developed almost from the start of the Attwood-Kanza meeting. Kanza called for a general cease-fire, and said the hostages would remain prisoners until the U.S. and Belgium forced Tshombe to halt the column of Congolese Regulars and mercenaries. Attwood replied he was there only to talk about the safety of the hostages.

For an hour, Attwood argued that international law prohibited the holding of diplomats and unarmed civilians as hostages. He urged that the Red Cross be allowed to fly the hostages out. Kanza refused. Attwood said he would have to seek further instructions.

Washington's answer was fast in coming: break off the talks, the State Department ordered. The rebel proposals were termed "outrageous blackmail."

* * *

The long paved (but seldom used) runway at Kamina, Katanga Province, was the scene of a two-day stop for the C-130 flyers and their passengers, while waiting for diplomatic attempts to free the hostages in Stanleyville. The planes took to the air on their final leg to Stanleyville in the pre-dawn hours of Tuesday, November 24, 1964.

The "talking bird" teletype clattered into action. Colonel "Grad" Gradwell stiffened and looked up from his desk.

"STAND BY," the first statement said. Gradwell called in Colonel Isaacson.

"STAND BY . . . STAND BY," the machine kept saying.

Finally the code signal, "B-I-G," came through from Washington. This was followed by a message from Brussels for Colonel Laurent, "P-U-N-C-H."

It was 10 p.m. Monday, November 23. Both governments had given their go-ahead. The understanding was that no action was possible until both words, B-I-G P-U-N-C-H, came through. Now it was official.

"DRAGON ROUGE is on!" The word spread rapidly among the American airmen and the Belgian paracommandos who had been holding three days at the hot Kamina base.

Gradwell called in his aircraft commanders. "We'll launch the first plane at 2:45 a.m.," he said. "The other planes will take off every ten seconds."

Aboard Chalk One would be Colonel Gradwell and Colonel Laurent, who would lead his Red Berets on the jump which was set for first light in Stanleyville—at 6 a.m. Hopefully, the Simbas would be asleep.

*   *   *

"TEN MINUTES," the navigator of Chalk One yelled into the plane's intercom.

"TEN MINUTES," the Chalk One loadmaster yelled out at the rear of the plane.

"DIX MINUTES," the Belgian jumpmaster repeated. The paratroopers nearest him, who heard the message, passed the word by hand signals to those adjacent.

Their Hercules, piloted by Capt. Huey Long, was skimming over the green Congo canopy at 700 feet. They were coming in from the west of the Stanleyville Airport, the side away from the city. This would provide the greatest element of surprise.

The 64 paratroopers in Chalk One, seated in four rows of 16, hitched up their gear. Some had general purpose bags containing ammunition and special weapons.

The low drop altitude was Colonel Laurent's wish. It was much lower than the jump altitude used by American airborne divisions. But it would get the commandos to the ground quickly, with a minimum of time dangling in the air. The low jump also meant the men would be less dispersed on the ground. The drop zone was a grassy strip 200 feet wide, paralleling the south side of the Stanleyville runway.

"SIX MINUTES!"

The navigator completed his final calculations and came up with the Computed Air Release Point—the CARP. Into his calculations had gone the temperature, the speed and altitude of the aircraft, and the direction and velocity of the wind.

Red lights started flashing over each of the jump doors.

The loadmaster reached down and with a heave pulled the left hand paratroop door open, and slid it up into the ceiling. He repeated the process for the right hand door, then extended wind deflectors in front of the doors and put jump platforms into place. Glancing out, he saw the dark green rain forest whirling by below.

"OUTBOARD STICKS STAND UP!" the jumpmaster ordered. The 32 men in the two lines on the outside stood up and folded their bench-like canvas seats. The roar of the propjet power plants could be heard distinctly, along with the whistling wind.

"INBOARD STICKS STAND UP!" The 32 paras through the middle of the airplane stood up and pushed up their seats.

"HOOK UP," the jumpmaster ordered.

All 64 Red Berets turned toward the doors at the rear and clipped their static lines to the overhead cables.

"CHECK STATIC LINES . . . CHECK EQUIPMENT."

Each man checked his own rig and that of the man in front.

"STAND IN THE DOOR."

The lines shifted to the doors in the rear on either side, and the lead men stepped directly into the doors, holding on to the sides.

Two minutes before drop time, the Chalk One command pilot, Capt. Huey Long, lowered the Herk's big wing flaps. The airplane shook a bit and groaned as it slowed to 125 knots . . . 145 miles per hour.

"ONE MINUTE!"

The lead paratroopers crouched and tensed, like track runners, with hands gripping the side of the doors. The lights started flashing green and the lead men dived into the Congo air, followed quickly by the other 62 paras. Parachutes popped open in a line along the runway, jerking the commandos upward momentarily. Within a half minute, all 64 men from Chalk One, including Colonel Laurent and Father Pierre Van der Goten, their chaplain, had departed the Hercules.

*   *   *

A line of tracers from a 50-caliber machine gun sprayed across the nose of Chalk Three, commanded by Capt. Keith McDonald. It came as a surprise. The crewmen had been briefed to expect only small arms fire.

Capt. John Ewing, McDonald's second in command, found the ground fire, which hit all five of the lead aircraft, a bit unnerving. Through it all, however, the pilots kept their cool, maintaining their exact heading and altitude. Any deviation could have been disastrous to the Red Berets. To climb would have left them hanging high in the air, an easy target for the Simba gunners. To dive would have not given them time for their chutes to open. If the planes had shifted to the right or left, the commandos would have landed in the jungle. Thanks to the cool, professional performance of the American Airmen, all 320 Red Berets landed right on target without receiving a single gunshot wound.

The five aircraft swept down the mile-long runway, then circled back to airdrop machine guns and ammo. Chalk Two through Five—the first phase of their work completed—leaped into the air at a fantastic 30-degree climb, clawing quickly to 10,000 feet for the flight to Leopoldville. Chalk One remained on the scene, circling at 2,000 feet, keeping a protective watch on the commandos and preparing to call in the next seven Hercules.

*　　*　　*

Donald Parkes awoke in the Victoria Residence. The whining sound of the C-130 propjets echoed from the airport 2 miles in the distance. Looking excitedly from his fifth floor window, he saw the parachutes billowing along the mile-long runway. "There's hell to pay now," Parkes said, as he shook his roommates, Ernest Houle and James Stauffer, the other radio code operators.

"The Simbas said they'd kill us if Stanleyville was invaded. Now they'll shoot us down, maybe here in our rooms."

*　　*　　*

The "talking bird"—code named Dragon Chief, with Colonel Isaacson aboard—screamed over the Stanleyville runway at 100 feet for a close look, then headed for Leopoldville. The whistling propjets sounded like a thousand banshees and may well have scared off some of the rebel defenders. The Red Berets likened it to the blast of Gideon's trumpets.

*　　*　　*

Colonel Laurent ripped off his parachute rig and quickly took command. His 320 commandos were strung out along the mile and a half of the runway and the adjacent golf course.

Laurent ordered his headquarters unit to roll the steel drums (filled with water) off the field. Ten-man teams were assigned to moving the dozen wheelless vehicles which had been left on the runway.

*　　*　　*

"Talking Bird" C-130 bearing Colonel Clayton Isaacson (above) roars over Stanleyville runway for a closer look. Below, C-130 waits in background to pick up wounded hostages while Red Berets mop up rebel snipers from runway area.

320 paratroopers, such as these, dropped onto the Stanleyville airport from the first five C-130s. (USAF)

From his fourth floor room at the Victoria, Paul Carlson watched the paradrop with hope and apprehension. He, along with two Mennonite companions, prayed at the edge of his bed. "If this is my day to die," he prayed, "then I am prepared." He asked God to comfort his family.

* * *

Chalk One, with Colonel Gradwell in command, kept circling the airport at 2,000 feet. He radioed Washington, by way of Kamina, that all 320 paratroopers were safely on the runway and were clearing the field for the next seven Hercules.

Down below, Company 11 quickly captured the airport control tower and the Sabena Guest House next door. Two dozen
Simbas fled from the tower after firing a few shots, and their com-
rades in the guest house also ran toward town.

. At 6:40 a.m., Laurent called Gradwell on his radio:

"The field is cleared," he said, "and ready for aircraft."

Chalk Seven promptly landed and disgorged two jeeps and
additional Red Berets. Chalks Eight and Nine followed shortly,
with 92 troopers each.

*   *   *

The telephone in the Control Tower kept ringing. Finally a
commando picked it up.

"Come quickly," stammered a man in French. "The Simbas
have rounded up all the white people at the Victoria Residence."

Major Jean Mine, commanding officer of the First Battalion,
ordered the 11th Company into Stanleyville immediately. Led by
two jeeps that had just rolled off Chalk Seven, the red berets—
with rifles at ready—took off at a trot.

The commandos leap-frogged into the city along Avenue Monsigneur Grison. While troops laid down heavy blasts of gunfire,
their colleagues would advance to the next corner. Along the two
miles, Simbas took shots at the Red Berets from the tall grass along
the road and from behind buildings. The paras responded with a
barrage of automatic gunfire. As the commandos reached the
intersection of English Avenue, the first white man rushed out.
"Hurry," he said, "murder is being committed."

*   *   *

"Your brothers have come from the sky," a Simba yelled to
the 300 foreigners herded in front of the Victoria Residence.
"You will be killed now." The Belgians and Americans, who had
been flushed out of their hotel rooms, were lined up in a column
three abreast. Nothcomb and Hoyt were near the front, Carlson
and the American missionaries in the middle. The crowd included
many children, some babies in their mothers' arms. The Simba
commander was Colonel Joseph Opepe, who had befriended
foreigners in the past.

The Simba soldiers kept asking permission to shoot down everybody in the column then and there. Opepe overruled them and ordered the column to start marching down Avenue Ketele.

*   *   *

The Red Berets were coming in from the airport, taking control of Stanleyville, a block at a time. A few whites warily emerged from their hiding places. Many answered the call of the commandos who called with their bull-horns: "We are here to rescue you. Come out and go to the airport. Planes are waiting."

Several blocks away, the whites from the Victoria House were not so lucky. They were being held by Simba soldiers. When the column reached Avenue Lothaire, Colonel Opepe ordered everyone to sit down. Red Beret gunfire could be heard moving closer. Nothcomb felt Opepe was stalling for time, so he could surrender the hostages to the commandos. A Simba deaf mute, "Major Bubu," high on hemp, drove up and wildly demanded that the hostages be shot. Opepe reprimanded him and again overruled other Simbas who wanted to conduct a mass execution in the street.

Exactly what happened next is not clear. Some said Bubu roared back in anger and began firing. Whatever set it off, Simbas suddenly started shooting wildly into the crowd on the ground, shouting "Ciguya, Ciguya" (kill, kill). Colonel Opepe screamed at his men to stop but he, himself, was shot down. The whites began running for cover, including Hoyt, who felt his legs weren't functioning right. He fell down twice. The man in front of him vaulted over a wire fence. The hostages did not scream; they were mute with stark terror.

As the firing stopped, Marcel Debuisson—playing dead on the ground—heard one of the rebels say, "Now we'll turn them over and finish off the ones left alive."

Marcel prayed for a miracle. To her amazement, Belgian paratroopers, submachine guns at their hips, came around the corner. When they saw what was happening, they raced across the square, shouting and shooting.

As the rebels turned and fled, Mrs. Debuisson, holding her daughter Monica in the dust, began bawling with tears of joy.

The hostages who had escaped to nearby buildings returned to the intersection and found 22 bodies scattered on the street and nearby. Two of them were American missionaires . . . Phyllis Rine of Bangs, Ohio, and Dr. Paul Carlson. Many others were wounded.

Father Van der Goten, the paratroop chaplain, came up to administer the last rites to the dead and dying.

Freed hostages rushed to the airport the best way they could. Some, particularly the wounded, were taken by available vehicles. Those who could walk hurried at a brisk pace down Avenue Monsigneur Grison (above) to board waiting C-130s.

At the airport, the armada of C-130Es buzzed like a swarm of angry bees. Capt. Huey Long and Colonel Gradwell circled the field in Chalk One, directing the air traffic. Chalk Six, piloted by Captain Secord, reached the scene and disgorged its four jeeps and paratroopers. Secord taxied to the terminal building and backed in to await refugees. He left his engines running, at idle, ready to make a quick getaway with hostages.

Although ground fire was heavy, Secord's plane escaped damage coming in. Two of his colleagues, however, were not so lucky. Capt. Jim Ostrem's C-130 received a direct hit on a wing fuel tank. His crew chief broke off a broom handle, wrapped it with a rag and plugged the hole. The patch held for the flight to Leopoldville. Simba ground fire blew a tire in the right wheel well of Capt. Charlie Gonzales' Herk. But Gonzales greased the aircraft in to a smooth landing at Leopoldville.

At 10:30 a.m., to the cheers of the Red Berets, a green flare rocketed across the sky on the south side of Stanleyville. The Congolese 5th Mechanized Brigade and Mike Hoare's mercenaries rolled into the city, climaxing an amazing, 23-day sweep from Kongolo. The commandos guarding the road block at Camp Ketele welcomed them with great joy. Together, they moved into Stanleyville and launched a house-to-house search for hostages.

*   *   *

Circling overhead at 2,000 feet, Chalk One was jolted by a strange thud.

"What's that?" pilot Huey Long asked.

"Smells like hydraulic fluid," said Burgess Gradwell, who got up from his jump seat and walked back to take a look. "We've been hit back here," he reported, "and fuel is pouring from a wing tank."

Altogether, Chalk One received seven hits, which knocked out the plane's hydraulic system and left gaping holes in two fuel tanks.

"Let's head for Kamina, Huey," said Gradwell. "This airplane's had it."

Amazingly, the bullet-riddled bird held together and, thanks to some skillful piloting, reached Kamina safely. There, USAF maintenance men set to work putting her back into shape so she could go back into action.

*   *   *

At the Stanleyville Airport, Capt. Mack Secord—the jovial, usually smiling "Red Baron"—had a splitting headache. But he stayed in his airplane and kept his props spinning at low idle. He had been told he'd have a load of hostages to take to Leopold-ville 15 minutes after landing. But 30 minutes went by, then an hour and still no hostages. From time to time, red-capped commandos rushed up to report, "They are on their way." But Simba ambushes had caused a big delay. Suddenly, three truck loads of wounded—mostly from the Avenue Ketele shooting—reached the terminal along with the first hostages walking in. Secord's load-master, Airman First Class Alvin Collins, became frantic. He rushed to the flight station.

"Captain, we've got folks bleeding all over the place. They need to be over on Chalk Twelve (the hospital plane), but I can't make 'em budge. They're sorta crazy." Frozen with fear, the hostages were in shock. They saw the Chalk Six props turning and thought the plane was going to leave first.

C-130s became flying ambulances on med-evacuation flights to Leopoldville. Doctors were kept busy tending the wounded rescued hostages.

"Do what you have to, Alvin, to get those people over to the other plane. March them over with your gun if you have to. They need the help of the surgeon. And tell them the other plane will be leaving just as soon as we get off the ground."

Collins managed to persuade 20 of the badly wounded to get in the hospital ship with the flight surgeon, Dr. Bob May.

Meanwhile, hostages running from town swarmed and jostled their way into Chalk Six. Airman Collins yelled to Secord to get moving. But Secord, seeing more people rushing up, decided to wait a bit longer. "We're not going to over-gross this bird with people," he said.

Still more hostages packed in—at least 125 anxious people. Secord finally ordered the ramp raised. It formed the rear door when it latched onto the upper half lowered from the ceiling. Secord taxied out fast, at 30 mph. Before he reached the end of the runway, Simbas jumped from four-foot high elephant grass; one fired his submachine gun straight up into the left wing. Another ran alongside, trying to climb into the paratroop door on the side, but fell away.

The pilot of the next Hercules, Chalk 12, seeing fuel gushing from the Chalk 6 wing, tried frantically to raise Secord on his radio, but got no response. Secord hung a sharp U-turn into the runway and pushed his throttles all the way forward. The Hercules rocketed ahead with a tremendous surge of power and bored upward at a ferocious clip.

As the plane climbed through 4,000 feet, the No. 3 engine oil gauge began fluctuating. Pressure was dropping fast. Loadmaster Collins spoke up on the intercom: "Captain, we're losing fuel like crazy from the right wing."

The C-130 on the ground, commanded by Capt. B.J. Nunnally, confirmed it.

"Chalk Six . . . Chalk Six. This is Chalk Twelve. Those guys just about shot your ass off . . . fuel is really cascading from that wing. I tried to tell you before you got airborne."

"Yeah, I heard you," Secord replied. "But I didn't want to hear you."

By now, Secord's headache had become a dull, painful throb all across his skull. But he was well in command of the situation. He feathered his right inboard engine and called his flight mechanic, Staff Sergeant Crawford Ingraham.

The last of 40 Paulis hostages arrive at airstrip for C-130 airlift to Kamina and thence by commercial aircraft to Elizabethville.

"We've got to decide how we're going to land this plane in Leopoldville," Secord said. He remembered that the Leopoldville runway was one of the longest in the world—well over two miles.

"We'll have to land without lowering the flaps," he said, "but we shouldn't have any trouble.

"And don't reverse your props, either," Ingraham advised. "You don't want to suck that fuel back up into the engines."

Their approach and landing—a three-engine, no flap, no reverse affair—was a resounding success.

Captain Secord, his head throbbing with what was later diagnosed as a concussion received the night before in Kamina, collapsed in his C-130 flight station. His crew had to lift him out of his seat and rush him to a doctor.

Throughout the rest of the day, the Hercules fleet roared back and forth between Stanleyville and Leopoldville in a never-ending shuttle. Transports from Sabena and Air Congo, as well as military aircraft from Italy, Britain and France, joined in the big airlift. Altogether, more than 1400 hostages were flown out of the rebel capital.

TIME magazine's report described the scene at the Leopoldville airport:

"By 10:27, the first transports were back in Leopoldville. They were chockablock with living, dead, dying and wounded. They kept coming all day: crisp white nuns and an old priest in a black Homburg: two little girls, blood-stained, holding tightly to their dolls; a mother and daughter in pajamas and no shoes; a baby with its feet sticking out of an airline bag . . ."

An elderly woman, the back of her head caked with blood, came off a Hercules, saying only "Oh God, Oh God." She could not summon her name for Red Cross people who met the plane.

*   *   *

Capt. Keith McDonald, flying the last C-130 into Stanleyville in the afternoon, winced when a mortar exploded only 50 yards in front of him as he came in on his approach.

"Do not land . . . do not land," the tower yelled.

McDonald firewalled his throttles, getting instant power, and his Hercules leaped quickly to 5,000 feet.

Forty minutes later, with the field resecured by the Belgians, McDonald came back in, landing on the other end of the runway. He brought his Hercules to a stop in 800 feet, reversing his props just at touchdown, and standing on his brakes.

A throng of whites was waiting at the terminal and 112 pushed and shoved their way aboard.

Co-pilot John R. Ewing was touched by what he saw. Most of the hostages were bruised, their clothing torn and dirty. Half had only the clothes on their backs. Others carried a suitcase or a gunny sack. They were all thirsty and hungry and they finished off the plane's supply of chlorinated water in minutes. Ewing opened two cases of C-rations and fed them to the women and children.

At dawn on Thanksgiving day—two days later, November 26, seven of Colonel Gradwell's Hercules fleet—including repaired Chalk One—moved into the second stage of the rescue mission, DRAGON NOIR*, at Paulis, 225 miles northeast of Stanleyville.

In many ways, it was a much more difficult and hairy mission than DRAGON ROUGE. The runway was only 4,100 feet long and it was thick with red dust. Due to the short runway, cut right out of the rain forest, and snipers, the pilots came in at a very steep approach, "pranged" their planes into the dirt, then threw their props into reverse. Some of the pilots went into reverse before touchdown. Major Joe Hildebrand's Herk hit the ground so hard, two of his engines flamed out. Every time a C-130 landed or took off, a cloud of thick red dust swirled for several minutes.

Also, fog hung low over the area. Despite it all, the DRAGON NOIR navigators directed their aircraft right into Paulis, and dropped 256 paracommandos.

"Dammit," said Colonel Laurent as he looked out from Chalk One, "I can't even see the ground!" He landed on the DZ nevertheless and his troopers were only 10 yards off target. The first four planes dropped the Red Berets and the last three landed with armored jeeps and equipment.

Capt. Jim Hunt brought out the first load of hostages—women and children. Shortly after takeoff, he called Leopoldville and asked for ambulances and doctors. Some of his passengers were hysterical.

Chalk One, which suffered such a beating at Stanleyville, received another dose of ground fire at Paulis—four hits.

Among the 355 hostage survivors evacuated was Mrs. Joseph W. Tucker, whose husband, an Assembly of God missionary from Arkansas, was killed by Simbas two days earlier. With her was her 10-year-old son. They sat in the flight station and Captain Ewing let the boy sit in the right hand seat for part of the way back.

*   *   *

The big airlift—headline news everywhere—was hailed around the free world as a magnificent display of military air power with

*i.e., "Black Dragon"

a great humanitarian objective.

At Melsbroeck base outside Brussels, King Baudouin presented both Laurent and Gradwell with the cross of the Commander of the Order of Leopoldville II, and praised the action of the Belgian/American DRAGON ROUGE team:

"The courage and determination which you showed in accomplishing your mission," the Belgian King said, "have gone right to the heart of our nation. In the space of a few days, you have averted a dreadful fate for 2,000 compatriots and friends.

"I salute with gratitude the crews of the U.S. Air Force who, by their mastership and their self-control, have carried out . . . with perfect success . . . this vast operation of transport."

For balding Colonel Laurent, the mission was a wonder. Only three of his Red Berets were injured, but none killed.

Colonel Burgess Gradwell—ever smiling and bubbling over with good will—hailed his crews and their Hercules. "What absolutely amazed me," he said, "we performed both the Stanleyville and Paulis missions right on time. We never missed a schedule. But what also amazed me was our Hercules—Chalk One. That plane really took a beating at Stanleyville. It was all shot up. But lo and behold, our maintenance people had it all repaired for our Thanksgiving day mission to Paulis."

On Friday, the day after the Paulis mission, the armada of Hercules took the commandos back to Kamina, first rest stop on the long flight back to Belgium and France.

Just after they landed, a thunderstorm came up, bathing the hot, 100-degree Kamina runway with a cooling shower. One of the Air Force crewmen—tired of living in his "Lockheed Hilton" and caked with a six-day accumulation of crud—stripped naked and ran out with a bar of soap and took a glorious outdoor shower.

The word spread quickly, and shortly 40-odd officers and enlisted men were lathering up and frolicking in the rain.

"I have never enjoyed a shower more in my life," said Captain Ewing. "Our squadron commander, Bob Lindsay, had a favorite expression—'We've got to be flexible.'

"That afternoon during the thunderstorm, we showed him just how flexible we could be."

*   *   *

For its heroism, the 464th TCW won the Air Force's coveted Mackay Trophy as the most meritorious flight of the year.

Captain Mack Secord of the 777th TCS—who despite a concussion airlifted the 125 hostages out of Stanleyville with a crippled aircraft—was awarded the Distinguished Flying Cross. He was cited for extraordinary coolness, courage and determination. The other flying crew members received air medals.

Thus was written one heroic chapter of a nation's struggle to establish a rule of order, and one more chapter in the life story of the stalwart Hercules.

Anguish showed on the faces of the freed Stanleyville hostages on their return to Leopoldville, where they were greeted by friends and relatives.

SAMARITAN OF THE SKIES

It has flown the overwhelming majority of its missions not with weapons and troops, but with food, medicine, hospitals, construction equipment . . .
—Martin Caidin

The Hercules . . . a marvelous Himalayan workhorse.
—Sunday Telegraph

Far up in the forbidding Himalayas, a propjet transport carrying the blue, red and white roundel of the Royal Air Force, its fuselage painted in caramel colored camouflage, threads its way over and through the snow-capped ridges.

The airplane's broad belly bulges with bags of corn and rice.

Reaching its destination over a valley in western Nepal, the aircraft turns and its commander prepares to launch a near "dive-bombing" drop of his precious cargo onto a target deep in the gorge ahead.

Aboard the flight is *Sunday Telegraph* reporter Duff Hart-Davis, and he gives a running account to his readers back in Britain:

"We slant into a twisting, wooded gorge, above a turquoise river that winds between the banks of white shingle.

"Depressurizing," says the captain. "Door and ramp clear?"

"Door clear," reports the loadmaster, in charge at the back.

51

" 'Gear down,' says the captain—a precaution in case we touch the ground during the dropping run. For a moment the air strip is visible far down to our right; but we swing left, round the marker. Then we wheel into a right-hand turn, heading straight for a precipitous, scrub-covered face. Head-on impact seems inevitable until, at the last second, we come 'round again.

"We skim a ridge and suddenly dive.

" 'One hundred percent flaps,' The captain demands, and down we go, plummeting 1,000 feet in 20 seconds towards the thin brown strip that strikes through the green of the valley floor.

"Warnings, commands and acknowledgements snap through the head-sets.

" 'Fifteen seconds.' says the captain.

" 'Your line,' says the co-pilot. 'Your line . . . steady . . . your line . . . steady.'

"We are down to 250 feet . . . 150 . . . 100 . . . We're hurtling straight for the runway at 50 feet and 120 mph.

" 'Ten seconds . . .' A searing blast from an alarm bell . . . 'ACTION STATIONS!'

" 'Action stations,' comes the echo from down below.

" 'RED ON.'

" 'Red on.'

" 'GREEN ON.'

" 'Load moving . . .Load gone.'

" 'RED ON.'

" 'Red on.'

" 'Lights out.'

"The village flashes below us and we lift steeply away into the circuit for the second run. Down in the back the dispatch crew is already maneuvering the next load along the rollers toward the tail—four baseboards with 24 sacks lashed on each.

"Beyond the huge square window framed by the open tail door, green hills, brown hills, blue sky and glittering snow peaks are rushing crazily past. It is impossible to tell which way the aircraft is heading. Only the loadmaster is in touch with the flight deck by intercom: for everyone else, the racket is so ferocious that signals have to be given by clinched fists, open hands and outstretched arms.

"Suddenly the floor stops tilting sideways. The ridge whips by a few feet below and the aircraft starts to dive. The loadmaster's fist goes up. Red light . . . green light . . . heave—and out go the 96 sacks.

"They hit the ground like a bomb burst and come racing along after us, vaulting end over end. One or two split and send spurts of golden maize flying back into the air. Behind the control tower a crowd is waiting to collect this priceless harvest from the sky . . ."

* * *

Heroic flying was displayed by RAF Hercules pilots as they negotiated over and between the Himalayan peaks in order to reach their targets in the high valleys of Nepal. (All photos in this chapter courtesy United Kingdom Ministry of Defence and the USAF.)

It was the Spring of 1973. A terrible famine had overtaken Nepal, the land of the Ghurkas nestled in the high Himalayas between India and China.

Torrential rain and hail in 1971, followed by a drought in 1972, had wiped out the mountain kingdom's crops; its granaries were bare.

Enough grain to fill the immediate need was pledged by the World Food Program, Canada and the United States. Katmandu decided to distribute the grain over the country on the backs of men and animals. But for one and one-half million Nepalese living in the most remote mountain valleys, that would be too slow and too late. Almost four million pounds of the grain needed to be taken in by air.

The challenge was formidable. Nepal, roughly the size of England and Wales, has a hostile geography. Six of the world's highest peaks—all of them over 26,000 feet—are within its borders, including 29,028-foot high Mount Everest.

Only one landing site in the region, a 3,100-foot dirt strip at Serkhet, could accommodate even small transport aircraft.

Helicopters would not do. They simply could not lift enough of a payload over the lofty mountaintops. Only a large payload transport aircraft nimble enough to get down in the dangerous gorges would answer the need. Drops would have to be made either "on the deck" or no higher than 700 feet due to the Pakli Hawa "mad winds" that sweep through the tunnel-like valleys off the North India Plains.

Complicating the picture, the monsoon season was approaching.

Nepal turned to its old ally, the United Kingdom.

London lost no time responding. Shortly, the RAF had fourteen plane-loads of vehicles, equipment and supplies and a team of 220 men on the scene in Nepal, together with four Hercules transports to airdrop the food right into the needed spots.

The C-130Ks, introduced to RAF service in 1967 as successor to the venerable Hastings, Beverly and Argosy aircraft, were by now thoroughly tested. They had seen tough UK service in Europe, Africa and Asia. At RAF Base Lyneham, seventy miles from London, the crews at Strike Command 46 Group had absolute confidence their "Herks" could do the job in Nepal.

Air-dropping of food by parachute was required in many Nepalese regions which had no landing strips. The RAF foodlift brought relief to more than a million Nepalese people living in remote mountain regions hard hit by two years of famine.

Children at Serkhet sift grain just brought to them by a United Kingdom RAF Hercules.

The food was provided by the World Food Program, Canada, and the United States.

Their confidence was quickly validated. The airbridge got off to a fast start. The "Brownies" took to the air and stayed in the air constantly, airlifting and airdropping enormous amounts of "khana" to the remote villages. Hungry Nepalese, migrating in search of sustenance, rushed to drop points when they saw the British Herks slipping back and forth through the mountains. Almost 2,000 tons of food were airlifted in 187 sorties into ten isolated places. One of the drop zones was about 30 miles from the Chinese border.

The skillful way the crews handled their 77-ton transports in negotiating the mountain passages drew praise from reporter Hart-Davis. "The other hero was the Hercules itself . . . ." Hart-Davis said. "In spite of its bulk, it proved so nimble that the speed of the airlift increased far above the rate originally planned."

The arrival of the first Hercules at the short strip at Serkhet was a momentous event. Fifty porters filed into the aircraft to pick up the sacks of grain: "All suddenly raised their hands, palms together, in front of their faces, spontaneously greeting the giant that had brought them deliverance," Hart-Davis reported.

The foodlift was an amazing success. RAF crews completed the assignment in five weeks—three weeks ahead of schedule, and well in advance of the dreaded monsoon.

Britain's Ambassador to Katmandu, Terence John O'Brien, was elated. The RAF, he declared, "plucked these people from the brink of despair."

*   *   *

Routinely carrying out such humanitarian missions around the earth over the past two decades, the Hercules has become an international goodwill legend . . . indeed, an angel of mercy. There are few areas of the world that, during times of disaster and human suffering—typhoons, earthquakes, famines, tidal waves, plagues and other disasters—have not received substantial succor from the stubby, scorpion tailed samaritan of the skies. . . .

—When a "killer quake," rated 7.7 on the Richter Scale, demolished the oasis town of Tabas in Iran's Davir Desert on September 16, 1978, claiming more than 20,000 lives, the Imperial Iranian Air Force immediately launched a C-130 airbridge to the devastated area. Twelve Hercules and a battalion of troops led the rescue operation. The Herks brought in medical personnel, tents, blankets, food, water, and medicines for the dazed survivors. Eleven hundred of the most seriously injured were airlifted to hospitals in Teheran and Mashad.

—When Cyclone Tracy struck Darwin, Australia, on December 24, 1974, the first aircraft to reach the devastated city December 25 was a RAAF C-130A Hercules which landed by the light of kerosene flares. For days, the Herks operated non-stop, bringing out the injured, evacuating women and children and hauling in urgently needed medicines and supplies. Flight Lieutenant John Pickett was taking a load of 180 passengers out of Darwin in his C-130A when he flew into a thunderstorm. "The plane was struck by lightning and those of us in the cockpit were blinded . . . we couldn't even see the instruments. The Hercules is a very forgiving airplane and we managed to get her down safely. If it were any other type of aircraft, I don't know what would have happened."

—When a highly infectious killer fever, Marburg (green monkey) virus, broke out in northern Zaire in 1976, causing 300 deaths in two weeks, a Royal Canadian Air Force C-130 rushed over a medical isolation unit from Canada. In Zaire itself, the Zairian Air Force utilized its own C-130s to airlift medical and other needed supplies into the Bumba and Lisala areas to fight the epidemic.

—In Saudi Arabia, four people were injured in late December, 1977, in an automobile accident in an isolated area 127 miles from Riyadh. The Royal Saudi Air Force flew a C-130 to the scene. Finding no landing strip in the area, the crew put the Hercules right down on the black-top road, picked up the injured and flew them to a Riyadh hospital.

—Four U.S. Hercules rushed in to the East Indian border state of Tripura in the Summer of 1971 to airlift thousands of refugees swarming in from what was then still known as East Pakistan. The American C-130s, responding to a call from the United Nations High Commissioner for Refugees, went to work moving the civilian victims of the war to more appropriate and safer areas deep into India's Assam Province. Performing double duty, the Herks carried a million units of cholera vaccine to begin with and then 21 tons of rice a day to feed the thousands of refugees

With tribesmen looking on, RAF Hercules swoops down a mountain valley preparing to drop one-ton loads of grain. Note sacks already collected in the foreground. Many places where food was desperately needed were considered inaccessible even from the air. But the RAF crews had confidence they could fly their Hercules into the valleys and out again. Drop zones were so small, food dropped from higher altitude on parachutes would drift into the hills. So they decided to drop the food without parachutes from 50 feet off the ground. The plan worked perfectly.

remaining in Tripura. On return flights, they hauled refugees to Gauhati, packing 192 people into the Hercules on each flight.

Many of the desperate refugees cried when crews welcomed them aboard their C-130s for the flight to Assam. Said Captain Bill Cowan, a navigator: "Some of them came up and kissed our feet. At times it was hard to keep from crying. I was glad I could do a little something to help these people."

Today, with the Lockheed Hercules being operated by 45 countries around the world (and the list still growing every year), it is not unusual to find C-130s in the colors of four or five nations flying virtually side by side to the scenes of disaster.

Following the Nicaraguan earthquake of December 23, 1972, aid came to Managua on the wings of C-130s from Italy, the United Kingdom, Peru, Venezuela and the United States. Precious blood plasma, medicines, blankets and tents were the main cargoes.

Earlier that year, when near-starvation panic swept through the new nation of Bangladesh, food-laden Hercules from New Zealand, Canada and the United States brought relief and hope to Dacca.

*   *   *

The continent of Africa, particularly the sub-Sahara, has been hard hit in recent years by extended drought. A precursor of major famine struck the region in 1966 and 1969. USAF C-130s airdropped and airlanded more than 700 tons of foodstuffs to distressed desert towns of Chad—Barai, Monto, Ati, Fada, Abeche and Faya.

The airlift commander, USAF Colonel Charles E. Turnipseed, found the situation to be in a critical stage: "Some of the tribes in the hills had already come to the cities searching for food. Believe it or not, I saw some people actually eating leaves, they were that hungry. Our job was to get the food there and that's exactly what we did."

Chadians, amazed that the airplanes flew all the way from America just to deliver foodstuffs to their people, would ask the identical question of C-130 crews at various strips: "Are you really from America?" They were curious and deeply grateful.

The relentless drought, worst since Biblical times, turned the one-time granary of West Africa into a dust bowl. It drove tens of thousands of nomads and their cattle southward in a massive migration. By early 1973, six million citizens of the entire 7,000-mile wide region—Mali, Senegal, Mauritania, Niger, Chad and Upper Volta—faced the danger of slow death from dehydration, starvation or disease. Their domestic animals were dying on their feet.

Proud, blue-robed, sword-carrying Malian Tuaregs were among

62/HERK: HERO OF THE SKIES

Hungry Hausa children have hands outstretched as Belgian C-130 lands with cargo of powdered milk in Tahoua, Niger. Belgium flew five of its Hercules to Africa throughout the summer of 1973, stationing them on a rotation basis in Niger and Upper Volta to deliver food to points within the various stricken countries. The Belgian Herks had delivered 9,000 tons of powdered milk by the end of June, 1973.

the most severely ravaged tribes. From their homelands above the great bend of the Niger River, they trekked hundreds of miles in fruitless search for food for themselves and grazing for their cattle, sheep, goats and camels.

The United Nations Food and Agriculture Organization (FAO) mounted a worldwide drive for grain and for transport planes and trucks. Canada, Great Britain, Belgium, Sweden, the United States and Switzerland—along with the FAO itself—contributed thousands of tons of grain and powdered milk . . . enough to feed the nomads a pound of food a day apiece for five months. But equally important, the six nations committed a combined total of 16 Hercules to airlift the food from African seaports into the remote interior.

From the Spring of 1973 through the fall, the multi-nation fleet of C-130s, working as a team in cooperation with local authorities, airlifted food by the thousands of tons into the hinterlands. Trucks—hauled in by the Hercules—retailed the foodstuffs into the remotest of starving villages. When rains turned many dirt roads into quagmires, the food was airdropped right into isolated villages.

The airbridge was a dramatic example of international cooperation and compassionate concern—a multinational war against hunger.

A leader in the effort, Canada pledged $6.8 million in food, three of its military C-130s, and 30 trucks. Its RCAF Hercules were assigned the job of getting the food into Niger.

It was June of 1973 when the Canadian C-130s went to work, logging 19-hour days flying 30,000-pound loads of grain, powdered milk and fodder to remote villages up the Niger River.

The foodlift took on a truly international flavor. Nigerian authorities gave priority to the food ships that swarmed into the busy Lagos harbor. They set aside a special area of the Lagos airport for the Canadian Hercules. Belgian troops drove the trucks of food from airhead centers into the hinterlands.

During the first two weeks, the Hercules bearing the maple leaf emblem airlifted more than two million pounds of grain and dry milk. Working from dawn to dusk, they flew whopping loads from Lagos to the interior towns of Kirkou and Arlit.

The tragedy of the seven-year famine struck the emotions of

the Canadian aircrews deeply. In Agadez, on the Niger River, they watched sadly as 12,000 refugees gathered quietly in 110-degree heat to receive their portions of just-received food. At Tahoua, dispirited Tuaregs straggled in from the desert, pitched their leather tents and waited patiently for their dole of life-saving grain. A Canadian reporter who accompanied the C-130 crews sent home this dispatch:

> "The faces of the once-proud nomads reflected their anguish; skeletons of cattle and animals lay in heaps in the desert and the rotting smell of death was everywhere. Children dressed in rags begged for clothing to keep them warm in the cold of the desert night; weakened by starvation, the very old and the very young fell victim to disease.

> "A once rich tribal chieftain, who had a herd of 100 cattle, is now down to ten, and the rest will die if the rains don't come. Their death would destroy the last of his breeding stock."

The importance of the airlift to the people was underscored by a Canadian C-130 pilot: "Powdered milk, particularly, was desperately needed. The Tuareg's normal diet of meat and milk was almost totally cut off by the death of their cattle by starvation. When we were at Tahoua, an emaciated tribesman was brought in on a litter to the hospital by four tribal brothers. He was suffering from malnutrition, dehydration and pneumonia."

Although the Hercules airbridge kept the food moving, there were difficulties. Red sandstorms—accompanied by temperatures soaring over 110 degrees (F)—swept across the Niger plains. Some of the Herks had to turn back to Lagos on occasion. A Canadian officer explained the reason: "Our crewmen are familiar with the whiteouts of blowing snow in the Arctic, so the red dust storms of the desert are not such an unfamiliar problem. But the whirling dust devils often climb to over 10,000 feet and cause most uncomfortable turbulence."

Two other problems plagued the Canadian mercy birds—bird strikes and foraging animals. To scare off goats and camels on the Agadez runway, the Canadians swooped over low with their propjets screaming, then came back around quickly to land.

One of the Canadian C-130s received 15 bird strikes, potentially a serious problem since an ingestion of a bird requires the engine be taken off and replaced. But the Canadians soon came up with a solution: They brought their Herks in to land very short on the runway, and immediately reversed their props, blowing the birds away with the reverse prop blast!

The humanitarian foodlift was a rousing success. More than eight million pounds of vital foodstuffs were hauled by the Canadians during their two-month stay and the crews received a deserved "well done" from the people of Niger as well as their own government in Ottawa.

In order to carry as many East Pakistan refugees from Tripura to Gauhti as possible, Hercules crews allowed them to pack into the airplane from wall to wall. Although designed to transport 92 persons, this C-130 took aboard 180 refugees. On return flights from Gauhati to Tripura, the C-130s hauled more than 1,750 tons of Assamese rice to feed the refugees remaining in Tripura. In addition, the four Herks carried in 190 tons of relief supplies from Bombay, New Delhi and Calcutta. The Americans nicknamed the operation "Bonny Jack."

*　　*　　*

Meanwhile, Britain's Royal Air Force had the job of hauling food in two sorties a day from Dakar to northern Mali. During the six-week airlift, the two RAF C-130s hauled 3,020 long tons of rice, maize and went into the remote towns of Timbuktu, Nioro, Nara and Bamako, the capital city.

John Smalldon of the London *Sunday Telegraph* was aboard one of the vehicles that took food from the RAF airplanes to a starving village in Mali:

> "The villagers turned out en masse to greet us. The women ululated their shrill cries of welcome, the children danced and the men in austere robes lined up to meet the visitors who were bringing the vital sacks of grain which their womenfolk would pound in their mortars to make coarse flour."

*   *   *

Belgium contributed the largest fleet of Hercules to the 1973 airlift—five of its fleet of C-130Hs. The Belgian birds rotated constantly between Brussels and Africa from May to September, hauling in heavy loads of food. Two of the Belgian Herks flew two weeks at a time on shuttle flights within the African famine region, flying out of Ouagadougou, Upper Volta, and between points in Niger, Upper Volta, Mali and Ghana. Every two weeks two more fresh Herks from Brussels would take the place of two planes that went back to Belgium.

The people of Upper Volta composed a song of thanks to the Belgians and their Hercules. It was understandable. Flying through severe sandstorms, the Europeans airlifted almost 20 million pounds of powdered milk, transported 3,000 women and children to better locations and also hauled some cattle. The Belgian Army put 45 vehicles and 30 drivers into the area.

When rains created quagmires of dirt roads across the interior, halting delivery trucks, the Belgians paradropped more than 450 tons of food directly into isolated villages. Many a Belgian parachute soon showed up as a new fashion for the desert women!

When a shortage of parachutes developed, the Belgians began airdropping sacks of grain from low altitude without parachutes. At first the plastic bags of sorghum burst on impact. Undaunted, the Belgians brought in a special sewing machine, placed four plastic bags inside a larger bag and sewed it up. The fix worked perfectly.

*   *   *

The UN itself, through the FAO, chartered two Pacific Western Airlines commercial Hercules from Canada—L-100-20s—which hauled 80 tons of sorghum seed a day from Khartoum into Chad, and later from Lagos into Niger. This seed grain enabled farmers to plant another crop. The UN's long-term effort was aimed at helping the people get on their feet again. They helped them drill wells, replant crops and replace their livestock herds.

*   *   *

The United States Air Force—well familiar with the sub-Sahara from eight years of previous foodlifts—sent three of its Tactical Air Command C-130s from Pope AFB, North Carolina. They first went to work in Chad. In mid-May, the Americans moved over to Mali, hauling 33,000-pound loads of sorghum, grains, wheat and rice from the capital city of Bamako to the more interior towns of Timbuktu, Gao, and Tessalit.

Flying two sorties a day with a cool morning 6 a.m. launch, the C-130 unit's objective was to "stay above the grain line"— 160,000 pounds of grain a day. That was the minimum amount of grain the people of Mali needed each day to survive.

On their first trip into Timbuktu, the Americans were greeted by a scorching 105-degree desert wind, with dust clouds boiling 10,000 feet high.

Working under auspices of the U.S. State Department, the U.S. airmen and their Hercules from May to early November hauled more than 12 million pounds of grain into the African interior, along with goats, barbary sheep and camp water buffalo.

Major John Correll recorded a typical flight into Goundam, Mali, in an article he wrote for *AIRMAN* Magazine:

"It was one of the afternoon sorties . . . that took the C-130 to the dirt/laterite landing strip on the edge of the desert at Goundam . . . As the rear door dropped open, a wave of stifling heat swept inside.

"First aboard was 'Cochise.' That's what the C-130 crews called him because of his spirited shouts and whoops . . . The other guys would try to keep up with him. He'd get a bag of grain on his shoulders, run to off-load it, and run back, passing people, to get another bag. And all the time giving out that whoop.

(Above) At the request of the UN refugee commission, four USAF C-130's from Pope AFB, North Carolina, carried out a 30-day humanitarian airlift of refugees from Agartala, Tripura inland to Gauhati in India's Assam province. Here refugees carrying their personal belongings line up to board Hercules. Many of them kissed the feet of the C-130 crews. *(Lower photo)* Timbuktu may be remote, but it is not too remote for the C-130. Timbuktu porters carry sacks of grain from a U.S. Tactical Air Command C-130, which hauled the cargo from Bamako.

"Colonel (Warren R.) Horney kept two engines on the leeward side of the airplane going. The wind blew the exhaust fumes and engine heat away from the workers.

"The last heavy sack of grain was out of the airplane in 25 minutes . . . Women clambered aboard to sweep out the floor of the C-130, so that not a grain of food would go to waste . . .

"After an hour and 20 minutes, the plane was back in Bamako . . . Ground crews began to ready the airplane to fly again the next day. The maintenance people, Colonel Horney avows, have been the miracle men of the Mali airlift. Working in intense heat and with limited facilities, they somehow found a way to keep the airplanes ready.

"That evening, Malian workers brought another 13-metric tons of grain aboard the C-130. The aircrews would be back out to the line by 4 a.m. tomorrow. Lunch would be at 6 o'clock . . ."

In addition to food, sheep and water buffalo, the Americans and their Hercules hauled missionary families, President Traore of Mali and Captain James Lovell, the former astronaut, who was serving as President Nixon's famine foodlift advisor.

Many of the Americans volunteered to return to Mali because they found the mission personally satisfying, knowing their work was helping to save lives.

"A lot of healthy people of Mali had moved to the south," said Colonel Horney. "The ones who stayed on and the ones who couldn't move were relying on us. Even though the temperatures remained above 100 degrees, all of our C-130 crews swelled with pride, knowing that they were accomplishing something highly worthwhile."

USAF Staff Sergeant Clint Brown, a C-130 loadmaster, was glad he could help out the starving people. "I've been on a lot of missions, but this one really touched me deeply."

Major Howard Seabolt, one of the first pilots of the airlift, who later returned for 30 days as mission commander, reflected the feeling of many of his colleagues: "After Vietnam, there are other people who need help and it feels good to be helping them."

The airlift undoubtedly averted starvation for millions of people. Robert Hunter, a senior fellow of the Overseas Development Council, viewed the U.S. contributions: "What forty men of

A nomadic Chadian watches from his camel as a C-130 from Dyess AFB, Texas, lands at Faya, Chad in support of "Operation King Grain." The airlift by U.S. C-130s saw 9,424 metric tons transported in 547 missions from June through October, 1974.

Frank L. Kellog of the U.S. State Department greets refugees from East Pakistan being airlifted by C-130s to India's Tripura state. (SIA)

the U.S. Air Force did here in Mali, from Bamako to Timbuktu and beyond, may be limited in terms of Mali's larger needs. But it still stands as an example of what can be done in the midst of human tragedy, by people from diverse countries."

The 1973 international foodlift to Africa was followed by another massive airlift, "King Grain," in 1974. Again the conditions were rough . . . frequent thunderstorms, sandstorms and temperatures ranging from 100 to 140 degrees (F). Yet, the USAF's 463rd Tactical Airlift Wing, Dyess AFB, Texas, got the food through. The Wing rotated 19 C-130s and 200 aircrew members in 30-day shifts. They hauled 9,424 metric tons of grain into Mali, Mauritania and Chad.

U.S. Secretary of State, Dr. Henry Kissinger, said that, "Once again it has been possible to assure that those who might otherwise have faced the very real possibility of starvation have received the food they required . . ."

As the American C-130 crews departed Africa, they chipped in $600 to purchase a grain mill for a Malian leper village. The villagers no longer would have to thresh their grain by hand in a long, and for them with their affliction, painful process.

*   *   *

Thus goes the story of the indefatigable Hercules, the world's true samaritan of the skies, whose helping hand has been hoisted to the hurt and hungry on every continent.

While the stories we've told in this chapter have received appropriate headlines of appreciation, thousands of smaller "helping hand" missions have gone unsung. To the individuals involved, however, they often have meant the difference between life and death . . . Two shark-bite victims from Eniwetok Island who will survive with their limbs intact, thanks to a C-130 airlift to the Naval Regional Medical Center on Guam . . . A child flown from Puerto Rico to Brooks AFB Hospital for medical care . . . An entire tent city airlifted to a Central American village demolished by a hurricane . . . The airlift of a 19-year-old youth with a broken back from the Canary Islands to Toronto for special treatment . . . Twenty-five tons of evaporated milk flown to Accra, Ghana . . . An emergency stop during a routine mission to fly a badly burned

"Operation Haylift," staged in 1971 by the 313th Tactical Airlift Wing, Forbes AFB, Kansas, resulted in the dropping of 30,000 bales of hay to 40,000 head of cattle stranded in Kansas' worst snowstorm since 1900. Civil Air Patrol and Future Farmers of America youth helped load the hay (purchased by the American Humane Society), and loadmasters "kicked" the bales from the C-130s to the cattle. (UPI, USAF)

missionary from Brazil to a U.S. hospital . . . Bales of hay air-dropped to cattle stranded in a blizzard.

Captain A.S. Quenneville of Canadian Forces Base Valcartier tells the story of an RCAF Hercules that landed at Frobisher Bay on Baffin Island far up in Canada's Northwest Territories. It was a mercy flight to save the life of a child:

"The mission was crucial for it involved transporting a young Eskimo girl who had sustained a skull fracture. It was imperative to land at Frobisher Bay, the site of the only hospital in this sector of the Great North with facilities for this type of injury.

"We were in the midst of a blizzard. Nonetheless, the crew managed to land the airplane without incident and without causing further injury to the child.

"Had it not been for the truly excellent Hercules, it is virtually certain that our landing would have been disastrous."

"Mercy bird of the world" is an apt title for the Hercules, as illustrated in part by this composite photo. Top left, Swedish C-130 delivers food for humanitarian agency to drought areas of sub-Sahara Africa. Top right, Italian Air Force C-130H takes aboard relief supplies for 1976 earthquake areas around Fruili in northeastern Italy. Lower left, Royal Australian Air Force C-130A drops hay in northwest New South Wales to sheep stranded by floodwaters in 1976. Lower right, Imperial Iranian Air Force C-130s rushed to earthquake areas in Iran in 1978, bringing tents, medicines and food and air-lifting injured quake victims to hospitals in Teheran. (Lockheed)

II

GENESIS OF A CLASSIC

The C-130 is a true
classic airplane. I
don't think it has
a peer and I don't
know that it ever will.

Lt. Col. Tim Brady

A MATING OF THE JEEP, THE TRUCK AND THE AIRPLANE

The front of the C-130 resembles a
goat, but it's nowhere near as stubborn . . . .

— Major Joseph P. Tracy
U.S. Air Force

Lockheed Corporation, headquartered 12 miles north of Los Angeles at the foot of the San Gabriel Mountains, has given birth to some of America's most amazing flying machines . . . the series of Vegas so well loved by Charles Lindbergh and Amelia Earhart . . . the "forked tail" P-38 fighter of World War II . . . the high-flying U-2 spy plane of Russian overflight fame . . . the L-1011 *TriStar,* the quietest of the modern day widebodies . . . and the SR-71 Blackbird, the highest-flying, fastest-cruising airplane of all time.

The turboprop cargo craft which waddled bashfully out of Lockheed's Hanger C-1 in Burbank, California, in August of 1954 did not seem to have a Lockheed pedigree. There were no swept wings. Its aerodynamic contours were dumpy, not flowing. Its nose was blunt and unshapely, giving the machine a mean, menacing appearance. Even Kelly Johnson, Lockheed's aircraft design genius, was not at all happy with the external shape that emerged in 1951 from the drawing boards of Lockheed's preliminary design organization, and he refused to sign the proposal for the C-130 to the Air Force. Lockheed's Vice President, Hall Hibbard, finally decided to let it go.

Birthplace of the Hercules: Lockheed-California Company at Burbank. Photo made in 1956. (Lockheed)

Despite it all, when the word spread in mid-August, 1954, that the new beast was going to take wings, excitement crackled through the Burbank air.

A first flight is the most crucial milestone in an airplane's career, and in the case of the prototype Hercules, its performance would figure mightily in the Air Force's decision about whether it would move into a production contract. The flight would climax three years of sustained effort by Lockheed's engineering, manufacturing and subcontractor team. Thus despite the smog that shrouded all of Burbank on the morning of August 23, 1954, all hands at Lockheed were psyched up for the Herk's big moment. Even the postponement of the 9 a.m. takeoff dimmed the excitement only slightly.

Shortly after 2 p.m., the sun broke out. As if by telepathy, workers began gathering by the hundreds along the Lockheed Air Terminal's north-south runway. People materialized on the factory roofs. Top Air Force and Lockheed officials took their reserved seats on top of the Terminal Building and in the control tower.

Outside Factory C-1, pilot Stan Beltz and his fellow crew members . . . Roy Wimmer, co-pilot, and Jack Real and Dick Stanton, flight engineers . . . fired up the C-130's shrill-sounding gas turbine compressor, the auxiliary power unit housed in the left-hand main wheel well. The GTC's ear-splitting crescendo was just the prelude. The APU in turn kicked off the plane's powerful propjet engines which, together with the 15-foot Curtiss-Wright propellers, emitted a distinctive, throaty, air-cutting sound that seemed strange to the ears of the people of Burbank, accustomed as they were to the piston-engined airplanes of the time.

For Beltz, a gutsy flyer of the old school, it was a moment to remember. Possessing a love for flying that transcended earthly pursuits, Beltz looked on a new flying machine as a special challenge. His derring-do was legendary even around Lockheed, which was known for the boldness of its test pilot corps. Beltz's trademark— a tip-off to his effervescent personality—was the large, two carat solitaire diamond ring which he displayed proudly on the third finger of his right hand. He was not an engineer and didn't want to be. He just wanted to show what he could do with an airplane.

Stan taxied the aluminum behemoth to the north end of the runway. He turned it into the wind and raced it down the strip, with the nose getting airborne momentarily, only to settle down with a roaring prop pitch reversal. Beltz performed another fast "skip-off" in the opposite direction, then turned the Herk aside to allow two chase planes to take off—a P-2V carrying Kelly Johnson, and a chartered B-25 loaded with photographers.

Crewmen in the YC-130 tensed up. With the huge, three-bladed props spinning at a constant 1,108 revolutions per minute, Beltz pushed the power levers forward all the way, giving the props a huge "bite" of air. But he kept his feet on the brakes and the aircraft "danced a jig," eagerly chomping to move out. As Beltz released the brakes, spectators gasped. The Hercules surged down the field, jerking the crewmen back in their seats. Eight seconds down the runway, at 855 feet, Beltz pulled back the control column and the prototype shot skyward at a startling speed.

"Just look at it climb!" exclaimed Lockheed President Robert E. Gross. The 15,000 horses in the T-56 powerplants, coupled to the Curtiss-Wright electric props, lifted the 54-ton machine in a 30-degree climbout. It was a startling shocker to the crowds who were accustomed to lumbering liftoffs by the piston planes of the time.

The takeoff, at 2:45 p.m., lived up to its creators' expectations and then some. The plane displayed amazing power and mobility.

High over Burbank, the daring Beltz—relishing the moment— had to suppress his own excitement. He leveled off at 10,000 feet and had his crew run a series of tests on the landing gear, flaps and control surfaces, and then ran stall checks. All systems worked fine.

Watching from his P-2V was Kelly Johnson, Lockheed's ubiquitous chief designer, who, despite his earlier misgivings, followed the baby bird on its 61-minute flight to Edwards Air Force Base in the Mojave Desert northeast of Los Angeles. There it was to undergo a series of Lockheed and Air Force flight tests.

Emerging from the plane at Edwards, Beltz* exploded in a torrent of enthusiasm.

*Beltz proudly showed off the YC-130 to Brig. Gen. Albert Boyd, commander of the Air Force Flight Test Center at Edwards AFB by landing the airplane quite short. "I could land it cross-ways of the runway if I had to," he told General Boyd.

Top photo: Stanley Beltz (R), Lockheed flight test pilot, and Jack Real, flight test group engineer, perform a visual inspection of YC-130 Hercules (AF serial Number 33397) prior to conducting in-flight air conditioning and cabin pressure tests. Photo was made at Edwards Air Force Base, Calif. (on June 21, 1955), where initial C-130 proto-type testing was conducted following the first flight on August 23, 1954. Beltz, a su-premely confident test pilot, told Air Force officials he could just as easily land the C-130 cross-ways on the Edwards runway if he took a notion to. Real later joined the Howard Hughes organization as its aviation director. Lower photo (L-R) Real, Roy Wimmer, Beltz and Dick Stanton. (Lockheed)

First flight of the prototype C-130 took place at the Lockheed Air Terminal at Burbank, Calif., on August 23, 1954, with Stanley Beltz and Roy Wimmer at the controls. Typical of the airplane's get-up-and-go characteristics from the first, the prototype was airborne in 800 feet from the beginning of takeoff roll. Lower photo shows plane heading for Edwards AFB landing after crossing Sierra Nevada mountain range from Burbank.

"I never saw such an eager airplane," he told the cluster of people who met him. "When we took off, it wanted to climb so bad, I had trouble keeping my air speed down. She's a real flying machine."

For the people back in Burbank, the excitement of the takeoff was unforgettable. Lockheed-Georgia engineer Sam Robinson, on temporary assignment in Burbank, went to his motel room and wrote an inspired report to the folks back home in Georgia:

"I wish all of you there (in Marietta, Georgia) could have witnessed this take-off as I did. For one brief moment, all the worries about flutter and shimmy and boost and lateral loads—all these were forgotten as the YC-130 flew out of sight."

*   *   *

The Hercules was born, in concept, in the better days following the June, 1950, invasion of Korea when it took the United States six agonizing weeks to move two Army divisions from the continental U.S. to the Korean front. The piston engine strategic transports of the time—the C-54 *Skymaster* and the C-124 *Globemaster*—were sorely lacking in range/payload capability. On the Korean battlefield area, the twin-boom C-119 *Flying Boxcar*, the venerable C-47 *Gooneybird*, and the C-46 flew yeoman duty, but could not accommodate the heavy support equipment necessary for the front line forces.

Pentagon planners—who knew the Allies had been deficient in airlift muscle even in World War II—decreed the U.S. had to have a powerful air transport capable of swiftly airlifting troops, supplies and equipment to any part of the world, and then have complete freedom from concrete.

The military's need for a C-130 type aircraft also reflected the changing state of U.S. military doctrine. Rapid mobility for Army ground forces was now the urgent requirement. Introduction of nuclear weapons helped stimulate this shift in thinking. The C-130 would be the medium-size transport to give the ground forces strike power in preference to large standing armies scattered over the globe.

The weekend after the war broke out in Korea, a hurry-up meeting was called in the Pentagon at the behest of Lt. Gen.

Gordon Saville. The assignment: Put together a $105 million supplemental research and development add-on to the Air Force budget. H.H. Test* of Bethesda, Md., who worked in the U.S. Air Forces Headquarters, was there and recalled the shirt sleeve session.

"As the meeting droned on, it became obvious that imaginations were beginning to dull before the magic and mysterious $105 million number had been reached. Suddenly, in mid-afternoon on Sunday, a colonel (and I wish I could remember his name) spoke up: "Hell, we need a medium transport that can land on unimproved ground, be extremely rugged, be primarily for freight transport, with troop-carrying capability, and carry about 30,000 pounds to a range of 1,500 miles.' "

The man on the adding machine asked how much money to put down.

"As I recall," said Test, "the number was an odd one in the low millions. That item stayed in and the funds appropriated. While the nameless colonel did not know it, he had just birthed the C-130."

Some weeks later, Lockheed—learning that an RFP (Request for Proposal) for the new transport was soon to be issued—sent design engineer Al Lechner and salesman Chuck Burns on an information gathering tour. They visited the Pentagon, Strategic Air Command Headquarters in Nebraska, Andrews AFB, Maryland, and the Army's Airborne Headquarters at Fort Bragg, North Carolina, where they witnessed air drops of paratroopers and equipment from the Air Force's main tactical transport of the time, the "Dollar Nineteen."

Said Lechner: "We were gathering comments from the men closest to the action. The colonel we dealt with at SAC told us that in his estimation, the winner of the competition would ultimately deliver as many as 2,000 aircraft."

The Air Force issued its GOR—General Operational Requirement—on February 2, 1951. Requests for Proposals (RFP) went

---

*Test, a former civilian and during the Korea War a military officer assigned to USAF Headquarters, had one additional comment about the "birthing" of the C-130: "Mine not to question the validity of the onerous paperwork now required to launch a new weapons system. However, I do feel that on this day the Department of Defense was well served by 'seat of the pants' flying."

out to Boeing, Douglas, Fairchild and Lockheed, calling for their designs for "a medium transport . . . to perform tactical and logistic missions." But there was more. The Air Force wanted "an advanced, all purpose, work-horse type, aerial vehicle that can go anyplace, anytime, without elaborate facility or equipment preparations." In other words, a super airplane—a speedy, high flying ocean-spanning strategic airlifter that could haul 90 troops in 2,000-mile stages, combined with a shortfield tactical transport capable of airlifting troops, supplies and 30,000-pound pieces of equipment on short hops right up to hastily prepared battlefront strips . . . being able to slow down to 125 knots for paradrops and even less for steep "assault" landings.

Many experts in industry and the military considered the requirements to be exceedingly harsh and virtually impossible to attain. Canadian pilot/historian H.G. Maxwell described the super aircraft envisioned by the GOR: "A plane that would fly the ocean with a healthy payload at a good rate of knots, land in a mudhole and get airborne out of it again, drop a tank, jump a goodly number of paratroops with their gear, carry a high percentage of the Army's bulky equipment, shrug off the failure of one of its four engines and, unless a guy was really hamfisted, land safely at its take-off weight."

Willis Hawkins, the brilliant head of Lockheed's Advanced Design Department, looked at the challenge from still another viewpoint. The winning contractor, he told his colleagues, would have to produce a hybrid mating of the jeep, the truck and the airplane. Hawkins and his crack cadre of creative engineers, including his deputy, Eugene Frost, Art Flock, E.A. Peterman and E.C. Frank, and, a little later, W.A. (Dick) Pulver, along with a lineup of whiz kid manufacturing specialists, accepted the challenge with a team spirit of innovative relish and gusto.

Lockheed intensified its effort to find out exactly what the customer—in this case the Tactical Air Command, the Military Air Transport Service and the Army—wanted. Their engineers consulted the Air Research and Development Command, the Joint Air Transport Board, the Joint Airborne Troop Board and Army Field Forces Board No. 1.

"It was obvious from the beginning," said the late Robert W. Middlewood, who became Lockheed-Georgia's chief engineer, "that the airplane would have to reflect the best judgment and service experience within the Air Force and the Army if Lockheed was to succeed in developing more than merely an acceptable airplane."*

Even when the Burbank designers were deep into building the prototypes, they continued to solicit comments. As H.G. Maxwell noted, "Just about anyone who could make an intelligent input was invited to look over the mockup and their comments were carefully recorded. If an idea was thought to warrant inspection, it was built into the mockup and the people invited back again."

Lockheed's engineers explored new avenues of design to come up with a configuration that would have a high survival possibility. Middlewood declared that "simplicity, reliability and rugged construction became the primary factors in our design philosophy. Other prime objectives were economy of manufacture, operation and maintenance."

This philosophy was pushed by test pilot Bud Martin, who admonished his colleagues to "Keep it simple . . . don't complicate it." He pounded home the theme that "this airplane is going to be used a lot out in the bush and in other austere situations."

Because operational economy was a goal, Lockheed and the Air Force chose a turboprop engine for its long range performance

---

*Middlewood gave his summary of Lockheed's C-130A design philosophy in a paper he delivered at the November, 1954 meeting of the American Society of Mechanical Engineers in New York that said, in part: "One of the early phases of an assault operation requires the use of an airplane capable of aerial delivery of such equipment as bulldozers, road graders, trucks and howitzers to forward areas. Paratroopers must be released into drop zones with an acceptable minimum of dispersion. Then, after hasty preparation of airstrips, the airplane lands with equipment too large to airdrop, with more supplies and with troop reinforcements. The return trip evacuates the battle casualties. The new performance requirements defined substantial improvements over existing transports. One-engine-out-capabilities over the drop zone were increased by factors of 1.5 to 2.0. Dependable controllability and stability at low speeds were essential. Design payload-range capabilities were multiplied by a factor of 8. Moreover, assault airplanes require exceptional takeoff and landing performance.

"Equipment and structural demands showed improvements of similar magnitude throughout the operating range. An 8000-foot pressure altitude for both crew and cargo compartments were now required. An integral ramp and rear door operable in flight for heavy equipment drops were specified. The limit flight-load factor was increased to three. Excellent crew visibility must be provided. The clear cargo volume asked for resembled a railroad box car (40 ft x 10 ft x 9 ft). The cargo floor had to be at the level of standard truck beds. The landing gear should be capable of enabling airplane operation in fields of clay, sand or humus.

"This is the air freighter the Air Force asked us to develop which it felt could meet the needs peculiar to modern tactical air-ground operations."

C-130 cruises over Lockheed-Georgia plant. Dobbins AFB in background. (Lockheed)

Two prototypes pictured on flight across California's Antelope Valley. Later they were flown from California to Georgia. Number 1001 is in the foreground with 1002 in the back. Both aircraft were dismantled some years after the completion of the Lockheed and Air Force test programs.

at high altitudes. Middlewood described other design considerations:

> The long-range and high-altitude factors meant a high aspect-ratio wing. A cargo floor at truck bed level placed wings high on the fuselage. We settled for a wing of 10 aspect ratio, 132-ft span, and 1745 sq ft in area. A relatively conventional arrangement of cargo space, which includes troop seating and litter tiers, was evolved after design studies proved again that simplicity is a virtue. Wind-tunnel tests solved the aerodynamics problem of fairing the aft fuselage containing the in-flight operable ramp and door.
>
> Soft-field tire flotation characteristics, smooth wheel-well profiles, and minimum structural weight all seemed to point toward a tandem-wheel arrangement of two large low-pressure tires in fuselage side blisters for the main landing gear. The more conventional wing-mounted dual-wheel arrangement was considered, but finally discarded in favor of the tandem arrangement. The somewhat modified tricycle landing gear was a reality.

Art Flock, later to become chief engineer and vice president at Lockheed-Georgia, was named the aircraft project leader in Lockheed's Preliminary Design organization. Al Lechner laid out the plane's general arrangements, including the wing and fuselage. The landing gear was done by Jack Lebold while Willard Tjossen and Merrill Kelly were in charge of the preliminary design of the power plant.

Flock made three-view drawings on a number of concepts. The ideas extended even into a gull-wing design, which prompted a laugh from Kelly Johnson. "You'll draw up anything, won't you, Art?" "Yes," Flock replied. "We're exploring all the possibilities."

Flock and his colleagues were quite apprehensive about sending in a proposal for a four-engine aircraft, thinking that it would be much higher priced than that of the competition. "But after thrashing it out and thinking it over—realizing the Air Force had some tough engine-out capability requirements—we settled on a four-engine design."

On July 2, five months to the day after issuing its RFP, the Air Force announced its decision. Lockheed, which came in with a proposal for a strange looking flying machine that it called its "Model L-206," was named the winner, and was given a contract to proceed with development of its unique approach. The Air

Force contracted with Lockheed to build two prototypes of its new creation. The aircraft, the Pentagon announced, would be designated the YC-130.

The world of aviation, meanwhile, was somewhat shocked by Lockheed's design, many features of which were radical for their time. These included:

–Turboprop powerplants, the first for an American airplane, and virtually a quantum leap forward in power and lightness over the reciprocating piston engines of the time. What Lockheed did was to marry the propeller and jet power. The four Allison T56-A-1A engines, each producing 3,750 equivalent shaft horse-power, were linked to a variable pitch, constant speed propeller, giving the Hercules a speed of 360 miles per hour, much faster than other tactical transports, and enabling it to exceed the speed of the then fastest passenger airlines while airlifting heavy cargo. Moreover, it was quite fuel efficient.

Weighing about 1600 pounds, the T-56 had a frontal area about half that of the then current transport piston engines, and developed 2.3 horsepower for each pound of engine weight. The small nacelles reduced drag and increased speeds.

The slim jet turbine had already proven more reliable than the "recip" engines, having less moving parts. Thus, coupling in the gearbox and a propeller gave the plane the benefits of the turbine engine's power and reliability combined with the propeller's thrust for take-off and climb. The prop's pitch could be reversed, giving crews the ability to stop quickly and back up an aircraft on a short field.

—An unusual airframe design. The plane's high angular wing was spread-eagled straight across the top of the "flattened" fuselage, providing good ground clearance on unprepared fields. The boxcar-like fuselage was unique in that it was not totally cylindrical like most pressurized aircraft but had a "fattened" cross section that provided a cavernous cargo hold measuring 10 feet wide, nine feet tall and 41 feet long. Moreover, the cargo floor was only 45 inches from the ground—truckbed height—and had a clear, wide-open back door, and a built-in ramp that could be lowered to the ground to enable trucks and heavy vehicles to move into the airplane on their own. The inward-opening top half of the cargo door would enable the Hercules to airdrop equipment and cargo

the width of the cargo compartment. As designer Charles Cannon described it, "You had one structure (the ramp) that served a dual purpose—it faired in the aft airplane and made a closure and it also served as a loading ramp.

—*The landing gear.* Here the Burbank designers went all out to provide the Hercules the ability to land, take off from and taxi on unprepared airstrips. A tandem main landing gear was created, featuring big, low pressure tires that retracted straight up into the wheel well. The front wheels would pack a solid path for the wheels behind, giving the aircraft traction to maneuver on and to operate from soft fields. The gear was housed in blister fairings situated proudly outside the fuselage.

—*A huge empennage,* particularly the vertical stabilizer. The towering, 38-foot high vertical stabilizer swept up scorpion tail-like from the fuselage, providing plenty of room underneath for the loading and unloading of cargo and personnel. The tall tail would give crews good control response on low speed approaches.

—*A unique nose* and roomy flight station with high "greenhouse" visibility. "The nose looked a little blunt," recalled engineer Cannon, "but there was a purpose . . . excellent visibility. We wanted the pilots to be able to have 20 degrees down vision for tactical approaches to unimproved fields." Another uniqueness of the big cockpit was that it had 23 windshield windows, including panes at the bottom of the flight station. Said Cannon: "We wanted the pilot to be able to turn around on a strange field, back up and maneuver around in safety. A remote field is quite different from a commercial airport where someone directs the pilot on the ramp." As to the big flight station, "We wanted the crew to have plenty of room for ease of operation."

Lockheed's Engineering Vice President, Hall L. Hibbard, was tremendously proud of what his team had wrought. He invited the company's top officers to his office in 1952 for their first view of a large model of the quaint looking transport then laboriously being born in Factory C-1 across the runway. When an engineer lifted the sheet off the big scale model, a resounding silence settled over the august assemblage.

Kelly Johnson spoke up first, objecting strenuously to the bulky design.

The trucking of the giant C-130 mockup from the port of Savannah to Lockheed-Georgia in Marietta (following its boat trip through the Panama Canal from California), was quite an event in Georgia in 1953. Activity stopped in cotton fields, traffic was backed up and there were a few tight squeezes in some of the Georgia towns.

Hibbard cleared his throat, a bit embarassed.

"It *does* have a beautiful paint job, don't you think?"

The Lockheed brass were not alone in their initial surprised reaction to the blocky bulldog shape of the new aircraft. Airplane aficionados around the world, who linked Lockheed in their minds with aerodynamically aesthetic air machines epitomized by the stately, elegant *Constellation* and the racy F-80, America's first production jet airplane, were shocked. Particularly when they saw photos of the doughty YC-130 that eventually rolled out from Burbank's Plant C-1. A colorful word picture of the new transport's appearance was woven by Martin Caidin in his book, *Long Arm of America*,* the definitive early history of the Hercules:

The airplane simply didn't "fit" into the concepts of jet power. It was squat and square; observers readily admitted that it certainly *looked* rugged. The wing sat high atop the fuselage in sharp contrast to almost every new airplane being produced. The only streamlining that could be seen was in the bullet nacelles that housed the four Allison jet engines. And almost as if to rob the nacelles of their graceful lines, four great propellers were clamped onto the needle-like spinners. This alone represented a radical departure from current thinking in the industry. Jet engines meant fabulous speed and the most graceful of lines. The Hercules seemed a step backward, since it used the jet engine but persisted in retaining the propeller. It was the first airplane in the country to enter production with the new system—the first of the turboprops.

The nose of the Hercules beggared aerodynamic law and challenged the senses. No rounded or streamlined shape there, but a huge, fat housing where the forward part of the cavernous fuselage ended abruptly. Later in the life of the airplane, the nose was to evoke even more comment, when it would be extended along the plane's lower half with a great, black and bulbous shape into which would go complex radar equipment.

The belly of the Hercules seemed almost to scrape the concrete of the flight line. No gear legs could be seen. From each side of the fuselage, about midway between the fat nose and the towering tail, there extended two huge bulges. These were the landing gear pods. The black tires weren't even fully revealed, and it seems that

*Published in 1963 by E.P. Dutton and Company, New York

the airplane rested more on caterpillar treads than it did on wheels. The Hercules didn't really rest on the ground; it hugged the concrete and glowered.

Despite the disappointment of some aviation buffs to the plane's dumpy external shape, the Lockheed design team in Burbank was undaunted. Utilitarian performance was the name of the game, and the designers were not about to sacrifice performance for sleekness. After all, the C-130 was destined to be a rugged, versatile, get-the-job-done aerial truck, with many tough and demanding tasks to perform and varied missions to fulfill.

"The C-130 called for a unique design job," recalled engineer Carroll Dallas. "We had always been in passenger airplanes or specialized aircraft like fighters or the P-2V. We had never been in the airlift business, and the C-130 required quite a different approach.

"The aerodynamic shape that evolved didn't look pretty to us, but then it didn't need to because of the plane's relatively slow speed. The Hercules grew on us because of its great utility. That finally got to us. But it took a while."

Along with giving the plane a businesslike external shape, Lockheed pushed the state of the aircraft art internally with numerous systems and manufacturing innovations. Among these was the incorporation of a high pressure, 3,000 psi (pounds per square inch) hydraulic system and high voltage AC electrical services. The fully boosted servo controls gave crewmen instant, light yet powerful control response—power steering, if you please. It was a welcome first for a transport aircraft crew.

Another trail-blazing feature was the incorporation of fuselage pressurization from front to back, enabling the airplane to cruise over six miles high with the equivalent of an 8,000-foot internal altitude. This was no small task for an airframe with so many "holes"—huge side and back cargo doors, two troop doors, a crew door and the huge 23-window "greenhouse" on the nose. Pressurization was essential to the C-130; one of its major assigned tasks was that of casualty evacuation. As a hospital ship, the plane was designed to accommodate 74 litter patients and two attendants in a battlefield area "quick change." The idea was that the C-130 would haul troops and cargo to the front and airlift casualties out.

Perhaps the greatest advances in airplane manufacturing techniques of the decade were launched with the C-130. Machined skins with integral stiffening were introduced. Designers called out machined panels for the upper and lower wing surfaces, including one section 48 feet long. This eliminated a lot of riveting and provided a much stronger and stiffer surface structure for the airplane. Three hundred pounds of titanium were used on engine nacelles and wing flaps, and high strength aluminum alloys—a new development—were used throughout the airplane.

Thanks to the economical design and the use of light-weight alloys and the integral milling of major components, Lockheed's proposal came in amazingly light, 10,000 pounds or more under competing proposals.

Summing up, a number of new trends in aircraft design were launched with the C-130.

1. It reversed the tendency toward more complex designs, being a relatively simple airplane made of approximately 75,000 parts.
2. By using new techniques of manufacture and new materials, the airplane was kept light, and, at the same time, rugged and tough.
3. Though a large aircraft for its time, the C-130 was designed so that it could operate from a grass field, ice lakes, and soft dirt. Large, low pressure, doughnut shaped tires placed in tandem like the wheels of highway vans made it possible for the C-130 to land and take off on quickly improvised air strips. Anti-skid brakes and powerful reverse prop capability helped to give the plane short field landing ability.
4. The entire fuselage was air conditioned, heated and pressurized, enabling the plane to be used as a flying ambulance, or a personnel transport, and giving protection to perishable cargoes. (The C-130 was one of the first transports to utilize bleed air from the turbine engines to feed the air conditioning and pressurization systems.)
5. The built-in versatility of the aircraft gave it many uses. It could be converted in a matter of minutes for paradrop of heavy equipment on platforms; as a paratrooper air-

Georgia Governor Marvin Griffin christened the first production C-130 at Marietta on March 10, 1955. It took four tries before he broke the bottle of Chattahoochee water on the Herk. Looking on: Dan Haughton, Col. Edward J. McRay, Jr.

plane; as an all-cargo transport, as a medical evacuation aerial ambulance; as a transporter of fully-equipped combat troops; or as a carrier of combination loads of troops and mobile equipment.

When the two YC-130 airplanes were completed, the airframes came out so light that Lockheed was able to meet the mission requirements at a gross weight of 108,000 pounds instead of the 113,000 it had proposed! Empty weight was 57,500 pounds and design payload was 25,000 pounds. On the redesign for production, the company's engineers added back in about a thousand pounds in areas they felt to need more beef.

By careful attention to design detail, Lockheed's engineers found they had bettered the minimum requirements for flying qualities as laid down by the Air Force. Predicted average cruise speed turned out to be 20 per cent faster; normal power, ceiling and rate of climb were 35 per cent higher; normal power, one-engine-out ceiling and rate of climb were 35 per cent better, respectively, and 55 per cent faster; take-off distance with maximum power was 25 per cent less and landing distance, using brakes only, showed a 40 per cent decrease. As Middlewood noted,

> The early hours of flight testing validated our predictions satisfactorily. The airplane, even with its relatively larger size and weight, has the flying qualities of a much smaller airplane. Large airplanes are usually slower in responding to the pilot's controls because of their larger inertias. The control forces on the C-130A are very light and even at low flying speeds, the combination of light forces with high inertia seldom gives the pilot any impression of sluggishness. There is always sufficient control.

Shortly after Lockheed won the contract to build the two YC-130 prototypes, the company's top management in Burbank decided that if the aircraft went into full-scale production, the work would be done at its new Georgia division, located at Marietta, 15 miles north of Atlanta.

The president of Lockheed, Robert Gross, later would tell the company's shareholders he wished he had a magic carpet so he could take each of them to Georgia "to see the remarkable operation there. It is one of the greatest aircraft establishments in the world."

The B-1 building alone, the keystone of the vast Air Force Plant 6 complex, is the world's largest aircraft plant under one roof . . . totaling 76 acres of floor space. Erected in just two years following Pearl Harbor, it was operated by Bell Aircraft (and affectionately dubbed the "Bell Bummer Plant") turning out B-29s during World War II. But with V-J Day, production was halted and the building converted to machinery storage.

Lockheed re-opened the facility in early 1951 at the request of the Air Force, to rehabilitate mothballed B-29s for use in Korea. Dan Haughton, one of Lockheed's brilliant young executives, moved to Marietta as assistant to General Manager Jimmy Carmichael and took with him a team of 275 key people. Soon a steady stream of B-29s (fresh in from Pyotte, Texas) were flying off to Korea. This was followed by a B-47 contract. Eventually, Lockheed-Georgia manufactured 394 copies of the six-jet B-47E bomber, under license from Boeing. Amazingly, the Georgia company was able to turn back to the U.S. Government several million dollars of budgeted funds that were not required, an unheard-of-performance by a defense contractor.

Thus it was that in October of 1952, with the production phase of the C-130 imminent, Lockheed's corporate officials, particularly Robert and Courtlandt Gross—pleased with the Georgia Division's astounding B-47 performance—decided to put the Hercules production in Marietta.

Al Brown was selected C-130 project engineer. A genial aircraft specialist with a long list of inventions to his credit, he was the company's B-47 project engineer and was former chief engineer of Bell's Georgia division. Brown and 40 of his top engineers moved temporarily to Burbank to pick up the program and bring it back to Georgia. They moved right in with the California company's C-130 organization in Plant C-1, headed by C-130 Project Engineer, E.A. Peterman, working side by side with their prototype counterparts. Later more group engineers, such as Juge Jaeger and Carroll Dallas, were recruited, with some difficulty, from the California Company.

By early fall, 1953, most of the design teams were back in Georgia, working at their big drafting boards on the mezzanine of the vast B-1 Building. Their return, along with a number of additional engineers who signed on from Burbank, coincided with the delivery of a 100,000-pound wooden mockup. The monster—a full size mobile replica of the Hercules—was lashed to the deck of a U.S. Army engineering transport, and was brought from Los Angeles through the Panama Canal, to Savannah, Georgia. Two tractor trailer trucks picked it up and brought it the remaining 275 miles to Marietta.

The move—directed by Lockheed-Georgia liaison engineer Roy Knight—was headline news across Georgia. Along the route, schools let out so children could watch the procession, mayors greeted the convoy with proclamations, and cotton pickers stopped in their tracks to view the whale-like monster. Telephone and power crews cut lines to let the mockup through, then spliced the lines back. Reaching Marietta at 3 a.m., trucks and crews placed the big model in Lockheed's B-4 Building. Thousands of manhours of engineering and manufacturing time were saved by the mockup. Aircraft systems could be fitted for physical tryouts before being committed to production.

The culmination of the C-130 shift to Georgia came with the rollout of the first production bird on March 10, 1955. Governor Marvin Griffin hoisted a bottle of water from the nearby Chattahoochee River and smashed it four times against the Herk's nose before it would break. "You also build tough airplanes," the Governor quipped.

Just 28 days later, on April 7, the airplane, Air Force Tail No. 53-3129, took to the air from the adjacent runway. Hundreds of employees took their lunch break outside to watch the 11:39 a.m. liftoff. The plane broke free of the concrete at 800 feet and made a spectacular climbout. By the time it reached the end of the 10,000 foot long runway, it had reached an altitude of more than 2,500 feet. Bud Martin and Leo Sullivan, who were at the controls, circled the field at 5,000 feet to give flight engineers Jack Gilley, Chuck Littlejohn and Bob Brennan an opportunity to check the systems. They raised and lowered the landing gear four times. All systems were go. From there, they pushed the plane on up to 10,000 feet for more checks.

Sullivan, the tall, red-haired Irishman who was the instructor pilot on the flight, and later to become the Georgia Company's chief engineering test pilot, recalled the day:

"The minute we moved the power levers forward to start the

takeoff roll, we gained momentum without the roaring noise associated with piston engines at near the same power range. The Allison T56 engines and their 15-foot three-blade Curtiss-Wright propellers gave the Hercules an acceleration that made other transports look like diesel trucks."

The flight went so well, before bringing the plane in to a landing, Martin and Sullivan made two fast passes over the runway at 1,000 feet. Sullivan, who had flown the prototypes earlier in California, came into the pilots' quarters in the B-4 Building with increasing confidence about the new bird:

"We knew that here was one of those happy combinations of shape, structure and propulsion system where everything fits together just right; 110,000 pound gross weight, 3,750-horsepower engines with instant response to power levers and a 3g load factor for rapid military maneuvers."

First production C-130 (LAC 3001, AF 33129, later changed to 53-3129) took to the air April 7, 1955, with the same sharp climb as the prototypes—lifting off after an 800-foot ground roll. Back on the ground, pilots Bud Martin and Leo Sullivan were surrounded by well-wishers. Martin called it "an aircraft for the future," and said it was "the finest, cleanest airplane I've ever flown." (Lockheed)

"It handled so easy, you could bend it . . . you could turn it into dead engines and move it around and do things like that no other airplane at the time would do. So I guess the Hercules advanced the state of the art of the flying business about 500 times over what we had prior to then."

Sullivan's admiration for the airplane was directed at praise for his fellow workers back up the line at Lockheed, who had designed and put the big bird together. "An airplane is a summation of a helluva bunch of work of a lot of people. The pilot who flies the airplane ends up with all the publicity. But it takes a lot of people and a lot of technical knowledge and background, a lot of energy and a lot of good decisions."

For Chief Pilot Bud Martin, the Hercules was easy to sum up. "In my twenty years of flying, I have never flown an airplane as easy to handle," he said.

Martin's and Sullivan's comments to the press were full of optimism, and their professional opinions, based on years of experience, matched their words. But a tough flight test program lay ahead for the C-130, and there would be a great number of hurdles to surmount before the plane could go operational. Some of them would be quite formidable.

Crew celebrates after successful first flight of first C-130 production aircraft. At fountain, Chuck Littlejohn. Others, L-R: Bud Martin, Leo Sullivan, Anthony Brennan and Jack Gilley. (Lockheed)

"FIRE ON NUMBER 2!"

> The Hercules came into being as a problem child . . . a pioneer into the jet age . . . fraught with many questions and few answers . . . .
>
> Lockheed Southern Star

> Some days you have flights and some days you have "frights." We had practically no frights during the C-130 testing program. Of course, there were some days when the pucker factor was pretty high . . . .
>
> Leo Sullivan

"I'm sick, Leo . . . I got to get to the ground."

The voice over the C-130 intercom sounded frantic. Turbulent thunderclouds were boiling across north Georgia that April 14, 1955, and airsickness had overtaken Carroll Fruth, a Lockheed flight test engineer. Ghostly pale in the face and wobbly in his legs, Fruth felt the need for solid earth beneath him as he sat at the airborne observer's desk deep in the fuselage of the Hercules aircraft as the test plane, Lockheed serial number 3001 . . . Air Force tail number 33129 . . . whirled past the Dobbins Air Force Base control tower on speed calibration runs.

A former P-38 pilot and a seasoned power plant specialist, Fruth was a key man at the engineering nerve center of the Hercules, Lockheed's first production C-130. The plane had made its first flight at Marietta exactly a week earlier. Now on its first data gathering test flight, and its third flight of record, Number three thousand-one was strapped up for action. Copper wire strain gauges were taped, octopus-like, inside the plane's wings, fuselage and empennage. They were designed to measure the "loads" on the various airframe parts—the grunts and groans the Herk would experience during increasingly severe flight regimes. The objective: To test the airplane to its very design limits, and beyond. The gauges fed data into the onboard data recorders.

Earlier in the two-hour, eleven-minute test flight, Lloyd Frisbee—Lockheed's studious chief development test engineer newly signed on from Boeing—had his engineering test crew to feather and air-start each of the plane's four propjet engines. This was a checkout of the C-130's emergency systems and procedures. All went well and on the flight back to Marietta, engineering test pilot Sullivan swung the new airplane by Stone Mountain east of Atlanta. There he rendezvoused with a chase plane for some air-to-air photographs, the first to be taken of the new airplane.

A seasoned engineering crew was aboard. In addition to Frisbee, Sullivan and Fruth, three other people were up front. Seated on the flight deck with clip board in hand was quiet-spoken Ed Shockley, ex-Douglas Aircraft flight engineer and a Georgia Tech grad, who was now Lockheed's lead flight test engineer and one of the original Georgia Company crewmen to fly the YC-130 prototypes in California. Co-pilot in the right hand seat was veteran flyer Art Hansen. Bob Brennan was flight engineer.

It was back at Dobbins Air Force Base, during the final bumpy thirty minutes of speed calibration runs, that Carroll Fruth incurred his motion sickness. The Herk hurtled repeatedly by the Dobbins control tower at an altitude of only 150 feet off the deck, giving the test engineers on the runway an opportunity to accurately record the parameters affecting airspeed such as wind, temperature, humidity, density, altitude, etc., while special ground cameras with calibrated lenses recorded the position of the airplane in space as it roared across the field. The runs ranged from 150 knots down to a loping 95 knots.

Sullivan answered Fruth's appeal for relief.

"Okay, Carroll, one more run by the tower and we'll go in."

The final tower-fly-by completed, Sullivan banked to the left and turned 180 degrees. Going into the downwind leg, he dumped his flaps and landing gear and sent Brennan back to the cargo compartment to visually check the main landing gear, to make sure it was down and locked.

"Gear looks good," Brennan reported. The crew ran through the landing checklist and Sullivan prepared for a short approach landing.

Just at the turn into final, Shockley, standing behind co-pilot Hansen, saw a faint flickering on the overhead panel. It was the Number 2 engine fuel tank boost pump. But the signal was not really distinct and, with the plane seconds away from touchdown, he saw no reason to call anyone's attention to it.

Unbeknownst to the crew, however, a quick disconnect fuel line had come loose and fuel was spraying from the trailing edge of the left wing. Two Lockheed engineers saw it clearly from the Planeview Restaurant on U.S. Highway 41 at the east end of the runway. R.H. Old looked up as the plane crossed overhead and saw JP-4 spewing from the Number 2 nacelle. The slipstream behind the Number 2 engine was a "bluish-white vapor," M.D. Rousso noted.

Descending steeply at 100 knots, with flaps hanging out all the way, Sullivan flared the airplane briefly as he crossed the end of the runway.

"FLAPS UP," Sullivan called out.*

Hansen reached down and pulled them up. Within seconds, the Herk touched onto the concrete and the plane's propellers were put immediately into reverse.

Back in the fuselage, Fruth, sitting at the AO panel, stood up with a start when the tachometer on engine number 2 "unwound" rapidly. Glancing out the small fuselage window, Carroll saw flames leap from the back of the left inboard nacelle. There was a "POOF"; the number 2 engine exploded in flames.

"FIRE ON NUMBER 2 ENGINE!" Fruth screamed into his headset. The plane continued rolling down the runway, with the

---

*Due to the configuration of the test airplane, flaps had to be retracted to land.

Shortly after this photo was made of 3001 circling around Stone Mountain on April 14, 1955, the airplane headed back to Marietta for speed calibration tests at Dobbins AFB.

Just after 3001 touched down, fire erupted in the back of the Number 2 engine. Lower photo, the crew is all out of the airplane but Sullivan is walking back up to take a look. Dobbins AFB and Lockheed fire trucks were on the scene within seconds. (Lockheed)

propellers roaring in reverse pitch.

Frisbee glanced at the panic handles and saw a fire signal light up on the number 2 panel and a blinking signal on Number 1.

"FIRE IN NUMBER 2!" Fruth yelled again.

"SHUT DOWN NUMBER 2" Shockley shouted . . . "PANIC HANDLE!"

Sullivan was already doing it. His arms were moving like a shuttlecock. He shut down the Number 2 engine condition lever then pulled the emergency fire handle—with its blinking red light— and pushed the fire extinguisher button. He did the same thing for Number 1.

But the flames did not abate; instead, they blazed white hot, and a column of black smoke belched angrily from the left wing.

Dan Haughton, Lockheed-Georgia's general manager, was walking out of his office on "the hill" to the northwest. He was accompanied by Courtlandt Gross, Lockheed Corporation president, there for the Lockheed Board of Directors meeting.

"My God," Haughton exclaimed, "an airplane is on fire!" They drove hurriedly to the flight line.

"It's *our* airplane," Haughton said as soon as he saw the Herk's unmistakable tall tail with the 33129 painted on it.

Sullivan turned the nose gear steering wheel sharply to the left and braked the machine to a stop in the grass near the 4,000 foot marker.

Lights were blinking across the instrument panels now . . . particularly those associated with engines one and two. Back in the fuselage, Fruth ran to the left hand fuselage window again. Heavy smoke obscured the view. He started to remove the AO camera that had been filming the entire episode but thought better of it and dashed forward.

"LET'S GET THE HELL OUT OF HERE!" Sullivan commanded as he and his crew feathered the Number three and four engines and shut off all electrical power.

"LET'S GET MOVING," Sullivan yelled again. Frisbee opened the forward crew door and saw that there was just enough room to get by the flames. Then a shadow went by "at about a hundred miles an hour." That would be Fruth. The remaining crewmen followed in quick order, dashing out with flames lapping to within two or three feet. Sullivan, checking to see all were out, was the last to exit the burning airship.

A blizzard of protein foam quickly squelched the blazing fire on the left wing of 3001, but the wing broke off nevertheless. The airplane (AF tail number 33129) was outfitted with a new left wing and went on to an outstanding career with the Air Force in the U.S., Europe and the Far East. It is still flying as a trainer aircraft with the Air Force Reserve.

Fire trucks from Dobbins AFB reached the plane about the time it stopped, and started pouring in an avalanche of foamite.

William B. Williams, the Dobbins fire chief, came up to Sullivan. "Anyone else in there?"

"No. I've counted them and they're all out."

Sullivan edged back up to witness the event from in front of the nose. By an act of providence, he stepped back just as the left outer wing melted in two and dropped to the ground with a sharp crack. The fuselage rocked to the right, then settled in a slump with the right wing tilted down where Leo had been standing seconds before.

Miraculously, within ten minutes, the Dobbins firefighters had the plane blanketed with foam and the flames squelched.

Spring winds quickly dissipated the heavy black smoke, leaving a gaunt, foam-covered bird slumped on the grass. Burned metal, rubber and foamite protein gave off a bitter stench. In the stillness of the moment, all eyes looked on in mute wonder. Lockheed Flight Line employees watching from atop the B-25 hangar and from the sides of the runway, along with some of the Lockheed directors who had come early, all were stunned. Word spread quickly through the flight line and among the swing shift workers in Lockheed's big B-1 assembly building up on the hill.

It was the saddest day up to then for Lockheed's fledgling, four-year old Georgia division. "It was worse than having a death in the family," recalled Dot Mauldin, a cockpit assembler.

Everyone concerned was thankful there were no casualties. But the dinner meeting of the Lockheed Board of Directors that night at Atlanta's Capital City Country Club was anything but a cheerful affair for Dan Haughton, the host. After all, how do you explain to your directors that the first production copy of your new transport had caught fire on its third flight and had come to within a hair of completely burning up?

*   *   *

The roughest period of a new airplane's life is in the "shadow zone" between its maiden flight and its later introduction to operational duty. The experimental period—when the two YC-130 prototypes underwent their initial testing in Southern California—had convinced the Air Force and Lockheed that the Hercules would be a winner. The USAF authorized full-scale production to begin.

Yet, as with any new airplane fresh off the drawing board, the machine was obviously far from ready for Air Force service and it was the job of Lockheed-Georgia's new engineering development test organization to prove it out, eliminate the bugs, and subject the bird to every manner of operating obstacle that it might encounter in service with the U.S. Air Force.

Developing an airplane is the result of a remarkable chain of circumstances. First, there is the preliminary design effort to get the best possible air frame/power plant combination. After that, the contractor builds the machine to acceptable standards; then he goes through a series of difficult ground and flight testing to prove that the original design meets its required standards.

"Today, we talk of aeronautical engineering as an advanced science—which it certainly is," said Sullivan. "But there's still room for a lot of breaks for everything to come out right, with so many demands, requirements and standards being integrated into that single final package." Then he added, "We wouldn't have jobs as test pilots if everything in engineering did come out right. The recognition of problems, and solving those problems, is the name of the game in our entire system."

As expected, problems did, indeed, crop up early in the Herk's engineering development. They were dealt with quickly and effectively. Had they not been, the C-130's blossoming career might well have ended then and there. The saying at the time among Lockheed-Georgians was that a minor problem would remain "minor" only if it were resolved quickly. Otherwise it could become a "major" problem and nobody wanted *that* to happen.

Of course, everyone—Lockheed and Air Force people particularly—realized that the wing fire was a very serious accident. But, as in the case of so many such mishaps, the culprit proved to be a tiny component, and a relatively easy problem to fix. An accident investigation team, headed by Lockheed's chief research development engineer, Gordon P. Thorn, quickly pinpointed the cause of the fire—a quick disconnect fitting on the fuel hose just behind the engine firewall. The device had been installed to meet an Air Force requirement that the C-130 engines be quickly changed in a few manhours. The probers found the Roylyn coupling apparently was not properly locked during assembly. During the turbulence encountered on the flight, and probably as a result of vibration of the hose with the loose coupling, the coupling disconnected, causing the fuel to leak during the base leg of the landing pattern. An engineering fix was quickly devised and Lockheed hauled the wounded bird up to its B-4 Building, put on a new wing and within a few months had "the first lady" flying again. To keep the test program on schedule, the heavy instrumentation from number one, all that could be salvaged, was pulled out and installed on number 3011, designated as the new structural test aircraft. The flight test program was not paralyzed, only delayed for a short time.*

*   *   *

The toughest C-130 development gremlin to emerge during the development was the plane's engine-propeller combination. Before the problem was licked, Lockheed's test pilots "flew through a succession of propellers."

As noted previously, the Hercules, as the first American aircraft ever to enter production with turboprop power and the Allison T-56 propjet engines, presented a complete departure from the piston powered planes of the past. Said Leo Sullivan, "Compared to what we had been flying, we had fantastic advantages in thrust capability, in takeoff acceleration and control of the aircraft under all emergency situations, because of the thrust-to-weight improvement of these engines. We had plunged into a completely new regime of flight."

Yet the marrying of the turbine engine and the variable pitch propeller presented frustrating difficulties to Lockheed's engineers. The big problem was the variable pitch Curtiss-Wright electric prop which failed to function properly. Harvey Christen, Lockheed's chief inspector, recalled, "When the propeller got an electric signal, it would over-compensate (on the pitch), then it would cut back, cut back, cut back." To test pilot Joe Garrett, the electrical

---

*As a testimony to the ruggedness of the C-130 airframe, Number 33129 went on to a spectacular career with the U.S. Air Force, first as a space vehicle tracker along the Atlantic missile range; then as a transport and later, following Air Force modification as a gunship in Vietnam. The airplane logged 4,500 flying hours in Vietnam alone.

impulses "would make the prop grab . . . change pitch all at once." Each engine had its own separate pitch control and the surges from individual engines gave the airplane an unpredicatble jerkiness. Leo Sullivan described the sensation:

"Flying the airplane, you'd be surging and you might surge fore and aft, or you might surge left or right, but you'd never see anything on the gauges; it would react so fast there'd be no RPM or fuel flow change!"

Frisbee put the blame on the reduction gear system which was under-designed. "Those gears would just turn into balls of metal. They were unable to handle the pitch control changes and last for more than a few hours."

Carroll Dallas, now Lockheed-Georgia's chief design engineer, described it as a mechanical problem with the propeller's clutch, and outlined the dimensions of the problem.

"The Allison T-56 is a constant speed engine—designed for constant speed. That's the key to its remarkable performance. But what is constant is its propeller speed. When you add more fuel, you start to develop more power and the prop takes more bite of air. It takes enough bite to keep the engine speed the same, even though you're pulling more power. As you reduce the fuel, you reduce the power in the engine, then the propeller automatically takes less bite. So really, the primary governor of the engine is in the propeller itself."

Ironically, Leo Sullivan greatly admired the hollow-steel turbo-electric props —*when* they performed right. "The Curtiss-Wright electric gave a great aerodynamic performance. But they would take signals and wouldn't turn them loose."

Sullivan's admiration would turn to anger when the props started misbehaving in flight. Harvey Christen went aloft with Sullivan several times during that period:

"To listen to Leo in the cockpit talk to those propellers was something I'll never forget. Leo had adjectives, but he had some special ones for those props. I remember vividly the time I was aboard while Leo made ILS (instrument landing) runs at Chattanooga. It was a Saturday.

"All of a sudden, two of the props started oscillating and Leo had to feather both of 'em. Next thing, the third propeller started acting up and Leo said, 'Harv, I think we can make one turn around the field . . . thank goodness we've got a light fuel load.' For a minute, it looked like we were going into Chattanooga one way or another. When we got around the field, the third prop quit oscillating and Leo cranked 'em up, one at a time, and boy, we headed straight back to Marietta."

At the beginning of the C-130 program at Lockheed-Georgia, the Hercules shared the production spotlight with the B-47 Stratojet bomber. First production C-130 is pictured on the Lockheed-Georgia flight line, then being expanded across the runway from the main plant. There too, it had to share space with new B-47s. (Lockheed)

Early in 1956, Lockheed and the Air Force scheduled a press demonstration to show off the new plane to the media. The night before the event, the demo plane developed *two* defective props. "The only thing for us to do was to replace them," Dan Haughton remembered, and it was done, between midnight and the 8 a.m. show time. Fortunately, the new props performed well.

But the people at Lockheed were worried. "We could see the whole (C-130) program going down the drain if we didn't get that prop problem resolved," recalled Carroll Dallas. "Strictly speaking, it was not our reponsibility; it was the Air Force's and Curtiss-Wright's. That didn't make any difference. We weren't going to get to build the C-130 any more, regardless of who was at fault."

Lockheed assigned one of its test planes, Number 3007, to a project dubbed "Let's try to make it (the electric prop) work." Another test plane, Number 3006, was assigned to testing out a new hydraulically-operated prop built by Aero-Products, a unit of GM's Detroit Diesel Allison Division.

By the time the tenth production C-130 rolled out at Marietta, the Air Force became convinced, as had Lockheed's engineers, that the electric prop wasn't going to hack it, and ordered a switch to the Aero-Products hydraulic prop, which worked well from the start. As luck would have it, once the switch was made, the electric improved and began performing consistently well. But the 49 "A" model Hercules that had stacked up in a horseshoe-shaped row at the Lockheed "Pea Patch" were retrofitted with the hydraulic prop, which turned in a great performance. (Beginning with "B" model Hercules, the propeller was opened to competition and the winner was the four-bladed Hamilton-Standard hydraulic prop, which has been used on all succeeding Hercules models.)

* * *

Meanwhile, despite the intermittent prop difficulties, Bud Martin, Leo Sullivan and their gang of gung-ho test pilots were having a ball wringing out the new airplane.

"It was fun flying the Hercules then," said Sullivan. "Everybody was interested in making sure you were selling the airplane. So the results were fantastic . . . what you could do with it was amazing compared to previous transports."

The Lockheed pilots took off and did near aerobatic maneuvers with their Herks, beginning with a high performance, 600 foot takeoff, coming around the field and stopping well within a thousand feet, and then backing it up on the runway a bit and taking off again! They'd fly a tight 360-degree turn at a 400 foot altitude around the Lockheed B-25 Building *at a speed of 80 knots* (a feat later performed with aerospace writers aboard) just to show the maneuverability and low speed controllability of the brash new propjet. One day Bud Martin used the *last* 1,000 feet of the runway to take off, and made it with ease.

"We'd climb the airplane up and go cruise around 35,000 feet," said Sullivan. "That was quite startling to the fighters. There was no other transport in the world then that could fly *that* high. The B-47 bomber could, of course, but it would startle people to see a prop-powered airplane *way up there at 35,000 feet.*"

One of Lockheed's bright young flyers, Walt Hensleigh, an engineering test pilot newly signed on from Fairchild, was especially impressed with the aerodynamic response of the Herk. Stepping up from the Fairchild C-119s that he had been flying, Hensleigh was visibly moved when he went up with Vern Peterson for his first 130 ride.

"It was very, very easy to transition to, and I was amazed at the tremendous power available. It was so terrific in its thrust versus gross weight—especially in the early days when we imposed strict upper limits on weight—that we never really had any emergencies. I had flown the twin-engined C-119 and C-123 loaded up to their maximum capacity. You lose an engine under those conditions and right away you were in trouble. Those airplanes were limited by power. The Hercules was a different story altogether. *Our* limitations were structural. We could carry just about anything up to its maximum allowable gross weight, and if necessary we could carry it just as well with only three engines operating. And once we really got up steam, we could do it on *two* engines . . . ."

Hensleigh, who conducted much of the C-130 stability and control testing as well as air drop testing at El Centro, California, quickly grew to appreciate the Hercules' responsiveness in short-field operations. He found it an ideal aircraft for survivability of a flight crew under almost all conditions. "It handled so easy; you could bend it, you could turn it into dead engines and move it around and do things like that, that no other airplane at the time would do. There's no pilot who flies it who will tell you that it isn't one of the nicest airplanes he's ever flown."

Hensleigh, today Lockheed-Georgia's director of flight operations with responsibility for both the engineering and production flight testing, found early on that the Hercules was capable of some amazing and quite unbelievable maneuvers never before done with an airplane—such as flying sideways and going into a powered "fin stall" *and coming out.*

As Lockheed test pilot Jesse Allen was to report, the C-130 "is the only airplane in which I've ever been able to make a level turn. Normally, to make a good turn, you've got to bank the wings. But with *this* thing you just kick the rudder, your wings stay level and she comes around smart and snappy in the turn. . . ."

The C-130 fin stall phenomenon was discovered by Vern Peterson flying with Roy Wimmer on Lockheed's first 80 per cent structural demonstrations with the YC-130 in California. Flight test crews developed the data to prove the extent of the problem and then conducted all the tests to prove that it wasn't harmful to the airplane and that you could get out of the stall without difficulty. But when Walt experienced his first fin stall it was quite a shocker. "We were flying at a sideslip angle of 17 degrees when all of a sudden, the plane went into severe buffeting from nose to tail. The rudder flopped over all the way and the plane went into a high rate left turn with a large bank angle to the right.

"That first time, it shook me a bit. I didn't know whether the airplane could possibly go all the way around in that sideslip, and that is one way of getting into a flat spin. The airplane remains basically level—its nose to the horizon—but it rotates around its axis with tremendous speed and you're completely out of control!

"It didn't happen that way . . . the bird slewed around to a 46 degree sideslip and it stopped right there. Everyone in the flight deck stared at everyone else in disbelief. I brought her out of the slip and then we tried it again. From then on we were able to repeat the test a number of times. It was simply amazing the way the big airplane, without any trouble at all, would go into this flight attitude, and, without any sweat, recover at once. Of course, there have been other airplanes that have had fin stall, but they would go completely out of control."

*   *   *

Meanwhile, a fleet of C-130A test aircraft was being tested by Lockheed and the Air Force to wring out the airplane's structure, stability and control, its landing ability on unpaved strips, and its airdrop capability.

Al Brown, first C-130 project engineer at Lockheed-Georgia, posed with two of his prides in 1953 . . . his Studebaker coupe and the newly arrived C-130 wooden mockup. Lower photo, the mockup is installed in Lockheed's B-4 Building where it was utilized for physical tryouts of various parts, systems and sub-systems.

Propellers were something of a problem during the early C-130 testing period. The decision was made to switch from the electrically-operated propeller to a hydraulic prop. Here then Lockheed marketing director "Gif" Myers (C) discusses the airplane with two USAF officers at Open House: Capt. Jim Sampson and Col. Edward McRay. (Lockheed)

The airplane's ability to land and take off from soft fields was a new airlift challenge. The C-119 had done some, and the 123 a little more on unprepared fields. But no U.S. airplane in history the size and weight of the C-130 had ever been landed onto unprepared fields and this requirement led to the Lockheed landing gear design that was unique and is still unique. The size of the tires was large for the airplane, but the uniqueness was that they were set in tandem. This was done purposely. The Lockheed designers had the idea that the front wheels would pack down the soil and the back wheels would run in the rut, both on landing and takeoff. Their idea was valid.

Lockheed's Vern Peterson took C-130s to Florida for soft field tests. The results were amazing.

At the same time, Lockheed delivered two C-130s to the U.S. Air Force in June, 1956, for the Category II performance and operational suitability tests. The Air Force's C-130 test director at Eglin was Major Russ Dobyns, a helicopter pilot who set a world helicopter speed and altitude record in 1953. Dobyns recalled the C-130 testing in the sandy, scrub oak fields.

"Our mission was testing the airplane in its operating environment. Since the primary mission was airdrop and assault field landing, we used some of the auxiliary fields at Eglin to perform our rough field tests. They were sandy, rough terrain with small scrub trees on them. The objective in a tactical assault was landing in the shortest distance going in and getting out in the shortest distance. All performance for that type of mission is based on coming in over a 50-foot obstacle, touching down and stopping in the shortest distance. We erected 50-foot poles with flags running across for our obstacles, and all our takeoffs and approaches were over them.

"On some of our landings, we hit some soft spots in the sandy soils and with max reverse and full braking, we ended up with some wheels so far in the ground that the belly would be just barely touching the ground! All we had to do was dig a little trench out in front of the wheels and apply power and the plane would pull itself right out. We did it at various gross weights and fuel weights, simulating mid-point landing weights for a 500-mile radius mission. At that weight, you didn't have a lot of fuel. We recorded data of all the landings and takeoff distances and most of that ended up establishing operational criteria."

Dobyns admired the Herk's stamina in the rough field environment. "We got a lot of wing waving (flexing) on those landings. And with full reverse on a dry field, it got dusty and visibility got critical. But ingestion of dust didn't really bother us."

Dobyns was quite impressed with the structural integrity of the Hercules. The test aircraft held intact while other aircraft being tested, including the P-2V flown by Lockheed's Stan Beltz, ended up breaking a wing on landing. "The C-130s came through those tests pretty well," Dobyns recalled. "We never did have any serious damage with it. The other two planes there at the time both crashed . . . one was lost and the other seriously damaged."

The Lockheed high wing design on the C-130 proved to be a valid one in the Florida tests, where the airplane rocked from side to side on the sandy strips.

"We cut up a few scrub bushes and trees with the props," Dobyns reported, "and they ran up to an inch or so in diameter. Scarred the props a bit, but that was all."

Dobyns, who got checked out in the C-130 at Lockheed-Georgia, tested the Hercules for about two years, starting out at Eglin, then at Pope Air Force Base, N.C., where all the drop missions and assault landings with troops aboard were made.

The Air Force "Prove It" campaign also included C-130 cold weather tests in the far north, with landings on ice runways. Other test Herks landed on PSP (pierced steel planking) laid on swampy lands. C-130 test birds went on flights into the Caribbean and Panama, throughout the U.S., Europe and Alaska. The Number 12 Hercules—carrying out continuous flying with shifts of crews—flew 41 hours out of 49, subjecting the engines and airframe to highly accelerated utilization. The Lockheed "tech rep," who lived with the airplane on its marathon missions, wired Marietta: "Number Twelve is wearing out the crews as fast as the USAF can supply them. Please send lots of stay-awake pills . . . ."

The C-130 was put through a tremendous variety of missions—as a paratroop transport, cargo-hauler, flying hospital, and assault troop transport. The airplane paradropped trucks, artillery pieces, field ambulances, food containers and supply packages. One of the biggest challenges was hauling 110 items of Army Engineers' equipment . . . 18-ton D-6 bulldozers, wheeled asphalt plants, tractor-excavators, 35,000-pound trucks and Baily Bridge sections. As Martin Caidin reported, "The Hercules came through in good fashion as a 'Can Do' airplane."

But still more tests—particularly in North Carolina—lay ahead. And even though Lockheed was getting ready to deliver the first production models to the Tactical Air Command, engineering development was still underway to iron out all of the bugs.

THE GEORGIA SKUNK WORKS

We had a strong team . . .
none of us were stars.
—Dan Haughton

The atmosphere around Lockheed-Georgia Company during the C-130 development years crackled with electricity.

"There were not many low dynamic people around," a development test engineer recalled. "We had a whole amalgamation of folks—Georgia Tech grads, people from other companies, Lockheed people who transferred from California and new employees from all over Georgia and the country. Everyone came to Marietta because they wanted to. So we didn't have a fixed pattern of decision making: It was a challenge system. If you told me something and I didn't think it was right, I'd challenge you and then we'd have an argument. But when we finished, we would have established what was the best course of action, and when we walked out of the room, that was the end of the dispute. If there were any unresolved question, we could go to a higher level and get an immediate answer."

The catalyst for the company's hard charging, innovative work force was General Manager Dan Haughton, a 41-year-old dynamo of a shirtsleeves executive who came out of the Birmingham coal mines by way of the University of Alabama, where he earned a degree in business.

"Dan always had the plant humpin'," recalled the engineer, "and when you were working with Haughton, you were humpin' all the time. There're not many people like him. There was only one Haughton, who could add, subtract, and divide as fast as he could—in people, personalities, planning . . . he even had a quick mind for scientific facts. Dan could separate the chaff from the wheat very quickly. His interest was movement: 'We've got a good product in the C-130,' he would say, 'Let's make it go.'

"Dan didn't figure he knew all things for all things. But he had a way of putting a team together—people from such differing points of view as engineering and manufacturing. He could cut through problems quickly. He could sit in a meeting with a varying number of talents and people, eliminate the parochial hangups *and get action.*"

While he was a strict exponent of disciplined teamwork, Haughton took a personal interest in his employees and encouraged individual initiative. Moving daily around the assembly lines, engineering shops and flight line, "plowing the orchard," Haughton knew hundreds of workers by name and issued snappy comments for the day, such as "It sure is fun building airplanes, isn't it?" He wore wide brim hats, summer and winter. Employees fresh off the farms across north Georgia idolized him, making him a legend in his own time. An engineer recalled Haughton:*

"With Dan as team leader, you had dynamics. You knew him and he knew you. When you had a problem you'd go see your boss and you and your boss would go see Haughton. There was no question that the end product was to make that the *best* gol-darned airplane that anybody could ever build, and we went at it that way. Not always were we successful. But more times than not we were."

During the crucial six months following the first flight of three thousand and one, Haughton held daily "steering meetings" with his key people to make sure the program was on the track. It was in these that he earned a well-deserved reputation for cracking the whip and putting on the pressure. Ed Shockley, now Vice President of marketing for Lockheed-Georgia Company, likes to tell the

---

*Haughton retired from Lockheed in 1977 after serving a long tenure as the corporation's chairman and chief executive officer.

Roominess and visibility from the flight station of the C-130 brought joy to flight crews. At the controls of one of the early C-130As were then Lockheed chief production pilot Lloyd Harris (L), and Don Mills, who later became chief of flying operations at Lockheed-Georgia. The C-130 has a glass area of 40 square feet. Significant is the downward view. The late Lloyd Harris was fond of calling the C-130 cockpit "our room with a view." (Lockheed)

Lockheed-Georgia Company flight line in early C-130 years. Blunt Roman Nose "A" models are lined up, with B-47 on the end. (Lockheed)

Hydrostatic testing of aircraft was pioneered by Lockheed in the U.S. with the C-130. This is an artist's rendering of the water tank Lockheed built for the Hercules fuselage. Lower photo, a below-ground pool was built to test smaller components. (Lockheed)

story about the time when hydraulic system problems were plaguing the C-130 test airplanes. Dogged efforts on the part of development test engineers had failed to find a solution. Haughton took the opportunity at a steering meeting to ask Shockley when he would have the problem licked.

"Well, I don't know," Shockley answered. "We really haven't defined the problem. When we get the problem defined, then the engineering folks will know how to correct it."

"That wasn't my question, I asked, 'When will you have it fixed?' "

Shockley started to repeat his previous explanation and Haughton interrupted him.

"What you're trying to tell me, Ed, is that you can't schedule an invention," Haughton said.

"I guess that's what I'm saying."

"Well, for your information, we do it every day. We scheduled building and delivering this airplane long before we had a final design and we do it all the time in this industry. Now, I'm going to ask you one more time, 'When are you going to have this problem solved?' "

"In three weeks."

"Fine. I'll check back with you then."

During those critical months, Shockley developed a lasting respect for Haughton and his tough managerial approach.

"Dan demanded action and if you committed to have something solved within a certain time span, you'd better do it *or you damn well better have a justifiable excuse.* You were expected to work as long as necessary and get whatever help or resources you needed to get the job done—and on time."

Haughton himself knew that if the Georgia Company was to become a permanent Lockheed division, it had to succeed with the C-130. His driving ambition was picked up by osmosis by his Georgia colleagues.

As Haughton recalled, "The thing we had pledged when we came to Georgia was to *be permanent.* After California won the C-130 prototype competition, we argued that the production should be moved to Georgia and the Gross brothers agreed. A lot of people had thought earlier that we couldn't build the B-47 at Marietta. The reason we succeeded was we had such a strong team

. . . as close a team as I've ever seen. One thing we tried to do from the beginning was to emphasize teamwork. There were very few things that somebody could get fired for at Lockheed-Georgia; one of them was failing to work with the team. We could have dissent during a discussion period, but once a decision was made, we expected teamwork."

Thus it was that the entire 10,000-person Marietta plant work force rallied behind Haughton to get the Herk through its birthing pains.

"Dan had a giant Skunk Works* behind him," said Jim James, a group engineer. "A glorified Skunk Works . . . an operation that could really *move*. All the problems that made the airplane the great plane it is today were addressed *then* . . . immediately. Nobody was allowed to think that a problem could be put off 'til tomorrow. Engineering Development Test, for instance, had a three-shift operation. We were developing fixes and we modified the airplane as we went along."

Leo Sullivan viewed it from the flight line:

"We'd fly today, come in with what we saw wrong with the plane. The next morning, we would be down to describe what we found wrong and what we needed to get fixed. Right there in that meeting, it was delegated who would do the job, and generally it had to be done that afternoon."

Haughton's hard driving management style—while tremendously effective—drew sparks on occasion, including the time he demanded faster work on a propeller test. At the time Engineering Development Test was conducting propeller vibratory stress surveys using highly delicate strain gauges on special propellers. Instrumented by Curtiss-Wright, the spaghetti-like maze of components would balk when they got wet and workmen would have to tediously remove the propellers and the hundreds of wires in a long, laborious process, dry them out, and replace them one by one. As luck would have it, a rainstorm came and the test aircraft

*The "Skunk Works" is Lockheed's highly acclaimed Advanced Development Project shop in Burbank, Calif., started by C.L. "Kelly" Johnson. From it have come such revolutionary aircraft as the P-80, U-2, YF-12, and SR-71, world's fastest airplane. The "Skunk Works" is noted for its unusual "vertical" management style where the development of aircraft is done on a fast response, individual responsibility basis in a self-contained environment. The "Skunk Works" term originated in the comic strip "Li'l Abner."

struck a puddle of water on the flight line, soaking the props. The plane had to go into layup, causing a critical delay.

At a steering meeting, Haughton wanted to know why the plane hadn't met its test schedule. Frisbee explained the situation and reported that the props had to be pulled, cleaned, and dried.

"How long is it going to take?" Haughton asked.

"Three or four days," Frisbee replied.

"I can't understand why it would take that long . . . Maynard Shumaker doesn't take three days to change a propeller." (Shumaker was maintenance supervisor for the production airplanes.)

Frisbee, new in Georgia and new to the Haughton style, started explaining the difference between an instrumented propeller and the regular production propeller Shumaker had to change. But he was not getting through. Frisbee could see Dan "pull down the venetian blinds, waiting for the noise in the corner to die down so he could get on with the meeting. And I could see he didn't accept it at all. He made some comments about engineering maintenance. Well, Charlie Smith was in the room. Charlie was a tremendous guy. He was superintendent for flight services in Engineering Development. He knew that airplane from A to Izzard. He had been out in California, gotten trained on the C-130 and trained all the Georgia maintenance people."

After the meeting, the company's chief engineer, the late Bob Middlewood, invited Frisbee to come talk to him and he explained how Haughton worked, and how he liked to put on the pressure and get things done.

"Well, Dan took a cut at Flight Services," Frisbee said, "and Charlie Smith is here morning, noon, and night and the guy never goes home and he won't take any pay for overtime and he's just dedicated. I didn't like the Haughton remarks and I thought I ought to explain that we had a different kind of problem than Maynard had. I understood what Dan was trying to do but I don't agree with him."

That night, Frisbee was sitting in his office on the fourth floor of the B-4 building, just under the control tower. It was about 7:30. Everybody else had gone. He heard someone coming up the stairs and in came Dan Haughton.

"I understand you weren't too happy with my comments in the meeting this morning," Haughton said.

Frisbee confirmed it and told Haughton why. He guessed Middlewood had talked to Haughton.

"Do you suppose Charlie is around?" Haughton said. "Maybe I was wrong about those propellers."

"Yes, I'm sure he's here, Dan. He's always around."

"You think we could call him up and I could talk to him?"

Frisbee called Charlie and he was, indeed, at work in the engineering test shops downstairs. When Smith came up the stairs and saw Haughton, he started to turn around and leave.

Haughton quickly apologized for his comments at the steering meeting and told Smith he hadn't understood the problem fully and that he appreciated Charlie's dedicated efforts.

Frisbee recalled that "When Dan got done with him, Charlie would have dived off the fourth floor of the B-4 building if Dan had asked him."

*　　*　　*

It was a seven day a week, 24-hour a day job, getting the bugs ironed out of the Hercules. Each problem that occurred was tackled then and there and direct responsibility assigned for getting it corrected.

Many Lockheedians felt the prop problem, which caused a stackup of dozens of airplanes on the unused north-south runway, gave the company a breathing spell to solve some of the design problems that had been identified on the C-130. One of these was the balky landing gear, which refused to come down on occasions. There was one such incident at Pope AFB, North Carolina, during a paradrop test flight in 1956. The crew was forced to land the plane on its belly.

Major Russ Dobyns, the Air Force pilot on the paradrop mission, had taken the Eglin test plane on a 20-minute paradrop flight over a Fort Bragg drop zone. Five U.S. Army colonels—the "Board Five" group which directed Army test and evaluation of airdrop systems—were aboard as observers.

After dropping the troops, Dobyns headed back to Pope AFB but, arriving at the air base, couldn't get the landing gear to budge.

Dobyns turned to the Army colonels:

"You men have your parachutes? I can go back over the drop zone and you can jump out if you want to."

The C-130 was subjected to extreme rough field conditions in remote landing strips at Eglin AFB. On this aircraft, the test engineers decided to take the doors off the main landing gears (see lower photo) in order to plow through the deep sands without dragging the doors. (Lockheed)

Early rough-field tests in Florida validated the Hercules' ability to operate into and out of sandy soils. The airplane, designed to land on "hastily-prepared runways," went further and made take-offs, landings and taxi-runs at 116,000 pounds weight across the soft, rough fields, with the airplane sinking deeper than 20 inches into the ground. Air Force and Lockheed pilots alternated in flying the tests at Eglin AFB, Florida. (USAF)

"We didn't bring any parachutes," a colonel replied. "We have confidence in the plane. We'll stay with you and ride it out."

Lockheed tech rep Herb Spring was on the ground and he patched a call directly from the distressed plane to Lockheed's engineers in Marietta. Dick Pulver, Lockheed's chief engineer, talked directly to the crew, but all efforts to get the gear down, even trying to crank the gear down manually, were fruitless. Later examination revealed a bushing had brinelled on the gear's jack screw. Even 3,000-pound per square inch of hydraulic pressure wouldn't budge it.

Dobyns burned off most of his fuel and came in to land. Just as he lined up on final approach, the wind shifted 180 degrees and the Pope tower instructed him to land from the other end.

The situation was critical. Fuel was down to minimum and Dobyns didn't know if he could make it. He made a tight downwind leg, and, fortunately, all four engines kept turning.

For Dobyns, it was one of the smoothest landings he'd ever made.

"Once we touched down solid on the foamed runway, we pulled all four fire handles for shutdown, skidded maybe 1200 feet, and ended up in a slight nose-left attitude. But there was less than an inch of fuel in the bottom of the wing tanks." A big fireball of sparks rose from under the aft cargo door when the fuselage scraped pavement. But the props didn't strike the ground and the Army colonels found the landing to be just like any other. While some of the skin was torn off, along with antennas, none of the airframe formers or stringers required replacing. Pope maintenance people patched the hole with temporary sheet metal and the plane was flown straight to Lockheed-Georgia Company the following day.

"We patched it up and had it back in the flight test program in about ten days, with a whole new belly (skin) on it," recalled Jim James. It was an early testimony to the ruggedness of the C-130 airframe and a test of the responsiveness of Lockheed's engineering shop.

*   *   *

In developing a new airplane, engineers who are plowing new

The wing fire of April, 1955, did not put 3001 out of business permanently. The indomitable aircraft, outfitted with a new wing, returned to the air in 1956 and went back into the Lockheed/Air Force test program, and subsequently into the Air Force inventory. The airplane is still flying as a trainer aircraft with the Air Force Reserve. (Lockheed)

territory with new materials and techniques run into what the aerospace industry calls "unk-unks"—the unknown-unknowns that are not revealed until the airplane is built and tested either on the ground or in the air, or both.

One such deficiency hit the C-130 early in the ground testing—the rear cargo door latching system. The problem surfaced in 1955 during a ground pressure test on the C-130 static test article in bay two of Lockheed's big B-4 test building. The C-130 was the first truly large all-cargo airplane ever built—and the first all pressurized *cargo* aircraft at that. The challenges were enormous. Complicating the problem was the huge rear cargo door—a complete 9 x 10 foot opening—plus four other large "holes" in the fuselage—forward side cargo door, crew entry door, and two paratrooper doors. The plan called for the airplane to be pressure-tested up to 15.0 pounds per square inch—200 percent of design limit, or twice the normal operating pressure. "That big rear cargo door represented an awful lot of square inches to put under pressure at that time," remembered Dan Haughton. Lockheed's engineers filled the plane's cargo compartment with hundreds of cardboard barrels, each of which had a small hole drilled in the end. Dean Cumro, engineer in charge of the ground tests, explained the reasoning behind the barrels with holes:

"When the plane was pressurized, the barrels would pressurize also. In the event we had an explosion, as we did, the air available would be entrapped by a small orifice in each barrel and couldn't all come out at once."

On the day of the big test, Cumro and his team cleared everyone from the bay and climbed into their iron box to watch what would happen. He gradually brought the pressure up to 12.7 pounds per square inch. The ramp door latches gave way, blowing barrels all over the ramp.

"We learned a great deal in those tests and from the British," said Lloyd Frisbee. At the time, Britain's Comet—the first commercial passenger jet—was plagued with fatigue problems. Several disappeared from the sky, a victim of decompression explosions due to fuselage failure. In the aftermath, the British developed a unique method for testing aircraft fatigue combined with the internal pressure required for high altitude jet flight. They did it by submerging the test articles in water!

Lockheed-Georgia became the first American aerospace company to adopt the English method and Georgia engineers "sent the Hercules to sea." The company built two pools. The first one, dug into the ground near the runway, was used to test fuselage components. This was followed with the construction of a large metal "swimming pool" which was built up 40 feet high around the static test aircraft on the B-4 ramp, enabling the entire fuselage to be enveloped in water. It was a funny looking box, with the C-130 wings sticking out the sides. But it did the job.

The advantage of the hydrostatic method was that any type of failure would not involve an explosion and therefore would preserve the test article, enabling engineers to analyze the failure and develop a fix. Under the old air pressure method, a failure could cause the fuselage to explode a quarter of a mile into space.

With the submarine type of pressure testing, and with the component pressurized with water, which does not compress or expand appreciably, the rip would merely go *clunk*. "You could go swimming underneath or drain the tank and examine the failure," said Frisbee. Lockheed engineers did just that.

The problem on the C-130 ramp door was found to be the material in the door latches which was too brittle. These were redesigned and more ductile material substituted. Subsequently the door as well as the entire fuselage passed the 200 per cent test in the "swimming pool." The entire aircraft meanwhile was subjected in the ground tests to the equivalent of four life-times of service life.

*   *   *

Simultaneous with the ground tests on the static and fatigue test articles, Lockheed-Georgia's C-130 flight test activity moved into high gear throughout 1956, and went on long after the delivery of the first operational planes to the Air Force late that year.

In the air, Leo Sullivan and his engineering flight test crews demonstrated the airplane to a three G load factor—subjecting the airframe to three times its own gross weight—in wing upbending maneuvers and minus one G in downbending.

The key maneuvers were designed to test the structural strength of the wings. "We demonstrated the 3G capability of the C-130 by carrying a full payload in the fuselage and by having hardly any fuel in the wing, affording maximum upbending. Then we pulled a 3G load factor, getting maximum bending because we had all the weight hanging in the fuselage. That's the *positive* load side of the structural testing.

"On the *negative* G side of the house, we went negative to Minus 1, putting the plane into a severe wing downbend, with maximum fuel load in the wing and hardly any cargo in the fuselage."

Sullivan described another wing-wringing maneuver of extraordinary range, "Moving from normal to positive G, on to the weightlessness of negative G, and then back down to extreme positive G." On such a maneuver, the internal structure and outer wing and all associated plumbing and wiring has to bend and flex also, just like the pinions of a great bird.

"You go through this structural program of critical maneuver points that no one in his right mind would get into operationally, except that in this business, you must prove the aircraft will fly safely to the limits of its design. And you can't do it sitting on the ground or as a daredevil in the sky. It's a serious step by step engineering effort that culminates in a complete investigation of the aircraft's design maneuver envelope in flight."

Sullivan described another maneuver: A rolling pullup, "A maneuver where you roll into a 60-degree bank at a given speed, and then rack in full opposite aileron to roll at maximum rate, with a full fuel load, through wings level to a 60-degree opposite bank." All of it was designed to measure the "loads" on all of the airplane components.

Measuring the airplane's tail loads was another interesting maneuver with the C-130, which was accomplished by "kicking the rudder." At a specific speed and gross weight, full rudder input is made resulting in max overswing yaw and return to stabilized side slip for max measured tail loads.

During a high speed "roller coaster" to ½G maneuver in Number 3011 to test the strain gauge accuracy, Sullivan encountered a classic case of "flutter" which caused buckling in the leading edges of the C-130's big horizontal stabilizer.

"We were accelerating to 340 knots pushing to a minus ½G," Leo recalled, "and I got 16.5 cps cycles anti symmetric on the tail elevators. We felt a high frequency buzz. I chopped the power, pulled two and ½G's almost straight up and reduced speed. When I got to 120 knots, it stopped and we flew home at 120 knots."

Looking in the records, engineers found that as far back as the original prototype testing, the strain gauge data did not give the correct load distribution. Sullivan explained the problem.

"Due to the peculiar (shape of the) back end of the airplane, the load distribution on the horizontal stabilizer was more outboard than anticipated, resulting in buckling the horizontal stabilizer. In the early prototype flight tests, we found that the Hercules would not stall at forward c.g. because we could never get enough 'up' elevator to stall the aircraft flap down."

As a result of the revealing test results, Lockheed's engineers increased the stiffness of the horizontal stabilizer. This engineering change was implemented from the "B" model forward. The Air

Force elected not to incorporate the change in the "A" Hercules, but instead limited the 'A' models to a speed of 287 knots.

The company's amazingly swift and successful response to the early engineering difficulties led many to describe the C-130 as the program that catapulted Lockheed-Georgia from just an "airplane assembly plant"—which it had been with the B-47 production—into a great aeronautical company. Lockheed's C-130 reputation was a major factor that led to Marietta's ability to compete to build the C-141 and C-5 strategic fanjet transports, and to become "the Airlift Center of the Free World."

The clean lines of the new C-130A were evident in this photo made just before delivery of the first operational plane to the Tactical Air Command in December, 1956. Photo was made from the open ramp of second C-130.

The first operational C-130s for the U.S. Air Force were delivered on a chilly Sunday, December 9, 1956, to the Tactical Air Command's 463rd Troop Carrier Wing at Ardmore, Okla. Five "A" model Herks—fresh off the line and outfitted with the new Aero-Products props—were flown that day from Marietta to Ardmore. The first one to arrive was Lockheed serial number 3050, AF tail number 5023.

General O.P. Weyland, commander of TAC, told the crowd of 5,000 people that "the C-130 will play a most important role in our Composite Air Strike Force for it will increase our capability to airlift engines, weapons, and other critical supply requirements."

General Weyland accepted the airplane for the Tactical Air Command from Lockheed Chairman Robert E. Gross, who said the

These C-130s were flown to Ardmore AFB, Oklahoma, on December 9, 1956, the first delivery of the Hercules to a Tactical Airlift Command operational squadron. A replica of an old Wells Fargo Concord stagecoach came out of the ramp of the first Hercules, pulled by four Shetland ponies. The first airplane delivered (LAC 3050, AF serial number 5023), is still flying with the Air Force Reserve, at O'Hare International Airport, Chicago. (Lockheed)

Crew on the flight of 3050 to Ardmore, L-R: Joe Garrett and Captains Gene Chaney, Richard Coleman and T/Sgt. Al Marchman, flight engineer. (Lockheed)

The C-130H-30 is the latest version of the Hercules aircraft. Fifteen feet longer than the standard C-130, the military "Super Hercules" transport has a near 40 percent increase in cargo volume, permitting the loading of two additional cargo pallets, and a capacity of 92 paratroops or 128 fully equipped infantrymen. The Royal Air Force (*photo top*) pioneered the "military Super Hercules" with the stretching of 30 of its fleet of C-130K's. Other nations operating C-130H-30's include, second to bottom: Algeria, Cameroon, Dubai, Indonesia and Thailand.

model symbolized "delivery of a new recruit—Hercules, the strong man of airlift—to the United States Air Force."

*   *   *

The C-130's first honest-to-goodness non-training operational mission wasn't quite as militarily dramatic as the Ardmore narrator had envisioned. The Pentagon needed troops airlifted to Little Rock, Arkansas, to enforce court-ordered school desegregation. The job went to a squadron of Herks from Sewart AFB, Tennessee, near Nashville. While it was merely a shuttle mission, the propjets pulled the mission without a flaw.

The C-130s became *the* airborne platform to haul paratroopers for similar displays of force in cities across the South. There was a humorous incident that developed when the University of Mississippi was being opened to blacks. The episode was recalled by then Capt. Tim Brady who later became a colonel and a C-130 squadron commander at Little Rock AFB, Arkansas.

"We had a briefing on what we had to do, going into Mississippi, the purpose of the mission, etc. When the briefing officer asked for questions, a black navigator raised his hand:

"Captain, there's just one thing I want to know."

"Yes, lieutenant?"

"Just *whose* side are we on, anyway?"

It brought an explosion of laughs and broke the tenseness of the moment for the C-130 airlifters.

*   *   *

In May of 1958, President Eisenhower ordered paratroopers into standby positions in the Caribbean in the wake of mob violence against Vice President Nixon in Caracas, Venezuela. The Tactical Air Command, responding to a "no notice" call from the Pentagon, rushed 40 C-130s from Sewart to Fort Campbell, Kentucky. There they picked up 577 battle-tough paratroopers from the 101st Airborne Division and flew them non-stop 1,600 miles to San Juan in an overnight deployment.

The Hercules took off in 30-second intervals and flew in-trail straight through a near continuous thunderstorm that got particularly vicious over Miami. Some of the paratroopers suffered bruised heads in the turbulence. The force was prepared to move in and rescue Nixon if required to do so. In addition to the troops, the Herks had aboard 44 jeeps, light and heavy trucks, ambulances, 17 machine guns, 22 rocket launchers, 115 land mines, 10,000 pounds of ammunition, a helicopter, three 106mm recoilless rifles, four mortars, and extra gasoline for the rolling equipment.

Fortunately, the requirement did not come; the screaming mobs melted away and the Hercules returned their charges to Fort Campbell. The C-130s received an "A" for swift action and dependability on a no-notice mission over a long distance.

The Puerto Rican airlift—a mere 3,200 mile round trip—was only a warmup for the crises ahead, that would test the mettle of the greenhorn C-130 and its valiant crews.

Troops of 101st Airborne Division prepare to board USAF C-130 at Fort Campbell, Ky., bound for Puerto Rico. This was on May 13, 1958. (UPI)

A TIME OF TESTING: 1958-1963

> We gave the C-130 a real shakedown
> during the Lebanon crisis . . . .
> —Col. Tarleton H. Watkins

> The C-130 has put speed, force, power
> and life into such words as "global
> mobility" and "jet age airlift."
> —Lockheed Southern Star

It was Monday, July 14, 1958 and midsummer's uneasy peace turned to alarm with news of the assassination of Iraq's King Faisal II and the overthrow of his pro-Western government. The explosion in the Middle East threatened the security of the free world. Lebanon particularly feared a Communist takeover and President Eamille Chamoun appealed to the United States for help.

President Eisenhower didn't hesitate. Within hours, the U.S. Air Force launched a tricontinental airlift that would become the largest in America's military history up to then. Eventually it would involve 100 red-tailed C-130s that would take to the air from bases in western Europe and the United States, along with other transports, fighters and bombers. The United States' response to Lebanon's request took many forms over the days that followed:

TUESDAY, JULY 15—U.S. Marines attached to the Sixth Fleet landed at Beirut, capital of Lebanon. At the same time

C-130s from Evreux-Fauville Air Base in France were humming nonstop across the Alps to Adana in southern Turkey with fully armed and equipped troops of the U.S. Army's 24th Division.

In the U.S., a fleet of C-130s from two Tactical Air Command Wings, the 463rd at Ardmore Air Force Base, Oklahoma, and the 314th at Sewart AFB, Tennessee, were streaking to staging areas in South Carolina. Under command of Colonel George G. Norman, the stubnosed 62-ton workbirds loaded equipment, supplies and men to support TAC's global composite air strike force.

WEDNESDAY, JULY 16—Major General Henry Viccellio, TAC air strike force commander, was flying a Hercules as his aerial command post en route to Adana, and TAC fighter-bombers already were in Turkey. C-130s from Evreux, operating around the clock, were hauling thousands of pounds of combat cargo and hundreds of paratroopers into Turkey.

THURSDAY, July 17—Less than 25 hours' flying time after takeoff, the TAC C-130s from the U.S. began landing at Adana. From their bulging fuselages swarmed the men, materiel, equipment and other logistics requirements to support the jet-age strike force from America. Although they had flown a third of the distance around the world, two Hercules flew quickly with 20 tons of perishables for troops at other Turkish bases. Next morning they were in Germany to pick up additional loads for U.S. forces. And General Viccellio's C-130 was dropping thousands of leaflets over Lebanon with a message of reassurance from President Eisenhower.

Special airlift requests cropped up throughout the July 15-25 period. For example, as the Adana build-up mushroomed, it soon became apparent that the Turkish base's water facilities were inadequate. The commander of the 322nd Air Division, Colonel Clyde Box, had ten of his C-130s pick up 224,000 pounds of iron pipe in Europe for airlift to Adana. Army engineers then built a twelve-mile water pipeline from Adana to the nearest water source. Another special airlift request came from oil-short British paratroop forces in Jordan. To handle the request, Colonel Box set up an oil shuttle between Beirut and Amman using thirteen C-130s and ten C-124s.

Within the short span of 96 hours, the C-130s performed feats of speed, range and payload never before possible in military airlift missions.

At Furstenfeldbruck Air Base, Germany (top photo) troops of the 24th Infantry Division board C-130s from USAFE's 322nd Air Division for airlift to Incirlik AB, Adana, Turkey (Lower photo). This was during the early days of the Lebanon crisis in 1958. (USAF)

The entire eleven-day airlift involved movement of eight million pounds of cargo and equipment and 5,870 personnel. Europe's 322nd Air Division alone flew 418 sorties without an accident, airlifting food, ammunition, weapons, tanks, bulldozers, jeeps, half-tracks and general logistic-type material.

In the words of General Paul D. Adams, the airlift "created enough visible military strength to defeat any military force that could be marshalled against it."

For the men of the 322nd Air Division, the C-130 was still new and they didn't have all the bugs ironed out. But they put them right into the Middle East support without hesitation, according to Major John Gomez III, the division's assistant maintenance officer:

"When the Beirut firecracker lit, we put almost every airplane we had into the sky. We were just green pilots and we just handled it the best we could."

While flying supplies into Beirut, one aircraft had an engine to go out. "The rules said you couldn't take off unless you had all four turning," Gomez said. "So we got it started and made the take-off roll and the damn thing quit. We just kept on going, to get out of there . . . ."

For the C-130 crews in the U.S., the Middle East crisis meant a quick change of plans, also.

"We were at Fort Campbell, Kentucky, and had just made a practice drop," recalled Russell Popejoy, a C—130 co-pilot. "The word came to stand down, something hot was coming. Then we were told to head home (to Ardmore)."

After his plane took to the air, Popejoy was ordered by the TAC command post to fly to Myrtle Beach, South Carolina, to pick up F-100 parts, "Seventy-odd hours later, we finally got a crew rest, after stops and layovers in Bermuda, the Azores, Evreux, Adana, Tripoli, and then back to Evreux."

Popejoy remembered that getting across the Atlantic was hairy. "When we arrived at Bermuda, it was late at night, the place was so full we couldn't get off the runway; we had to park down at the corner and let airplanes go by us so they could get off. Tankers were there and others—all with jobs to do."

After arriving at Adana, Turkey, and off-loading the F-100 spares, Popejoy was told to fly on to Wheelus (in Libya). "So we went to Wheelus, a six hour trip, and finally got ourselves three beers, went to bed and passed out. Everybody slept for 20 hours. When we got up, they told us, 'Go back to Evreux' (for another load)."

Another Ardmore-based C-130 pilot, Capt. Lloyd Adsit, had a similar experience. He and his crew flew to Fort Campbell and picked up an ambulance and miscellaneous supplies. With stops along the way, the augmented crew—using celestial navigation and direction finding systems—flew on through the 6,400 miles to Adana. Once they landed at Incirlik and had their cargo unloaded, Adsit's crew flew on to Chateauroux, France. It was only then that the intrepid Ardmore flyers, dog tired after 36 hours of continuous duty, were able to leave their airplane and get some rest.

Colonel Box, then commander of the 322nd Air Division, who later rose to major general, gave credit to the newly-operational C-130s as being the key to the amazing show of power.

"I can promise you that without those C-130s, we never would have done the Lebanon operation as successfully as we did. It took us only about two days to get 1,600 troops—one full regiment—down to Adana, along with their 7,000 tons of equipment. From there to Lebanon, it was only a shuttle."

It was, indeed, a swift and sharp projection of U.S. military power at a distant point, sustaining the independence of a nation without killing any of its people, and eventually leaving the country as the first armed force ever to be there in 7,000 years of history without leaving death and destruction in its wake. Evreux's C-130s were the exclusive departure airlift aircraft. The withdrawal was swift and efficient.

*　　*　　*

In August of 1958, another major crisis popped on the other side of the world.

Colonel LeRoy Stanton, the C-130 wing commander at Ashiya, Japan, heard about it first in a call he received from General Lawrence S. Kuter, commander in chief, Pacific Air Forces, with headquarters in Honolulu. The general had a terse request:

"We've got a problem brewing in the Straits, Roy. I want to know what kind of support you'll need to make every C-130 in your inventory operational. Don't answer off the cuff; come up with the right answer and call me back in about two hours."

The mainland Chinese were pouring artillery rounds into the Nationalist Chinese islands along the Taiwan Straits—Quemoy and Matsu—threatening to invade. It was a case of the Communists "pulling both triggers of their shotgun, aiming carefully on opposite sides of the globe," as Martin Caidin was to report it. President Eisenhower was in no mood to be intimidated and with his growing fleet of C-130s, he had the airlift muscle to back up his determination. As in the case of Lebanon, the Pentagon quickly deployed entire fighter and bomber wings into the theater. Again, it was the C-130s that hauled in the bulk of necessary armaments, maintenance and support personnel. Two squadrons of Herks from Ardmore moved to Ashiya on "CASF" (composite air strike force) alert. Seventeen additional C-130s from Sewart AFB, Tennessee, came roaring across the Pacific into the Philippines.

Stanton, meanwhile, was working frantically to get his own squadron of 17 Hercules at Ashiya on full time operational status. Although the 483rd Troop Carrier Wing at Ashiya was essentially just beginning its program to train crews to operate and maintain the C-130s, the commander was determined to get every C-130 he had on his base primed for action.

Stanton and his staff huddled and listed the help needed to accomplish the task. He told General Kuter that two dozen aircraft specialists from the Air Force's maintenance center at Robins AFB, Ga., and from Lockheed, plus additional qualified pilots TDY from TAC, were required. Within two days, the help started arriving at Ashiya.

"We had 17 planes operational almost overnight . . . it was unprecedented," Stanton said.

The Ashiya and Ardmore Herks began a massive airlift out of Japan and Okinawa into Taiwan, hauling everything imaginable. Herb Spring, a Lockheed "tech rep" assigned to Stanton's wing, was on the scene: "Those C-130s were hauling just anything and everything they could pile on. Nobody weighed anything. One plane I went in on was five tons overgrossed. We landed on cobblestone runways in Taiwan . . . nothing but cobblestone! It was miserable."

The scenes at the Taiwan bases were unforgettable. "You'd go in there at 2 o'clock in the morning, taxiing through, and all

Colonel George Norman, commander of the 463rd Troop Carrier Wing, Ardmore AFB, Okla., bids a formal goodby to TAC Crews bound for Ashiya Air Base, Japan (top photo). The eight C-130s and crews departed Ardmore March 1, 1958, for six months temporary duty in Japan. The group was in Japan when the crisis erupted in the Taiwan Straits. Lower photo, unit personnel bow during prayer for their safety during the Far East mission. (USAF)

Minelayer C-130? That possibility has come closer following successful aerial gravity drop trajectory testing of mines carried out from a C-130E in Lockheed/Navy tests. Using a C-130 on loan from the U.S. Air Force, the Cargo Aircraft Minelaying System (CAML) tests were conducted at Eglin AFB, Fla., as part of a development program conducted by Lockheed for the Naval Surface Weapons Center.

C-130/L-100 flight simulator in the new Hercules Flight Training Center near Atlanta went into operation in 1985. Here technicians from the Singer Company's Link Flight Simulation Division land at "Hong Kong's International Airport." The new flight training center is jointly owned and operated by Lockheed-Georgia Company and Singer/Link.

the (Nationalist) Chinese fighter planes were lined up with pilots sitting in the cockpits, on the alert. How many hours they stayed right out there in those planes on alert, I'll never know."

At Sewart AFB, Tennessee, Colonel Harry S. Dennis, Jr. was ordered to get his 50th Troop Carrier Squadron deployed *immediately* to Clark Air Base in the Philippines. "We had only six airplanes on alert, but all of our squadron had to go," Dennis recalled. "We had to make up crews." Within twelve hours, seventeen planes of the 314th Wing were winging across the Pacific, by way of Hawaii and Kwajalein.

C-130s of 37th Tactical Airlift Squadron are lined up for 15-second interval takeoffs at Rhein-Main AB, Germany. (USAF—Emmitt Lewis Jr.)

"It was," said Air Force Colonel A.G. (Tommy) Thompson, "a dramatic demonstration of airlift support. The swift mobilization of the composite strike force calmed down what could have escalated into a major shooting war." It was the Tactical Air Command's first large scale composite force exercise in the Far East and turned out to be just as successful as the Lebanon operation.

There was no war—brushfire or otherwise.

*   *   *

The Little Rock, Puerto Rican, Lebanon and Taiwan airlifts proved to the Air Force that even on perilously short notice, its new C-130 could do the job for which it was designed: Pack a global logistic punch into the same transport that served as an airlifter and airdropper for troops, cargo, weapons, vehicles and supplies.

The Hercules had become a cornerstone of the Air Force Tactical Air Command's newly developing Composite Force concept—a forerunner of the STRIKE Command and today's Readiness Command. This concept is based on "short notice" mobility of tactical ground and air units over long distances. The C-130's long range and speed—compared to the C-119s then in use—made the CASF plan possible.

"In the Adana airlift," said Air Force Lieutenant Colonel Otis Winn, "the Hercules proved to be one of our finest weapons." Martin Caidin put it another way, "The 'longest arm' (Hercules) had emerged from the mists of concept and entered the arena of reality."

*   *   *

Over the next five years, America's new airlift machine would receive an extended testing in fire, both as a military transport and as a mercy bird as well.

While the U.S. military, in ordering the C-130 in the 1950s, demanded and got a multitalented tactical transport with strategic legs, the plane's outstanding features as a military airlifter gave it unique adaptability for humanitarian purposes. The Herk's ability to haul heavy war material and manpower into undeveloped strips, and convert quickly to a hospital ship, helped the bird to become, in the words of *Aviation Week* Editor Bob Hotz, "an emergency system (able) to respond to natural disaster in all parts of the world."

The Hercules' first big sustained test as a "mercy bird" in a tough environment came in the summer of 1960 when the 322nd Air Division was pressed into duty airlifting a United Nations peacekeeping force into the strife-torn Republic of Congo. Violence had erupted across the heart of the continent and UN Secretary Dag Hammarskjold issued an emergency call for joint United Nations action. The United States committed sixty C-130s to the record-breaking aerial bridge of UN troops, food and supplies into

A fleet of Lockheed Hercules "mercy bird" transports from at least four nations rushed in millions of pounds of vital foodstuffs and medicines in 1984 and 1985 to relieve the suffering of six million people caught in the grip of the worst drought in the sub-Sahara's history. C-130 and L-100 propjets from Botswana, Italy, the United Kingdom, the United States, and other nations in Europe and the Middle East flew an aerial food pipeline into the disaster regions. Each Hercules aircraft loaded with 14 tons of grain feeds about 20,000 people a day at a cost of 37 cents per person, according to officials of a sponsoring international Christian relief agency. Larger, long-fuselage "Super Hercules" transports haul in the foodstuffs at the rate of 24 tons (48,000 pounds) per flight. In photo above, Ethiopians at a remote famine area unload 48,000 pounds of flour from a Transamerica Airlines Lockheed L-100-30. The workmen accomplished each offloading in only 30 minutes while chanting all the while. *(Photo courtesy Transamerica Airlines)*

the Congo, and, on the return trip, a humanitarian pipeline for refugees being evacuated out.

Hercules started pouring into the Congo in a seemingly endless stream, landing in two-hour intervals on their mission of mercy and peace-keeping. And the job continued for a long time. Beginning on July 18, 1960, the airlift extended into 1961. Altogether, the Evreux C-130s delivered more than 48,000 UN troops from seventeen nations, plus sixteen million pounds of vital supplies, particularly food. Thousands of refugees, many of them victims of beatings and rapes, were brought out.

Throughout the long, gruelling airlift deep into Africa, with missions extending to 3,500 miles and with many landings at dirt and grass fields, the 322nd operated without a single flying accident. It was a magnificent performance: 33,000 hours of flying were logged in nearly 1,300 "sorties." It was during this period that the C-130's true capability as a transport was tested to the ultimate and fully validated. "In-service commission rates became matters of life-or-death," said Lockheed tech rep Jack Pruett. "The reliability of the old bird was real good." Credit also went to teams of maintenance specialists who flew in along with the airplanes and, like the flight crews themselves, worked night and day to keep the airlift going.

There *were* some system failures in the intense heat. "But we didn't put a single Hercules out of commission out there in the bush when something failed," a USAF officer reported. "When something went haywire, the crews just kicked in the backup . . . They were beating up those airplanes so badly without a worry in the world."

Colonel Bob Crow, USAF retired, recalled the ingeniousness of one crew. "They changed an engine in the bush with two trees . . . pulled them together and formed an 'A' frame and then just taxied the plane up, lifted the bad engine out and put in a new one."

The major problem at the beginning of the airlift was not the airplane, but the exhausted crews, who were flying 20 and 30 hours without a break. Colonel Tarleton (Jack) Watkins, the chief of the 322nd, flew in and ordered his men to limit their continuous flying to 18 hours.

During the Congo airlift, John Gomez was ordered to remain the night at the Addis Ababa military field to load up Ethiopian troops the next morning, to take to Leopoldville. Gomez protested having to spend the night in Ethiopia but was told by the Ethiopian authorities in no uncertain terms that he *would* stay. The next morning, he found out why. His manifest was made up of Emperor Haile Selassie's palace troops, and the "Lion of Judah" wanted to bid his men a personal goodbye.

It was during that operation that the Hercules gained an unusual distinction in the African continent. The first planes to fly in from Europe brought in food for the starving natives as well as for the refugees. Without asking, hundreds of delighted Congolese pitched in to help unload the airplanes. The tall red tails of the C-130s soon became the talisman for safe flights across the troubled region. Being carriers of food—including 28,000-pound plane loads of fish from Norway—the C-130's image rose dramatically in the eyes of natives.

A U.S. Air Force pilot had his own rationale: "Their communications may mystify us, but they got the word around fast. Our Hercules went into strips where they had never heard of us, and where many people were getting cut to pieces, and not one of our men was ever molested or threatened."

But the six C-130s that hauled those big loads of fish into the steaming Congo carried memories of the mission for months. Said one pilot: "My airplane stank on and on . . . ."

During Congo airlift, USAF 1st Lt. John Gomez III was sent to Addis Ababa to pick up Ethiopian troops for the United Nations peacekeeping force. He was forced to remain overnight and the next morning he found out why. Emperor Haile Selassie came to the plane to give a personal sendoff to his palace troops. Here Selassie (in white hat) looks over C-130 cargo ramp with his sons. At left is Lieutenant Gomez. (Lockheed)

The ultimate early test of the Hercules came in late 1962 when the Chinese Communists invaded India's Assam Valley and its mountainous Kashmir region high in the Himalayas.

The Indians, who were having difficulty meeting the threat with their fleet of Russian AN-12 transports, called on Washington for help. President Kennedy responded by making available 12 C-130s from Evreux. Flying "over the hump" into crude mountain strips two miles high, the 322nd Air Division Herks mounted a massive airlift of men and materiel.

Colonel Charles W. Howe, the commander of the 322nd, led his pack of courageous C-130s on the mission, spanning virtually uncharted peaks across the spine of the Himalayas into the cruel region of Ladakh. The air at the high altitude was so rare that cigarette smokers turned blue and nonsmokers gasped for breath, seeing red spots leaping in front of their eyes. Russian helicopters were ineffective at that altitude.

Before it was over, the Hercules would remain on the India project for nine months. But in the beginning, the prospect that the airlift would last very long was somewhat remote, and the first chore was much less demanding than the Himalayas. At the start, the Indian air vice marshal was somewhat disappointed at the peculiar looking air machines President Kennedy had sent to his aid.

"After a series of minor delays," Colonel Howe said, "He got around to telling me about 5,000 troops he wanted moved into the Assam Valley."

"Will it take you about two weeks to do it?" the air vice marshal asked.

"Oh no," Howe declared, "we can do it in four days; we'll just put 100 troops in each of the 12 aircraft, fly them out, drop them off and come back. The next day we'll take another 1,200 and in four days we'll have 5,000 on the ground."

When the troops were removed even ahead of Howe's announced schedule, the air vice marshal was astounded. And no wonder, because it took *less* than four days. One reason was that the Indian officers packed upward of 120 soldiers into each airplane for the 7½-hour flight! One of Howe's squadron leaders, Harry S. Dennis, Jr. recalled the flights:

"They put those troops in shoulder to shoulder, right on the cargo floor, not in the seats. They ordered them not to move, to stay seated for the entire flight. They were well disciplined and did

While flying to the Congo with a load of fish fron Norway, 322nd Air Division C-130 No. 464 became lost due to radar/radio equipment malfunctioning. The crew found an emergency airstrip at Ghuru, Nigeria, and made a normal landing on a dirt field. While waiting for fuel, the crew passed the time with a game of cards, which drew an interested group of spectators. (USAF)

Leader of the long range United Nations mercy missions into the strife-torn Congo in 1960 was Col. Tarleton H. Watkins, commander of the USAF 322nd Air Division. The Hercules fleet transported 2,000,000 pounds of food to stave off a famine in the new republic, hauled in a large contingent of UN troops from 15 nations, and evacuated hundreds of refugees out. (Lockheed)

Aerial heroes of the 1983 Granada resue operation were USAF crewmen of three versions of the Lockheed Hercules aircraft — the AC-130H *(center photo)*, MC-130E Combat Talon *(lower photo)* and standard C-130E/H transports such as the one on top taking off from Greneda runway. The Air Force awarded to MC-130E aircraft commander, Lt. Col. James L. Hobson, Jr. of the 1st Special Operations Wing, Hurlburt Field, Fla., the Mackay trophy for "the most meritorious flight of the year." Hobson piloted the lead MC-130E Oct. 25, 1983 in a night paradrop of Rangers into Port Salines at 500 feet. Despite heavy anti-aircraft gunfire, Hobson flew a precise path across the drop zone until the last ranger had left the aircraft. Meanwhile, AC-130's stayed on target supporting the U.S. forces for eight and one-half hours. Col. Hugh L. Hunter, commander of the 1st SOW, said, "This was a rescue mission and the AC-130H was the perfect vehicle for it. The idea was not to destroy half the country but to go in and surgically take out enemy targets. That's what minimized civilian and American military casualties."

it. But when we landed and they filed out, you could see where many of them had wet their pants . . . ."

After seeing how well the American propjets had performed on the Assam airlift, the air vice marshal came up with his main feature event—the Himalayan airlift.

But Colonel Howe, before committing his Herks to the sustained mission over the Hump, made a pioneering flight up into the rugged mountains to the Ladakh strip of Leh where most of the missions would terminate. With the air vice marshal aboard, Howe probed his way down through the thin air, descending at 2,000 feet per minute, dodging peaks and abutments with 90-degree turns, then—after a 270-degree turn into the approach—slammed down on the pierced steel planking (PSP) that covered the strip. Leh was the key staging area for the Indian Army battling the Chinese nearby.

The Chicago Daily News' Paul Hermuses, who later flew into Leh aboard one of the C-130s, found the strip "the worst ever to challenge the American planes and the skill of their pilots. Situated at a 10,500 foot elevation, it has been lengthened from 3,000 to 5,000 feet. One end of the strip is 300 feet higher than the other. Surrounding the strip are snow-covered peaks 7,000 feet above the valley. In Air Force parlance, the landings and takeoffs are hairy . . . ."

One of Howe's pilots, Major Lloyd Adsit, detailed the hazards of going into Leh. "There were no navigational or radio aids on the ground. We were on our own with our airborne radar and our own navigation. The mountains jutted up well over 21,000 feet. We'd be flying at 25,000 feet and just be skimming the mountain tops. When it came time to land, we'd have to dive into the valley at a maximun descent. We had a procedure where we could descend to 20,000 feet, on our own radar—and if we couldn't get out of the soup at 20,000 feet, we'd have to go back up and return home (to New Delhi.)"

Another pilot, 2nd Lt. James P. Morgan, recalled that "the approach was made from west landing east; downwind was to the south, with the turn to base heading us directly into the rapidly rising northern edge of the valley. From base until final, all you could see out the windows was sheer gray mountain. On final, the approach was over a monastery on a small hill about a mile from the runway. There was 5,000 feet more or less of rusted old PSP. Every time we touched down—controlled crash would be more appropriate—a bow wave of PSP would form ahead of the aircraft reaching a height of four feet or so. Eventually, when the airplane caught up with and rolled over the wave, it would lurch and roll drunkenly . . . ."

Once the Herk pilot had committed himself to land in the valley, the loss of an engine precluded climbout via the normal return route. The 322nd operations people devised an elaborate escape route, a maze down through the valleys until a long enough stretch was found to climb up and out. But one wrong turn and that was it . . . because it was too narrow for a turnaround and too high to get up and out. At least one Hercules crew used the "maze" departure route successfully.

The Leh runway itself was a bitch, particularly for nose gears. There was a dip between the main runway and the extension that required planes landing to execute a precise touchdown pattern.

M/Sgt. Claude Ferrand, a loadmaster, was on the first crew to go in. "You'd come zipping down through there at 150 knots and you had a two-foot jump to get up on the main runway. They had told us to hold the nose up so it wouldn't hit the lip of the extension. Well, we did . . . we held it a little *too* high and we experienced a *tail skid*!" Fortunately, not much damage rubbed off on the aircraft, but one of the C-130s slammed across the dip and caved in a nose gear. As Martin Caidin reported it, the airplane "got snagged between the shock-absorbing action of its nose gear and the hazards of the airstrip; steel forgings collapsed, metal ripped with a high, screeching sound, and the airplane plowed forward on its nose with the gear mangled into junk." The intrepid 322nd maintenance men rigged up a nose gear from a disabled C-119 and flew the Herk back to New Delhi for major repair.

After Colonel Howe got his first look-see at the Leh situation, he and the air vice marshal returned the 800 miles to New Delhi.

"Well, Colonel, what do you think?"

"We can start tomorrow, sir," Howe replied. "We'll fly 15 tons per airplane and operate 11 sorties a day with the 12 planes." (That was 165 tons, or 330,000 pounds a day.)

The air vice marshal was astounded, but at the same time he was perfectly delighted.

Flying "over the hump" of the Himalayas, 322nd Air Division C-130 is pictured (top photo) in late 1962 on way to Ladakh province in support of the Indian Army. Lower photo, airplane lands in the icy Leh runway, situated at over 10,000 foot altitude. (USAF)

Leh airstrip in India's Ladakh province in the Himalayas near the border with China. It's an "uphill" runway, with a convent on a small mountain at one end of the strip. Note C-130 on ground at center right. Landing at Leh was quite "hairy," Hercules pilots found. Lower photo, C-130s brought in Indian troops, trucks and supplies to the Himalayan strip. (USIS, USAF)

As it turned out, the mission turned out to be a good display case for the C-130 versus its Russian equivalent—the AN-12, a four-engine turboprop with a fuselage cargo hold about the same size as the Hercules.

Harry Dennis' first sight of the AN-12 came on a flight to Leh when his co-pilot yelled out, "Looka there, there's one of those AN-12s." "They were flying at about 28,000 feet, and he went by us like we were standing still," Dennis said.

But aside from speed, the Russian transport was sorely lacking in payload capacity, range and short field capability, the prime ingredients required in a tactical airlifter. Moreover, the AN-12's cargo compartment was not pressurized, which meant that hauling troops over the Himalayas was completely out of the question. But its really big drawback, reducing its ability to land on a short strip, was that it could not reverse its propellers. And the tires, unlike the low-pressure, pliant C-130 tires, were rigid, and subject to being cut up severely by PSP.

"They were having one hell of a time stopping on the Leh strip," Howe said. "We were landing uphill and taking off downhill. But the AN-12s were having to land downhill and the strip wasn't all that long."

But the big difference was in the payload. The Russian propjet couldn't carry much of a load into Leh. "They had to go light on payload to take enough fuel to get out ."

The Himalayan airlift left no doubt as to which airplane was the winner. "It really revealed the wide disparity between the two planes," Howe said.

Joseph Manship, commander of Howe's 42nd squadron, went aboard one of the Russian propjets and was struck by the lack of sophisticated instrumentation. "In the cockpit, you almost had to be a cat-walker to get around the wiring. There was hardly any flooring and cables were all around you."

Lloyd Adsit, having come up from the unpressurized C-119 ranks, was grateful for the Herk's pressurization, which came in handy in the Himalayas when Indian troops developed cases of "bends" (altitude sickness). "We'd bring in the C-130 at Leh, put the sick troops·aboard, and pressurize the plane to sea level. That would help them snap out of it."

Manship loved the C-130's reverse thrust—a capability that

allowed pilots to taxi their Herucles *backwards* on a runway or taxi-way. If there wasn't room for the plane to turn around for takeoff, the pilot could just back his bird up on the runway where he landed!

"The reverse-thrust capability was a terrific thing, really. When you came in to land on a strip such as Leh, as soon as you got the plane firmly on the ground, you could reverse it and stop quickly."

For nine months, the U.S. Air Force kept 12 C-130s continuously on duty on the Indian airlift, rotating them and their crews in from Evreux on 30-day tours. In addition to hauling in troops and supplies—ammunition, drums of fuel, vehicles and hay for Army mules—they air-dropped many items, including bags of grain, right up to the frontline Indian troops.

It was, indeed, an airlift that proved to be a Godsend for India, which was able to stave off the northern incursions. Prime Minister Nehru and his daughter, Indira, rode up to Leh aboard the Herk and expressed their gratitude for the Americans and their funny looking flying machines. Brigadier Eric Sen, the commander of one of the frontline Indian brigades, told the Herk crewmen that without the 130, the Indian defense activity could never have been maintained.

It was an equally gruelling test of the C-130, whose manuals up to then documented its operational parameters for airports no higher than 6,000 feet!

*   *   *

While the Indian operation proved to be an effective use of tactical airlift muscle in a brushfire war environment, the C-130, as in so many similar operations around the world, proved itself to be equally as effective as a winged samaritan.

The most heart-warming episode to come out of the Himalayan operation was the airlift south into India of 104 Tibetan orphans whose parents had lost their lives on the battlefront. The USAF crew men collected their little passengers at the snow-covered Leh strip. Lloyd Adsit, the mission commander, brought in two Hercules for the project. "Many of the children were barefooted, and they had stood in the snow for sometime. But they appeared to be under no discomfort."

U.S. Ambassador to India John Kenneth Galbraith (L) paid a visit to C-130 unit at the New Delhi Airport during the airlift program and met with the commander of the 322nd Air Division, Colonel Charles W. Howe (R). Altogether, 12 C-130s were dispatched to India's aid by President John F. Kennedy. Lower photo, Russian equivalent of the C-130, the AN-12 is pictured at New Delhi. The propjet airplane is somewhat speedier than the C-130 but does not have a pressurized cargo compartment, and its payload is much smaller than that of the C-130. The AN-12s, part of the Indian Air Force airlift inventory, had a difficult time landing in the Himalayas due to the rigidity of their tires. Note the tail gun turret. (USAF)

Orphans from Tibet—victims of the border war with China—were airlifted by the C-130s from Leh in the Himalayas to a convent in India in early 1963. Top left, C-130 crewman hands out sweets to the little ones, who were soon to be reunited with their Dalai Lama, then in exile in India. (Lower left), Major Lloyd Adsit (second from left) was commander of the Tibetan orphan airlift mission involving two C-130s. 104 children carried prayer books on their backs and small bundles of clothes. The plucky youngsters stood barefoot in the snow (lower right) and sang Tibetan folksongs while waiting to board the Hercules. (USAF)

Pat Dana Hagen of the *San Francisco Chronicle* rode back with the kids and reported on the plucky youngsters and their American benefactors:

> The children carried small bundles of clothes and oblong Buddhist prayer books when they boarded the planes. They had never flown in an airplane before. In fact, they had never seen anything like these huge shiny monsters before. But, although their eyes were round with staring, nobody cried. Instead, these brave little waifs, many of them barefoot, sang Tibetan folksongs and waited for whatever would happen to them next.
>
> What did happen next brought lumps to the throats of many observers that day. The American airmen, most barely out of their teens, shepherded the children aboard, lifted them gently into the plane's bucket-seats and buckled seat-belts around them. They did it so calmly and with such careful kindness that not one child resisted or seemed afraid.
>
> The airmen smiled reassurance to their passengers and the planes roared aloft to fly over the endless stretches of uninhabited jagged mountains, down to the safety of India's Himalayan foothills. There, emissaries of the Dalai Lama welcomed the orphans to their new home and the transports rose again to return to Delhi.

The C-130, meanwhile, came out of India a real winner. Having conquered the extreme climates of Africa and the Himalayas and having successfully negotiated unpaved landing strips there and elsewhere around the world, the C-130, U.S. Air Force observers agreed, was an aircraft of unusual talents.

It had met the toughest challenges an air machine should ever expect to face, and it came through, like Job of the Old Testament, stronger and tougher than ever.

III

THAT MOST AMAZING FLYING MACHINE

Trash Haulers have fun.

—Captain Les Walz

THUNDERWEASELS AND CARRIER LANDINGS: A PILOT'S AIRPLANE IF THERE EVER WAS ONE

> The C-130's like a beautiful woman. If you treat 'em right, there's nothing finer.
> —Lt. Col. Wilbert Turk,
> U. S. Air Force Retired

> It's the most fun airplane I've ever flown.
> —James E. Hunt, USAF Retired
> Delta Air Lines pilot

It is no wonder that pilots fell head over heels in love with the Hercules from the first moment they took over her controls.

The "A" model Hercules, with 15,000 powerful propjet "horses" pulling a gross weight of only 124,000 pounds, would roar from the starting line with a ferocious burst of energy. Being an air machine that knew virtually no limitation to her prowess, the Herk was endowed with super amounts of acceleration . . . deceleration . . . nimbleness . . . maneuverability . . . but particularly *power*.

"It's a pilot's airplane if there ever was one," retired USAF Brigadier General Tarleton (Jack) Watkins told me recently from his home in San Diego. "I don't think I've ever flown an airplane I've liked better. I'd like to own one."

Thus, despite the C-130's dumpy, dolphin-like superstructure, crewmen became hopelessly enamored of her from the start, once they had taken her for a ride. "She may look like a truck," the saying went, "but she handles like a *Cadillac*."

There was the C-130 pilot's wife at Langley, Virginia, who, with tongue in cheek, wrote of her jealousy for the winged beast:

> All brown and green, clumsy and fat
> I'm surprised that you'd be attracted to *that*!
> *
> I'm not referring to Mable or Gertie
> I'm talking about that darn C-130!*

The reception the C-130 received when it touched down for the first time at Evreux-Fauville AB, France, on September 6, 1957, was typical of its introduction elsewhere around the world. First impression was one of doubt and disappointment.

"They came in one evening and parked them on the back side of the base," recalled Major John Gomez III. "People came by on the way to work the next morning. We all went out there to look at the big old ugly thing. When you've been used to looking at an airplane with a big gear and wide tread and you see this thing with a narrow tread and it's kinda lop-sided. Matter of fact, one of the struts was a little low and the wing was kinda low. Well, we said, 'Geez, what an *ugly* airplane.'

"But I'll tell you, it didn't take long to fall in love with her. Every time we got in that thing it was a *go*-er. I liked the 'A' particularly. It was a lightweight airplane and had the high speed gear box. That thing would go like a screaming eagle. Up to then, we were used to flying only 165/175 knots cruise in the C-119. Then going into the C-130A was all the difference in night and day. Right then and there was when I went into C-130s and I flew the devil out of 'em from thereafter until the day I retired."

With the arrival of the first C-130As, the flying horizons of the Evreux crewmen suddenly opened wider.

---

*Written by the wife of Capt. Edward W. Hamilton and noticed on the bulletin board at Clark AB, Philippines by Lockheed Tech Rep Hal Clary.

"Everyone seemed to walk straighter," an officer recalled, "and for sure we were able to fly in a manner we'd never dreamed of." The case was clinched when Evreux' ex-fighter jocks started asking for rides on C-130 training flights! A young lieutenant remembered the exuberant mood:

"We'd take the 130 up to 12,000 feet and hold it up with the nose in a steep climb until the airplane scrabbled for life. Finally we'd go into a complete stall. Then . . . just slam the throttle forward. The props would chew their way straight on out and up from that stall. It's the only big airplane I know of, anywhere, that can do that . . . ."

Evreux' excitement was repeated in the Far East. When the first Herks arrived at Ashiya, Japan, just before Christmas of 1957, Col. LeRoy Stanton and his airmen of the 483rd Troop Carrier Wing lined up to fly in the new bird.

Stark amazement was the reaction of then Lt. Jim Alexander. "The plane just leaped off the ground exactly like a T-33. Flight controls were so easy. If you wanted 45 degrees of bank, you just touched it and there it was. *Fantastic.* We flew around the outskirts of Tokyo and they let us all go up to the flight station and get a feel of it. It made everybody sense that *something was coming, really.*" As soon as Alexander got down, he put in his papers to go to a C-130 unit when he returned to the States. Now a bird colonel, Alexander is the vice commander, 374th Tactical Airlift Wing, Clark AB, the Philippines.

The powerful, maneuverable C-130s, coming on the heels of the C-119, boosted the morale of the airlifters everywhere. "The C-119 was a good old workhorse in its day," said Stanton, "but if you got in trouble with it, you damn well had to unload it if you wanted to stay up there. And you had to be quick not to get on the back side of the power curve."

Stanton's men, who up to then had evidenced a bit of an inferiority complex, blossomed dramatically. "They became confident to the point of arrogance," Stanton grinned.

Stanton himself liked to show off his new bird. He took a C-130 down to North Borneo to pick up a Colonel Lee whose T-33 was disabled on a short dirt strip. Roy "chandelled" the Herk right off the deck in a spectacular, sharp liftoff. His passenger bounded up to the flight deck to ask:

If you'll look closely at lower photo, you'll see USAF C-130E is not climbing without engines, as a quick glance might indicate. Actually, the No. 2 turbine and propeller are powering the climbout. Feathering three props while making a fast fly-by and pull-up was a highlight of the Hercules "E" demonstrations to European air forces in 1963. This particular picture was made by a Spanish photographer at Getafe Air Force Base, near Madrid, Spain. (USAF)

These cartoons come from the pen of the world's greatest Herk fan, the irrepressible Dave Davenport of Spring Lake, N.C. A retired C-130 flight engineer who works as a civilian photographer at Pope AFB, Davenport's cartoons have given a distinct personality to the Hercules aircraft.

Back from distance record flight, Lt. Col. Edgar Allison Jr., mission commander, and crew are greeted by Military Airlift Command's General Jack Catton and Lockheed Corporation's Larry Kitchen, then president of the Lockheed-Georgia Company. The USAF Aerospace Rescue and Recovery Service Hercules flew 8,790 miles, from Taiwan to Scott AFB, Illinois, to set a long distance record for turboprop aircraft. The flight took 21 hours and 12 minutes. The non-stop, non-refueled flight topped a 6,842 mark held by the Hercules' turboprop Lockheed cousin, a U.S. Navy P-3. (Lockheed)

World record airlift of external weight by a turboprop aircraft was set by this DC-130H as it took off from Edwards AFB, California, in July, 1976 with four remotely piloted vehicle test units weighing 44,510 pounds. The aircraft, modified by Lockheed Aircraft Service Company, is designed to carry future vehicles weighing up to 10,000 pounds each. The record external airlift for the DC-130 was flown by Carl Hughes of Lockheed and Major Paul Stephen of the U.S. Air Force. (Lockheed)

"WHAT KIND OF PLANE IS THIS, ANYWAY?"

The Ashiya airlifters pulled other amazing feats with their new machine. They would take the C-130 to altitude, then put it into a stall with the two inboard engines at cruise and the two outboards at flight idle. They then would bring the outboards back in and would climb right through the stall.

Many "A" flyers likened the Hercules to a fighter plane, and some reported they could out-run an F-86 Sabrejet momentarily in a flat-out acceleration "drag race." Even the subsequent "B" model, whose gross weight was increased to 135,000 pounds (along with an overall 1,200 hosepower boost) was considered to be a "helluva sports model."

For H.G. (Aussie) Maxwell, a pilot with the Royal Canadian Air Force, his first encounter with the C-130 nearly blew his mind. It was on September 30, 1960, when he went up in a "B" model with Lockheed instructor pilot Bill Jones:

> "Bill dropped the throttles into flight idle, the high-pitched howl dropped to a powerful hum, brakes were released, power applied and away we went! DAMN THAT BILL, HE HADN'T TOLD ME TO HANG ON HARD—the airplane went hurtling down the runway as I ended up in a heap on the crew rest bunk at the rear of the flight deck. Nothing in 18 previous years of military flying had prepared me for this monster. Not even the Mustang had accelerated at this rate."*

Later, "Aussie" learned just how powerful and maneuverable the Hercules was. When he first arrived at the Canadian Fighter Wings in Europe, the newcomers were told by the Canadian Sabrejet pilots that the new USAF C-130s then deploying to the European bases could turn *inside* the Sabres. Maxwell later went on to prove that the Hercules was *indeed* a match for a fighter trainer, and claimed that his C-130 beat a RCAF T-33 (higher powered than the USAF version), "from a standing start to 25,000 feet."

My own first-time flight in the C-130 was one *I'll* never forget, either. It happened in 1966 during an Armed Forces Day Open House at Lockheed-Marietta. I was allowed to ride with a Lockheed crew that put on a C-130 "maximum performance" takeoff/

*From AIR CLASSICS Magazine, June, 1974

landing demonstration. The plane used only 800 feet of the west end of the Dobbins AFB runway. When we took off, I was fortunate to have a seat at the back of the flight station with a solid bulkhead behind me. Before taking off, Lockheed pilot Jack Dunn locked his brakes at the end of the runway and built up the propeller bite until the bird was shaking and shimmering, literally pawing the ground with pent up power. Finally, he cut the brakes; we rocketed forward like a bullet, plastering everyone aboard to the back of their seats. At about 800 feet, the pilot "rotated" and the Hercules shot skyward at an amazing angle of 40 degrees or so. By the time we crossed Highway 41 at the east end of the 10,000 foot runway, we were a mile in the sky. But that was just the beginning.

After some high speed fly-bys, Dunn brought the Herk back in on an "assault" landing, the type that was then being made almost routinely in Vietnam.

"Better hold on," Jack told me as we plunged from the sky on final like a dive bomber, at a sink rate of 2000 feet per minute. *BAM* . . . we smacked into the concrete in a controlled crash. Suddenly, the props were roaring in reverse; Jack stood on the brakes. The safety belt burned me a bit as the plane skewed to a stop in 500 feet. DAMN!

*　　*　　*

Captain Les Walz of the USAF at Howard AFB, Canal Zone, has had his share of pleasure flying the one-thirty, which he claims is more fun than any other big plane flying today. "You can rack that bird around . . . and do things that just doesn't look like you should be able to do. It's just a *good* damned airplane. And it's fun."

But, as Walz will attest, even the best airplanes and the best pilots sometimes have bad days. "I made a really shabby landing in a C-130 once in Poland, and later in Athens. I was in the righthand seat and my AC* was nice enough to let me land. He was a real understanding guy, the AC was. He was training me to be an AC. It was the *worst* landing I've ever seen *any*body make in a C-130.

*aircraft commander

A USAF C-130B helped Walter Schirra's Sigma 7 space capsule complete its "orbit" back to Florida after it landed in the mid-Pacific. (USAF)

Landing C-130 on an unopened section of a highway south of Stuttgart, Germany, General William G. Moore launched Autumn Forge 78 NATO exercises in Europe. There were crosswinds of about ten miles per hour. The commander of the Military Airlift Command flew the Hercules from Rhein-Main AB, Germany, for the "assault strip" landing. "This gives you a highway to drive on in peacetime and an airstrip during war," General Moore said. (Photos courtesy Europe Stars & Stripes—Gus Schuettler).

The BLC-130 — the "boundary layer control" aircraft *(upper photo)* — was a Lockheed modification of the Hercules to provide true STOL landing and takeoff capabilities. The seventh production C-130B was used for tests in the early 1960s. Two T-56 pure jets were placed on outer wings, feeding air through ducting across both wings, providing high energy lift, and enabling the airplane to take off and land at speeds of 50 to 70 knots, instead of 80 to 100 knots that C-130 pilots usually counted on. National Aeronautics and Space Administration acquired the C-130 as a research aircraft, and it is still flying today, *(lower photograph)* as an NC-130B "flying laboratory", developing techniques for remote satellite sensing, operating out of the NASA-Ames facility at Moffett Field, California.

Two of the world's largest helicopters, the U.S. Marine Sikorsky CH53-E "Super Stallion," get a refueling drink simultaneously from a new Marine Corps Reserve KC-130T refueler transport from the Marine Reserve's Air Control Group 48, 4th Marine Air Wing, Glenview, Ill. The new KC-130T gives the Marine Reserve the capability of simultaneously refueling by drogues two fighter planes or two helicopters. *(Photo courtesy United Technologies Sikorsky Aircraft.)*

It was almost backwards. You're sorta supposed to make the airplane land straight, but I landed it almost backwards, *I swear*.

"There was a pretty good cross-wind, so I said, 'Well, we'll just circle and land on the other runway!' I was about half way through the circle and Jerry says, 'Ahhh. We can land there,' (on the first runway). I said, 'Yeah, you're right," and called out, 'Give me flaps of 100.' The landing was *awful*. It was just a matter of where you were gonna be in that flutter and where you hit. I was all over the runway. I was pretty thoroughly humble, 'cause I always prided myself on being a fairly decent stick man.

"So the next day, I got out there and I said, "Goddammit, give me that airplane and I'll show you guys what I can do."

"What happened? I took off *in a crab*. You just *can't* screw up a takeoff in a one-thirty. No way. I don't know what happened, but I took off in a crab. It was like this . . ." he said, as he pictured with his hands the awful angle of his takeoff, shrugging as if to say, "Well, some things in life you just can't explain."

But even so, Walz admits to a great love affair with the Herk. "God, it would be great to have a squadron of C-130s. I love that thing. I grew up with it. I love the sound of it. I like the feel of it. I just *know* it. I don't want to fly anything else . . . ."

*   *   *

The race car performance of the "A" model Hercules was so spectacular that it inspired the Tactical Air Command's pioneering Herk pilots at Ardmore AFB to show off their new transports in style. It came in the early days of the C-130's operational career, in 1957, when four gutsy captains with the 463rd Troop Carrier Wing at Ardmore decided to put together a Thunderbird type demonstration.

"We had five or six airplanes at Fort Campbell," recalled Hubert (Gene) Chaney," and one day our drop missions were cancelled; there was a stand down. So four of us got together to see what we could put together in a little demonstration."

The four aircraft commanders had more time in the new C-130 than anyone else in the Air Force. In addition to Chaney, they were James Akin, David Moore and William Hatfield. They put on quite a show that day at Campbell, taking off about five seconds apart, then flying in formation for fast fly-bys. Another stand-down by the Army later that week gave the Ardmore foursome another opportunity and they flew additional formation maneuvers, gaining experience and confidence.

"Then we got an invitation to go down to Sewart, which was awaiting its first C-130s, and they had a fit when they saw us perform." From there, the Hercules demo team became the hottest new act in the flying world, and ended up with their picture on the cover of *Aviation Week* magazine.

In the beginning, the Herk quartet called themselves the "Thunderweasels."

"We had an ops officer with the 774th squadron who called us weasels," said Billie Mills who became one of the alternate horses, "and me and another crewman went to the library and found a picture of a weasel that looked kinda mean—standing on a bank looking over a creek, kinda humped over. The librarian drew up a sketch of a weasel. We were sent to Japan two months later and had a Japanese seamstress make a patch. It became our squadron patch."

In a short time, the "Thunderweasels" became "The Four Horsemen" (of the Apocalypse)—a more fitting title—and they wowed audiences over the United States and in Denmark and Japan with precision formations.

Martin Caidin, who had flown with the Thunderbirds, was astonished when he saw the Horsemen perform the "Dance of the Heavies." "Their maneuvers—with airplanes each weighing 100,000 pounds—followed a series of elaborate and precisely executed aerobatics that left veteran transport pilots shaking their heads in wonder. Precision is not only a requisite, but a key to survival when you fly these behemoths with the fluidity of a ballet presentation at speeds of 340 miles per hour—*with the wingtips only six feet apart*."

Zoom-bum-bum-zoom-bum-bum-zoom-bum-bum-zoom.

Lt. Col Tim Brady described a typical show beginning with a four-ship, two second interval takeoff which made it appear that the takeoffs were simultaneous. "Take-off roll was less than 2,000 feet. The gear came up on all four aircraft simultaneously and the flaps were milked up while climbing out."

As they crossed the end of the 10,000-foot runway, the

"The Four Horsemen" made C-130 history with their amazing aerobatics that wowed audiences over the U.S. This composite photograph shows the horsemen sweeping over the Ardmore runway and, inset, comparing notes. L-R: Captains Gene Chaney, William Hatfield, James Akin and David Moore. (USAF)

C-130 from Ashiya Air Base flying formation with F-86 Sabrejet in Thailand. Some Herk pilots claimed they could out-run a Sabrejet in a flat-out acceleration drag race. C-130A flyers at Ashiya and Evreux-Fauville performed amazing aerobatics with the first "A" model C-130s that arrived at their bases. (USAF)

"horses" would be in a diamond formation and passing the 1,500-foot altitude while climbing at 4,000 feet per minute. This was followed by a high speed pass over the runway in a diamond formation, a diamond chandelle, the "arrow head" fly-by. The grand finale was the "bomb burst" from the diamond formation, with the slot man making a steep climb with a 45-degree left bank. Almost simultaneously, the leader pulled up sharply and to the right at 45-degree bank while the wingmen broke off to their respective sides with 90-degree banks.

As an example of the aircraft's tremendous power, Chaney flew one entire demonstration with one of his outboard engines caged! "Unfortunately, they got some pictures of it," Chaney laughed as he recalled the incident recently. "I was flying lead. The lead had a set power setting. Shortly after takeoff, I had to shut an outboard engine down. But it didn't hurt the performance at all!"

As the world's only four engine (per plane) precision flying team, the Four Horsemen—sandwiching their practicing and performances on their own time between such airlift missions as Lebanon and Quemoy-Matsu—continued their performances right on with the move of the 463rd wing to Sewart AFB, Tennessee, where they became part of the 839th Air Division. But in the Spring of 1960, due to the press of airlift duties, the Air Force denied the Horses' request to be made an official demonstration team and the foursome had to disband.

"We were sorry about it," Chaney said, "but the Air Force decision was understandable. It was difficult to justify using an aircraft as versatile as the C-130 for demonstrations."

*　　*　　*

Dissolution of the Horsemen did not mark the end of Hercules demonstrations, however, and spectacular C-130 shows popped up around the world as Herk crewmen showed off their flying skills with their frisky birds. In 1961, during a 16-plane, mass formation C-130 flyover at Naha, Okinawa, four planes fell out and put on a few low-pass demonstrations.

In 1959 in Oslo, Norway, a USAF C-130 from Evreux, France, stole the show in a six-country aerial event. Nicknamed "the

The Four Horsemen had a number of formations never before flown with an airplane so large. Top photo, the airplanes go into a "bomb burst." Lower illustration depicts some of their favorite formations. (Lockheed)

beast" by its crewmen, the Hercules did its stuff during a five-minute segment of the air show. Some 30,000 spectators gasped when they saw the spectacular C-130 takeoffs and landings. A similar occurrence happened at the Fifth International Air Show at Spa, Belgium, when a Hercules from Lockbourne AFB, Ohio, was simply listed as "USAF C-130 Show" scheduled between jet fly-bys, helicopter formations, parachute demonstrations and the "Red Devils" and "Red Arrows," respective Belgian and British jet demonstration teams.

Captain Nils Larson, Jr., and his four crewmen agreed at a pre-show meeting to land the Herk on the 2,700-foot grass strip. Up to then, the largest aircraft to land there, and with much difficulty, was a DC-3. The Hercules performed spectacularly, causing the crowd to shriek with delight. After the Herk finished up and flew out, the Belgian tower radioed them congratulations on being the hit of the show. Belgian newspapers termed the Hercules performance "the crowning event of the meet."

"As far as I am concerned," said Lt. Col. Joseph B. Bilotta, USAF retired, "that little beast has been all over the world and it's getting more popular all the time. It was a plane I could do all sorts of things with—fly on three engines, for instance. We used to take off on three engines frequently although it was officially illegal. When we were in the Congo delivering goods, one of my birds flew every day for a week with only three engines, because we couldn't get spare parts."

Bilotta, who retired some years ago after commanding a MATS C-130 Squadron at Charleston AFB, South Carolina, transitioned to the Hercules from the Lockheed Constellation. The shift was a bit traumatic. "I lost all my stewardesses . . . all 30 of 'em. I was flying an airline. They took me out of the airlines and they put me to work!" Soon, however, when Bilotta found out what the Hercules would do, he became one of its most ardent boosters, and eventually flew the A, B, and E models.

"When you knew the bird and its capabilities, you couldn't help but love it. In Vietnam, I would land the Herk and turn off the runway at 1,200 feet. Some people can't do that with a Piper Cub."

Vietnam, indeed, turned out to be the finest hour of the C-130, and, in the largest airlift in history, provided the ultimate

The Royal Air Force utilizes one of its C130K Hercules for meterological research. The flying laboratory's 26-foot long nose boom, painted red and white, houses instrumentation to measure and record the still air ahead of the aircraft. Marshall's of Cambridge modified the transport to accommodate 22 scientists and sophisticated equipment, including a laser projector and camera which can take three-dimensional pictures of cloud samples. On top of the aircraft is a weather pod. (RAF)

Skimming just ten feet above the ground, parachutes pull a 50,150-pound load from a C-130 near El Centro, Calif. in the spring of 1967. It was an unofficial world record for a low level airdrop of a single package. Load skidded to a stop after 700 feet. The record came during tests conducted by the 6511th Test Group (Parachute) near El Centro. In a LAPES (low altitude parachute extraction system) mission, the Hercules climbs quickly to altitude (lower photo) after completing the drop. (USAF)

testing ground for the machine. (See chapters 13 and 14). Going into the short strips in Nam, Bilotta would pull off all of his power when he was downwind and had crossed the end of the runway, "drop that wing and that mother would go straight on in and be on the ground in seconds."

"High up in the Himalayan Mountains at Kathmandu (Nepal), I landed a group of Army technicians and a complete radio station. We made just one turn and dropped it in and offloaded the radio station. I did the same thing landing at La Paz, Bolivia, at 13,500 feet. The bird doesn't know any limitation. It will do anything you tell it to. During all of my experience with it, that one-thirty never hesitated a bit. All you had to do if you got into trouble was to apply more power and keep on going. That Hercules is the best advertising Lockheed ever had, because that bird has landed in everybody's back yard."

Mack Secord of Atlanta got *his* first yen for C-130 flying as a T-33 pilot at Itazuke AB, Japan, in 1963 after hearing his base commander, Colonel John Roche, talk about the plane's virtuosity. Roche was former ops officer of the 463rd TCW at Ardmore, the first Air Force base to get Hercules in 1956. Up to then, Secord had been oriented to fighters. "But I was about to get smart and say, 'Why not fly in comfort?' I like to have folks around . . . eat a meal; I was tired of carrying that 40 blasted-pound parachute around on my back and being wedged in a little old cockpit for two hours and sweating every minute and worrying if I had enough fuel. I was ready for a gentleman's plane. So I put in for a transfer. It was my dream plan . . . to go to a Hercules squadron. I specified E's . . . they were just coming out."

Secord ended up at Pope AFB, North Carolina, with the Herk-flying 464th Troop Carrier Wing. "It was a different world. Everything I could ask for in an airplane: Responsiveness . . . a world of safety features. The Herk turned out to be the most 'fun' airplane I've ever flown. It would do anything you wanted.

"The thing that impressed me about the C-130, other than performance and speed, was the human engineering. Just the way things worked. Have you ever looked at the engineering panel? You could almost take a man off the farm and make him a C-130 engineer. He's got the diagrams up there and the handles all lined up with the diagrams. The way the instrument panel was laid out, and the way the knobs and switches are placed, it's just hard to go wrong. The Hercules was the first time where the human factors people had a role in the aircraft design."

The props: Didn't the props cause him some problems? "No, props didn't bother me. I always considered the Herk a jet airplane with props." But Secord did have a bit of trouble when he completed his Phase II C-130 training at Pope. He was told by his instructor at Sewart that, to obtain his certification as combat ready, he had to simulate an assault landing.

"Pope had a 5,500 foot asphalt runway, with an 800-foot concrete extension on each end. My instructor told me, 'I want you to simulate an assault landing. If you've not stopped by the time you get to the asphalt, you have flunked the course.' Which meant you had to touch down and stop within 800 feet. I said, '*I don't know if I can do that.*' Of course, the beauty of it was you had anti-skid brakes on the Herk. You could touch down and lock the brakes and go in full reverse and the wheels wouldn't skid. Well, I did it." It proved to be well worth the effort when Secord ended up in the mission to Stanleyville, Belgian Congo, the episode described in Chapter One. Later on, Captain Secord imparted his assault landing experience to his own C-130 students at Pope AFB. He would give them all the assurance in the world that their Hercules would get them in and out safely and surely.

"What you are doing is flying strictly a controlled rate of descent with the throttles, and you're not interested in putting in a roundout. If you want to put in a little roundout, that's okay; the object is to get pretty close to the end of the runway, get the mother on the ground and get it stopped . . . drive the airplane into the ground and lock the brakes."

The only serious problem Secord encountered in teaching C-130 students came at a dirt strip at Fort Bragg. One student had made his second landing on the 2,000-foot strip and had taken off. "I told him, 'After you touch down, go into full reverse, then just tap the brakes to make sure you got some brakes, then pull off. That's what we did. We got off the runway, and all of a sudden, I see a fire truck roaring up and people making all sorts of signs. They were yelling, "Wheelwell's on fire!" The fire was put out promptly, but the student was given a few more lessons in landing.

As *Aviation Week's* Bob Hotz has noted, the C-130 "has outstripped all its original requirements in a fantastic manner . . . it has landed on dirt strips, grass, desert sands, aircraft carrier decks and picked up and delivered cargo by aerial systems without ever landing at all . . . ."

Even the C-130's high altitude antics in its early years caused raised eyebrows, particularly among commercial airline pilots. "Aussie" Maxwell tells of the DC-8 at 31,000 feet, calling by a C-130 at 33,000 feet:

"We're going by that Air Force traffic—*God, it's got propellers on it.*"

Or the time one busy evening over Washington, D.C., when an empty C-130, flying at 37,000 feet, was cleared to 39,000 feet. The pilot messaged he'd rather not go any further since "these props will only do so much." An unidentified airplane piped up, "I'd like to know how the hell he got to FL370 in the first place."

When one reviews the encyclopedic range of accomplishments by the Hercules and its valiant aircrews over the years, surely one of the most astounding took place in October of 1963 when the U.S. Navy decided to try to land a Hercules on an aircraft carrier: Was it possible? Who would believe that the big, four engine C-130 with its bulky fuselage and 132-foot wing span—could land on the deck of a carrier?

Not only was it possible, it was done, in moderately rough seas 500 miles out in the North Atlantic off the Boston coast. In so doing, the airplane became the largest and heaviest airplane to land on a U.S. Navy aircraft carrier, a record that holds to this day.

When Lt. James H. Flatley III was told about his new assignment, he thought somebody was pulling his leg: "Operate a C-130 off an aircraft carrier? Somebody's got to be kidding," he said.

But they weren't kidding. In fact, the Chief of Naval Operations himself had ordered a feasibility study on operating the big propjet aboard the Norfolk-based *Forrestal*. The Navy was trying to find out whether they could use the big Hercules as a sort of "super CoD"—a "Carrier onboard delivery aircraft." The airplane then used was the Grumman C-1 Trader, a twin engine bird with a limited payload and only a 300-mile range. If a carrier is operating in mid-ocean it has no "on board delivery" system to

Hopping on and off the Navy attack carrier U.S.S. *Forrestal* in the Atlantic Ocean off Boston, a Navy/Marine KC-130F Hercules set an aviation record as the heaviest and largest aircraft ever to perform the feat. Naval Air Test Center pilots from Patuxent River, Maryland, flew the tests. The Navy was investigating use of the C-130 for increased logistic support of the U.S. fleet. (U.S. Navy)

The seas were choppy when Navy test pilots flew the Hercules onto and off of the U.S.S. *Forrestal.* Gross weights for the first landings were 85,000 pounds and were raised by increments by refueling to 121,000 pounds. Landing distances ranged from 270 feet at 85,000 pounds to 460 feet at 121,000 pounds. One landing during a rain squall with a gross weight of 109,000 pounds required only 495 feet to stop. (U.S. Navy)

fall back on and must come nearer land before taking aboard even urgently needed items. The Hercules was stable and reliable with a long cruising range and a high payload.

The aircraft, a KC-130F refueler transport (Buno 149798), on loan from the Marines, was delivered October 8. Lockheed's only modification to the original plane was to install an improved anti-skid braking system, remove refueling pods from the wings and install a smaller nose-landing gear orifice.

"The big worry was whether we could meet the maximum sink rate of nine feet per second," Flatley said. As it turned out, the Navy was amazed to find they were able to better this mark by a substantial margin.

In addition to Flatley, crewmen consisted of Lt. Cmdr. W.W. Stovall, co-pilot, ADR-1 E.F. Brennan, flight engineer, and Lockheed engineering flight test pilot Ted H. Limmer, Jr., safety pilot. The initial seaborn landings, on October 30, 1963, were made into a 40-knot wind. Altogether, the crew successfully negotiated 29 touch-and-go landings, 21 unarrested full stop landings and 21 unassisted take-offs at gross weights of 85,000 pounds up to 121,000 pounds. At 85,000 pounds, the KC-130F came to a complete stop within 270 feet, about twice the aircraft's wing span! The Navy was delighted to discover that even with the maximum load, the plane used only 745 feet for take-off and 460 feet for landing roll. The short landing roll resulted from close coordination between Flatley and Jerry Daugherty, the carrier's landing signal officer. Daugherty, later to become a captain and assigned to the Naval Air Systems Command, gave Flatley an engine "chop" while he was still airborne, enabling him to reverse thrust on the props while still three or four feet off the deck.

Lockheed's Ted Limmer, who checked out fighter pilot Flatley in the 130, stayed on for some of the initial touch and go and full-stop landings. "The last landing I participated in, we touched down about 150 feet from the end, stopped in 270 feet more and launched from that position, using what was left of the deck. Still had a couple hundred feet left when we lifted off. Admiral Brown was flabbergasted . . . ."

The plane's wingspan cleared the *Forrestal's* flight deck "island" control tower by just under 15 feet as the plane roared down the deck on a specially painted line. Lockheed-Georgia's chief engineer, Art E. Flock was aboard to observe the testing.

"The sea was pretty big that day. I was up on the captain's bridge. I watched a man on the ship's bow and that bow must have gone up and down 30 feet." The speed of the ship was increased 10 knots to reduce yaw motion and to reduce wind direction. Thus, when the plane landed, it had a 40 to 50 knot wind on the nose.

"That airplane stopped right opposite the captain's bridge," recalled Flock. "There was cheering and laughing. There on the side of the fuselage, a big sign had been painted on that said, "LOOK MA, NO HOOK.' "

From the accumulated test data, the Navy concluded that with the Hercules, it would be possible to lift 25,000 pounds of cargo 2,500 miles and land it on a carrier. Even so, the idea was considered a bit too risky for the C-130 and the Navy elected to use a smaller CoD aircraft. For his effort, the Navy awarded Flatley the Distinguished Flying Cross.

For a bulky transport, the Hercules holds an inordinate number of world records. For instance:

—It is the largest operational ski-and-wheel equipped aircraft. As such, it holds all ski-lift records for transports, being the largest airplane ever to operate from 10,000-foot high "Dome Charlie," in the Antarctic and the Greenland Ice Cap.

—It holds the world record for the longest first flight by a commercial aircraft. The L-100 Hercules, commercial derivative of the C-130, flew 25 hours one minute on its maiden flight from its takeoff at 11:29 a.m. Monday, April 20, 1964, until its landing at 12:30 EST on Tuesday, April 21. Joe Garrett, Lockheed's chief production test pilot, was at the controls much of the time. Taking turns in the left hand seat were pilots Ralph I. Evans and Hank C. Price.

—The C-130 holds the record as the world's highest flying paradrop aircraft. Nine U.S. Marine Corps parachutists jumped from a Hercules flying at an altitude of 44,100 feet.

—The world's heaviest low-altitude cargo extraction—50,150 pounds—was made from a C-130 skimming ten feet above the ground at El Centro, California. This record Low Altitude Parachute Extraction System (LAPES) drop took place in March, 1967, and the load skidded to a stop in 700 feet. Capt. Floyd

Lockheed chief production test pilot Joe Garrett emerges from record-breaking first flight on red and white Lockheed demonstrator Hercules aircraft, with a big smile. Named "old reliable" by its crew, the airplane stayed aloft 25 hours, one minute and eight seconds on its maiden flight on April 20 and 21, 1964. This also was a one-of-a-kind world aviation first flight endurance record, and also broke the endurance record for its type, formerly held by a USAF C-130B.

First USAF C-130 modified for in-flight refueling is pictured here above California's Mojave Desert being refueled from a KC-135 aerial tanker. In the 1978 flight, the aircraft established a C-130 airborne record of 27 hours and 45 minutes. Plane was modified by Lockheed Aircraft Service Company. (Lockheed)

"Baby birds leaving the nest" could be the caption for this shot showing Navy Blue Angel fighters taking off at a Dobbins AFB, Ga., air show, leaving behind the Blue Angel "mother hen," a KC-130, on the ground. The Marine Corps Herk accompanies the aerobatic team wherever it goes, providing spares and logistic support. *(Photo courtesy Marietta, Ga.,* Daily Journal).

First of a fleet of new HC-130H surveillance aircraft acquired by the U.S. Coast Guard is pictured patrolling coastline of Florida. Delivery of the first aircraft took place in 1983 at USCG Station Clearwater, Fla. The Coast Guard is launched on a major fleet modernization program. The new HC-130H's feature numerous improvements over the Coast Guard's earlier "B" models, including 1983 model airframes, as well as modern state-of-the-art avionics and numerous systems and structural updates.

Stroup of the 1611th Test Group (Parachute) was the aircraft commander. (For a time, the Hercules held the world's record for the heaviest weight extracted in a single package by parachute from an aircraft—41,740 pounds. But this was later eclipsed by a C-141 Lockheed StarLifter, the Herk's younger fanjet brother).

—In July, 1976, a drone-launch DC-130H set what is believed to be a world record for lifting external weight by a turboprop aircraft when it took off from Edwards AFB, California, carrying on its wings four remotely piloted vehicle test units together weighing 44,510 pounds. Pilot was Lockheed-Georgia engineering test pilot Carl Hughes. The modified aircraft is designed to carry future vehicles weighing up to 10,000 pounds each.

—A long distance flight record for turboprop aircraft was set on February 20, 1972, by a Military Airlift Command HC-130H rescue aircraft which flew 8,790 miles from Taiwan to Scott AFB, Illinois. The non-stop, non-refueled flight wiped out a 6,842-mile mark held by a U.S. Navy P-3. Aircraft commander was Lt. Col. Edgar Allison, Jr. The crew flew in a jet stream at an altitude of 37,000 to 39,000 feet. "We hoped to make it to Andrews or McGuire" (on the east coast), said MAC photographer M/Sgt. Yuen-Gi Yee, "but the winds died down just past Midway Island." The plane landed with 4,500 pounds of fuel in reserve.

*   *   *

Over the years, numerous extra long distance flights have been logged by C-130 crews, particularly across the Pacific. In 1961, for instance, a U.S. Coast Guard SC-130B, piloted by Lt. Cmdr. Vance K. Randall, zipped nearly 4,000 miles non-stop, from Tachikawa AB, Japan, to Barbers Point, Hawaii. The new search and rescue bird, carrying 16 passengers and 9,000 pounds of cargo, averaged 453 miles per hour on the 3,900-mile stretch, the fastest ground speed recorded up to then for a C-130 on a long distance hop.

In December, 1966, a Military Airlift Command C-130E, commanded by Capt. Clovis T. Lightsey, set two MAC records when it flew nonstop from Midway Island in the Pacific to McGuire AFB, New Jersey, covering the 5,700 statute miles in 16 hours. Maximum altitude was 33,000 feet.

After the arrival, and while Lightsey and crew were being

congratulated and photographed, the standardization folks were checking their fuel gauges!

Earlier, a MATS C-130E of the 1611th Air Transport Wing at McGuire flew the 5,000 miles from Hickam AFB, Hawaii, to McGuire in 13 hours . . . five hours less than usual. Commanded by Capt. Andrew W. Biancor of the 29th ATS, the Hercules "step-climbed" to 37,000 feet, taking advantage of a healthy tailwind and had an average ground speed of 450 mph.

On September 1, 1960, a U.S. Coast Guard SC-130B flew non-stop and unrefueled from Shemya Island, Alaska, bordering the Bering Sea, the 5,253 nautical miles back to Elizabeth City, North Carolina, in 14 hours and six minutes. Average ground speed exceeded 370 miles per hour, but was as high as 430 miles per hour on some segments. The plane cruised from 32,500 feet on up to over 40,000 feet while crossing over Washington, D.C. This is believed to be a distance record for the "B" model. Aircraft commander was Lt. Cmdr. Lloyd Kent.

A MATS C-130E on duty as a Project Mercury recovery aircraft in the Pacific, set a distance record for the "E" in 1963, covering 6,400 statue miles nonstop from Wake Island to Wayne County Airport in Detroit. The aircraft and project commander was Lt. Col. Joe Bilotta, the aforementioned commander of the 41st Transport Squadron at Charleston.

"While at Wake Island, a couple of my younger officers said, 'Why don't we fly non-stop all the way back to Charleston?'

"I said, 'Figure it out.' They sat down and figured we could make it. We had an auxiliary tank, but we had a lot of people and equipment aboard. We started at 16,000 feet. As you burn fuel you go higher and higher, and the higher you go, the less friction, possibly better winds and better speeds, and you burn less fuel. We ended up at 36,000 or 38,000 feet. We actually had some adverse winds, though, and we landed in Detroit and got a load of fuel. We had enough to get to Charleston, but we didn't want to stretch it." The flight took 19 hours and 40 minutes.

In 1966, a Marine KC-130 flew from Atsugi, Japan, to MCAS El Toro, California, in 15.9 hours, but the U.S. Navy claimed to have beaten this record with two earlier C-130 flights. L. A. Price flew from Tachikawa AB, Japan to Norton AFB, California—4,854 miles—in 14.8 hours. But the record holder at that

A 35,000-pound Sheridan tank is delivered by low altitude parachute extraction during NATO exercise "Certain Shield" in late 1978 near Lauterback, Germany. In the LAPES drops, the Hercules skims over the ground at five to ten feet (with wheels down), makes the drop then climbs quickly to altitude. (Top photo, USAF/Paul Hayashi; lower photo, European Stars and Stripes/Jim Cole)

In what may have been the world's shortest delivery flight, a new C-130H transport built by the Lockheed-Georgia Company was handed over to the 94th Tactical Airlift Wing, Air Force Reserve, across the Dobbins AFB runway in Marietta, Ga., Oct. 2, 1982. Air Force pilots gave the airplane a short test flight prior to landing at Dobbins for the delivery event. Named the "City of Marietta," the camouflaged transport was the first direct-from-the-factory C-130H model to be delivered to the Reserve. Aircraft is pictured above in flight over downtown Atlanta.

Nigerian Air Force Group Captain U.S. Abbas *(c)*, Defence and Armed Forces Attache from the Nigerian Embassy, Washington, D.C., accepts his nation's third C-130H-30 "Super Hercules" transport in ceremonies in March, 1985, at the Lockheed-Georgia Company. Making the presentation in behalf of Lockheed was Vice President-Marketing Charles Ray *(l)*. The three new Lockheed propjets are based at Lagos, and will be used for military logistic support as well as for country-building missions. Altogether, the Nigerian Air Force has a fleet of nine Hercules aircraft — six C-130H's and three C-130H-30's.

time was Lt Commander P.E. Sturdevant who flew a C-130E from Tachikawa to NAS Moffett Field, California, in 12.9 hours. This flight, on January 8, 1966, covered 4,520 miles at altitudes of 21,000 to 27,000 feet; tail winds exceeded 220 knots and maximum ground speed approached 500 knots! The aircraft burned 40,000 pounds of its 63,000-pound fuel load.

*   *   *

There were times, however, when attempts at long distance records didn't quite come off. Retired USAF Col. Chuck Howe, the aforementioned commander of the 322nd Air Division in Europe, recalled trying to set a distance record with his Sewart-based "A" model on a flight from Newfoundland with a 25,000 pound load.

"We filed for Rome. The forecast winds were favorable and we had plenty of fuel. We kept going farther and farther north, but we never found that wind. We got up to the coast of Greenland. That's when our *first* difficulty arose. We encountered what was later explained as 'harmonic yaw' of the propellers. The prop tips went through the speed of sound. When they did, they began to fluctuate and the fuel flow indicator just went wild. I guess it was scheduling fuel on and off to keep up with the resonance in the propeller.

"We finally staggered into Prestwick, Scotland . . . we had burned up all of our fuel."

But that wasn't the end of the story and Chuck Howe takes up the narrative:

"Unbeknownst to us, on our takeoff from Newfoundland, the landing gear had frozen in the well. That was a little bit common on the 'A' model.

"We had about a 1500-foot ceiling. While we were still on instruments, we went through the check list; *that's* when we found out about the gear."

Even though the fuel was getting short, Howe wasn't about to panic. He had faith in his Herk, even though she had a few cranky idiosyncracies.

"We monkeyed with the gear for a while and we finally got it down.

"We asked for the prevailing winds and *that's* when we found out about our other problems: Prestwick had 30-knot cross winds at a 45-degree angle *and the runway was a sheet of ice!*"

Howe was yet to lose his cool.

"We just held the wing down into the wind. That airplane is *so* fantastic, you could actually almost do a dance on the slippery runway, just by playing those reverse prop levers. We had complete control all the way, manipulating the conditioning levers—popping them in and out of reverse. Everything worked, but it was a big drill, I'll tell you."

*   *   *

What may be a speed record for a Hercules was set on February 9, 1960, when an RC-130A from the 1370th Photo-Mapping Wing, Turner AFB, Ga., attained gound speeds of 541 miles per hour in a flight from Tucson, Arizona, to Albany, Ga. The Georgia pilot was Capt. T. L. Smith.

A high speed flight across the Atlantic was recorded on December 2, 1960, by an RCAF C-130B flown by the aforementioned Aussie Maxwell; "It was the first trans-Atlantic crossing of a Canadian turboprop and at one stage, we were making 508 knots ground speed, which converts to 585 mph. I've never seen winds like it before or since." The flight, from Gander to Marville in northern France covered 2289 nautical miles, averaging 371 knots, or 2640 statute miles at an average of 429 mph. The distance was spanned in 6:35 chock to chock.

Endurance, another hallmark of the C-130, was given a good run in 1961 when a C-130 from Tachikawa AB, Japan, set a turboprop record for three and then two engine operation by continuous flight for more than 16 hours. Following takeoff, the aircraft, under command of Lt. R. Young, climbed to 23,000 feet and the Number 4 prop was feathered. The Hercules continued on three engines for three hours. After five hours, the Number 1 engine was feathered and the aircraft descended to 20,000 feet. The remainder of the 16 hour, 20 minute flight was on two engines, until start of descent, when the outboard engines were restarted.

The all-time C-130 airborne endurance record of 27 hours and

These stamps testify to the popularity of the C-130. They are from the Ross Dependency, Indonesia and Ascension Island. They depict, respectively, a C-130E, C-130B and C-130K. (Courtesy *Stamp Collector* magazine).

WHY NOT—THEY USE US FOR EVERYTHING ELSE!

This cartoon, by retired USAF M/Sgt. Dave Davenport of Spring Lake, North Carolina, is one of hundreds he has drawn and had published in the *Hercules Herald* at Pope AFB. Dave's cartoons humorously depict the human element of Herk's labors, such as this one showing the C-130 pulling a snow plow during the severe winter of 1977-78. (Courtesy Dave Davenport and *Hercules Herald*).

Versatility of the Hercules was demonstrated in 1978 by Air Force Reserve C-130s operating out of the Canal Zone. Top left, C-130 lands on strip in South America. Top right, crew arrives at La Paz, Bolivia, world's highest altitude airport. Center left, C-130 circles ship in distress while calling in a rescue ship to its aid. Center right, Hercules drops U.S. Army paratroopers in Canal Zone training exercise. Lower left, plane offloads cargo at Rio de Janeiro, while lower right, passengers prepare to board C-130 at La Paz. (USAF, Lockheed)

"Thanks, Admiral," was the appreciation expressed by Russian Scientist Leonid Kuperov, who was rescued on April 11, 1961, from Byrd Station, Antarctica by a Navy crew flying an LC-130 ski-Hercules. Below, smiling scientist bids Rear Admiral David Tyree goodbye after his recovery at Christchurch, New Zealand. The pioneering rescue flight pierced the "Antarctic winter darkness" for the first time. Kuperov was suffering a bleeding ulcer. (USN)

45 minutes was set in 1977 by a C-130 outfitted with a new in-flight refueling system. The aircraft was refueled three times during its record-setting flight, including two night hookups. The in-flight refueling system was developed for the Air Force by Lockheed Aircraft Service Company at Ontario, California.

*　　*　　*

When the final story of the C-130 is written, it will be replete with examples of stamina never before seen in a transport, and certainly never again in an aircraft of its size and type.

When the Hercules first appeared on the Air Force operational scene around the world, people had their doubts as to whether it would live up to its advance notices. Colonel Bilotta recalled that "People told us when we first got the C-130 in MATS, 'Hey, you've got a half breed.' But this little beast is fantastic getting in and out of unimproved runways. Oh, God, we've been in some places I wouldn't even take a C-47 in. In fact, this bird will out-perform a C-47 on landing, takeoff, and everything else.

"I can take that 130 here and cut all four engines at any altitude, normally a thousand, but this is what we call almost dead stick. I can cut four engines, pull the power back and without much power I can land on end of runway and I won't exceed 1,000 (ft.) from end of runway. It's nothing but a fighter plane. Honest to God. It *is* a fighter plane."

*　　*　　*

What has amazed many fliers has been the plane's stamina to keep on flying, and hauling, even without scheduled maintenance.

The experience in the Congo in the early 1960s, as mentioned in an earlier chapter, was a good example. The USAF and the Royal Canadian Air Force got the assignment to carry out the bulk of the United Nations peacekeeping airlift support, shuttling troops and food from Europe and the Middle East into Leopoldville and inland areas and bringing out refugees. It was a monumental, long range assignment that went on for more than a year, but thanks to the C-130, the task went off without a hitch. The inspection schedules were temporarily abandoned and Air

Force people were pleasantly surprised that the plane operated right on. Brig. Gen. Tarleton Watkins (ret.) was thankful for the fleet of new Hercules in his European airlift inventory. The Congo airlift came during a series of crises—the Lebanon presence, plus earthquakes in Morocco and Iran—which required a superhuman airlift effort. Throughout, there was not a major or minor C-130 accident. Said Watkins: "Our utilization rate went sky-high with the arrival of the C-130. We'd been dead without it. We operated well over a year without an accident. Fact is, I don't remember ever having an accident. We won the Air Force Flying Safety Award every year."

Which brings us around to the C-130's safety record, which is considered to be one of the finest of any military transport in the world. This is all the more remarkable in view of the many thousands of hazardous flights, under all sorts of grim flying conditions—in the Arctic and the Antarctic and considering the plane's super hazardous role in Vietnam.

Chuck Howe, as related previously, appreciated the Herk's generous and forgiving nature. "The margin for getting yourself out of bad conditions (with the 130) was more than on any other aircraft I've ever flown. You just had that raw power.

"If everything else was against you, you still had the power to just push every throttle forward and get the hell out of there in a *helluva* hurry—4,000 feet a minute in a near vertical ascent.

"Most cargo aircraft, when you get within 15 feet of the ground on a landing approach, you're going to have to go on through with your landing. But on the C-130, it made no difference when you decided to go away from it, even landing in the mountains at 11,000 feet above sea level. If you decided you didn't want to complete a landing—uphill or whatever—you'd just pull up and go around. No problem."

A U.S. Marine Corps group—VMGR 252 at Cherry Point, North Carolina—set the current longest safety record in Naval Aviation history by flying a squadron of KC-130 Hercules 18 years and 204,000 hours without an accident. Third Aerospace and Recovery flew 125,000 accident-free hours in 30 months in Vietnam. Two Royal Australian Air Force squadrons—flying "A" and "E" model C-130s—accumulated more than 250,000 hours of safe flying and now, with their "H" models are building even further on that record.

The "typhoon chasers" of the 54th Weather Reconnaissance squadron on Guam—flying their HC-130 search and rescue aircraft in some of the most turbulent atmospheric conditions on earth—including more than 5,000 flights into the eyes of more than 300 tropical storms—have logged well over 100,000 hours of accident free flying. (This same outfit for several years now has performed fog-seeding operations in Alaska. Using crushed dry ice, they successfully disperse dense fog which often closes the northern bases to air traffic.)

The key to flight safety is two-fold: flight crew professionalism and a well built aircraft. In the case of the C-130, crews have established an outstanding record of aircraft operation and maintenance. Then too, Hercules crews are the first to confirm that the C-130 is a solidly built machine. The first person to log 1,000 hours in the Hercules, Lockheed flight engineer Roy Reynolds, has often told his colleagues at Marietta with appreciation that they build "the most forgiving airplane ever made."

A quiet, bespectacled professional with a long experience in aircraft, Reynolds recalled "a little landing incident" that occurred at a foreign base in 1958. At the time, Roy was assigned to the U.S. Air Force in Japan to help train pilots and navigators transitioning to the C-130. During a routine landing approach, 1,200 feet above the airstrip, a USAF pilot got a fire-warning on engine Number 3. The aircraft commander ordered the co-pilot to pull the fire handle. Instead, he pushed Number 3's conditioning lever, feathering the prop. In the excitement of the moment, the aircraft commander mistakenly pulled the fire handle on Number 2, while the co-pilot, trying to redeem himself, pulled Number 1.

"There she was, in her approach with three engines feathered. But she came in smooth as silk, making a normal landing on one engine. Any other airplane in a situation like that would have clobbered us into the ground."*

As LeRoy Stanton recalled, "The Hercules was a godsend. It had such tremendous performance, it was tremendously safe, and if you lost an engine, you didn't damned near have to have a heart

---

*RCAF's Aussie Maxwell confirms the no-sweat reaction to an engine out. "Our skit was a rather crude gesture . . . we'd pick at one part of our nose, flick some imaginary thing into space and say, 'What else is new today?' But we did have a case out of Thule where

attack. You could say, 'Well, I believe we've lost Number 4; how about feathering it and clean it up' and you'd roll in about a degree of trim and drop off 20 knots and keep on going."

Pilots who have landed at wrong (and extremely short) airports have thanked their lucky stars that they had the Hercules to get them in and back out safely.

On New Year's eve, 1966, U.S. Coast Guardsmen in San Francisco flew one of their HC-130Bs into Baja, California, Mexico, to pick up an injured tuna clipper captain. Arriving at Cabo San Lucas, pilots Lt. Cmdr. Clyde Robbins and Lt. Chester Wawrzynski were shocked when they saw only 2,500 feet of irregular surfaced gravel. A large hotel sat at one end of the strip and a hill jutted up at the other.

"Surely they aren't going to land here," a hotel guest exclaimed as he saw the Hercules circling. "Quick, bartender, give us another, I think he's going to try."

Try and succeed they did . . . bringing the big propjet to a stop in 1300 feet! The takeoff with the injured captain, George Souza, was equally spectacular. "Our plane roared down the gravel pit, neatly clearing the hotel and on to San Diego," Capt. J.K. Rea said. "The patient fully recovered."

Robbins was the pilot on another amazing mission to pick up an injured woman at a 2800-foot long 40-foot wide airstrip in the Sweetwater Mountains of the California-Nevada border at Bridgeport, California. Extremely high mountains made the approach even more difficult. The max performance landing went off well but the plane did not get to carry off the rescue flight when the patient died in an ambulance. Nevertheless, Robbins used his JATO bottles to get out of the strip, which was at a 7,000-foot altitude. The C-130 landing and takeoff left the manager of Bryant Airfield awe-struck. "We've been trying for some time to get this airport lengthened for light aircraft," he said. "Now how am I going to convince anyone we need it after this giant comes in and out of here with such ease?"

That same month, June, 1966, people at Norton AFB, Calif.,

a fully loaded (i.e., overloaded) B model lost two engines on one side. (The pins locking the oil filter caps on both props hadn't been properly seated. The caps came open and out went all the oil.) The failures took place at about 200/300 feet after takeoff. They drove her around without much trouble."

got a big chuckle when a Navy pilot destined for Norton landed by mistake at the tiny unpaved Tri-City strip nearby. The *Redlands Daily Facts* reported the incident thusly:

> The red faced Navy flyer, identified only as Lt. Johnson, landed his C-130 Hercules at Norton 30 minutes late after an unscheduled stop at nearby Tri-City. Lt. Johnson apparently landed the big cargo aircraft without difficulty on the short 3,500 foot unpaved Tri-City strip at 11:15 p.m.—his scheduled arrival time at Norton to the east. The Norton control tower gave the Navy pilot his landing instructions and then lost contact. After landing, the pilot commented that the runway seemed a little short.
>
> A San Bernardino sheriff's deputy advised him he was at the wrong airport. The nonplussed flyer made a short field takeoff and landed at Norton where he received a full cargo load and proceeded to Hickam AFB, Honolulu.
>
> "The C-130 has a short field capability," an AF spokesman said, "but they usually don't fool around in that kind of area." AF pilots agreed that the Navy pilot had performed a remarkable feat.

*　　*　　*

Actually, it was more like routine for a C-130, although embarrassing.

Meanwhile, testifying to the endurance of the valiant bird, the first production test model to roll out of the Lockheed-Georgia Company plant at Marietta, Ga., in 1955 (which survived the wing fire on landing) also is still on duty, serving as a trainer aircraft with the Air Force Reserve's 919th Tactical Airlift Group, Eglin AFB, Florida. It, too, has seen action in the U.S., Japan, the Mideast, the Atlantic missile range, and in Vietnam as a transport and subsequently as a highly effective gunship.

USAF Major Bob Killam recalled that the aircraft, tail number 33129, received its severest test in Vietnam, hauling extremely heavy loads into and out of short, rough strips. "But through it all," he said, "the plane was super. Lots of time, we carried loads on the Herk that were heavier than we were supposed to carry. The Army had equipment for us to haul and we had no idea how much they weighed. We'd carry anything we could fit into the Herk, and fly into and out of short, rough fields, sometimes taking off on three engines. The Herk is a beautiful airplane on three-engine takeoffs and I've done it because of mortar fire and the like."

Killam remembered hairy days flying the AC-130 gunship down the Ho Chi Minh trail, destroying hundreds of enemy vehicles in one night. But enemy gunfire also was intense.

"The plane got hit many times in combat . . . had all kinds of holes in it . . . and yet it would always bring me home."

Number 129's most serious battle injuries were received on March 26, 1971, when the plane took a 37mm shell just aft of the nose wheel. The shell exploded, seriously damaging the wheel well and the area beneath the flight deck. Several hydraulic and electrical components were damaged, but the plane made it back to the base.

Major Killam, meanwhile, has retired from the Air Force Reserve, leaving the "first lady" behind.

"The airplane," he said, "has outlasted me. It's a great airplane. It's been rebuilt several times and we pilots can't be rebuilt. It'll probably be here for more years . . . I love the airplane. They'll have to go a long way to replace the Hercules."

"This C-130 has outlasted me," said USAF Major Bob Killam as he bade goodbye to the first production Hercules, USAF serial number 33129, on his retirement from the Air Force. The airplane, which has seen action in the U.S., Europe, the Mideast and Asia, was still flying as a training aircraft with the Air Force Reserves as of January 1, 1986. (Lockheed)

THE LABORS OF HERCULES: "A" TO "K"
AND VARIATIONS GALORE

Sure, the Hercules was strong, but who could know that a short haul, tactical bantam rooster would have roles of recon, rescue, strategic airlift and aerial refueling.

—Major Orlen L. Brownfield
(MAC FLYER magazine)

Quite possibly, the C-130 is the most versatile airplane ever built.

John Pennington
Atlanta Journal-Constitution
Magazine

Hercules, the hero of Greek mythology noted for his strength and courage, had an appearance that suggested he was "waiting for yet another superhuman task to fulfill."

The description aptly described the winged Hercules, whose labors soon exceeded by far the 12 accomplishments of the Greek-Roman god. No four-engine transport aircraft in aviation history has ever performed so many different aerial tasks—and so well—as the Lockheed Hercules. Its catalogue of missions is thick and dramatic:

C-130 Derivatives

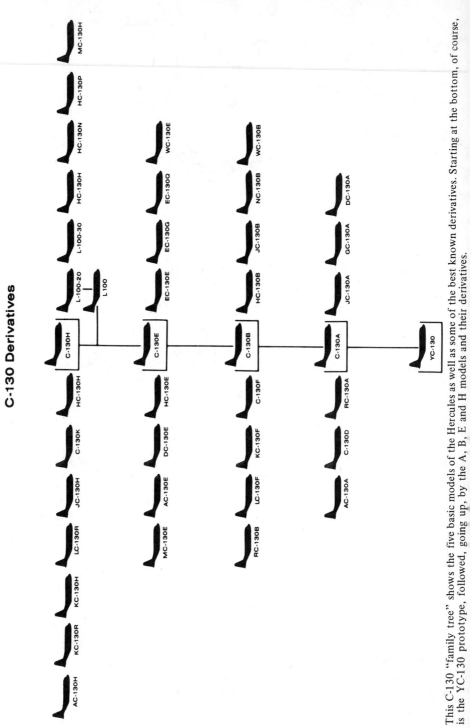

This C-130 "family tree" shows the five basic models of the Hercules as well as some of the best known derivatives. Starting at the bottom, of course, is the YC-130 prototype, followed, going up, by the A, B, E and H models and their derivatives.

From snagging satellite nose cones in mid-air to "skyhook" snatches of people from land and sea . . . from chasing typhoons in the Pacific to "busting fog" in Alaska . . . from refueling fighters and helicopters across the Atlantic and Pacific to launching drone targets off Puerto Rico, the roles of the C-130 seem endless.

Lockheed people answering inquiries about the Hercules often respond by asking, "Exactly which model are you talking about?" There are versions for hurricane-hunting, forest fire-fighting, photo-mapping, iceberg patrolling, and rescue and recovery of men and spacecraft.

New roles emerge almost yearly for the rugged aerial platform, far beyond its original task as a transport for troops and their supplies and equipment.

Except for the "stretching" of the fuselage for the later commercial versions, the airplane's external appearance and dimensions have remained nearly the same since the rollout of the original model: It is 97.8 feet long, has a 38.4 foot vertical tail height and a wingspan of 132.6 feet. The squat, low slung fuselage is only inches from the ground.

As Lockheed's Ed Shockley noted, "The C-130's basic design turned out to be very reliable and the engines had growth capability. Another factor that was a key one was the cargo compartment design. That's true now of all three of our (Lockheed-Georgia) airplanes, the 130, the C-141 and the C-5. It gave them so much flexibility for uses other than just hauling cargo. The fact that we had a wide open compartment, we could drive on and drive off, so to speak; we could put anything in it. Most cargo aircraft design prior to that time had small doors and you really couldn't utilize the available space. Take all of the versions of the airplane . . . You can put fuel tanks in the inside, to give it additional range or to refuel other airplanes. You can use it as a drone launcher. It is amenable to hanging those big drones on it. The plane has adequate power to handle the additional weight and drag.

"It's such a flexible design for almost any use, including the current look at hauling passengers. And, of course, the fact that it can operate into and out of airfields too small for jets—that's a key factor."

Not only is the plane adaptable to many uses, it can be

converted quickly, in minutes for cargo-carrying, personnel transport, paradropping of personnel or cargo, the latter configuration for aerial ambulance duties, search and rescue, and similar missions. Other conversions, or modifications, make possible low-level extraction, inflight refueling, ski-and-wheel operations, photo-mapping, fuel transport with removable 3,600 gallon fuselage tanks, weather observation and air sampling, aerial recovery of missile nose cones, drone-launching and direction, and other missions.

When C-130 flyers and ex-flyers get together, the inevitable subject arises as to which of the various Hercules models is the "best." From the pilot's point of view, the "A" and "B" models were the unanimous favorites, with the exception of the high noise associated with the "A."

"I thought the earlier 'A' and 'B' models were much better to fly," stated Lt. Col. Wilbert Turk, USAF Retired, "because of their horsepower to weight ratio. The later models which had so much added to the aircraft in gross takeoff weight perhaps didn't have the performance of the earlier versions."

Col. Jim Alexander of Clark AFB, Philippines, flew the "A" model from 1958 to 1963 and has flown the "E" since. "The only real complaint I had with the A was the fire protection system. The sunlight would set it off. One of the procedures, if you were

Early C-130-B model test flights included jet assist takeoffs (JATO). Here, the C-130B, grossing 135,000 pounds, roared off the runway at Eglin AFB, Florida, with assistance from eight JATO units, during prop stress tests on new four-bladed Hamilton-Standard propellers. This flight took place March 18, 1959. Lockheed's engineering flight test crew included Walt Hensleigh, aircraft commander; Bernie Dvorscak, pilot; Bill Harris, flight test engineer, and Bob Brennan, flight engineer. (Lockheed) flying with the sun at your back, if you had a fire light, the first thing you did was to turn ninety degrees to your track to see if it went out. It usually did."

Col. Bruce Mosley, commander of Altus Air Force Base, Oklahoma, found the "B" "the closest to a fighter of any transport plane that's ever flown—just beautiful. Put a couple of fingers (on the controls), put in a sixty-five degree bank and go right on around." Mosley has never rolled a one-thirty but doesn't doubt at all that it would easily do it. As pilots in the Vietnam War will attest, the airplane was indeed rolled there, on several occasions. "Split S" performances were reported, particularly Herks trying to escape SAM missiles or MIG fighters.

Lt. Col. Charles Simons felt that the "A" model, with the clean wing, enabled pilots to get a higher "true." Later "B" and "E" models "did everything they were supposed to do, but when you get the N and P (rescue and refueling) versions, with the two tanks and also the refueling pods on the outer wings, It got to be a little bit of a hog."

Lockheed's Walt Hensleigh agreed that while the newer "E" and "H" models have tremendously increased range, payload and power, it was the "B" that seemed to have the edge as to flying quality.

"Of the C-130 series, the 'B' is the best airplane from the pilot's viewpoint. It had more power but the gross weight (135,000 pounds) wasn't nearly as high as later models and it was a more stable airplane and not as noisy as the 'A.' Let's face it, the 'A' was an awfully noisy airplane due to the bigger diameter three-bladed props.

"When the 'E' was modified to put long range tanks on them and long range refueling pods, you reduced the directional stability of the airplane. And as we progressed from that and got bigger cargo payloads and longer range, the plane's flying qualities were reduced. From the utilization standpoint, of course, the 'H' is a very good airplane."

Yet Air Force pilots were delighted with the E's. The flyers in MATS were quite excited when they got the long range "E" model, which retained a great amount of the flying qualities of the earlier hot-rod versions. Colonel Simons, as mentioned earlier who is now with the U.S. military group assigned to the American

Embassy in Bolivia, recalled the excitement at McGuire AFB, New Jersey, with the introduction of the C-130Es.

"We flew tactical missions when we first got them. We flew 'V' formations, 250-knot low level routes, overhead patterns, assault landings. We'd descend at 500 feet a minute and never round it—land right on your speed . . . come right down and drive it in. The translation of angle when you hit the runway caused you to lose 15 to 20 percent of your airspeed. But the airplane was beautiful for that kind of thing. You could really stop it.

Colonel Charles Howe also liked the "E" better, due to its more modern instrumentation. "It handled a little heavier, but it made short field landings just as well as the A's did . . . in 1500 feet with no problem."

Hensleigh noted that the "B"—with a change in the gear box reduction and a shift to the shorter, four-bladed Hamilton-Standard propeller—brought about a reduced noise level. "The 'B' had a somewhat better cargo carrying capability, yet the plane was still way over powered.

"When we went to the 'E,' the gross weight was upped to where it wasn't the over-powered airplane as the 'A' and 'B.' "

Gordon Forbes, Lockheed-Georgia's chief enginner—test and electronics, described the "A" model Hercules as "more like a hot rod than the 'B.' We didn't have such a big gross weight on the 'A.'

"The Hercules had a great basic design, really, when you think of the derivative improvements over the years. The horizontal stabilizer, for instance, was beefed up between the 'A' and ' B. ' And there was considerable beef-up between the 'B' and 'E' to accommodate the extra gross weight of 20,000 pounds."

The 1958 deployment of C-130s into Lebanon—almost 10,000 miles—demonstrated to the military the need for greater range and payload, which brought about the development of the "B," the really long-ranged "E" and the even longer range "H."

The improved range and payload began with the C-130B, which had a boost of 300 horsepower per engine. The airplane ended up with the capability of airlifting a payload of 36,000 pounds nonstop over a long haul distance of 2,300 statute miles. For short trips, the B's payload capacity rose to 45,000 pounds.

In addition to noise reduction, the crews were delighted with the redesign of the flight deck, providing for additional window area up front, double-deck crew bunks and a galley complete with an oven, hot food containers, refrigerator and sink.

The latest advanced "H"—with the higher-power engines, the stronger wings and updated avionics as well as an in-flight operable auxiliary power unit—represents the near ultimate in the design state of the art, and gives the plane a good balanced combination of payload, range performance, and life service expectancy.

*　　*　　*

Lockheed's design philosophy with the Hercules from the start emphasized product improvement—"developing an ever new aircraft in a proven framework."

Based on this maxim, Marietta's engineers—between the original "A" Hercules and the current "H"—have boosted the C-130's payload 26%, its speed 11%, range 52%, and decreased takeoff distance by 17%. Another amazing gain: The airplane's service life expectancy has risen remarkably.

"Of course, we had a good base from which to start," noted Lockheed-Georgia's retired Director of Engineering, Carroll Dallas. "Our designers of the prototype Hercules in Burbank were very radical and bold in their thinking. The YC-130 concept was years ahead of its time."

Dallas, who was a group engineer in 1952 on the YC-130 Hercules prototype in Burbank, transferred to Lockheed-Georgia in July 1953, and was present in Marietta for the first flight of the production aircraft in April, 1955. Said Dallas: "I have had a chance to see just how a great plane can become even greater and reach for its real potential through state-of-the-art improvements brought about by a continuous production string."

*　　*　　*

Here follows two by-lined accounts of the C-130 on completely different missions—typhoon reconnaissance, and a rescue-and-recovery effort that resulted in the bringing out of Charles Lindbergh, Jr. from the jungles of southern Mindanao.

*　　*　　*

C-130 GENERAL ARRANGEMENT

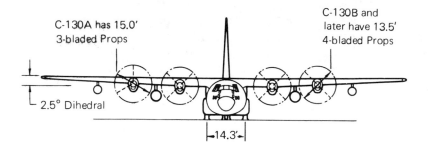

C-130A has 15.0'
3-bladed Props

C-130B and
later have 13.5'
4-bladed Props

2.5° Dihedral

14.3'

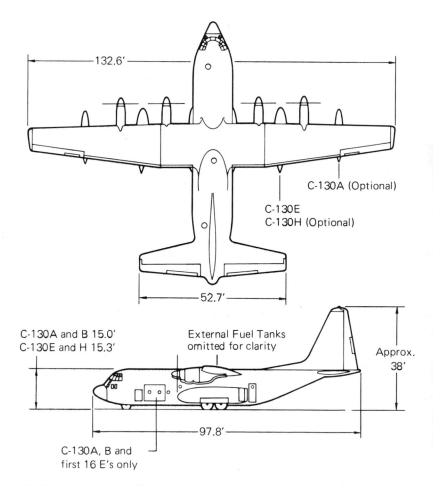

132.6'

C-130A (Optional)

C-130E
C-130H (Optional)

52.7'

C-130A and B 15.0'
C-130E and H 15.3'

External Fuel Tanks
omitted for clarity

Approx.
38'

97.8'

C-130A, B and
first 16 E's only

As this three-view drawing illustrates, the A model Hercules had 15-foot long three-bladed props while subsequent models had four-bladed 13.5-foot propellers. The large side cargo door was a feature of the A, B, and the first 15 Es only. (Lockheed)

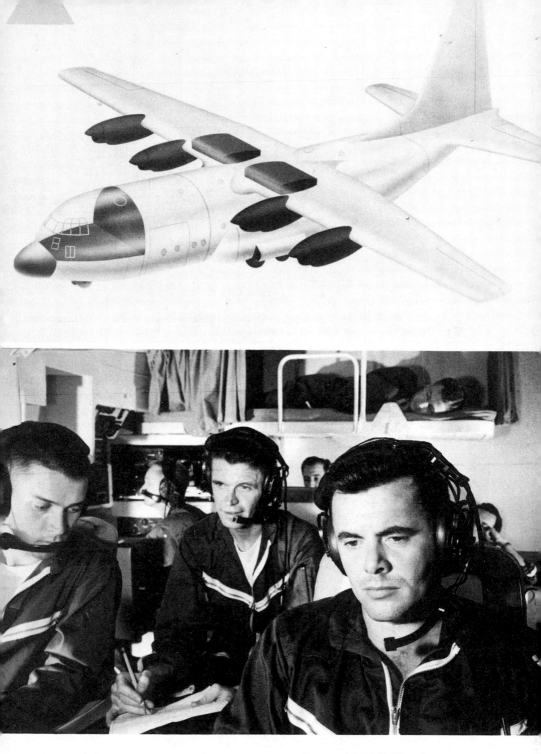

Dark areas (top photo) show where changes were made on the B model C-130. The plane had larger, more advanced Allison engines, additional tanks in the wings containing an additional 1,820 gallons of fuel, stronger landing gears and a more spacious flight station (lower photo) to accommodate multiple crews on longer-range missions. While one crew flew the airplane, another could relax on newly-installed bunks. (Lockheed)

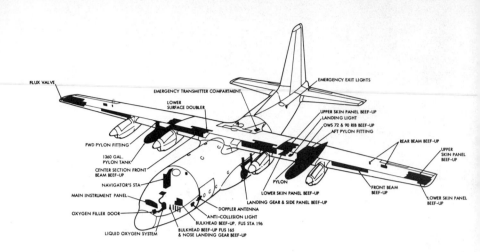

FLUX VALVE

EMERGENCY TRANSMITTER COMPARTMENT

LOWER
SURFACE DOUBLER

EMERGENCY EXIT LIGHTS

UPPER SKIN PANEL BEEF-UP
LANDING LIGHT
OWS 72 & 90 RIB BEEF-UP
AFT PYLON FITTING

FWD PYLON FITTING

REAR BEAM BEEF-UP

UPPER
SKIN PANEL
BEEF-UP

1360 GAL.
PYLON TANK

CENTER SECTION FRONT
BEAM BEEF-UP

NAVIGATOR'S STA

PYLON

MAIN INSTRUMENT PANEL

LOWER SKIN PANEL BEEF-UP

FRONT BEAM
BEEF-UP

LOWER SKIN PANEL
BEEF-UP

OXYGEN FILLER DOOR

LANDING GEAR & SIDE PANEL BEEF-UP

DOPPLER ANTENNA

ANTI-COLLISION LIGHT

BULKHEAD BEEF-UP, FUS STA 196

LIQUID OXYGEN SYSTEM

BULKHEAD BEEF-UP FUS 165
& NOSE LANDING GEAR BEEF-UP

■ INDICATES CHANGES

C-130E HERCULES

Sketch shows the improvements and changes made with the C-130E model Hercules. The beefed-up airplane boasted a gross takeoff weight of 155,000 pounds—ten tons more than the C-130B. The pylon fuel tanks added between the engine nacelles each carry 1,360 gallons, giving the airplane total fuel capactiy of 9,680 gallons, enabling the airplane to cruise non-stop from East Coast U.S. bases to European points, carrying 92 combat troops or 17 tons of outsize cargo. The airplane also was able to fly fully loaded across the Pacific to Japan with only one stop. (Lockheed)

Ground-to-air live pickup utilizing the Fulton Recovery system was demonstrated on "E" model Hercules in 1965 at Pope AFB, North Carolina. Man on ground at left is hooked to a cable pulled up by balloon. Right photo, the airplane's scissors hook picks up the cable, which is latched onto a winch at the back of the plane's cargo compartment. Amazingly, the person on the ground is snatched vertically 200 feet before he is reeled in horizontally. (Lockheed)

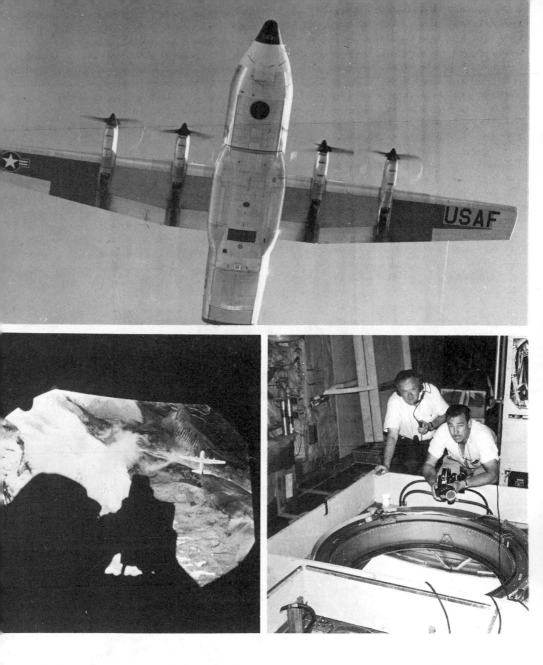

With a television viewfinder bubble under the nose and a large camera window on the bottom of the fuselage (top photo), the RC-130A "seeing eye" photo-mapping Hercules helped to correct world maps in the early 1960s. Cuba, it was found, was misplaced by 1200 feet on standard charts, and Iceland was 600 feet off. Most surprising was the discovery that the Grand Bahamas Island was misplaced on most maps by six miles!

One of four RC-130A's utilized to the photo-mapping Colombia is pictured below another Hercules. Silhouette at left is movie camera operated by Lloyd McCumber. Lower right, McCumber (R) and the late Kermit Echols look at the world below with the "big eye" camera removed from its circular mount. (Lockheed)

These Air Force crewmen from the 463rd Troop Carrier Wing were the first to take C-130B training at Lockheed-Georgia. Joe Garrett (second from left), Lockheed's chief production test pilot, posed for this photo with the USAF flyers from Sewart AFB, Tennessee. At left is Captain Richard (Stumpy) Coleman. (Lockheed)

Successful first transfer of fuel from HC-130P Hercules tanker to an HH-3E was recorded on film at Wright Patterson AFB, Ohio. The "wet" transfer in late 1966 culminated a year-long test program by the USAF and Lockheed. Lockheed subsequently modified twenty HC-130Hs to the "P" model for the Aerospace Rescue and Recovery Service. Two ARRS HE-3Es were flown non-stop across the Atlantic for the 1967 Paris Air Show, being refueled by two HC-130Ps. (USAF)

High above the Pacific, a USAF JC-130B cruises with boom poles extended, ready to snare a parachute holding a Lockheed Agena capsule. The Air Force's satellite nose-cone chasers—the 6593rd Test Squadron based at Hickam AFB, Hawaii—converted to the C-130 from the C-119 in 1961, giving the unit greater speed, range and agility. In lower photo, Captain Edward H. Hosher, and his crew smile after successfully snatching a simulated Discoverer satellite capsule (foreground) in mid-air over Randolph AFB, Texas, and 25,000 people looked on, including the president of Pakistan and Vice President Lyndon Johnson. Their modified C-130B is in background. The Honolulu-based satellite recovery unit roams the Pacific "ball park" recovering space capsules. (USAF)

Captain Gerald LyVere became the first human picked up by an HC-130H ground-to-air recovery system in a test May 3, 1966, at Edwards AFB, Calif. Above, Lockheed test engineers M.R. Edwards, T.C. Hollingsworth and W.T. Yarbrough welcome LyVere aboard after reeling him from the desert floor 400 feet below. Two people were lifted simultaneously by the same plane later in the day. Then, on May 5, three men were "rescued" from the Pacific Ocean surface off Point Mugu, Calif., in two flights. Pilot on the flights was Lockheed engineering test pilot Carl Hughes. (Lockheed)

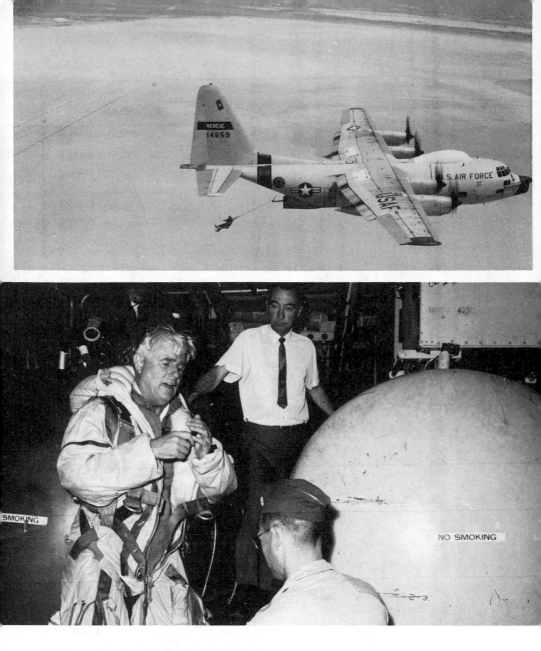

Most spectacular role for the HC-130H—first major derivative of the C-130H—was live pickups utilizing the Fulton Recovery system. As shown in the upper photo, Colonel Allison C. Brooks, commander of the USAF Aerospace Rescue and Recovery Service, and pararescue jumper A3/C Ronald Doll are reeled into the airplane after being snatched from the ground 400 feet below. In the ground-to-air recovery system test at Edwards AFB, Calif., the plane flew overhead, clamped onto a balloon-suspended nylon cable attached to a harness dropped earlier by parachute. A winch in the back of the cargo compartment quickly reeled the pair into the airplane. In the lower photo, Colonel Brooks catches his breath while taking off his recovery gear. In background is E. (Mitt) Mittendorf, Lockheed's director for the test. The Air Force test director was Capt. John D. Bell while Lockheed engineering test pilot Carl Hughes was the pilot on the demonstration flight. This simultaneous pickup of the two men on May 3, 1966, came after the first single pickup of Air Force Captain Gerald T. LyVere. The ARRS ordered 63 of the HC-130Hs for worldwide search and rescue duty, particularly during the Apollo Moon program. (Lockheed)

This U.S. Navy EC-130 is part of its TACAMO communications network, an airborne system for radio contact with the nuclear submarine ballistic missile fleet. Its primary role is to receive messages and relay them via Very Low Frequency (VLF) radio to the submarine fleet. The TACAMO III system is integrated into the C-130 aircraft, reducing system weight while providing improved crew comfort. TACAMO, by the way, derived as an acronym from the Marine challenge to Take Charge and Move Out. The system was developed by the Collins Radio Company. (Photos courtesy Rockwell International)

Weather reconnaissance was an early role assigned by the USAF to the Hercules due to its stable platform and rugged performance in adverse conditions. The C-130B, E, and H model aircraft have been configured to the weather observer role. The weather bird's most dramatic service is "hurricane hunting" in the Gulf of Mexico and the Atlantic, and "typhoon chasing" in the Pacific. Above, the hurricane hunters of Keesler AFB, Miss., are pictured flying into Hurricane Caroline in 1975. (Lockheed, USAF)

The U.S. Marines utilize their KC-130 refueler/transport Hercules to move entire fighter wings across the Atlantic and Pacific oceans. Here a Marine/Navy KC-130F (based on the C-130B airframe), feeds two F-4 fighters at 20,000 foot altitude near Cherry Point, N.C. Initially the Marine tanker version was called the GV-1, later the KC-130F. The latest version is the KC-130R (based on the C-130H) which features the addition of 1360-gallon wing mounted fuel tanks, adding an 18,000-pound fuel giveaway capability for aerial refueling of tactical aircraft. The KC-130 can refuel two fighter planes simultaneously at the rate of 300 gallons per minute each. (Lockheed)

The "Labors of Hercules" around the world are many and varied. Top photo, Royal Australian Air Force Hercules offloads plastic water pipe to hurricane-devasted Port Vila in the New Hebrides in 1960. Center, Argentine AF C-130 takes aboard fuselage of another aircraft at Marambio Base, Antarctica. Third photo, Canadian troops disembark from Hercules during military exercises in the Arctic. (Lockheed)

Flying at an altitude of 200 feet, an Air Force Reserve C-130 lays down a pressurized stream of retardant a quarter mile long and 90 feet wide to help contain a forest fire raging in California. The standard C-130 can be converted quickly into an aerial fire truck with the installation of Modular Airborne Fire Fighting System (MAFFS) units which are positioned in the western U.S. In less than ten seconds, the C-130 can spray 3,000 gallons of retardant on an area the size of five football fields, fireproofing trees and brush. (U.S. Forest Service)

Shadow of a low-flying C-130 from the National Oceanic and Atmospheric Administration research center in Miami, Florida, flashes across the surf zone of a North Carolina beach. The instrument-laden airplane probes the clear, windy weather behind a passing winter storm. A joint NOAA/NASA experiment was testing new radar and laser ocean-wave sensors for use on sea-watching satellites. (NOAA)

U.S. Coast Guard HC-130s ice patrol plane, hedge-hopping row of icebergs off the coast of Labrador, has selected the berg in foreground for marking with a chloride-rhodamine "B" dye bomb. This aircraft was originally designated the SC-130. The USCG's latest Hercules version is the HC-130H. Lower photo, Captain L.H. Seeger (R), then Coast Guard chief of aviation, checks the scanning door of new patrol Hercules with Captain A.E. Harned, then commanding officer of the Goast Guard Station at Elizabeth City, North Carolina. The large glass doors on either side of the aircraft permit wide-ranging scanning as the Coast Guard performs sea rescue and search missions, as well as iceberg patrol, pollution patrol and the monitoring of America's fishing zones. (Lockheed)

GOING TO THE HEART OF TYPHOON GLORIA

Typhoon Gloria was about 50 miles north of Guam island in the Pacific. Most of the WC-130E weather reconnaissance aircraft had been evacuated to Okinawa. The storm was intense, with surface winds of more than 175 miles per hour.

Capt. Al Gideons, a veteran aerial weather reconnaissance officer with the 54th Weather Reconnaissance Squadron,* Andersen AFB, Guam, was the weather officer on the last WC-130 aircraft launched to "take the pulse" of Typhoon Gloria. Gideons, who has flown into the eyes of more than 50 full-blown typhoons and hurricanes and dozens of tropical storms, recalls his thoughts while flying into the eye of "Gloria."

BY CAPT. AL GIDEONS

Now into Gloria for the first fix. It *is* turbulent. The radar shows many heavy returns—cumuloform clouds—with heavy rain. I must move about the flight deck to perform my duties . . . checking wind, observing clouds and surface wind, and taking various readings from meteorological instruments. It looks good; we're on a course for the center.

I have to hold on now because of the heavy turbulence. Things not tied down are being tossed around on the flight deck. We experience positive g forces and then negative g forces.

This is a rough one. We've all been through many typhoons, but the strong ones such as this demand our respect. We have to think of aircraft limitations . . . . A flight bag weighing about 40 pounds suddenly flies up to my eye level. I'm holding on!

Papers are scattered, work implements tossed about. Let's be careful on this one, it may be smart to get out and make a radar fix. Up to now we're okay, but if it gets much worse . . . .

We want that fix; that's why we're here. We plug on.

*Other Hercules-equipped weather reconnaissance squadrons—units of the Military Airlift Command's Air Weather Service—are the 53rd Weather Reconnaissance Squadron, Keesler AFB, Mississippi, (known as the "hurricane hunters") and the 55th WRS, McClellan AFB, California. The National Oceanic and Atmospheric Administration also flies a WC-130B Weather Hercules (affectionately dubbed "NOAA's Ark") out of Miami, Florida.

There it is on radar. We're heading straight in toward the "eye" or calm center. Only one problem left. The wall is a solid, circular band of heavy cumuloform clouds complete with thunderstorms, screaming winds, excessively heavy rain. Maybe hail, too?

The eye is eight miles in diameter. We know we're in for a real jolt when we hit the wall cloud. It's just massive. We try to bore straight into the wall cloud. The airplane is literally tossed out and forced parallel to the wind flow around the wall cloud. Okay, regroup. Try it again, this time crabbing into the wind more. Wham!! Once again we're rejected by the wall cloud. Again we try, this time with 40 degrees of crab.

We slam into the wall. The noise from the rain is deafening. Outside it looks like we are in a waterfall. Severe turbulence, the worst I've experienced. It happened so quickly, nothing to do but hold on and hope the airplane stays upright. It won't last long. A minute or so later and we're through it.

Total serenity, calm, smooth air . . . sunny, hot. And all around us that boiling storm. It takes constant turning to stay inside the tiny eye.

What an awesome sight . . . . The black, ominous wall cloud is all around but it's bright inside the eye. Looking up, there is a perfectly circular hole in the high cirrus clouds. The sunlight is pouring through that cylinder. Like looking at a bright light held at one end of a tube or pipe with you inside.

Far above there is beautiful blue sky. Below, a little stratocumulus topping at about 2,000 feet. The surface of the ocean is nearly calm . . . .

Looking under the wall cloud the wind has the sea churned into a frenzied froth. Strange . . . how in a distance of less than half a mile the wind changes from calm to in excess of 150 knots! We call a storm like this a classic typhoon! It's fourteen degrees centigrade warmer in the eye than just outside the wall cloud! We ask for more cool air from the flight deck air conditioner.

Back to work gathering data and readying for a radio broadcast that we'll make from the eye. We're all set up for a radio phone patch with the Armed Forces Radio on Guam. We expect many interested listeners.

A JOB IN THE JUNGLES OF MINDANAO:
FIND CHARLES LINDBERGH
By CAPTAIN MARC L. SHERRILL
HC-130 Navigator

I was on Easter weekend alert at Clark Air Base, the Philippines, with the 31st Air Rescue Squadron, when the call came in on Sunday, April 2, 1972. We had a State Department mission to southern Mindanao Island in the Philippines. When I attended the briefing along with aircraft commander, Capt. Kent Tatom, we learned that our task was to retrieve Charles Lindbergh, Jr. and his research party from the jungle where he had been visiting the Tasaday stone age tribe. The expedition's helicopter had broken down; Mr. Lindbergh and his group were stranded. It was not a life or death situation, but without our help, it would have been a long, long walk out to civilization for Charles Lindbergh and his party.

Our HC-130P escorted the HH-3 helicopter, navigated for it and refueled it on the 650-mile flight to the southern end of Mindanao. Never before had the helicopter been that far out from Clark.

When we arrived, we found the terrain to be extremely rugged mountains covered in large timber. Our search was hampered by low clouds hanging in the valleys, which made flying hazardous. There was a solid overcast above, so higher altitude flying was out of the question.

After about a half hour, we spotted the tribe's rattan platform sticking out of the tall trees. The Jolly 33 picked up four persons a trip and transferred them to a small strip down the valley, a twenty-mile flight. We had to air-refuel the helicopter on every other trip up the valley so it could complete the job. These refuelings were a real challenge for the pilots of both the HC-130 and the HH-3.

As soon as the Jolly had picked up all thirty members of the research party and delivered them to the strip, it then picked up Mr. Lindbergh and two aides and flew under our escort to Mactan Philippine Air Force Base.

On the way to Mactan, we gave the Jolly one refueling; it left us quite low on fuel. Although we could have flown faster and at a higher, more economical altitude, we chose not to separate from the Jolly since one of our primary jobs was navigating for him. Part of the trip was over water and the weather was marginal on some segments of the route. Our landing at Mactan didn't come too soon. We had minimal fuel—enough, but low enough that we didn't want to dip the tanks to find out *how* low.

Mr. Lindbergh transferred to our Hercules for the flight back to Manila. After dropping his aides off at Manila, Mr. Lindbergh wanted to go on to Clark to thank all those involved in the mission. We had to slow down a bit to make our block time good; all the senior officers from the 13th Air Force would be out to greet our distinguished passenger. When we arrived, right on schedule, the spotlights came on, but Mr. Lindbergh did not leave at once. He waited at the plane to personally thank every man on our crew. While he was doing this, he noticed some of our crewmen waving to their families. He decided he would speak to them before greeting the generals and colonels. To efforts to steer him to the official greeters, he said, "I'll be there in a minute," and went on with us.

A couple of months later, each of us—the crewmen of both the Hercules and the helicopter—received from Mr. Lindbergh a signed picture (made in front of our aircraft in Mactan).

(For additional detail on the wide ranging and unique missions of the Hercules, photos in this chapter, and on the pages that follow, depict the missions just described as well as many more offbeat roles.)

Charles A. Lindbergh poses with crews of HC-130H and HH-3 helicopter which brought him and his party out of the jungles of Mindanao, Philippines in April, 1972. (USAF photo courtesy of Capt. Marc L. Sherrill)

THE FLYING DUMP TRUCKS OF ALASKA

The Herks are just the workhorse of the
arctic.

–Helen Atkinson,
Fairbanks *News-Miner*

"Numbers fail to reveal the real truth of the (Alaska Haul Road) effort. For the
road is truly a monument not to equipment, but to individual men; to pilots who
herded huge planes over rugged mountain ridges in almost all kinds of weather,
and to construction workers who didn't quit until all the work was completed."

–*Alyeska Reports,* published by the Alyeska
Pipeline Co., Fairbanks, Alaska

It was an amazingly warm day in Fairbanks, Alaska—a crisp and
clear 20 degrees (F). Yet a thick carpet of ice clung stubbornly to
the sidewalks and streets of America's northernmost city. The busy
flight line at the Fairbanks International Airport lay draped in a
blanket of white. Swirls of snowdrifts shrouded the sides of the
airport buildings, a reminder that winter had not yet loosed its
grip in the Alaskan interior.

Out on the ramp at Alaska International Air, two silver and
blue Hercules—sporting big white "As" on their tall tails—were
taking on loads of cargo through their wide open rear ramps.

231

Hurdling over Alaska's Brooks Range, Alaska International Air Hercules heads to North Slope oil exploration territory. Lower photo, view from Hercules windshield shows gravel landing strip in valley at Dietrich, surrounded by jagged mountain peaks. The aircraft landed there a few minutes later. Note the oil pipeline "haul road" in the valley. During 1974-1975, AIA's L-100s flew a seven-day-a-week, 24-hour-a-day airlift of fuel, supplies and equipment to ice and gravel strips along the pipeline and to North Slope oil exploration areas. They hauled an average million pounds of cargo a day. (AIA-Lockheed)

A couple of pilots and a flight engineer, dressed in heavy, fur-lined parkas and thick, "muckluck" type boots, walked gingerly across the oil-blackened ice from the AIA building.

As I climbed aboard, Captain Steve Foss, a youngish 35 years old but a veteran Alaskan flyer, was buckling into the left hand seat of Herk Number 32-R. I found a spot to sit in the roomy flight station, behind the flight engineer.

"Let's get something started," Foss yelled out.

Co-pilot Jim Colburn and Flight Engineer Bing Downing swung into action, methodically running through the system of checks with the maze of switches, instruments and dials spread over the instrument panel and across the top of the plane's huge, "greenhouse" windshield.

The shrill crack of the gas turbine APU pierced the chilly calm; power coursed through the aircraft. The propjet engines began their throaty high whine and the four-bladed propellers whirled into action.

Groaning with its heavy payload which had been secured by the loadmaster, the aircraft rocked a bit as it crossed the ramp and taxied quickly to the south end of the runway. In the cargo hold were 25 drums of oil and a skid load of five-inch steel drill pipe—a total payload of 44,000 pounds. The loadmaster, who had been busy for a quarter hour getting his load lashed in, came forward to complete his record-keeping.

The Hercules lifted smartly from the runway, gained altitude over the snow-draped city, then climbed quickly northward toward the Yukon River, the first big landmark we would see on the way to our destination, a wildcat rig on Arctic Alaska's "North Slope."

The Yukon, immortalized by Jack London, was a mighty spectacle. It was frozen solid, and spread out in big white loops like taffy. I remembered that the big river was larger even than the Mississippi. For decades the Yukon, along with hundreds of smaller streams, had posed a major barrier to the development of the vast, untapped regions of northern Alaska. The rivers, that is, along with the harsh climate *and* the Brooks Range of mountains which cut a 50-mile wide swath across northern Alaska from Canada west to the Bering Sea.

As we climbed to 10,000 feet, I sat in wonder at the vastness of Alaska, draped in its mantle of winter white, and spread out before us as far as the eye could see. I remembered that the two mighty obstacles—the rivers and the mountains—had led the oil companies to introduce the Lockheed Hercules to this huge, unchartered state in the first place. The rugged propjet, like Superman, able to leap Alaska's mountains with ease, then bring its superhuman loads down gently into rough strips, quickly won the hearts of Alaskans.

But there was not time to muse. Within 45 minutes we had crossed the shark-tooth peaks of the Brooks Range . . . over Dietrich Pass, Galbraith, Toolik and pipeline pumping stations 3 and 4. The North Slope came into view before us—a magnificent Arctic desert which descends gently as a vast plain down to the Arctic Ocean. In the winter, the slope takes on a blanket of wind-blown snow; in the summer, it becomes a sea of green tundra. Underneath it all is permafrost—permanently frozen earth 18 inches under the surface.

"Look at the caribou," Foss called to my attention as we dropped to 2,000 feet. The herd grazed serenely across the valley below. Off to our left, the oil pipeline Haul Road loomed into view—a long, thin, gray line, going as far as the eye could see in both directions. Tractor-trailer trucks were rolling north with long, four-foot diameter pipe—three to a truck. They had crossed the Yukon's frozen "ice bridge" and were heading to the pipeline route up north.

"There's the rig," Foss said, pointing to a steel tower and a trailer complex on our right, silhouetted against the snow on a plateau. The landing strip, Lupine, was only four miles away, lying on the line that the oil pipeline would take.

Foss banked our plane sharply and lined up with the runway, descended quickly and made an uneventful landing. Despite the ice, the Hercules, with its prop blades roaring in reverse pitch, came to a solid stop in less than half of the 5,000 feet.

After taxiing to the S&G Construction Company complex next to the strip, Foss left his engines running, and it was understandable why.

"These people have unloading an airplane down to a science," Foss declared as we bade him farewell. "We'll be here only a few minutes," he added.

Echo Bay Mines' L-100-20 leaps off the Port Radium gravel-ice strip, a former glacial lake adjacent to Great Bear Lake in Canada's Northwest Territories *(top left),* and later makes a hairy landing at 4600 foot strip, surrounded by 1,000 foot hillsides and ground *(top right).* Echo Bay was cited for using its L-100-20 as a "flying railroad" to establish a gold mining complex at Lupin on Lake Contyoto. In a 12-month period, the plane hauled more than 47,000,000 pounds of freight, fuel and cargo, much of it heavy, oversize equipment, such as the shaft, mill and smeltering plant, along with equipment and fuel. In center left photo, insulation for the gold mine complex is offloaded, while the photo at center right shows silver float being loaded aboard the plane at Port Radium. In photo montage below, Echo Bay L-100 takes aboard worker housing. Sequence shows modular dormitory, containing three rooms and eight beds, being inserted into the plane's cargo bay. Arriving at Lupin, the building was rolled out into a waiting truck and hauled to its new foundation in the gold mine city of Lupin.

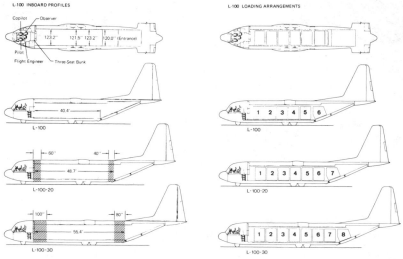

Photo and sketches at bottom show how Lockheed-Georgia has stretched the Hercules to the L-100-20 and L-100-30 Super Hercules configuration. Plugs are inserted fore and aft of the wing. The Dash 20 is 100 inches longer than the standard C-130 and the L-100-30 is 180 inches longer. All of the commercial Hercules now built by Lockheed are either the Dash 20 or Dash 30 size. All of the original L-100s have been stretched. (Lockheed)

From the rear, a giant tinker toy of a steel dock on skids came rushing toward the Hercules, being pushed by a bulldozer. Measuring three feet, six inches high, the transportable dock matched up precisely to the plane's ramp, being one of the simple engineering miracles wrought by the skilled cargo handlers of Alaska. The bulldozer operator then winched the skid load of drill pipe out of the plane onto his mobile dock, then pulled the entire rig off to the side.

Foss pushed a button in the flight station, lowering the Herk's rear ramp down to the ice. The loadmaster and two helpers from S&G rolled out the drums of oil with ease.

It was only 12 minutes from touchdown when Foss "buttoned up" his Hercules and taxied off. I hastened around behind the load of drill pipe with my camera and awaited the takeoff. Foss rotated his empty Herk and it leaped into the air, a scene I captured with my 35mm Pentax—the drill pipe in the foreground with the Hercules boring skyward at a 40 degree angle.

"Ah, that Hercules," said H.E. (Bunky) Snider, the blocky, quiet spoken oil boss from Forest Oil Company's headquarters in Denver, who was visiting his company's wildcat rig for a few days. "That bird brought in all of our supplies and pipe. Fact is, our entire camp and all of our drill rig was airlifted to this site last year," he said. I learned that the rig move, which took more than 200 flights, is a routine type operation for AIA and its flying trucks, which carry out a dozen such moves a year for the oil companies.

Around the Forest Oil campsite could be seen the results of the Hercules labors of previous days—a high mound of "drilling mud," in sacks, and stacks of steel pipe.

"This drill pipe you just brought in," said Bunky, "we'll use it to send our drill bit several hundred additional feet into the earth."

*   *   *

It was April of 1965 when the Lockheed-Georgia Company, in a pioneering effort, dispatched its commercial L-100 Hercules demonstrator and crew to Fairbanks on a 30-day lease to Alaska Airlines. At the time, seven exploration parties were combing the North Slope for oil. But they had run into problems: How could they get the necessary oil-drilling equipment and supplies into the country north of the Yukon (where there was no roadway) and through the jagged, snow-covered Brooks Range? The only other alternative at the time was to haul the goods by barge through the long, ice-clogged seacoast of Alaska'a Arctic Ocean. But that was risky, too, and far from a real solution. Only for a few weeks in the summer could barges get through.

Engineers considered various schemes for solving the monumental problem. They envisioned a monstrous "snow machine," a caterpillar train. But it would cost upwards of $1 million and would require a year to snake its way slowly through the mountain passes. And in the summer, the fragile surface of Alaska's earth—the tundra—posed additional problems on the ground.

Airlift seemed to be a possibility. But what plane could do the job? It would take a tough flying truck that could withstand the rigors of the Arctic, take on outsize loads, negotiate undeveloped landing strips, and get the job done with little downtime.

Alaska Airlines told the oil companies it had the answer, and "wet-leased" a Hercules—crew and all—from Lockheed.

The Hercules acquitted itself with great distinction, completing the big job quickly, and for a reasonable cost. The airlift became known in Alaska as "the 30-day miracle." Lockheed journalist Pete Roton, who covered the entire project, filed a glowing report on what he had witnessed.

"With 45,000 pound payloads secured in its huge cargo hold," Roton wrote, "the Hercules touched down with ease on Lake Edna's ice strip, on the snow and ice-covered gravel runway on a sandbar beside the Sagavanirktok River (SAG-1), and the snow-covered tundra at Dahl Creek. All are above the Arctic Circle!"

The first company to utilize the Hercules that month was Richfield, which subsequently struck oil at Prudhoe Bay, setting off Alaska's great oil rush. It was one of history's greatest oil discoveries.

During the month lease, the Herk and its Lockheed crew hauled prodigious loads such as the following items into Richfield's oil-drilling staging area at SAG-1 . . . a 45,000 pound D-8 Caterpillar, a fuel storage tank, three sleeping trailers weighing 24,710 pounds, three trucks loaded with 20-foot pilings, three belly-loading trailers and 26,000 gallons of diesel fuel.

First commercial Hercules was this demonstrator "One World Hercules" which was developed from a C-130E and certificated by the FAA to operate as a commercial cargo-hauler. The aircraft was flown around the world on demonstration flights by Chief Production Pilot Joe Garrett and crew. On its first flight, the airplane flew 25 hours and one minute. The plane flew all but 36 minutes on only two of its engines. While the airplane can fly 360 miles per hour, the record flight was made at "loitering speed" of 130 to 140 mph. Center, pilot Leo Sullivan and master scheduling coordinator Jim Hogan have a brief chat after the successful flight of the experimental aircraft. (Lockeed)

First flight of stretched L-100-20 Hercules is pictured as plane climbs by Lockheed-Georgia's B-1 Building.

Cavernous maw of an extended fuselage L-100-20 aircraft features rows of rollers, part of advanced, high-speed cargo handling system developed by Lockheed. The system is certified for 9g restraint—nine times the force of gravity—eliminating need for a barrier net. Lower photo, 40-foot-long railway van goes from truck into Hercules. Van is eight feet high and eight feet wide. (Lockheed)

When a 12-ton earth-mover and a six-ton "Nodwell" tractor emerged from the plane's belly at SAG-1, and rolled down the adjustable ramp under their own power, a sourdough yelled in excitement: "Look man, they're already made! We won't have to put them back together!"

During the four-week airlift, the lone Lockheed propjet transported more than two million pounds of outsize and general cargo to Alaska's wilderness areas. It was understandable why Charles F. Willis, then president of Alaska Airlines, was ecstatic. He told the press that the Hercules would be a boon to Alaska, representing as it did a new concept in transportation. "This aircraft," he said, "can airlift heavy machinery, large, earth-moving equipment and prefabricated structures *on the same day* at less cost than by conventional surface means."

Today, Mr. Willis' comments seem to fall in the area of prophecy. Many Alaskans credit the Hercules with being one of its most effective instruments of progress. One official of Alaska told me: "The pipeline wouldn't be where it is today and the oil fields would not be where they are had it not been for the help of the Herk. I can say that unequivocally."

During 1974, at the height of the pipeline buildup, AIA dedicated six of its L-100s to the oil airlift, hauling a fantastic million pounds of goods a day. During the year, their Herk "tankers" transported 22 million gallons of fuel to distant points over Alaska, including 14 million gallons to pipeline camps alone, providing the heat and power for the pipeline construction effort. The AIA birds literally created a dozen "instant towns" along the route of the oil pipeline by hauling in 1,200 boxcar size mobile homes from Fairbanks and Anchorage.

I flew to Alaska in March, 1975, to see the amazing airlift first-hand. I found the cargo airline was literally supporting the modern day oil rush on the wings of its commercial Dash 20 and Dash 30 Hercules.

"AIA is hauling a fantastic tonnage for us," Alyeska Pipeline Company's Les Bays told me shortly after I got to Alaska. "They're putting those Herks in on 5,000-foot strips that are gravel in the summertime—frequently wet and muddy—and frozen snow and ice in the winter time—so slick it's difficult to walk on. What other airliner in the world is around that could do it?"

As I landed at Fairbanks in an Alaska Airlines jet, I could see the "Big A" Herks landing and taking off, climbing over the frozen Chena River headed for points north. That first afternoon, on my first visit to the AIA complex down the runway from the airport terminal, I found the airline's flight ops nerve center and the ramp area bustling with activity. Dispatchers were busy scheduling flights. Skid loads of cargo were being assembled in the buildup yards for quick loading onto the planes. AIA, I learned, was hauling an average of 25 loads a day, averaging 20 tons a flight! And the loads: Everything from bulk fuel to drill pipe, drilling mud and cement, igloos of food, big earth-moving machinery and entire units of prefabricated ATCO housing.

During that one week—March 10-16—the six AIA Herks logged 504 hours of block time, with each plane averaging 12 hours in the air. This was all the more remarkable considering that one of the aircraft spent part of the week undergoing "C-Check" maintenance overhaul.

"Our motto is '12 Hours a Day' for each of our planes," said then Executive VP George Kamats, pointing to a sign on his wall. "But that is just the average. We have gotten up to 21 block hours in a day."

The high time aircraft for the week was No. 106, which logged 17 hours on Wednesday, March 12. All of the flights went to Alyeska Pipeline camps north of the Yukon. These included a fuel flight to Galbraith; three flights of supplies for Franklin Bluff, a supply run to Deadhorse (Prudhoe Bay), and a flight with supplies for Happy Valley, on the North Slope. Altogether that day, five Herks on duty logged 29 flights to such destinations as Umiat, Deadhorse, Sparrovhon (a military Dew Line base), Point Barrow, "Lake 186," (a frozen lake on the slope), Karupa, Lupine, Prudhoe Bay and Barrow Village. While Alyeska was the biggest customer at the time, other clients during the week included United Geophysical, Atlantic Richfield, Texaco, British Petroleum, Amoco, Parker Drilling, Lounsberry Associates, the military and GSI.

Shortly after arriving in Fairbanks, I met Doug Miskinis, AIA's quiet, efficient, stringbean traffic manager, who was busy jockeying loads and destinations, keeping a sharp eye on the weather map and the availability of aircraft and crews. At the time, 28 complete crews were on the payroll, each crew consisting of a pilot, co-pilot, flight engineer and loadmaster.

A major objective of the visit was to fly with AIA and Miskinis suggested I get aboard a Thursday flight to a wildcat oil rig on the North Slope.

In Northern Alaska, one must prepare for the treacherous weather, which during winter can drop overnight to 50 below. Lloyd McCumber, my photographer colleague, and I called on a Fairbanks landmark, the Rocket Surplus Store. There we completed our Arctic winterizing by purchasing Arctic-pak boots, thermal long johns and knit ski-masks. The boots, providing insulation for the feet and good traction on the ice, proved to be indispensable.

Arriving the following morning at AIA's flight ops complex, we found Herks lined up taking on loads, and taxiing across the oily black, ice-covered ramp. But they didn't stay long. "If our planes stay on the ground at either end more than 30 minutes," said Miskinis, "we call it a delay and we have to answer for it to the executive vice president." Ten-minute turnarounds are not unusual on the AIA loop, thanks to the skid-load system, the expert loadmasters and the truck-like characteristics of the Hercules. Steve Kline of the *Anchorage Daily News* heard of a minute-and-a-half turnaround.

On this particular day, Flight Ops was having problems up the line with weather. Pilot Ron Moore strolled into the crew lounge. He had been on earlier flights to Galbraith, Franklin Bluff, Old Man and Prospect, and had to wait while his aircraft took on a new load for a new destination.

"We were going back to Old Man, but the weather went down," Moore said. "An ice (fog) bank rolled in. They're changing us to Coldfoot."

Moore poured himself a cup of coffee and relaxed a bit.

"Unusual loads?" he asked. "Oh, I don't know. When you work around the Herk very long it gets to where *nothing* is unusual. We haul *anything*. If it'll fit in the Herk, we'll haul it. They call it The Good Old Alaska Flying Dump Truck."

Moore, a flight instructor in Fairbanks for a number of years before joining AIA, remembered his first days piloting an AIA Herk. "When you start out, it's all new and weird and different. A lot of difference in driving around in a Herk and driving around in a 206 Cessna. We have to have super checked out people."

Moore described some of the interesting destinations. "A few of the strips are real narrow, particularly the geophysical camps. They just gouge them out of the ice. They move them around every three-four days and do seismographic work. They lay out the Herk strip in a day and we land on it." He recalled his first days guiding his Hercules through the narrow mountain passes into Dietrich and Galbraith. Those valley strips are carved out of the ice in the shadow of 7,000-foot-high Brooks Range peaks. "We have to have decent weather to go into Dietrich," Moore said. "And the same is true for Prospect Creek and Old Man. They're situated down in a pocket of mountains."

Utopia is an interesting strip to the Herk pilots, where the aircraft must land uphill on a 6% grade.

Despite the rough strips, high mountain ranges and fantastically harsh weather, including whiteouts, Moore had never had any close calls flying the Herk. "Of course, there's been a lot of change for the better in the flying situation here," he said. He explained that a full Instrument Landing System (ILS) is now in effect at Deadhorse, the main landing strip at Prudhoe Bay, and at Galbraith. Several of the camps south of the Brooks Range have VASIs (Visual Approach Systems.)

"And, of course, every place has good runway lights now. A year ago, a lot of them had nothing but flare pots."

The interview ended abruptly when flight ops told Moore his plane was ready for boarding. He ended it with a comment heard often around Alaska. "I'll just say that the Hercules is a fantastic machine . . . a fantastic aircraft." With that, he pulled up his parka and walked out into the chilly breeze to board his Herk for another day of "hauling everything to everywhere" in Alaska.

*   *   *

At 10:10, Flight Ops gave us the word. Our plane had clearance to take off for the Brooks Range. We joined the crew in walking to the aircraft. We had aboard a load of oil drilling equipment.

A consultant for Forest Oil Company, Dr. William Long,

greeted us on our arrival and served as our escort for the day. Following a hearty lunch at the cook house, along with several cups of steaming hot coffee, Long drove us in his four-wheel drive Blazer the four miles up the gentle slope to the oil rig. The tower was clearly visible four miles away, and seemed nearby. "On a clear day such as this," Long pointed out, "you can easily see 20 miles away . . . actually a hundred."

Bill Long, a professor of geology at Alaska Methodist University, declared himself to be a great admirer of the Hercules. "It has taken me and our scientific parties into the remote mountains of Antarctica in the years 1961, 1962, and 1964," he said. "We landed where no one had been before. We conducted the original exploration there." He would never forget, he said, the time Navy ski-Herks dropped a turkey to his eight-man team on a Thanksgiving.

In the afternoon, after a thorough inspection of the oil camp, we returned to the runway, to await the arrival of the next Hercules. Another L-100 was landing at Happy Valley on the other side of the Sagaranirktok River, only 10 miles from the SAG-1 area where the Hercules flew demo flights 10 years earlier for the oil companies. A quick trip over to Happy Valley resulted in our hitching a ride back to Fairbanks.

During succeeding days, I caught three additional flights on the AIA Hercules. On Friday, it was to Dietrich, where the pipeline reaches its highest elevation, 4,800, in a mountain pass. Captain Clint Schoenleber skillfully threaded the big transport like a fighter plane through the narrow pass until we reached the wide open valley. After he had deposited our load—36,762 pounds of Cat parts and 54 drums of lubricant—Schoenleber on the flight back to Fairbanks recalled his flying experiences. "On many strips, particularly farther north," Schoenleber said, "they just smooth off the frozen lake surface and we land on the ice. No problem . . . even though some of them get pretty slippery, we get good control with the Herk all the way down.

"We can do a lot more with the Herk than with pure jets," Schoenleber said, "runway-wise and every other way. We get better braking . . . better stopping. Just like our maneuvering around those mountains and down through the valley. I don't think you could do that with a 727. I don't know of another airplane that can compete with the Hercules."

It was a bone-chilling 30 degrees below zero at Deadhorse, when I arrived there on Saturday morning. The wind was whistling off the Beaufort Sea at 30 miles per hour, giving me a quick case of cold feet. Visibility was extremely limited when we landed with our Nodwell tractor (for United Geophysical), and several barrels of drilling cement.

My photographer colleague and I wasted no time at Deadhorse. After getting our pictures, we caught another Hercules heading south, and interviewed loadmaster Dale Garrels, who told us all about Hercules shuttle flights. "We had one just night before last," Garrels said. "We came up here and landed at one lake, where they had a GSI outfit, and unloaded a load. Then we flew up to Deadhorse and loaded a Nodwell and a forklift. We took the forklift to Barrow and dropped it off and then we took off to another lake and unloaded the Nodwell. We made seven flights, taking whatever needed to be hauled."

A Southern Air Transport Lockheed L-100 sprays dispersant across the Arizona desert testing out a new oil spill dispersal system. The 22-flight, two-day test — sponsored by the American Petroleum Institute — sought to determine if the Hercules aircraft could effectively neutralize an oil spill on the high seas. Utilizing a 5,500-gallon tank in the cargo compartment and sprayer arms sticking out of the rear ramp of the airplane, the system laid down a 150-foot wide swath of detergent, blanketing almost 800 acres in 12 minutes. Designed by Biegert Aviation, Inc., Chandler, Ariz., the system is built to fit into the 9-foot high, 10-foot wide C-130/L-100 cargo compartment.

And so it goes. Just a minor glimpse into just a part of one week's AIA Alaska airlift.

The AIA Hercules have hauled many unusual cargoes besides oil pipeline equipment . . . trees for the BP operational center at Prudhoe Bay . . . post offices for outlying villages . . . drilling mud for all the oil companies . . . fresh fish from the western and northern coasts to Anchorage canneries.

In the spring of 1975, AIA was tasked to airlift 300 homes built for Alaskans in the bush country, from Fairbanks and Anchorage. It was reminiscent of the 1974 airlift of 1200 huge ATCO housing units to the oil pipeline camps.

"That was quite a challenge for us to get those camps in before the haul road was completed," said Ed Rogers of AIA. Each of the ATCO units was a Herk load. Measuring 9½ feet wide by 48 feet long, the Canadian-built structures were designed to fit inside the L-100. The Dash 20 Herk has a 48.7 foot long cargo hold while the Dash 30 measures 55.4 feet long. The ATCO units left only six inches to spare on each side of the 10-foot wide Hercules compartment.

When Alyeska Company needed a replacement engine to drive the pumps along the 800-mile Alaska oil pipeline in late 1977, Trans International Airlines got the assignment to haul a 43,000-pound gas turbine unit from the manufacturer in Ohio right to the oil pipeline. The package measured 45 feet long, nine feet high and just under ten feet wide, the cargo compartment dimensions of TIA's L-100-30 Super Hercules, with ten feet of length to spare. It was a close fit but just another routine task for the workhorse Hercules. (Cooper Industries)

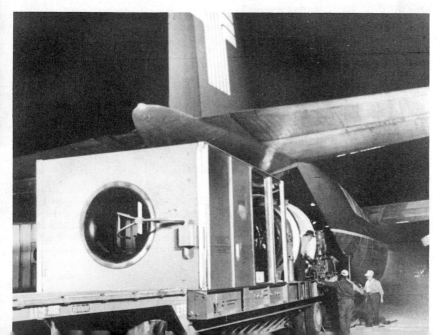

On my last day in Fairbanks, I paid a call on AIA headquarters. Officials spoke with bullishness about the future of Alaska as well as the cargo airline. They were particularly high on the Hercules.

"It has been the right aircraft at the right place at the right time," said Neil Bergt, the chairman of AIA. "The Hercules was just the right vehicle for the oil pipeline work. Although jets can beat hell out of our Herks in speed, they can't land on short fields, and they don't have the fast loading and unloading capability.

"The beautiful thing about the Hercules is that it is equally capable as a short range aircraft as well as long range . . . it can operate with full payload at distances of 2,500 miles as well as 250 miles."

* * *

When Lockheed's engineers designed the C-130 for the U.S. Air Force in the early 1950s, little did they realize that the military airlifter some day would become almost as famous as a civil transport.

Yet today, as the Alaska International Air example illustrates, the C-130's commercial derivative—the L-100—has found a secure niche for itself as an airfreighter for airlines and governments around the world.

There are two commercial versions of the Hercules currently being built—the L-100-20, which is 100 inches longer than the standard C-130, and the L-100-30, which is 180 inches longer. Yet, despite the "stretching" modification, which adds 33 percent more cargo capacity, the elongated Hercules retains the C-130's ability to haul "awkward cargo into awkward places" and can land and take off with ease from dirt, sand, gravel and/or frozen lakes!*

A number of carriers operating stretched Herks such as AIA have made a speciality of airlifting complete oil drilling rigs from one drilling site to another. One of these is Pacific Western Airlines, whose L-100-20 Hercules have been the dominant airlift force in Canada's oil region development. In 1977 alone, PWA

---

*Hercules flown by TIA, AIA, and PWA—flying oil related missions in the arctic—routinely make wheeled landings on frozen lakes. It was a James Bay Energy Corp. L-100-20—flown by Quebecair pilots—that made what is believed to be the southernmost ice landing. This occurred on February 3, 1974, when CF-DFX landed on an ice runway 42 inches thick and 4,500 feet long, located at LaGran-3, a James Bay construction site northwest of Montreal.

Herks accounted for the movement of 72 million pounds of freight for just one oil development firm—Panarctic Oils, Ltd. (For further details of PWA's arctic activities see Chapter 12.)

Due to the Dash 30's increased productivity and low ton-mile costs, most commercial Hercules being sold today are this latest model. The L-100-30 carries eight large pallets, providing 4,700 cubic feet for palletized cargo, a dramatic increase over the standard Herk which holds six pallets.

Features which have made the C-130 such a popular military airlifter have figured in the airplane's adaptability by commercial carriers. The straight-in loading aft door at truck-bed height, common to all current Hercules models, has proven advantageous for quick turn-arounds and easy loading and unloading. This is particularly true of outsize items too long for side-loading aircraft.

Equipped with a roller system, the L-100 can quickly take on palletized cargo, as well as special trailer-type modules. The rear ramp can be lowered to the ground to allow roadable equipment to drive directly into and out of the cargo hold. Another factor is the Hercules' wide and tall compartment which enables it to airlift 8 foot by 8 foot containers and pallet loads up to 106 inches in height. This assures maximum use of its cube in the large aircraft it can feed, such as the nose and side-loading widebody jets.

Altogether, more than 60 commercial stretched Herks are being operated by 10 carriers around the world. The L-100 is the major cargo liner for six commercial carriers—the aforementioned Trans International Airlines of Oakland, California; Alaska International Air of Fairbanks, Alaska; and Pacific Western Airlines of Calgary, Alberta; and Southern Air Transport, Miami, Florida; James Bay Energy Corp., of Quebec, whose Hercules is operated by Quebecair; and SAFAIR, Johannesburg, South Africa. In addition, L-100 Hercules are operated by governments or civil carriers in Angola, Gabon, Indonesia, Peru, Pakistan, Kuwait and Uganda.

TIA operates the largest U.S. based fleet of L-100-30s, carrying out schedules freight airlift service for the U.S. military as well as charter work worldwide. The late 1976 merger of Trans International Airlines and Saturn Airways, two of America's strongest charter airlines, created what is the world's Number one supplemental airline. Saturn's fleet of 12 Super Herks formed the backbone of the merged airline's cargo fleet.

TIA's Hercules* are based not only in the U.S., but Europe as well, which enables the airline to respond quickly to unusual airlift requirements in the Middle East and Africa as well as in Europe. The airline also carries out unscheduled freight haul jobs in North and South America. Some examples:

- QE-II, the Cunard ocean liner, lay in a New York drydock with a broken engine, its cruise departure date uncertain. Cunard called in TIA. The Oakland-based carrier dispatched one of its Super Herks and delivered the 45,000-pound replacement engine from Europe to New York within 11 hours after receiving the order.

- An oil company needed to get an oil drill rig delivered deep into the Guatemalan jungle, to a site so remote no surface carrier could get within a hundred miles of it. In a dramatic airlift, TIA's Super Hercules hauled the complete, 900-ton base camp, rig, and related heavy oil drilling equipment to the landing strip hand carved out of the dense Central American jungle. The airlift put the oil drilling team in operation in 15 days.

- When an explosion at a pumping station closed down the Alaska Oil Pipeline in 1977, TIA was asked to fly a replacement turbine from the manufacturer in Ohio. A TIA L-100-30 airlifted the massive, 45,000-pound unit in a matter of hours to the pipeline site in Alaska.

In recent years, many industries have been turning to charter airlines such as TIA for fast, money-saving movement of high priority freight ranging from turbines to teddy bears.

*A TIA L-100-30 was the first aircraft in the C-130/L-100 fleet to top the 30,000 hour mark in the air. Tail Number N19ST reached the milestone in 1977 on a LOGAIR military supply flight between Tinker AFB, Oklahoma, and Hill AFB close to Ogden, Utah. Lockheed delivered the airplane originally to the Delta Air Lines in 1966. Delta had the airplane stretched 8.3 feet to the Dash 20 configuration in 1968. Saturn Airways subsequently acquired the airplane and had it stretched in 1974 to the Super Hercules length. It became a TIA aircraft in late 1976 when Saturn and Trans International Airlines merged.

Pilot's view from cockpit as Hercules descended toward the Zorillos landing strip hewed out of the Amazon jungle ahead, alongside and to right of the Aguaytia River in Peru. The Alaska Airlines L-100, under contract to Mobil del Peru in 1967, operated around the clock, making five trips a day between Lima and Zorillos with 20 ton loads of oil drilling equipment. (Lockheed)

Sparrevohn Air Force Station, Alaska, where C-130s and L-100s fly into with regularity, conditions are quite adverse. It's a 4,000-foot gravel runway, but the worst aspect is the rugged terrain which limits takeoff to one end of the runway and landings to the other end. Frequent winds of more than 20 knots can cause turbulence approach in the descent point. Lower photo, C-130 touches down on runway 34, after making a quick descent from the nearby ridge of hills. (USAF photo courtesy MAC FLYER magazine).

Such a case came in early 1978, when an Alaska International Air L-100 airlifted a killer whale nicknamed "Big Mama" almost to the front door of a wildlife park in central Japan. The monster whale, weighing 9,000 pounds and measuring 21.4 feet long, had too big a girth for a DC-8 airfreighter. The DC-8 also was too noisy for the Osaka airport which it would have had to use to make delivery. Flying Tigers solved the trans-Pacific stretch by flying "Big Mama" across the ocean from San Francisco in a 747. The crucial final lift from Tokyo went to the AIA Hercules, which simply ignored Osaka and flew directly on to Shirahama, site of the park. The whale easily reached its new home well before the 24-hour deadline for being out of its element and the Hercules used only a portion of Shirahama's 3,900-foot runway.

TIA's predecessor, Saturn Airways, made history with its Super Hercules when it airlifted an entire television station to China to provide live color television coverage of President Nixon's visit. The airplane's 55-foot long cargo compartment easily accommodated the two 8 x 8 x 14-foot electronic shelters, a 24-foot diameter dismantled antenna and two diesel generators. In another unique flight, a Saturn Super Hercules airlifted a complete Walt Disney movie production unit to four continents on an around-the-world filming of a travel documentary.

A major Hercules role in recent years has been the delivery of complete telecommunications systems to developing nations. TIA carried out around 100 such flights in moving a system from the U.S. to Lagos and Kano, Nigeria.

Southern Air Transport and its Hercules also have flown numerous high priority cargoes around the world . . . helicopters from Louisiana to Australia, computers from Minnesota to Libya (computers operate much modern oil drilling equipment), and bulldozers from Ohio to Labrador.

Meanwhile, the future of the commercial Hercules seems to be especially bright as the world seeks to open up new energy and mineral resources. The L-100 appears to be just the right air machine at the right time. The United States, for instance, is considering opening up Petroleum Reserve Number 4 in Alaska. Once that happens, the next step will be to call in the Hercules to haul in the heavy equipment to get the job rolling.

IV

HUMANITARIAN HERCULES

At a time when violence and
disregard for the law is accepted as
a normal part of daily life . . .
the C-130 is a reminder that the
majority of people are still motivated
by a spirit of "What can I do to help?"
when disaster strikes.

—INTERAVIA

MERCY MISSION TO McMURDO

> Seven globe-girdling giants from Sewart (AFB), wearing two-ton sets of skis, are opening a new frontier at the bottom of the world . . . .
>
> —Nashville Tennessean,
> January 29, 1960

> The C-130 has revolutionized our efforts . . . . It has been the greatest tool we've ever had for the permanent development of Antarctica.
>
> —Rear Admiral David Tyree, Commander
> Naval Support Forces Antarctica

It was June 23, 1964, and the polar ice cap that is Antarctica, measuring miles thick in some spots and blanketing an area almost twice that of the United States, lay in subzero darkness. The dark winter—five months of continuous night—held the great white continent in its icy grip.

At McMurdo Sound, the main American base on the edge of the Ross ice shelf, the "wintering over" contingent of 53 scientists and Navy support personnel were virtually locked into their cocoon-like complex of Jamesway huts. Outside, McMurdo's thermometers registered 20 degrees below zero (F), and the sudden gale force winds that sweep down from the trans-Antarctic mountains whipped the powdery, age-old snow into blizzard-like density.

In the station's fire house, McMurdo's fire marshal, Builder First Class Bethel McMullen, a 30-year old Seabee from Port Hueneme, California, was perched on top of a thirty-foot high ladder splicing a faulty wire. As he put his weight on one foot, McMullen lost his footing, slipped and plunged to the concrete floor below. He landed on his back and head, nearly scalping himself. The blow also gave him a cerebral concussion and a broken back, paralyzing him from the waist down.

McMurdo's doctor, Lt. Thomas Bates, was called in and went to work on the scalp wound and immediately put the Seabee in traction. But the young doctor quickly concluded that McMullen would die unless he got emergency surgery. Unfortunately, McMurdo, with a skeleton staff and limited facilities, was not prepared to do it.

Moving quickly, Bates wrote out a message and instructed the McMurdo radio center to put through an 11,000-mile short-wave radio transmission to the Pentagon in Washington. He addressed it to Rear Admiral James R. Reedy, the commander of the Navy's Antarctic Support Forces.

In his message, the doctor outlined the serious extent of McMullen's injuries and said emergency help was needed immediately. The Seabee was having difficulty breathing because of his spinal injury. Bates' message was desperate:

"UNLESS McMULLEN MOVED AND OPERATED ON AS QUICKLY AS POSSIBLE, HE WILL NOT SURVIVE MORE THAN A FEW DAYS."

In the Pentagon, Admiral Reedy read the message and knew that action was required, and now.

"Place a call to Quonset Point—get me Commander Gallup at VX-6!" Admiral Reedy commanded Lt. Alan Blanchard, his aide.

It was a pleasant June day at the Quonset Point Naval Air Station, located on the water's edge below Providence, Rhode Island, but Commander Frederick S. Gallup, the skipper of AirDevRon 6, was jolted when the admiral's voice came on the line.

"How soon can you get a ski plane off to McMurdo, Fred?"

"Sir?"

"They've got a serious emergency down on the ice. A Seabee

McMurdo Station, America's permanent base camp located on the edge of the Antarctic continent, pictured (top photo) during a "hot" summer day (with 24 hours of sunlight). The Williams ski-way is located some distance away. Airplanes with skis can land on the snow skiway around the year. Wheeled aircraft can land on the ice inlet runway during certain months of the year. Map below shows distances to major U.S. outposts on the frozen continent. (Lockheed)

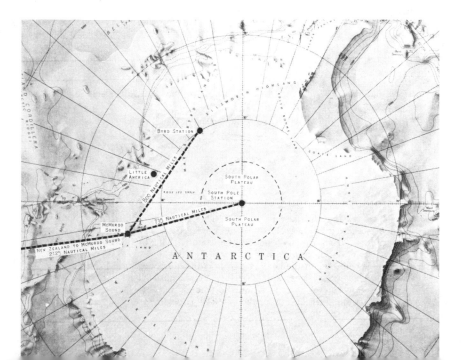

SKI-130 GENERAL ARRANGEMENT

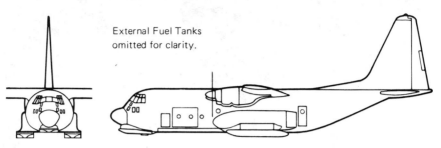

External Fuel Tanks
omitted for clarity.

Landing Gear Retracted

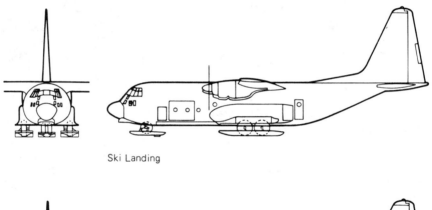

Ski Landing

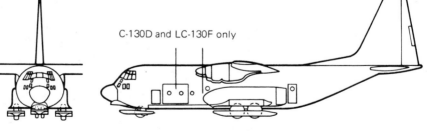

C-130D and LC-130F only

Wheel Landing

One of the early derivatives of the C-130A was the ski and wheel modification which resulted in the Air Force ski Hercules designated the C-130D. The largest ski system ever incorporated on an airplane enables the crew to land or take off with either skis or wheels. The one-ton, 20-foot long skis, attached to the conventional landing gear, can be raised or lowered when the landing gear is in the down position. Both the nose and main skis have eight-degree nose-up and fifteen-degree nose-down pitch capability to enable them to follow uneven terrain. When the landing gear is retracted, the skis are drawn up against the streamlined fairings of the fuselage. (Lockheed) fell and broke his back. He can't make it unless he is brought out. We'll need volunteers to go in to get him."

"I feel sure we can do it, Admiral."

It was noon, but the Admiral asked if Gallup could have his crew and plane ready to launch the mission the next morning.

"Yes sir, Admiral Reedy, I'm confident we can."

"That's fine," Reedy replied. "I'll get a medical team lined up here ready to go with you."

As soon as Gallup hung up the telephone, he called in his new operations officer, Commander Dan Balish, and then put through a call to "Bull" Mayer—Lt. Robert V. Mayer—his most experienced polar pilot who had been to the Antarctic ice with him during the previous season, DEEP FREEZE '64.

Mayer was on his way to lunch at his home at North Kingstown, and Gallup left word for him to report immediately to his outfit.

As soon as Mayer received the message, he bussed his wife and bounded back into his car for the trip back to Quonset.

He walked into the VX-6 Ops Room and took a seat as Gallup and Balish were poring over a big map of Antarctica.

"We'll need two planes for this mission," Gallup was saying. "One to go in to McMurdo to bring out the Seabee, and another one in Christchurch as the SAR back-up."

SAR stands for Search and Rescue—and VX-6 never used a single plane to perform an extra-hazardous mission. And this, in the dark of austral winter, certainly was one—without having a back-up bird standing by.

"Is 319 in good shape?" Gallup asked. "Okay, then, let's get it checked out, refueled and ready to go. Paty and Mo Morris should be in from Paris at about 2000 hours in 318. We'll use it as our SAR plane."

VX-6, the Navy's crack "Antarctic airline" then based at Quonset Point, had the demanding job every year of providing the aerial transportation for America's scientific exploration on the white continent. But the unit had only recently, in March, returned to its home base in Rhode Island after "closing up the continent" for the Antarctic winter. No airplane had ever before penetrated Antarctica's curtain of midwinter darkness, and it would be a mission fraught with danger. The closest anyone had come to a winter fly-in was in April of 1961—during the continent's "late Fall"—when a VX-6 ski-bird flew in to Byrd Station during a six-hour "window of twilight" and rescued a Russian ionospheric scientist with a bleeding ulcer.

"Well, men, Admiral Reedy wants volunteers for this one," Gallup said. "We're tasked to get that Seabee out, and we're the only outfit in the whole Navy that can do it. What about it, Bull?"

"You've got it, Commander," Mayer spoke up. "And I'm sure my crew will go, too, to a man. I'll get them rounded up."

"That's fine," the skipper declared. "All right, then, let's get our show rolling."

As soon as Mayer notified his crewmen, he went out to the flight line to look over his plane, a squat, LC-130F Hercules ski-bird with a big bull painted on its nose.

VX-6 had four of the Lockheed propjets—largest aircraft ever equipped with skis—and while Gallup and Mayer were a bit apprehensive about the unknowns of the mission ahead, they felt confident about their flying equipment. As Gallup often told the new men joining VX-6, "I've got an awful lot of respect for that airplane. The plane just handles beautifully. And it's so stable, it's a joy to fly."

Introduced by the Air Force and Navy into Antarctica just four years earlier, the Hercules was the near perfect answer to Antarctica's fierce challenge. Boasting beefy propjet engines and a great appetite for big loads, the Hercules was the jet-age solution to the South Pole environment, where 100-mile-an-hour blizzards and whiteouts and zero-zero landings are not uncommon. Lockheed had put skis on the new C-130A in 1957, to enable the Air Force to fly supply missions to Dew Line stations across Greenland. The result was the C-130D, an unusual ski-and-wheel system that Fred Gallup was fond of calling "an engineering masterpiece."

The Navy quickly realized the big new Air Force ski-bird was just what it needed for its Antarctic support mission, where it had been struggling along with two-engine C-47s and P2Vs. It ordered four of the new aircraft.

The man chosen by Gallup to lead the dangerous midwinter flight into Antarctica, forty-one-year-old Rober V. Mayer, was VX-6's oldest pilot. While most of the officers his age had risen to

On March 12, 1985, the first of four new LC-130H ski-Hercules aircraft of the 109th Tactical Airlift Group, New York Air National Guard, made its first landing at DEW Line radar station on the Greenland Ice Cap. Pilots were Capt. Giles Wagoner and Maj. Graham Pritchard. Photo was taken by the pilot of the chase LC-130H, Capt. Elliott H. Marchegianai. The Schenectady, N.Y., based unit has four new LC-130H's and four C-130H's, replacing its 24-year-old C-130D's *(lower photo)*. Lt. Col. Tom Leonard said crews were pleased with the increased power, performance and payload: "We really like the new birds. I tell my fellows to be patient. . . they don't have a Porsche anymore, but a Cadillac." In times of national emergency, the 109th and its Herk-fleet become part of the Military Airlift Command's tactical airlift force.

USAF C-130Ds lined up at McMurdo's Williams Field in early February, 1960. Seven of the Air Force ski-birds swooped into Antarctica to help the U.S. Navy resupply its inland stations during "Operation Deep Freeze 60." Lt. Col. Wilbert Turk flew the first C-130 into the South Pole Station. The 62-ton Lockheed propjet became the largest transport and first turbine-powered aircraft to land in inland Antarctica. The scientific exploration of the frozen continent was advanced at least a year by the ski Hercules that season. Lower photo, the weather grounded air operations on the Sewart ski-birds' first Sunday in Antarctica (January 24, 1960). Colonel Turk invited the Navy chaplain to conduct a service for his unit. It was held (lower photo) alongside Turk's lead plane. (Lockheed) commander or captain rank, they had not attained it through the tough enlisted steps the way Bull had. Heavy-set, with a powerful physique and an enthusiastic manner, Mayer joined the Navy at age 18, just out of high school, and served during World War II as a crew chief on patrol bombers in the Panama Canal Zone. He rose to chief. At war's end, he elected to make the Navy a career, went to flight school and became one of the service's few enlisted pilots, as an aviation pilot first class.

Bull won his commission in 1955 and became, in his words, "the oldest ensign in the Navy." His crewmen enjoyed flying with Bull. Flights with him were exciting. He was a tough yet flexible airplane skipper. Now a lieutenant, he was a VX-6 pilot and proud of his assignment. He took a possessive pride in his Hercules—which explained the bull painted on the nose. And he enjoyed strolling around with his blue flight jacket on—a bull painted on the back—just looking over his airplane.

Mayer and Gallup were there at the flight line when 318 landed on its non-stop flight from Paris. The pilot, Lt. C. Robert Paty, knew something was up when he saw Gallup coming up to greet him.

"We must have done something wrong," Paty told his co-pilot, the squadron's new exec, Commander "Mo" Morris.

"How's the aircraft?" Gallup asked Paty as he emerged from the crew door.

"Okay."

"Want to go to the Antarctic tomorrow?"

"Are you kidding? Nobody goes to the ice this time of year."

"I know, it's dark down there, but we've got to go into McMurdo and bring out a Seabee. He suffered a terrible fall and broke his back."

"Sure, I'll go."

"Then you'd better get home and get some sleep. We'll be leaving at eight in the morning."

Paty was assigned as Mayer's co-pilot, and their backup pilot would be Commander Balish. The navigators chosen to go on the mission were Lts. Fred Wright and James E. Stanley. Navigation would play a crucial role in the mission—particularly on the long flight from Christchurch to McMurdo.

The two ski-birds took off at 8 a.m. on June 24. Mayer headed directly toward the West Coast, while Gallup took 318 to Andrews AFB near Washington, where he picked up a four-man medical team from Bethesda Naval Medical Center.

Except for an overnight crew rest at Hickam AFB near Honolulu, the two planes drove straight through to New Zealand. At Hickam, the medics took aboard a striker frame, a stretcher designed for broken back cases. They also got an update on the injured Seabee: McMullen was slowly sinking. The Navy radioed Dr. Bates that "help is on its way by C-130. Do what you can to get that skiway cleared."

Around the world, alerted by press reports, people waited anxiously for developments in the drama of this race against death. Wire services were reporting on the dangerous mission into the Antarctic night.

On June 26, the two Hercules touched down on their wheels at Christchurch within minutes of one another, at 1 a.m.

The senior doctor on the plane, Lieutenant Commander Dick Millington, came out and was greeted by a Navy liaison officer.

"What's the latest on the Seabee?" he asked.

"We've just received this from McMurdo."

"McMULLEN STILL CRITICAL. NOW IN STATE OF SHOCK AND SINKING. HAVE CONSIDERED EXPLORATORY SURGERY BUT FACILITIES HERE ARE LIMITED. REQUIRE WASHINGTON SURGICAL TEAM AT EARLIEST POSSIBLE TIME."

"How quickly can we take off, Lieutenant Mayer?"

"Tomorrow morning, Commander."

"Why can't we leave now?"

"Because we're heading into the toughest part of the mission. We've go to get the plane checked over thoroughly, place survival gear aboard, and we'll need a detailed weather briefing."

As the other two physicians and the medical corpsman came up, Fred Gallup expanded on the uncertainties of this last, and longest, leg.

"Bull will have an overwater flight all the way and the headwinds can be awfully rough. Sometimes we get a hundred knots on the nose. The general weather circulates all around and off the polar cap. Conditions can change very rapidly. You can go

While seven of the ski-Hercules from Sewart AFB were in Antarctica in January, 1960, two others had a special mission to perform in the Arctic: Evacuate 30 U.S. scientists and 230,000 pounds of equipment, vehicles and supplies from a floating ice island within the Arctic Circle that was breaking up. Above, a snow vehicle is readied for loading aboard airplane from Sewart. Pilot of the lead aircraft was Capt. William A. Culling. Earlier, the scientific base at "Ice Island Charlie" was installed on the island by the Sewart-based Hercules. (USAF)

Lt. Col. Wilbert Turk (L), and four of his crewmen from the lead ski-Hercules, pose for a photo at Sewart AFB, Tennessee, after returning from their 1960 mission to Antarctica. Note the outline of Antarctica painted on the aircraft along with nine penguins—representing nine supply flights to the South Pole by this aircraft, affectionately dubbed *Frozen Assets*. L-R: Turk, Captain James Whitener, Captain John Phelps, M/Sgt. Klukas and S/Sgt. Ireland. (USN)

VX-6 LC-130F is pictured (top photo) being unloaded at Plateau Station, Antarctica on November 18, 1967, during the first fly-in of Deep Freeze 68. It was the first fresh food, mail and new faces that the remote station had seen in nine months. Rear Admiral J. Lloyd Abbot, the Navy's commander for Antarctica, and Capt. H.A. Kelly were aboard to greet the wintering over party and officially open the station. Lower photo, first stringer of an eight-man Jamesway hut is erected November 8, 1969, during the building of a camp at Lassiter coast on the Wetmore glacier. VX-6 C-130 in the background had just brought in the construction materials. (USN)

from a ceiling unlimited situation to absolute zero visibility in an hour."

"Exactly," said Mayer. "And we have limited nav aids. If we reach McMurdo and the situation is zero-zero with cross-winds, we've got a badass situation. We're going to put on enough fuel so that if worse comes to worst, we'll have enough to come back if we can't get in."

At McMurdo, the winds had calmed down somewhat and some Navy crews emerged from their quarters in the glow of the silvery moonlight, heated up their scrapers and started knocking down some of the heavy drifts of blizzard snow that had accumulated on the Williams Field Ski-Way.

Back at sunny Christchurch, Navy ground crews went over 319 with a fine tooth comb and loaded the bird up with fuel. Even the GV-1 tank inside the fuselage was filled, plus the wing tanks and reserve tank. Mayer had to get approval from Lockheed and the Admiral to take off with such a heavy gross weight—155,000 pounds, 10 tons over the 135,000 max gross weight specified for the LC-130F. The McMurdo Navy had radioed, "Heavy on the eggs," but Mayer was unable to take them on. He did put aboard a few sacks of mail and 80 pounds of fresh apples donated by the Salvation Army.

Before taking off, Mayer had his fuel tanks topped off with still additional fuel. Before buttoning up the plane, Mayer spoke to New Zealand reporters:

"I have no fears," he said. "I'll just be talking to the Man Upstairs and let Him guide me." Before taking off, Mayer accepted a telegram from the school children at Taranaki which said: "May God go with you, gallant gentlemen."

*　　*　　*

The C-130 made its debut in Antarctica four years earlier, on Saturday, January 23, 1960, in the austral summer.

Under a brilliant sun hanging high in the southern sky, Lieutenant Colonel Wilbert Turk, a lanky, professional, pipe-smoking Air Force squadron commander from Tennessee, led a fleet of seven ski-shod C-130Ds into McMurdo Sound.

Even from a hundred miles out, thanks to the clear polar

air, Turk could see through the lead plane's windows the stark Antarctic panorama—a spectacular, vast expanse of ice, snow and mountain peaks.

"Awesome, would you say, gents?" Turk said as he surveyed the shimmering blanket of white behind the green Antarctic Ocean.

The polar cap reminded Turk somewhat of the Arctic, 13,000 miles to the north. There, his 12 C-130Ds of the 61st Troop Carrier Squadron, Sewart AFB, Tennessee, had tasted polar flying for the first time the year before, shuttling vital fuel and supplies from Sondestrom Air Base to DEW Line stations being constructed on the Greenland Ice Cap.

Turk guided his Hercules "down through the slot" between McMurdo Bay and volcanic, 14,000-foot Mount Erebus. The plane descended gracefully, touched down lightly on the Williams Field ski-way, and swished through the snow to a stop.

Following behind, in thirty-minute intervals, six more of the Lockheed ski-birds swooped down onto the Antarctic ice. It was a historic day, one that had Rear Admiral David M. Tyree literally jumping with joy.

With four more weeks remaining of Antarctica's summer season of 24-hour-a-day sunlight, the Navy's Antarctic boss knew that those big ski-birds would be able to haul a helluva tonnage to the inland scientific stations. Several of the stations were desperately low on food and fuel. Now the admiral had big help—in abundance.

Two days later, on Monday, January 25, Admiral Tyree climbed aboard Turk's lead aircraft as it launched a fantastic series of 58 shuttle runs to the Byrd and Pole Stations. Turk's ski-birds completed the entire mission of airlifting 400 tons of supplies and equipment in just two weeks—10 days ahead of schedule. The airlift was credited with pushing the U.S. Science Foundation program one year ahead of schedule. Despite temperatures that ranged from 40 degrees below zero to a high of eight below, the seven planes kept right on flying. On February 7, with their job completed, the Herks returned to Christchurch, and were back at the home base in Tennessee on the 13th. One month later they were back on the Greenland ice cap mission.

Antarctica would never again be the same. Virtually overnight,

Photo of Navy-operated ski Hercules was made in 1960 as the airplane painted Antarctic skies with vapor trails. Giant 20-foot aluminum skis, coated with Teflon, are highlighted. During the five month austral summer, the Navy's VXE-6 squadron operates fleet of National Science Foundation ski-birds in all types of treacherous polar weather, supplying the National Science Foundation's research stations across the 5.5 million square mile continent. Lower photo, Herk takes aboard a prefabricated building for airlift to inland station. (USN)

"Sacked out" on the long flight from Christchurch, New Zealand, to McMurdo Station, Antarctica, dozen or so personnel get sleep on mattresses spread out on cargo floor of LC-130 ski Hercules (top photo). Lower photo, new LC-130R version ski Herks were delivered to the National Science Foundation and U.S. Navy's VXE-6 Squadron in time for Operation Deep Freeze 74. The first of the new models (lower photo) discharges a contingent of scientists at the South Pole Station. (USN)

the scientific exploration of the 5.5 million square mile polar desert, the world's last geographic frontier, took a quantum leap, from an era of dog-sleds and long overland traverses to a jet age mobility never before imagined. It was, indeed, a revolution, bringing to realization Admiral Byrd's prophecy that if the colossal continent were ever conquered, it would be by air. Admiral Tyree later would point to the arrival of the Hercules that year as "the beginning of permanent development of Antarctica."

Admiral Tyree was completely won over by the C-130's fantastic capabilities and by the beginning of DEEP FREEZE '61 in October of 1960, the Navy had its own fleet of ski-Hercules—four red-tailed C-130BLs that were later designated LC-130s. Excitement rippled among the flyers of VX-6 Squadron—the Navy's proud "Penguin Airline"—as they brought their powerful new flying machines to the ice.

Among other things, it meant that the days were numbered for the strong-hearted but fragile C-47 and R-4 "Goons," whose skeletons dotted the Antarctic landscape like radar reflectors. The same fate of obsolescence was in store for the squadron's other slow-flying, unpressurized piston aircraft such as the P2V, C-54 and C-117, even the more modern C-121 Constellations.

Despite the ski-Hercules' cumbersome looks, made more so by the addition of boat-like skis tucked under her broad belly, she quickly won admiration as a hefty, can-do polar draft horse, uniquely designed and equipped to master the continent's adversities. The agility of the 70-ton flying machine amazed scientists and sailors, particularly when they saw the plane come in to land on unprepared snow surfaces as deftly as a bird. Some old salts compared her to a gull. "Our old Globemasters look like a sausage," they added. While the C-47s had to use jet assist (JATO), the C-130, on a gross weight of 124,000 pounds, seldom needed the bottles. (Later, however, with heavier loads and visits to the thin air of higher elevations, JATO was put into use frequently).

Admiral Tyree led the songs of praise for the Navy's new Antarctic workhorse, and he summed up his enthusiasm in *The National Geographic:*

> The C-130s, which thrive on cold temperatures and high altitudes, have become the backbone of our air operation. Carrying ten tons of cargo, they easily clear the (Polar Plateau, Beardmore and

Glacier) mountains, and climb over the weather . . . . Even when loaded with cargo, the C-130 can leap into the air in 20 seconds and cruise at 25,000 feet. Jet turbines, driving four propellers, thrive on thin air that make piston engines pant . . . .

The arrival of the big-bellied Herks with their unique "ski-and-wheel" landing gear meant that, unlike during the era of wheeled transports, the Antarctic resupply runs would not have to terminate with the thawing of McMurdo's ice runways in the sunny days of February. The Herks merely would shift over a few miles to the snow ski-way and switch to their skis.

For another thing, the Navy was able to haul all of its equipment and supplies to inland stations and unload right at the scientists' door. In the earlier era, the Navy had had to call on Air Force for that mission. MATS' wheeled C-124 "Old Shakies" had to parachute their cargoes—including scientific instruments, "the crown jewels of the Antarctic"—into inland stations. "That cost a million dollars a year in parachutes alone," Navy officials said, "to say nothing about the time lost in hunting down and recalibrating the instruments." The Herks could gobble up tremendous loads, up to and including big 15-ton Sno-Millers, D-8 tractors, ski-mobiles, even dog teams, and haul them swiftly to their destinations across the continent.

A similar revolution occurred in the delivery of fuel oil—the life blood of the Antarctic outposts. Previously, the C-124s air-dropped 55-gallon drums of oil, four to a pallet. The C-130, fitted with cylindrical internal tanks adapted from the Marine tanker version, toted the equivalent of 66 drums of fuel on one load. Arriving at an inland station, they could pump the fuel into receiving bladders or tanks in seven minutes.

But the Hercules' major advantage was its superb ability to give mobility to scientists. Admiral Tyree observed: "Vehicles for scientific traverses no longer need to crawl hundreds of profitless miles to reach the area in which the scientists wish to begin their studies."

The admiral pointed out how, during DEEP FREEZE '62, the Herk for the first time gave polar technologists the legs and speed to move quickly around the continent—particularly to areas never before accessible:

Last season (DEEP FREEZE'62), seven scientists flew 1500 miles

Photos depict historic first wintertime landing of the Navy's ski-equipped LC-130F Hercules at Byrd Station, Antarctica, on April 11, 1961. The plane had arrived to pick up a Russian exchange scientist, Leonid Kuperov, suffering from a duodenal ulcer. Top photo, Kuperov is taken on a stretcher at Byrd Station to the waiting plane. The Navy flight commander, Lt. Don Angier, timed his arrival at Byrd Station during a five-hour "window" of murky twilight. Bottom photo, airplane is readied for takeoff in darkness on final 2100-mile leg from McMurdo to Christchurch, New Zealand. (USN)

> east of McMurdo to Camp Minnesota. There they began the
> Ellsworth Land Traverse, which significantly altered the map
> locations of many mountains and produced new discoveries about
> the great trench under the ice which seems to split Antarctica.
> Only the C-130 could have delivered this expedition: Seven men
> with supplies and equipment for a two-month, 1,000-mile traverse;
> eight sleds and a hutlike Wanigan equipped as a galley; three
> sno-cats weighing nearly four tons apiece; and a rolli-tanker with
> four huge rubber tires used as fuel tanks.

Soon after, VX-6 and its Herks went even further by taking entire scientific villages, including prefabricated buildings, designed to fit inside the Hercules, deep into the continent. A good example came in late 1965 when the "Puckered Penguins" airlifted a complete station to Antarctica's No Man's Land—the desolate, 13,000 foot high Polar Plateau 1,200 miles from McMurdo. The high, windy plateau—coldest spot on earth— gave scientists a perfect platform to study the earth's magnetic field, the aurora australis (southern lights), and the weather.

John R. Dantzler, Lockheed's senior tech rep with VX-6, recalled the first flight to the plateau region "never before touched by human hand, foot or aircraft:"

> The landing of the LC-130F (piloted by Cmdr. M.E. Morris) was a
> noteworthy accomplishment. However, there was grave concern
> whether the aircraft could get airborne after its cargo was
> unloaded. The soft snow and extreme altitude combined to present
> the Hercules with a formidable task. After a long bout with the
> clutching snow, the veteran Hercules, past master of many Ant-
> arctic pitfalls, gently lifted skyward for the trip home to McMurdo
> Station.

One Puckered Penguin attempted 12 Plateau takeoffs before getting airborne. He arrived at the South Pole Station "on E and that doesn't mean Enough."

Despite the adversities, the intrepid VX-6 flyers completed the plateau camp delivery in one month, including 66,000 gallons of fuel and all the housing and equipment to enable Dr. Jimmy Lee Gowan and his scientists to "winter over" for seven months.

Establishing the Plateau camp was only part of VX-6's task that season. During an unusual period of good weather, the squadron set a one-day airlift record. Dantzler reported it this way:

In a 24-hour period of 28 December, the (four LC-130F) planes delivered more than 267,000 pounds of cargo over 7,500 miles to various Antarctic scientific stations. After several warm-up operation days of 60 to 65 flight hours, the four ski-130s flew a grand total of 85.5 hours in one day for a single plane average of 21.4 hours. The four planes made three missions each, delivering much needed fuel to the South Pole Station, Byrd Station and Camp Neptune. On-ground time was kept to a minimum, and the loading and unloading of cargo was done in less than a half hour in most cases . . . .

It was thus understandable why the Navy, which for years had operated a wide variety of fixed wing aircraft such as the Neptune, Albatross and Skymaster, decided to go all out for the Hercules, "the biggest and best."

Since acquiring the Hercules, the squadron—now known as VXE-6, has carried out an astounding annual airlift, retailing virtually all the supplies and personnel from McMurdo, on the Ross Ice Shelf, to the Antarctic interior. This has been its job since it was commissioned in 1955 as a logistic arm of America's Antarctic research programs. For 17 years, the squadron was based at Quonset Point, but moved in 1972 to Point Mugu, California. Every September, the Puckered Penguins "deploy" their fleet of icebirds to the Navy's advance staging base at Christchurch, New Zealand, and, in early October move on to the continent for the five-month DEEP FREEZE season. In addition to moving the bulk of men and material on the continent, VXE-6 handles Antarctic aerial mapping, search and rescue, and scientific reconnaissance support.

From early October when VX-6's first C-130 "opens up the continent," the Herks shuttle continuously across the polar cap, stockpiling enough supplies to support more than 2,000 sailors and scientists for a full year, including the seven-month wintering-over parties.

Despite all of the environmental hazards, the big airlift is only temporarily deterred by whiteouts and high winds. Jim Hunt, former Lockheed tech rep with VXE-6, recalls an incident to illustrate the improvisational spirit of the Puckered Penguins:

"One day we were on a routine flight from McMurdo to Byrd Station, up on the 9,000-foot plateau. It's a crevasse-free area, but the wind blows quite a bit, creating whiteouts. It takes only a twenty-knot wind to whip up the snow; it's light, dry powder, like flour. So when we went out, the Byrd meteorologist radioed us they had a whiteout and that the wind was blowing at a 90-degree angle to the ski-way. So the skipper decided he would land before he got to Byrd and just taxi in . . . .

"That's like lighting out here in a field someplace north of Atlanta, and getting on a freeway and taxiing downtown. Well, we landed about 10 miles out. We found a good place, we had our radar on, dropped a smoke pot to show the wind direction, and landed. Then we taxied the ten miles up to the station. It's weird when you are taxiing in a Herk in a whiteout; you can't tell whether you're moving, because of the engine noise, unless your compass needle moves when you make a turn."

The people who appreciate the Hercules most in Antarctica are the scientists from 17 nations who use the C-130 flying taxicabs to go anywhere they feel a need to go. Besides logistic support, the ski-Hercules serves as an aerial platform for scientific projects including glaciology, mapping, magnetic surveys, seal population surveys and weather charting.

A.N. Fowler, with the National Science Foundation's Office of Polar Programs, stated flatly that the VXE-6 Squadron and its C-130s "have made the U.S. Antarctic Program what it is.

"Five major inland stations, not to mention uncounted remote camps, were built because VXE-6 brought the materials and the people to build them. The thickness and the below-surface terrain of a good part of the ice sheet have been measured accurately and swiftly because of the aircraft. Major efforts like the Dry Valley Drilling Project would not have been considered without the knowledge that the Navy Ski-Hercules were there to provide support. . . ."

*　　*　　*

Lt. Bull Mayer's C-130, heavily laden with fuel and grossed out at an overweight 155,000 pounds, lifted ponderously off the Christchurch runway in the twilight hours June 26, and headed out toward the Antarctic darkness.

"Good luck, Bull," were the last words Commander Gallup spoke to Bull as he buttoned up 319. The VXE-6 skipper would be standing by with 318 at the Christchurch Airport, fueled up and ready to take off on a moment's notice in the event of trouble.

In the 319 flight station, all was calm. "We'll cruise-climb all the way," Mayer told Paty and Balish, as he leveled off at 16,000 feet. "We should be up to about 30,000 feet when we reach the continent." (In cruise-climb, the airplane floats up in altitude as it burns off fuel.)

Although all the weather reports were good as far as they knew, Bull was well aware of the potential perils ahead. He had flown this route many times—all of it in the Antarctic summer, however—and on occasion he had to abort missions due to the strong headwinds coming off the polar cap.

Should the forecasts become invalid (and the meteorology from the ice was not all that accurate this time of year), Bull knew he had enough fuel to reach McMurdo itself as the point of no return, and still get back to Christchurch. But still . . . .

At McMurdo, Seabees were working frantically by the light of the moon in a bone-chilling minus 20-degree "day." Blizzards had piled tons of snow on the unused Williams ski-way, and the two-mile long course looked in many ways like a roller-coaster. Fifty gallon oil drums were brought out by Sno-Cats and sleds and positioned along a half-mile of the runway. They would be set afire at the proper time. The new Zealanders at nearby Scott Base cut on their lights, just in case. Out on the Antarctic Ocean, the U.S. Navy ordinarily kept a picket ship at the halfway point between New Zealand and McMurdo—at about 1,100 miles, to provide on-station weather reports and to be there in case of an airplane ditching. But the ship had departed from the rolling, windswept sea in April. New Zealand did dispatch some of its Navy vessels off the New Zealand coast to give what help they could.

Meanwhile, 319 had moved up to 24,000 feet altitude and was cutting through the Antarctic night. The last rays of sunlight had flickered out just after the plane departed Christchurch. It would be the last sunlight Bull and crew would see for some time. Up over the 319 flight station, a sign summed up the present mood: "Antaractic flying consists of hours of sheer boredom, interrupted by moments of stark terror."

With the propjet engines droning in the background, the crew talked quietly as they moved over the icy dark ocean. They had heard the standing joke among Navy men who pulled Antarctic duty: "If you ever ditch your plane in that ocean, just take a tool box in hand and jump overboard . . . follow that tool box down. Get it over in a hurry." In that icy water, all agreed, you wouldn't last five minutes.

But Mayer and crew had no such worry. As 319 approached the continent, the skies became brilliantly clear. The moonlight got so bright that Paty got up and taped maps onto the upper windows of the flight deck, to cut down on the glare.

"This sure is a beautiful night," Paty remarked. "Just perfect for this sort of thing. I can't believe it."

From 200 miles out, Mayer got a TACAN lock on McMurdo, and the VX-6 controller on wintering-over duty, Lt. Cmdr. John A. Morton, came on the radio.

"Hello, Bull. Do you have us on your radar? We're going to light up the barrels now."

From 150 miles out, the 319 crew could see with the naked eye through the clear polar air the two rows of flares as they brightened up.

"How do you see us, Bull?" Morton asked.

"Beautiful, John, Beautiful. You're lit up like a Christmas tree. But keep that radar on me."

As 319 slowed down to make its approach, a note of anxiety rang out as Lt. Paty spoke into the intercom.

"Gear on the starboard side must be frozen stuck, Bull. It won't go down."

Bull called on the instantaneous power of the C-130 and pulled up quickly for another approach. The Allison propjets answered quickly and powered the plane up sharply on a long turning curve.

"Must be condensation we got taking off from Christchurch," Paty said. "The screw jack on that gear must be frozen." Outside, it was 110 below zero.

"Keep trying to cycle it," Bull ordered.

After holding his breath for a long minute, Paty broke into a smile as the ski broke loose on the third try and the green light flashed on the panel, showing it had lowered and locked into place.

Bull called the controller and announced he was coming in on

Backup SAR aircraft to Lt. "Bull" Mayer on his long overwater midwinter flight from New Zealand to McMurdo was this Hercules (number 318), pictured at the Christchurch airport on the night of June 26, 1964. (USN)

Injured Seabee Bethel McMullen is pictured being lifted from Hercules following flight from McMurdo. Navy hospital corpsman holds blood plasma bottle. Thus ended another successful mercy flight for the Hercules. (USN)

another ground control approach. "What do you expect from an airplane that's been summerized in Rhode Island?" he joked to the McMurdo voice, who had left his family at home near the Quonset Naval Air Station.

"Okay, Bull, let me see you get her down here this time," the ground replied.

Down over the McMurdo Sound Approach, alongside the Royal Society Mountains, came the big Hercules, lining up with the flickering lines of oil drums which were sending up plumes of black smoke. Quickly, 319 settled onto its skis and went bounding down the roller-coaster for 3,000 feet.

The surgical team was met by a helicopter which took them the seven miles up to "the hill"—the McMurdo main base. Inside the station's one-room dispensary, they found Seabee McMullen, who had regained consciousness.

"Hi, Sailor, we're here to take you home," Commander Millington said.

A smile crossed McMullen's face. This was the first he'd heard about the rescue flight. Dr. Bates hadn't mentioned it to him in the event bad weather kept the mission from getting through.

Although 319 had enough fuel to get back to Christchurch, Mayer had his wing tanks topped off, just in case. And it was a good thing. Just after leaving McMurdo, when Bull switched over to his auxiliary tanks, the fuel booster pumps burned out. But there was no problem. That extra fuel was adequate.

Arriving at Christchurch, McMullen was taken to the hosptial were he was X-rayed. Four vertebrae had been crushed and he would be paralyzed in his legs for life. Later he was flown to a stateside hospital.

Bull Mayer and his crew were awarded the Navy Commendation Medal by the Secretary of the Navy, and Mayer himself got the Distinguished Flying Cross.

At Christchurch, Bull quipped to reporters, "Just another routine Antarctic first."

Back at Quonset Point, however, he went a bit further.

"The crux of the whole situation is that we broke the back of the Antarctic winter. The men who winter over—and I've been there myself—know now that if anybody gets hurt, the Puckered Penguins will bring them out."

THUNDERBALL: MIRACLE AT ENTEBBE

> It was an operation to remember . . .
> longest in range, shortest in time and
> most daring one can imagine.
>
> —Israeli Defense
> Minister Shimon Peres

It was 12:15 p.m. Sunday, June 27, 1976, and a festive air of excitement rippled through the jam-packed Air France Airbus as it taxied out at the Athens Airport. Its destination: Paris.

But back in the theatre-like tourist cabin, an undercurrent of anxiety was stirring. Stately, silver-haired Dora Bloch, 75, was uncharacteristically fearful. She squirmed anxiously in her seat on row 25 and nudged her son, Ilan Hartuv, seated alongside.

"I don't feel right about them somehow," Mrs. Bloch whispered. She motioned with her eyes to the two dark-haired young men who had just taken seats in row 28 behind them. One wore a red shirt; his hair draped his shoulders. The other, mustachioed, had on a yellow sport shirt and slacks. Both carried large leather shoulder bags. They came aboard, along with 56 new passengers, at Athens Airport, a collection point for Mideast flights to Europe. From the Athens control tower came the final clearance:

"AIR FRANCE FLIGHT 139, YOU ARE CLEARED FOR TAKEOFF."

Captain Michel Bacos wheeled his A-300 onto the runway and spooled up the two fanjet engines to get the full benefit of their 102,000 pounds of thrust. Sporting a blue seahorse on its side, the Airbus buzzed down the runway, took to the air into the grayish-blue haze, whirled past the white rooftops of Athens, and gained altitude over the blue-green waters of the Corinth Gulf. It was 12:28 p.m.

Just as the seat belt light went off and the attendants scurried to prepare lunch for the 243 passengers, Dora Bloch turned again to her son, a Tel Aviv economist. "I'm *afraid*, Ilan," she whispered ominously. "Did you see their huge bags?"

Scattered across the vast cabin, at least a half-dozen other passengers, mostly Jews who had gotten on Flight 139 at its Tel Aviv origination point, shuddered on seeing the two young men swaggering down the aisles with the big bags. Pasco Cohen's gut reaction was: Terrorists!

Up front in the first class cabin, a young German-speaking couple had come on at Athens and taken front row seats. The girl, despite her petite ponytail, had masculine mannerisms. Her face was marred by acne pockmarks. She had on a blue blouse, a blue skirt and blue stockings. Her companion, a lanky six-foot Nordic blond with a German accent, sat beside her, quietly sipping his champagne.

Suddenly, the blond young man stood up and hoisted his empty glass, a pre-arranged signal. Almost simultaneously, hysterical screams rang out in the tourist cabin. The youths in row 28, waving Beretta pistols, bolted from their seats and ran up to the to the galley separating the two cabins.

It was 12:33 p.m. and Air France Flight 139 was being hijacked.

The blond German up front—Winfred Bose—one-time member of the Baader-Meinhof gang—broke into the flight station and pointed his pistol at the head of Captain Bacos. In his other hand was a grenade with the pin removed. "No tricks now. Turn this plane around—to Benghazi," he said as he handed Bacos a map.

The tall, greying captain, seeing that Bose wouldn't hesitate a minute to blow up the plane, put the A-300 on a banking turn 90 degrees to the south-west over the blue Mediterranean.

Back in the tourist section, the red-shirted youth, an Arab, turned to the passengers with a grenade in his hand. He deftly removed the grenade's firing pin and hooked the loop on his little finger.

With her ponytail swinging wildly, the German woman screamed angrily at the 26 first class passengers and herded them into the tourist cabin. The two Arab youths took canisters from their handbags and placed them by the emergency exits. Yellow fuses stuck out the top.

Pandemonium swept through the cabins as the jet roared upward at 550 miles per hour. Many of the women screamed madly, and some of the passengers went into shock, terrified by the sudden turn of events. The eight flight attendants obeyed orders and stretched out on the floor.

Over the din, the public address system squealed to life.

"This is Captain Basis el-Koubeisi of the Che Guevara Force, the Gaza Commando of the Palestine Liberation Forces."

It was the voice of Wilfred Bose, commander of the hijackers, speaking from the cockpit.

"The plane has been hijacked . . . I would advise you to behave quietly . . . ."

* * *

In Jerusalem, the Israeli Cabinet was in session when the first word of the plane's strange flight pattern came through from Air France's office at Lod Airport. Before Prime Minister Yitzsak Rabin concluded the meeting at 4 p.m., he was handed an update.

"The plane landed at Benghazi at 2:58," Rabin announced. As the cabinet members filed out, the prime minister convened five of the ministers to help him handle the crisis. Rabin feared political blackmail; he knew many Israelis were aboard the airbus which now sat on an airstrip in Libya.

* * *

At mid-day on Monday, twenty-four long hours after the

hijacking began, the passengers and crew of Flight 139 were hustled off the Airbus between columns of Ugandan troops at Entebbe, in deep South Central Africa, 2,400 miles from Tel Aviv. Inside the airport's old terminal, amid swirls of accumulated dust, the tired, motley travelers learned they were in the hands of the PFLP—the Popular Front for the Liberation of Palestine. Higher-ranking terrorists were now on the scene and in command.

*   *   *

In Tel Aviv, Defense Minister Shimon Peres, weary from a five-hour vigil at Lod Airport, was fighting mad. If Uganda and its president were collaborating in the aerial kidnapping, Peres told his colleagues, it would mark the first time in history that a nation and its highest authorities had become accessories to a terrorist hijacking. A hawk, Peres made it clear to his associates that the Israeli Defense Force probably would have to get the hostages out.

*   *   *

Idi Amin, standing six-foot four and weighing 280 pounds, darkened the terminal's doorway with his massive bulk.

"I think some of you know me. For those who don't, I am Field Marshal Doctor Idi Amin Dada, the man responsible for them allowing you off the plane to stay in Uganda . . . ."

The passengers applauded loudly as Amin, grinning broadly, strode into the terminal, wearing his Israeli paratrooper wings, and surrounded by a phalanx of Palestinian and Ugandan guards. After he departed, the captives realized just how precarious their predicament was. Amin was not only cooperating with the terrorists, he was a major link in the entire scenario. It should have been obvious earlier in the day when the four hijackers got off the Airbus at Entebbe and were greeted with kisses by Ugandan troops.

*   *   *

Tuesday at 4:15 p.m., Jerusalem received the hijackers' demands, relayed by the French ambassador in Kampala, Pierre

Renard: By noon Thursday, 52 terrorist prisoners held in jails in Israel, Switzerland, Germany, France and Kenya, must be handed over in Entebbe. Forty were in Israeli prisons.

Rabin's crisis committee met at 5 p.m. It was a tense affair. Lt. Gen. Mordechai Gur, military chief of staff, was flown in by helicopter and asked point-blank what suggestions the military had.

"At the moment, we don't have any suggestions," the general replied. "Quite frankly, gentlemen, our biggest problem is the distance. Uganda is some 2,400 miles from here. We've never taken a military operation more than a few hundred miles. At this point we don't have any hard intelligence about Entebbe. But we could certainly come up with a plan . . . ."

*   *   *

Rivulets of sweat ran down the backs of the 243 hostages held captive in the cramped old terminal. It was understandable. The equator crosses Uganda just to the south of Entebbe. But fear chilled the atmosphere. More terrorists were now on hand . . . Antonio Bouviet, a diminutive, white-suited Peruvian, and Faiz Abdul Jaaber, a native Palestinian. Both were chums of international terrorist chief, Carlos the Jackal, and equally as cruel. Still on the scene were Wilfred Bose and his pony-tailed pal with the pock-marked face.

*   *   *

"Get me Colonel Bar-Lev," Shimon Peres asked his secretary.

"Baruch, we need your help. I understand you made friends with Amin when you headed our military mission in Uganda."

"Yes, that is true, sir. I still correspond with him."

Baruch Bar-Lev had directed the Israeli mission to Kampala until all Israelis were kicked out in 1972 when Amin switched allegiance to Libya.

"Can you reach him on the phone?"

"Certainly. I have his telephone number."

"How about coming to the Defense Ministry and put through a call."

*   *   *

Ugandan soldiers lolled around the old terminal with their strange array of weapons, Russian Kalashnikovs, Beretta pistols and UZI submachine guns. One Israeli woman went to the rest room to find a Ugandan soldier staring through the window. It was obvious that the hijacking force consisted not only of the so-called "terrorists"—but Uganda's Army, headed by the dictator president.

* * *

Although Rabin and his defense secretary, Shimon Peres, desperately longed for a military solution, the deadline of Thursday noon, looming less than 40 hours away, dictated their move toward negotiation. But they agreed that a military plan should be mapped out anyway, just in case. And Rabin ordered his intelligence chief to get his Mossad organization busy.

The Air Force chief, General Peled, had already done a lot of thinking. He told General Gur what the Air Force could do:

"We could easily airlift a sizeable strike force to Entebbe non-stop with our C-130s, Mota. It's not beyond our capabilities at all. With a payload of, say, 30,000 pounds per plane, we could even go 3,000 miles. Our only problem would be getting refueled for the flight back. If we could seize control of the Entebbe airport, we could fuel up from the Ugandan Air Force pits."

* * *

The hostages looked on with fascination as Ugandan troops ripped out the plywood wall creating an opening to the next room, then nailed a bar across the gaping hole. Wilfred Bose strode in with his loud-hailer and ordered all hostages with Blue Israeli passports and Jewish sounding names into the next room. One by one, the Jews, many of them weeping, crawled through the opening. Air France Captain Bacos and his crewmen insisted on joining the Jews segregated in the side room.

* * *

Shimon Peres pleaded everywhere he could—particularly with government and defense officials—that military action had to be taken. Late into the night Wednesday, he was making an appeal:

"If Israel gives in, I fear a tremendous disaster for our nation. When we talk about the danger to the lives of the hostages, I regard them as if they were IDF soldiers in a war. We can't let them down."

* * *

AMIN: Who's speaking?

BAR-LEV: Colonel Bar-Lev.

AMIN: I'm very happy to hear your voice today.

BAR-LEV: I heard what has happened. My friend, can I ask you for something?

AMIN: I agree . . . you are my friend.

BAR-LEV: My friend . . . a lot of people are writing bad things about you. You have an opportunity to show them that you are a great peacemaker. If you liberate the people, you will go down in history as a very great man . . . .

AMIN: I have spoken satisfactorily with the Popular Front for the Liberation of Palestine. They have freed 47 of the hostages. Now they have 145 Israelis and Jews together, and other hostages.

BAR-LEV: What about the Israeli hostages?

AMIN: The PFLP have now completely surrounded the remaining hostages . . . . They say that if the Israeli government doesn't answer their demands, they will blow up the French plane and all the hostages at 12 noon Thursday . . . .

* * *

The hijackers treated the hostages in different ways. Wilfred Bose, the determined, quiet-spoken German, stayed on duty inside and just outside the terminal, his Scorpion submachine gun slung nonchalantly over his shoulder. While businesslike, he spoke courteously to the captives. His German girlfriend—dubbed the "Nazi bitch"—spewed hate continuously, screaming at the captives through a loudspeaker. The terrorists relented a bit, however, allowing the children to play on a small grass plot in front, and allowing the women to hang clothes outside to dry.

* * *

In the Israeli Defense Force's underground war room in Tel Aviv, planners sat down to devise a rescue plan. Their problem was monumental. How do you bring off a military strike so far away? Virtually a 5,000-mile round trip? There were a thousand and one questions to resolve.

*   *   *

El Al Airlines Flight LY 535 landed at Nairobi's Embakasi International Airport late Wednesday night. Among those aboard were 50 Israeli "businessmen" in suits and ties. Most of them were agents of Mossad, the crack Israeli CIA. They moved quickly to set up an intelligence gathering command post in the home of a Nairobi trader. Black operatives, posing as tourists, started out Thursday on a seven-hour drive to Kampala, 380 miles across the Rift Valley. Other agents went to Wilson Field to rent light planes to fly to Lake Victoria.

*   *   *

"Our Hercules can easily get to Entebbe," General Peled was saying. "If the IDF wants us to haul a force there, the Herks could do it. They have the range, the short-field capability, the bulk size and plenty of takeoff power. My only concern, besides getting refueled, would be the chance of being fired on after we land. But I would imagine the IDF would solve that problem."

*   *   *

Idi Amin visited the hostages Wednesday to bid the 47 non-Israelis goodbye.

"Don't forget your friends remaining here. When you get to wherever you are going, please tell your governments to release the (terrorist) prisoners they are holding. I wish for you happy landings . . . ."

*   *   *

Only three hours before the deadline expired at noon Thursday, the Israeli Government bit the bullet and voted to negotiate with the terrorists over the fate of the hostages. The consensus was: What else can we do?

An hour later, France's Ambassador Pierre Renard drove up to Entebbe's old terminal and passed on the Israeli decision. Terrorist "Faiz" Jaaber leaped into the air with a gleeful shout. Air France Captain Bacos and flight engineer Jacques Lemoine rushed to the door to see what was happening.

"Israel has surrendered," Faiz shouted. "Israel has surrendered."

Captain Bacos walked back in to give the word to the captives and was met with an explosion of excitement. Passengers hugged one another in joy. There were some, however, who greeted the development somberly, regretting the government cave-in to terrorist hijackers.

*   *   *

Excitement reigned Thursday night, also, at Israeli Defense Force offices in Tel Aviv, with the word that the terrorists were postponing their ultimatum four days—until Sunday—and were releasing another 101 non-Israeli hostages. On top of this good news, word came that Idi Amin would be leaving Uganda to attend the Organization of African Unity in Mauritius, far out in the Indian Ocean. He would be gone until Sunday.

Meanwhile, intelligence pouring in from Paris, from Washington, and from Nairobi (even from Entebbe itself) strengthened the spirit of the IDF hawks. The big news (obtained from freed hostages landing in Paris), was that the security at Entebbe was lax, with seven or eight terrorists taking turns just outside the terminal room, and with only perhaps 60 to 80 Ugandan troops—many of them unarmed—guarding the airport complex.

From Washington came sharp photos taken by satellites, giving a precise depiction of the Entebbe layout. But it was the word out of Nairobi that was most encouraging. Quiet arrangements had been made so that Israeli rescue planes, if required, could refuel at Embakasi International Airport.

The intelligence reports had one ominous overtone, however: The terrorists were planning to start executing the hostages, one at a time, beginning at noon Sunday . . . .

*   *   *

ENTEBBE
ELEVATION
3789 FT

758 ADDIS ABABA
304 1230 ADEN
BOMBAY
SINGAPORE
NAIROBI

This photo, made in the 1960s in front of Entebbe's old terminal, depicts the airport's elevation. In the distance is a U.S. Air Force C-130 stopping off on its way to the Congo during the UN peacekeeping effort. (USAF)

USAF C-130 received curious stares by Ugandans as it stopped at Entebbe for refueling en route to Leopoldville. This was in 1960 when the 322nd Air Division C-130s from Evreux AB, France, were carrying supplies and equipment to UN forces in the Congo. In background is the old terminal and tower, the precise scene of the liberation of the hostages by the Israeli commandos in 1976. (USAF)

At Tel Aviv's Capriccio Restaurant, Peres spotted Moshe Dayan and called him aside to inform him of the latest developments. Dayan encouraged him to move ahead boldly.

"Shimon, I'm with *you*. If your people develop a military option that makes sense, go with it, even if it's risky."

*   *   *

In Paris, an American physician released with the batch of hostages, agreed to be put under hypnosis. His amnesia vanished and he came up with some startling recollections about Entebbe, which added to Israel's broadening mosaic of intelligence. This information, combined with facts brought out by Mossad and interviews with international pilots familiar with Entebbe, gave revealing clues to the airport's runways, fuel tank locations and control tower alertness. Help also came from Solel Boneh, the Israeli construction company which built the original Entebbe airport. All in all, the airport appeared to be quite naked to a commando raid.

*   *   *

In Entebbe, Dora Bloch served as the interpreter for the Libyan doctor who visited the hostages. As she passed out anti-malaria tablets and other drugs, Dora shifted easily from Arabic to German, to English and French. Captives willingly took the anti-malaria pills. Mosquitoes were swarming by the hundreds from nearby Lake Victoria.

*   *   *

In Kampala, Somalia's Ambassador to Uganda, Hashi Farah Abdulla, made a telling remark to a western diplomat. "The hijackers are circulating very easily," he said. "It has been a week now and they have relaxed to the point that good troops could storm them with minimal loss."

Several miles away, two Piper Cub type aircraft circled over vast Lake Victoria, flown by young Israelis with cameras. It was a clear day and the views of Entebbe were spectacular, particularly the runways, the new control tower and both the old and new terminals. The planes landed first at their flight plan "destination"—Kisumu on the Kenya side—then streaked out for Nairobi. Couriers met them, picked up the film and drove off hurriedly.

*   *   *

On Friday, July 2, Israel's government/military machinery —drawing encouraging signs from its intelligence tentacles—began shifting inexorably toward military action.

Defense Minister Shimon Peres had Chief of Staff, General Mota Gur, as a guest at his home in Tel Aviv. This was the time for boldness, Peres declared; to give in to the terrorists would be disastrous. "The future of Israel hangs in the balance," he said.

General Gur agreed for a model of Entebbe to be set up in the desert and for actual practices of a rescue to begin. He assigned Brig. Gen. Dan Shamron to direct the ground planning. But the chief of staff had yet to be convinced of the C-130's ability to get into Entebbe undetected. Furthermore, he needed a guarantee that the hostages could be brought out without a great loss of life. A massacre was the last thing he needed in Entebbe.

*   *   *

Thunder from the MIG fighter plane afterburners echoed through the old terminal as Idi Amin's student pilots "dive-bombed" the building. The children ran inside; everyone put his hands over his ears, bracing for the next "bomb." It was a bit of psychological intimidation ordered by the Ugandan president.

*   *   *

General Shamron picked Lieutenant Colonel Yanathan Netaniahu to concentrate on the old terminal rescue strike. The Harvard-trained philosopher was popular among his soldiers, being known as "the Man of the Sword and the Bible." Tall, dark and handsome, "Yoni," 30, was a decorated veteran of the Six-Day War and the Yom Kippur War. He would command the first of three elite Israeli commando units that would hit the ground at Entebbe in a run. The objective: Eliminate the terrorists, and quickly.

The ground force would come from three sources: Paratroopers from the 35th Airborne Brigade, commandos from the Golani Brigade, and hand-picked counter-guerilla force troops.

* * *

Ugandan troops dragged mattresses and chairs into the second room. Israeli lawyer Akiva Lakser, trying to be helpful, began parceling them out, giving first choice to the older hostages. Faiz Jaaber, his eyes blazing with anger, rushed up and slammed the butt of his pistol into Lakser's right kidney. The lawyer doubled over in pain and hobbled to the side.

* * *

It had become obvious, and Shimon Peres expressed it, that the ideal time to stage a rescue strike into Entebbe would be Saturday night, July 3rd, no less than six hours before sunrise Sunday. There would be no commercial air traffic into Entebbe from noon Saturday until 2:30 a.m. Sunday—the arrival time of a British Airways VC-10 from London. Peres explained the rationale:

"Nothing is going to be happening in Entebbe on Friday night and Saturday, while Amin is presiding over the OAU in Mauritius. And we can't wait until Sunday. That's when the terrorists may start their executions."

* * *

Lights burned throughout the night in the IDF underground pit. Officers and aides pored over maps and photos, making detailed plans for every eventuality. The computer, given the job of picking a code name for the mission, scored on the second try with THUNDERBALL. Everyone thought it quite appropriate; the strike seemed to be something that only a James Bond could bring off.

* * *

In Entebbe, the departure of the second batch of 105 hostages gave Amin a chance to make another speech to the remaining Jews before he, himself, left for the OAS meeting in Mauritius. It was 7 a.m. Friday and Big Daddy, wearing a wide-brim white hat, was accompanied by his stunningly beautiful wife and seven year old son.

"Israel so far has not accepted the demands (of the terrorists)," Amin said. "Your situation is critical. The men who brought you here have mined the building with TNT and if their demands are not met, will demolish it . . . ." Amin suggested the passengers write a letter of appeal to Jerusalem.

*   *   *

It was Friday morning when Yoni Netaniahu's deputy—one of the brains involved in planning the ground operation—came up with the plan for a Mercedes. "All Ugandan Army officers drive black Mercedes," he declared. "And, of course, Idi Amin himself."

It was a bold idea. The Mercedes would help Yoni's commandos reach the terminal quickly under the guise of a Ugandan vehicle. The car could be taken to Entebbe easily in the hold of a Hercules and could be driven out right onto the runway . . . .

*   *   *

Prime Minister Rabin still had caution flags up about THUNDERBALL.

"Just exactly how do you propose to get your commandos into Entebbe without arousing the Ugandan Army?" Rabin asked.

General Gur looked over to his Air Force Chief, Benny Peled, who answered them both.

"Gentlemen, we can get the commandos there with four of our C-130s, efficiently and quietly. I'm going to give General Gur a demonstration tonight, to show how we can put the Herks down in much less than 2,000 feet."

"And how will you make it all the way without being detected? Remember that's over *3,500 kilometers*." The question came from a member of the crisis committee.

"We'll go right down the Red Sea for more than a thousand

miles," Peled said. "That's a 200-mile-wide stretch of water, and an international air route. But we'll fly low most of the way to avoid radar on the coasts. Once we start to cross land, north of Djibouti, there just won't be much ground radar. That's remote territory. Even if they see a blip on the radar screen, who would imagine what our mission is?"

Gur noted that the Israeli C-130 navigators—using their ground mapping radar and INS (inertial navigation) would be able to go directly to Entebbe.

"Our lead Hercules will be the pathfinder. The other three will be able to come behind in exact intervals by squawking with their SKE (station-keeping equipment). They can tell immediately the position of the other three aircraft at any point along the way. And, of course, we plan to send four F-4 Phantoms on high-altitude cover for at least 700 miles."

General Gur spoke up. "I agree with the decision to go with only four Hercules rather than 10 or 12 as proposed earlier. But I'm not really convinced you can get those big C-130s down into Entebbe without alerting the whole base."

General Peled knew that the brawny, nimble Hercules, in the hands of his skilled airmen, was the perfect vehicle for THUNDERBALL. But General Gur needed to learn the fact for himself.

"You'll see tonight, general," Benny Peled declared, trying to withhold a grin.

*   *   *

Twilight was deepening across the landing strip in central Israel when the white Mercedes, a one-time taxicab on Jerusalem's west bank, reached the THUNDERBALL practice site. The arrival of the white car created quite a stir. The team looked on with astonishment and reported the error to Colonel Netaniahu. Yoni took it calmly. The Army could repaint it tonight, he said, when it was being serviced for its big moment.

The old taxicab was put right into the practice routine. It was backed up into the open belly of the hulking Hercules, which was situated about 4,500 feet from the old terminal model. The distance would provide the commandos the element of surprise.

Traveling at 50 mph, Yoni's force, led by the Mercedes, took less than a minute to reach the terminal site from the parked Hercules.

* * *

Black Mossad operatives, driving into Uganda as tourists, penetrated the Entebbe Airport and learned the night routine at the complex, along with the dispersal of Ugandan and terrorist guards. Other agents came in boats across Lake Victoria from Kenya, right up to the shore alongside the runways.

In Entebbe, the hostage committee finished its letter to Jerusalem, written with great reluctance.

> "We are grateful to Idi Amin for his good attitude .... We ask the Israeli Government to respond positively to his efforts to try and bring about **the release of all of the people who are still here ...**"

Ilan Hartuv inserted the last phrase to let the world know that the hostages were all still alive.

Despite the increasing cases of food poisoning, the captives sang sabbath songs far into the steaming African night. After all, it was the Jewish Sabbath eve.

* * *

Friday night was a warm one, also, in Port Louis, the capital city of the volcanic island nation of Mauritius. But the breeze from the Indian Ocean cooled the delegates to the Organization of African Unity at their opening reception. Big Daddy Amin, the OAS presiding officer, was the standout in the throng, fresh in from his jet flight from Entebbe. Dressed in his blue field marshal's uniform covered with medals, Amin was in splendid spirits. Describing with a flourish how he had handled the hijack affair, he revealed that he had disarmed half of his troops at the airport. After all, as his listeners would appreciate, he didn't want to risk any problems with an armed revolution.

* * *

Yoni Yetaniahu was proud of his men . . . the elite Golani

volunteers. During the THUNDERBALL rehearsals at the desert strip, Yoni kept thinking of the British Army quotation he kept on a wall in his office: "He who dares, wins." Yoni's force was made up of young men, none of them more than 25 years old and most not over 21. Many had been tested in battle. Those who hadn't would soon get their baptism in fire.

*　　*　　*

Dora Bloch began to turn blue. She was eating a piece of meat and it lodged in her windpipe. Ilan slapped her on the back, but Dora, heaving uncontrollably, doubled over. An ambulance was rushed in to take her to a Kampala hospital.

As Ilan got up to accompany her, he was pushed back. "You will stay here," Bose declared, firmly.

Ilan kissed his mother goodbye and looked through the terminal's tall French doors a long time after the ambulance drove off.

*　　*　　*

It was shortly after 9 p.m. Friday when Benny Peled brought Chief of Staff Gur aboard the C-130 and introduced him to the crew. The Herk's big, variable pitch paddle props were already whirring on the stems of their silver, bullet-shaped nacelles. As the plane taxied to the end of the runway, General Gur was given the flight engineer's seat just behind and between the pilot and second pilot. Advised to buckle in securely, the general gave his seat belt an extra tug.

The flight that followed was an eye-opener for the general. It was described in an unforgettable sketch by William Stevenson, in *90 Minutes at Entebbe:*

> (General Gur) sat on the huge flight deck while the four-engine Hercules was put through tests that would try a thoroughbred jet fighter . . . . The Hercules, though clumsy in appearance, had the handling qualities of a fighter . . . .

> Benny Peled, who had been flying since boyhood, knew these things were possible from experience. General Gur knew it from reports. But he had yet to feel the immense power and flexibility of this huge machine. That night the Chief of Staff's Hercules flew

in and out of the desert and between mountains in what seemed to him total darkness. In jump-takeoffs, with the four turboprops at full power . . . the 77-ton transport climbed more like a helicopter. Landing on the invisible desert, it seemed to drop out of the sky . . . . Several times Gur found himself gripping crossbraces, fighting sudden acceleration or deceleration. Once he burst out: "Where the hell are we going?" Peled gave him a comradely punch in the shoulder. "To Entebbe, we hope."

. . . Gur was treated to a short field landing that felt more like a falling elevator. The distance eaten up during landing was never more than 700 feet, which would perch the Hercules on the outer edge of Entebbe Airport . . . .

The Hercules was put through these paces because Entebbe would demand a swift, near-silent arrival, the minimum use of the runways and the shortest and steepest possible getaways . . . . The Hercules was ideal for these tasks . . . .*

* * *

From British sources in East Africa, came confirmation Friday night of the increasing threat to the hostages in Entebbe. The terrorist leaders in Kampala were becoming uneasy, and were defintely thinking of launching their execution plan over the weekend, unless their demands were met.

But there was one consoling report. Contrary to Idi Amin's boasts, agents found the old terminal was not wired with explosives.

* * *

Back from his dizzying, roller-coaster Hercules ride, General Gur stopped off at the Entebbe model and observed Yoni Netaniahu's commandos in rehearsal. The Golani brigadeers, wearing rubber-soled boots, raced quickly from the Hercules on Land Rovers and on foot, being prodded by Yoni to move faster. The entire exercise—eliminating the terrorists and rescuing the hostages—took 55 minutes. Gur urged Yoni to keep practicing, and they kept it up until past midnight.

The chief of staff got on the phone to Peres. "I believe it just

90 Minutes at Entebbe, by William Stevenson, published 1976, by Bantam, New York.

might work." As to the Hercules, General Gur voiced no reservations whatsoever.

*   *   *

The hot rays of the Saturday morning sunlight spread over the 26,848-square-mile Lake Victoria and on over Entebbe. In the old terminal, many of the captives, stricken with food poisoning, were vomiting and writhing in pain. Hana Cohen lost consciousness. Her husband Pasco knelt over her but he, too, had terrible abdominal pains. Only the orthodox Jews, who refused to eat the meat, were free of the misery.

*   *   *

Buzzing across central Israel this sabbath morning was a strange assortment of military vehicles. The convoy began its trek before dawn to the IDF airbase. Israeli-built "Rabbi" field cars led the way, followed by Land Rovers, a grey Peugeot pickup truck and an armored personnel carrier. In the Rabbi up front were Dan Shamron and Yoni Netaniahu. Back in the line was a shiny black Mercedes that looked factory fresh . . . .

*   *   *

The mood among the crisis committee—meeting at 11 a.m.—was a strong "go." Hercules airlift force and the commando team were all set. All the problems had been worked out; all the intelligence signs were positive.

Yet, when General Gur laid out his final report on THUNDERBALL, Prime Minister Rabin remained noncommittal.

Shimon Peres spoke up strongly in favor of the military plan. If THUNDERBALL succeeded, as he felt it certainly would, Israel's resolve against terrorism would stiffen, and so would that of other nations around the world.

"What time will the planes have to leave?" Rabin asked.

"They must take off at 1:50 p.m. from central Israel for Ophir." That was Sharm el Sheikh, on the lower tip of the Sinai Peninsula, facing the Red Sea. There the C-130s would top off their fuel tanks for the long flight to Entebbe.

It was 2:01 p.m. when the four Hercules—splotched with camouflage green and brown—snapped up their big rear hatches. Two minutes later they were airborne. Their broad bellies were jam-packed with 245 elite Israeli commandos and their equipment, plus an array of rolling stock—jeeps mounted with 196mm recoilless guns, heavy machine guns, bazookas, grenades, UZI submachine guns, satchel charges, rockets and radiophones.

The lead C-130—the pathfinder—had aboard the key THUNDERBALL unit, Yoni Netaniahu and his hand-picked commandos, their faces and hands blackened for the old terminal attack. Some of them were seated in the old Mercedes that would take them to the scene of combat. Also aboard, seated on the rows of canvas seats along the plane's interior walls, were dark-skinned Moroccan-born Israelis whose task would be to seize control of the airfield and lay out 48 portable landing lights along the runway for the other three Herks.

*   *   *

At 2 p.m. Rabin and his team moved on into the cabinet room for the final government hurdle. General Gur went into the details again:

"We'll use four C-130s and 245 commandos in seven squads. Two of the planes will land on the international runway, and the other two on the shorter parallel runway.

"We have several big objectives . . . achieving surprise on arrival, getting to the old terminal building as quickly as possible, eliminating the terrorists, neutralizing the Ugandans, then stabilizing the area so that the hostages can be airlifted out in safety."

General Gur went into further details, pointing out the respective jobs of the various squads.

Prime Minister Rabin complimented Gur on the bold plan.

"Gentlemen, it is obvious that this is the only solution to our problem. To try to negotiate with the terrorists will be more dangerous than this military action. I recommend we take this action that General Gur has suggested." Peres sat back in his seat, breathing a sigh of relief.

There were questions. Several cabinet members were hearing about THUNDERBALL for the first time. The clock was moving relentlessly. Around 2:30, Rabin scribbled out a note and handed it over to Peres. "Release the planes for the first leg."

The fact was, the Hercules were already airborne, headed for Sharm el Sheikh.

At a break in the questioning, Rabin spoke up:

"Our C-130s are already in the air, gentlemen. If the government should decide against the project in the next few minutes, we can call them back. But I recommend highly that we approve the mission."

All 18 ministers held their hands high.

It was 3:30 when the Defense Ministry flashed the word to the Hercules fleet:

"Zunek."

THUNDERBALL was on . . . .

*   *   *

The IDF C-130s, their wings bulging with 62,000 pounds of JP-5 fuel, took off from the tip of the Sinai and headed out over the Red Sea in one-minute intervals. It was a clear day as they climbed over the waterway between Ziba on the Saudia Arabia coast, and Bar Safajah, on the Egyptian side.

"We'll stay relatively low for quite a way down," the flight commander of the lead Herk told the second pilot. Overhead, climbing to 25,000 feet, were the F-4 shepherds. Ahead of them, being refueled on the ground in Nairobi, was the IDF 707, painted in El Al colors. It was General Peled's flying command post, a former TWA jetliner loaded with electronic and communications gear. On board was ECM equipment that would be used to jam the Entebbe tower at the appropriate time. The 707 would orbit high over Entebbe throughout the raid.

*   *   *

In Paris, General Rehavam (Gandhi) Zeevi, Israel's negotiations coordinator, was about to climb the wall. He had been told nothing of THUNDERBALL. Here it was Saturday afternoon and the highjackers' ultimatum would expire at noon Sunday. Yet he had no direction from Jerusalem.

Zeevi called Rabin and demanded some instructions.

"Don't ask us what to do, Gandhi," Rabin replied, "*You're advising us. Return to the French and ask if they've heard anything of our proposal to set up the exchange in Paris.*"

Zeevi was still furious as he slammed down the receiver.

* * *

"We've just lost our Phantom cover," the pilot of the lead Herk commented. It was a casual reference, but his message was clear. The C-130s were now on their own. It was 5:30 p.m. Port Sudan could be seen on the radar screen on the Egyptian side 100 miles to the west. Coming up on the left was Al Qunfudhah, Saudi Arabia. So far, flying low, they had run into no problems. Just to be safe, the fleet skirted around a line of ships headed north. Now, to avoid radar ahead, they dropped even lower, down to 50 feet over the water.

The flight commander took a break and got out of his seat for a few minutes. He glanced back in the plane's belly. The young commandos were completely relaxed. Several, Yoni Netaniahu among them, were snoozing inside the Mercedes, which was tied in with restraint harness. Some of the soldiers were stretched out under the Mercedes and Land Rovers. The vehicles were pointed toward the back door, ready for their moment of destiny . . . .

* * *

It was the Jewish Sabbath, and the five Orthodox Jewish families gathered in a corner of the terminal passenger lounge in Entebbe and quietly recited the evening prayers. "Out of the depths have I cried unto thee, Oh Lord, hear my voice."

* * *

"Must be Djibouti coming up on the right," the pathfinder pilot said, looking on the amber radar scope. It was 7 p.m. and they had logged 1,100 miles down the Red Sea, mostly at low altitude. His navigator gave him a new reading and he banked to the southeast and began climbing to 20,000 feet, to get over Ethiopia's Eritrea mountains. The other C-130s followed in loose trail . . . strung out over the next 20 miles.

"As soon as we clear this range," the navigator said, "we can pick up the Awash River and follow it right into northern Kenya."

The seeing eye aboard the Hercules was the AN/APQ 122 radar. Parabolic and fan beam dishes were housed in the bulbous black radome ahead of the cockpit. Covering a two hundred and forty degree sector forward of the aircraft, the dish, in the map mode, projected a fan beam over the terrain ahead on an x-band frequency. The radar displayed a sharp pictorial definition of the terrain on the Pilot's 5-inch radar scope perched on top of the main instrument panel, and on the 7-inch cathode ray tube at the navigator's station, behind the second pilot.

Both scopes displayed terrain features, in particular waterways, lakes and mountains. Switching to the parabolic dish, in the weather mode, a pencil beam was projected at the aircraft's altitude to highlight any weather in the aircraft's path.

Inside the Hercules' office-like flight station, all was quiet and business-like as the crew looked ahead into the moonlit African night through the big greenhouse window panes.

*   *   *

Idi Amin came back from Mauritius that Saturday night; Big Daddy's limousine swung by the old terminal for a quick visit. The sick captives, stretched out on their mattresses, were in no mood to greet him. The food poisoning was pervasive. Amin stayed only a few minutes, just long enough to tell the Jews he was expecting Jerusalem's answer by midnight. Little did he realize how the answer would come . . . .

*   *   *

"We've got storms ahead." The second pilot confirmed what the flight commander had noticed on the radar. They were flying over Kenya's Rift Valley, nearing the equator, and this was the summer storm season. Lightning streaked across the skies.

"Should we try to divert?" the second pilot inquired.

The navigator and flight engineer, huddling behind the pilots, recommended driving straight through at perhaps a higher altitude. The navigator spoke up. "We need to go to our destination as straight as possible to meet our timetable, and to conserve fuel."

The flight commander put his Herk in a climb to 26,000 feet and kept on course. Rain and hail from one dark thunderhead caused the Hercules to buck a bit but the Lockheed "flying truck" plowed ahead steadily as it had on countless other missions, a stable and sure platform, contemptuous of the weather.

The other Hercules, following in the loose trail formation, climbed to the higher altitude.

On the scopes of all four C-130s could be seen the huge Lake Victoria, source of the mighty Nile river. The lake lay dead ahead, and beyond it, on the western shores, Entebbe . . . .

*   *   *

In Nairobi, an "El Al Airline 707" landed at 10:26 p.m. Inside the airliner were four operating rooms and 30 medical personnel. The 707 taxied to the El Al area for refueling.

*   *   *

In Tel Aviv, an impatient Prime Minister Rabin could stand it no longer. He left his apartment and rushed to the Defense Ministry.

"What have we got?" he asked Shimon Peres.

"The 707 is orbiting Lake Victoria at 30,000 feet. The Herks should be over the lake soon."

Rabin pulled out a cigarette and looked intently at the six-inch square squawk box on a shelf over the bank of telephones. It was linked with Dan Shamron's radiophone by way of Benny Peled's high-flying 707.

*   *   *

High over Lake Victoria, General Peled and General Kuti Adam eyed the 707 command post radar scopes intently and

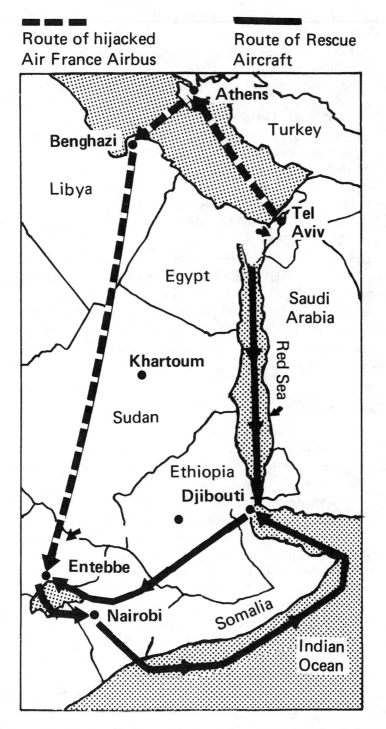

Route of hijacked Air France Airbus ---

Route of Rescue Aircraft ▬▬▬

Athens

Turkey

Benghazi

Libya

Tel Aviv

Egypt

Saudi Arabia

Khartoum

Red Sea

Sudan

Ethiopia

Djibouti

Entebbe

Nairobi

Somalia

Indian Ocean

The route of the hijacked A-300 (dotted line), and the rescue Hercules fleet (solid line)—shown in sketch at right.

listened on earphones for reports from the little armada that was six miles below them.

"The planes are over Jordan (Victoria)," Peled reported to Tel Aviv.

The 707 radar showed four blips approaching from the east. The first blip was at 1,000 feet and was descending at a moderate clip. The planes were coming in pairs. Two would land on Entebbe's long new international runway. The other two on the short, old runway.

The first Hercules broke the radio silence and made a routine-sounding request to land, identifying itself as a charter flight from an East African airline.

The Entebbe tower responded quickly and routinely. But before the approaching pathfinder Hercules came into its final approach, an eerie silence enveloped the control room.

Suddenly the radar scopes inside the Entebbe tower went "snowy." The 707 overhead had started jamming with its ECM. The four Entebbe controllers eased back from their scopes, waiting for the temporary interference to clear up.

* * *

The pilot of the pathfinder Hercules, locked on to Entebbe's radio beacon, cut his speed to 150 mph and descended gently through the swirls of mist over Lake Victoria. The windshield wipers flapped in a rhythmic beat. Suddenly, through the flurry fog patches, the lights of Entebbe's two and one-quarter mile long runway blazed up ahead. On his approach, the Herk was virtually skimming the lake, only 40 feet over the water.

Back in the hold, Yoni Netaniahu's men hoisted their battle gear. The bell rang out loudly—a giant alarm clock announcing touchdown was imminent. Yoni got into the right front seat of the Mercedes and poked his carbine through the window. Eight of his black-faced companions climbed aboard. Behind them the other commandos got into the Land Rovers. They pulled on their white sailor type caps, and turned down the brims.

The pilot of the lead Hercules, skimming at 20 feet over Lake Victoria's waters at 130 mph, got to within a few feet of the asphalt and pulled his power. Smacking down on the lip of the long runway, the Herk glided quietly (without the noisy prop reversal), and came to a stop in 1200 feet. From the cockpit, the flight commander pushed a button and opened the rear hatch to within a foot of the ground. Twelve Israeli commandos popped out and began placing flashlight torches alongside the runway lights. Shamron broke radio silence for a short report:

"I am on Yuval," he said.

* * *

Inside the old terminal, hostage Claude Silvers asked Bose—who was on guard duty at the front door along with the German woman—if he could cut off the overhead lights. The sick captives were having a hard time getting to sleep. Bose shrugged and walked away. Patrolling the halls inside were two Palestinians. Three other terrorists were asleep upstairs.

* * *

The lead Hercules taxied quietly with only two engines running, on down the long international runway, past the new terminal and turned onto a mile-long taxi strip crossing between the two runways, toward the old terminal. He eased his Herk to a stop, just about 4,500 feet from the old terminal and far out of ear-shot of the terrorist guards. The pilot lowered the rear ramp to the tarmac. When he cut his engines and looked back into the hold, the commandos were gone. Yoni's black Mercedes and the two Land Rovers had sped down the ramp in the direction of the old terminal. It was 11:03 p.m. Israel time . . . just past midnight in Entebbe. The plane's contingent of doctor/soldiers took up sentry posts around the C-130. Altogether, 33 of the unique physician/soldiers were aboard the four Herks. They were equally skilled in the use of the scalpel and the rifle.

Dan Shamron jumped out and directed a squad that moved on to take over the control tower. The "dead silence" of the place was overwhelming. Only the quiet buzzing of tropical insects and the noise of the Israeli vehicles violated the stillness of Entebbe. Was this a trap, perhaps?

Within a minute, the second Hercules—its propjet engines emitting a muffled whine . . . slipped in over Lake Victoria's waters and landed on the shorter parallel runway. The plane stopped behind a 200-foot rise that effectively hid it from the Ugandans in the new terminal.

Just as the third C-130 reached the end of the new runway on its approach, the Entebbe controllers panicked. Their excited voices could be heard over the Hercules radios. The airport lights suddenly went off, plunging the airport into darkness. This caused the pilot of Hercules Number 3 to land with a heavy plop, being shaken by the sudden disappearance of the bright lights. The controllers had cut the lights as they fled the tower and ran out into the night. The Israeli commandos found the control room deserted. Hercules Number 4 came in gracefully on the short runway, being guided by the portable torches set up by the first Israelis to land.

Overhead, Generals Kuti Adam and Benny Peled pushed their earsets tightly. In Tel Aviv, Yitzsak Rabin and Shimon Peres and 10 cabinet members and aides were hypnotized as they watched and listened to the squawk box. They could hear shooting in the distance through Dan Shamron's ground radio and they heard Shamron barking out commands to his various units from his command post near the control tower.

The crucial fight—the battle at the old terminal—was over in less than two minutes. Yoni's black-faced marksmen—sprinting from their Mercedes the last 200 feet on their rubber-soled boots—wiped out seven terrorists in an awesome display of speed, surprise and firepower. Two of the hostages were fatally wounded in the cross-fire, and several injured.

Shamron received word from Yoni's unit and passed it on over his radiophone. "Transgressor eliminated." In Tel Aviv, the smoke-filled office of Shimon Peres broke into shouts and back-slapping. A relieved General Moda Gur received hearty handshakes from all in the room.

Israel's white-hat commandos from the four planes were now spreading all over the airport and the Ugandans, seeing fireworks in every direction, were confused and didn't know which way to turn or fire. As Amin had revealed, over half of them had no weapons anyway.

Units from the second Hercules raced in their vehicles to the

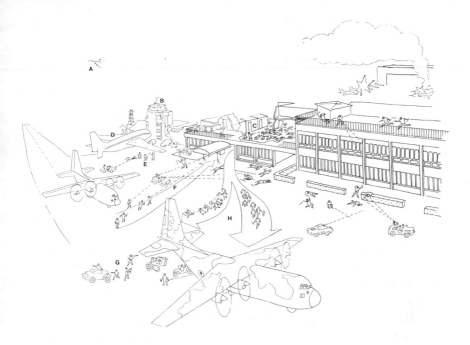

Sketch of Entebbe old terminal and tower. While the 707 communications aircraft circled high overhead (A), commandos (F) burst into the old terminal building (C), and killed guerillas while hostages tried to take cover. Israeli commandos met opposition from Ugandan soldiers (E) who were guarding the Air France Airbus (D), Ugandan marksmen in the old tower (B), killed the Israeli commander. Commandos led rescued hostages (H) out of terminal to the C-130s which had taxied up to the old terminal. Diversionary blasts were set off against Ugandan fighter aircraft at a hangar in the distance. (Sketch by Bob Karr).

The Entebbe airport has two runways and two terminals and control towers. The newer runway and control tower are at the left with the older, shorter runway at the right, with the old terminal and old control tower on taxi strip between the main runways. The Israeli Hercules landed on both runways. (Sketch by Bob Karr).

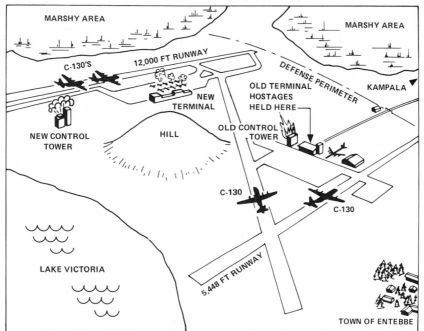

MIG fighters lined up at the far end of the old runway. The third group drove their half-track to the airport perimeter and braced for the arrival of troop reinforcements. "Reinforcements" never arrived, but a Ugandan truck coming in on a routine trip was blasted into the sky by Israeli bazookas.

At the old terminal, five civilians and four soldiers were wounded. Colonel Netaniahu himself was cut down by a sniper in the old tower when he went outside to direct the loading of the hostages aboard the Hercules.

The pilots aboard the four Hercules were talking to one another, now that one of the birds was being refueled from the Entebbe pits with one of the three pumps the Israelis brought with them.

But the gassing up was going slowly. The one Herk, after what seemed an eternity, was only one-quarter full. Shamron agreed with the crews that waiting for refueling at Entebbe was too risky. He ordered the crews to prepare for immediate takeoff. They would refuel in Nairobi. The Herks had adequate fuel anyway to get to Embakasi International Airport in Nairobi, just 50 minutes away.

*   *   *

Taxiing up to within 900 feet of the old terminal, the pilot of the first and second Hercules went hurriedly through their pre-flight check list. They could see coming across the taxi strip a stream of more than 100 liberated Jews, still confused yet jubilantly amazed at the miracle that was happening to them. They piled onto the Land Rovers and the stripped down Peugeot pickup. Others ran and walked hurriedly between the columns of Israeli troops, up the Hercules ramp into the plane. The wounded, including Pasco Cohen and Yoni Netaniahu, were brought aboard in stretchers and were placed in special litter equipment aboard that enabled the aircraft to be converted quickly into a flying ambulance. Doctors immediately went to work on the wounded, giving them blood transfusions on the spot. Special oxygen lines were also available . . . again part of the standard equipment aboard the C-130.

Within minutes, the first Hercules took off with its precious cargo and rendezvoused with General Peled's 707 over Lake Victoria. It was 11:43 p.m. Israel time, only 40 minutes after the first THUNDERBALL plane had touched down. The other three Herks followed shortly. The only items left behind were the three Israeli fuel pumps and the black Mercedes taxicab.

Aboard the C-130, Ilan Hartuv had a heavy heart. He kept thinking of his mother, Dora Bloch, now in Kampala's Mulango hospital.

Shortly after 1 a.m., while the wounded were being transferred from the Hercules to the waiting 707 hospital plane in Nairobi, the wire services were already teletyping to the world the first word of the Entebbe rescue.

In Tel Aviv, Prime Minister Rabin rang Golda Meir to give her the good news.

On the way to Israel, the lead Hercules was quiet and subdued. But one of the hostages, an old woman, kept repeating, "Ness! . . . Ness!" (A miracle! A miracle!)

Indeed it was a miracle, and for the Israeli Air Force and its valiant Hercules crewmen, the airlift portion of THUNDERBALL was especially gratifying, although, in their crew's eyes, nothing really out of the ordinary—merely a bit more distance and a bit more unusual than other flights.

Benny Peled was anything but blase, however. He was proud of the men of his transport squadron and their on-time navigational accuracy. The first Hercules, he noted, reached the Entebbe runway right on its ETA—estimated time of arrival—after a seven-hour flight through unfriendly skies, equal to a trip from Chicago to Panama.

The biggest message of the THUNDERBALL episode to Israel's potential enemies was quite dramatic: With its fleet of rugged, dependable Hercules—designed for long range missions as well as short field maneuverability—Jerusalem demonstrated its ability to move its forces swiftly in response to any attack . . . not only against aggressors nearby but even those far away.

Arriving back in Israel, the Herk crewmen received a thunderous reception at Ben Gurion Airport, as they returned the liberated hostages to their homeland. The huge throng welcomed everyone with outstretched arms and hoisted the C-130 fliers onto their shoulders in grateful appreciation. Israeli pride and joy exploded in a great outpouring of love.

It was July 4, 1976 and Israeli and American Jews were celebrating the American bicentennial. The President of B'Nai B'rith, David Bromberg, expressed the gratitude of the occasion.

"The IDF," he said, "has given the world a birthday gift on this occasion of America's 200th birthday . . . . The gift is the eleventh commandment: Thou shalt not bow down to terrorism."

The happy scene at Tel Aviv's Ben Gurion Airport as crowd marches one of the pilots around on their shoulders. The flyer's face was darkened on photo to disguise his identity. The C-130s brought the rescued hostages home to a triumphant welcome. (UPI)

MENDOZA'S MIRACLE

> It is possible now to bypass conventional arteries of steel rails or concrete ribbons, to build a bridge in the sky. It is this mission that the Hercules will best serve . . . .
>
> —Martin Caidin
>
> This road means the whole future for this part of the country . . . . There is room here for hundreds of farms on land that has never been cleared . . . .
>
> —Christina Del Aguila
> Tarapoto, Peru

"Viene el 'ercules?" It was a question that occupied the thoughts of Rodriquez de Mendoza, population 800, in Peru's Amazon back country. "Will the Hercules come?

*   *   *

For three years, the Indians of Mendoza, located in South America's lush heartland, had waited patiently for their Miracle.

Isolated behind the four-mile high Andes mountain chain,

315

Coming in to Mendoza's postage stamp runway, the Hercules pilots were confident they could make the landing okay . . .but it would be a bit hairy. Earlier that day, a C-47 landed and skidded into a ditch. (Lockheed)

Taxiing the rest of the way, the Hercules stopped half way down the strip and taxied on to the end where the crowd of townspeople waited expectantly. (Lockheed)

Mendoza was a Latin Brigadoon, centuries removed from Peru's capital city of Lima, 300 mountainous miles to the southwest.

But as May Day, 1965, dawned, the little village's fortunes seemed to be taking a decided turn for the better. On a scale of one to ten, Mendoza's mood was a high eight and rising. Barrels of bubbly native brew shimmered under the morning sun, ready for The Celebration. A barbecue was cooking on a side street. Palm fronds fluttered from the adobe huts. Womenfolk pulled out their most colorful finery.

The first sign that the Miracle was *really* about to happen came shortly after 1 o'clock when a two-engine Peruvian Air Force C-47 circled within the lap of mountains and came in to land on its pasture-like airstrip. The pilot touched his C-47 down a third of the way and immediately stomped on his brakes, trying to effect a "U" turn to avoid plunging into the jungle and the river beyond. The plane slalomed and made two ground loops, ending up in a ditch, with one wing tip stuck in the black Andean mud.

The Peruvian crewmen and four *Norteamericanos* emerged from the ancient Gooney Bird, none the worse for the unusual landing, and the word quickly spread through Rodriquez de Mendoza that the slim, crewcut gringo in the red shirt, holding a little box in one hand, was The Man Who Could Bring Them Their Miracle. An hour behind, the Miracle was winging over the Andes. It was aboard a big air machine, about which the people of Mendoza had heard many stories. The airplane was three times larger than the C-47, up to then the biggest man-made machine ever to come to Mendoza.

As soon as the muscular menfolk of Mendoza had grunted and shouted the C-47 out of the ditch, attention turned to the red-shirted gringo. Reynolds found the strip quite wet (from a day of boiling rain), a bit narrow (only 70 feet), and somewhat short (around 2,400 feet). Moreover, a range of mountains surrounded the village. It was not the ideal landing spot you would choose for a large aircraft such as the 70-ton, four-propjet Hercules. Expert flying would be necessary to get the heavily laden plane down accurately, to avoid the fate of the little C-47.

But slender, quiet Roy Reynolds, having flown the C-130

through countless short landings and takeoffs from similar dirt runways, was not at all dismayed, and his infectious grin was not lost to the villagers. After tramping over the springy grass, Roy Reynolds felt pretty confident. He walked to the edge of the strip and lit up a cigarette.

Even so, to the people of Mendoza—long denied their Miracle—there was a subdued mixture of hope and fear.

"Viene el 'ercules?" ("Will the Hercules come?")

It was a question that surfaced continually as the crowd swelled. Reynolds grinned and nodded constantly to the mayor and talked through a photographer interpreter. The crowd clung to his every word and movement.

Through the patches of cumulus clouds swirling across the valley, a speck loomed in the distance, from which came the unmistakable muffled whine of propjet engines.

"EL ERCULES VIENE! . . . EL ERCULES VIENE!" the Mendozans shouted, justling for the best vantage point.

The plane didn't come in immediately, but cruised at 2,000 feet inside the cup of mountains. Sixteen hundred eyes in Mendoza flitted back and forth between the gringo on the ground and the Hercules circling overhead.

Suddenly, a voice crackled from the little box in Reynolds' left hand, turned to the Herk's high frequency channel.

"This is Armstrong in Lockheed Eleven Thirty Echo. Do you read me, Roy?"

"Loud and clear, Ken. Go ahead."

The multitude grew silent.

"That strip looks awfully short, Roy. Whatta you think?"

"Little wet on top, Ken. Rained here all yesterday. But it's solid underneath. And it's long enough, well over 2,000 feet. But keep it straight coming in; it's pretty narrow. COME ON IN!"

Mendoza exploded in emotional pandemonium. The villagers hoisted the Miracle Man onto their shoulders, while singing and chanting, and marched him triumphantly around the field.

Overhead, Pilot Ken Armstrong winked at Peruvian Air Force Col. Frank Tweedle in the right hand seat, signaling for him to brace for a roller coaster descent on his great American scream machine. Armstrong banked the big bird 50 degrees and circled to the far end of the valley.

Awe shows in the eyes of Mendozan (top photo) as he watches bulldozer coming from the rear ramp of the Lockheed Hercules. Lower photo, operator backs bulldozer out of the Hercules as the people of Mendoza look on in wonder. (Vernon Merritt III)

The "Miracle man of Mendoza" was Lockheed's advance man, flight engineer Roy Reynolds, who was swept off his feet by the villagers when he called for the 382B Hercules to come on in and land on Mendoza's short, wet strip. (Vernon Merritt III)

Peruvian Air Force Colonel Frank Tweedle and Lockheed pilot Ken Armstrong receiving the emotional tribute of Mendozans after emerging from the Lockheed propjet. (Lockheed)

As the squat Hercules swooped down on its approach, its high slung wings and flaps made it appear all the world like a monstrous Jonathan Livingston Seagull. Mendozans held their breath, many crossing themselves in a prayerful gesture.

The doughnut soft tires bit into the turf with a gentle thud, leaving a track six inches deep. Traveling down the bumpy strip, the Flying Whale's elastic wings flapped up and down four feet. As Armstrong reversed the props, the plane slammed to a stop only 900 feet from touchdown.

The crowd, now chanting, cheered and gave out lusty whoops, swarming toward the machine as it taxied to the side.

"Caramba! Un milagro!" (Heavens! A Miracle!)

As the propellers stopped whirling, Colonel Tweedle stepped out into a flurry of *abrazos*, being hoisted onto the shoulders of the men. Now the crowd was singing the national anthem, chanting and crying.

"GET SENOR ARMSTRONG, ALSO," Tweedle shouted.

The Lockheed pilot was plucked from the plane's steps, and accorded equal honors with his Peruvian co-pilot. Filled with spontaneous emotion, the sobbing citizens of Rodriquez de Mendoza broke into more singing. They poured their *cerveza* brew on one another and on the plane.

But the best was yet to come. The Herk's rear hatch was lowered to form a ramp. Mendozans looked on reverently as Marcos Leon Roldan, the government's tractor instructor from Lima, drove the eight-ton dozers down the ramp, out of the belly of the big bird.

It was a great moment for Rodriquez de Mendoza, and there were few dry eyes. Congressman Isaias Grandez, who came in on the Hercules, mounted the bulldozer and made an impassioned speech, bringing greetings from the President of Peru, Fernando Belaunde Terry. These tractors, the Congressman said, would enable Mendoza to build an important link in Peru's 1,000 mile long *Carretera*, the marginal highway skirting the fertile Andes/Amazon plateau. Peru's highway, to connect with similar highways in Ecuador and Bolivia, would help create on the east side of the Andes "a new environment rejuvenated by modern transportation, energy and medicine." The *Carretera* would have a connecting link to Lima and other cities on the coast. In Lima,

President Belaunde was optimistic. "If the Mendoza section of the *Carretara* is finished by July, it will be due almost entirely to this aircraft," he said.

To Mendozans, long denied hopes for a better life, being cut off from the developed part of their nation by the towering Andes, the graders meant a road to market for their tea and coffee, sugar cane, tobacco, cotton and cattle. Many products they had not even tried to raise, for lack of a market. But the significance went far deeper. Hope, and a brighter future. That's what the arrival of the Hercules with the bulldozer meant to Mendoza.

*   *   *

The Hercules was introduced to Peru's over-the-mountains montana land four years earlier, after a study showed that the nation's treasure chest of natural resources in the interior could be tapped only with a network of roads. To ship the necessary road building equipment by barge required a two-month, 7,000-mile trip from Lima—up the Pacific, through the Panama Canal, south on the Atlantic and then up the Amazon through Brazil. A flying truck such as the Hercules could reduce this vital job to 66 minutes.

When Peru appealed to the United States, five "A" model Hercules came winging from the Panama Canal Zone—the famed Blue Eagles of the U.S. Air Force's 773rd Troop Carrier Squadron, 463rd Wing, Sewart Air Force Base, Tennessee.

Led by Captain Lewis Senter's inaugural C-130 flight to Tarapoto on August 2, 1961, 300 tons of the heavy equipment were airlifted to Juanjui, Tarapoto and Yurimaguas. The Peruvian Air Force Chief of Staff, Lieutenant General G. Van Oordt, credited the airlift with "hastening this road-building project by three years, and opening up this previously inaccessible area."

The USAF commander of the operation, Lieutenant Colonel Frank L. Weatherbee, was enthusiastic, also. "The success of this mission proves two things conclusively," he said. "We can operate from unprepared strips if we have to, and our planes can be used to as great an advantage for peace as they can for war."

*   *   *

The use of C-130s in the 1960s—on lease from the U.S. Air Force—cut months off Peru's road building programs in the Amazon interior. Top photo, the scene at Tarapoto was typical. Cargo is offloaded from plane which had just hopped over the Andes from Lima. Cargo is offloaded from C-130s at other Peruvian communities in lower photo. (Lockheed)

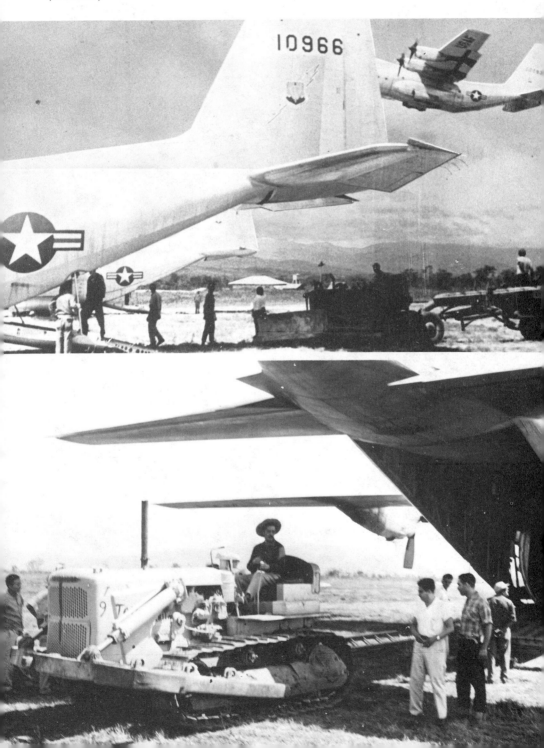

When GTE's Spacenet II communications satellite was fired into orbit Nov. 9, 1984, from Kourou, French Guiana — on the "hump" of South America — it marked the bird's second "flight". First boost into the air for the RCA-built spacecraft occurred earlier when it was transported over 2,800 statute miles inside a Transamerica Airlines Lockheed L-100-30 airfreighter. The flight, reaching altitudes of up to 28,000 feet, took the multi-million dollar satellite from Philadelphia International Airport to Cayenne, the capital city of French Guiana. In photo above, French gendarmes keep eye on satellite as it is offloaded at the Cayenne Airport. The loading of Spacenet II and support equipment in Philadelphia took around an hour while the offloading in Cayenne took even less time. An earlier L-100 flight took electronic ground test station and command equipment to Cayenne.

Every day, in scores of countries around the world, Lockheed Hercules airlift equipment to help build roads, explore for oil or otherwise develop nations. It has helped Abu Dhabi launch a "green revolution," has enabled the Philippines to speed up . development of its southern territories, and has helped Peru reduce the price of fish for the people in its interior regions. Malaysia utilizes its fleet of Hercules to bridge East and West Malaysia, while Denmark has put its C-130s to work supporting the scientific development of Greenland. Thanks to the Hercules, which airlifted brood catfish from Arkansas, the citizens of the Azores now have a good protein diet during winter months when the Atlantic Ocean is too rough for fishing. Italy utilizes its C-130s to fight forest fires. Indonesia's 3,000 mile long archipelago of islands are linked in a strong C-130 aerial network.

Natural resource extraction in Alaska, Canada and across remote regions of the Middle East, Africa and South America has been speeded up enormously with the help of the Herk.

The Trans-Gabon Railroad, the Trans-Alaska Pipeline, the Trans-Amazon Highway and Peru's Trans-Andes Oil Pipeline all owe a debt of gratitude to the logistic might of the powerful propjet.

The airfreighter, now being operated by dozens of Third World countries on the move, has proven to be a valuable economic vehicle, a "flying truck" that gives even the smallest of nations a big edge in pulling themselves up economically.

Take the mountainous, landlocked Republic of Bolivia. Taking delivery of the first of two C-130s on July 23, 1977, Bolivia lost no time putting it to work. Hurdling the Andes from La Paz, the lone Hercules—in a two-week airlift—transported 523,000 pounds of trucks and earth-moving machinery to Rurrenabaque down in its lush Beni agricultural region, enabling construction to begin immediately on a sugar cane mill. Cargo included 14-ton earth movers, 17 ½-ton D-85 Caterpillars and 14-ton D-6 Caterpillars.

Another big job for the Bolivian Hercules is airlifting farm products out of the agricultural provinces—formerly difficult due to a lack of railroads—to La Paz and to other countries. On its first return trip to the U.S., the Bolivian C-130 had aboard commercial cargo—35,000 pounds of ladies shoes which it airlifted from Montevideo, Uruguay, to Miami.

A similar success story has occurred in the Philippines. Receiving its first L-100 aircraft in April, 1973, with two subsequent aircraft going into service in July and August, Manila put its Herks to work immediately. After four months, the three Herks airlifted more than four and one-half million pounds of cargo and personnel in 383 sorties. Agricultural products—corn, rice, tomatoes and bananas—were hauled from areas of plenty to places of scarcity. In the same manner, millions of fingerlings, seedlings and plants were transported over the nation, in support of its Green Revolution.

Thanks to the Hercules, thousands of books were distributed quickly to school children in the southern Philippines. The nation also utilized the Herks to transport cargo, equipment and personnel to the south for massive construction programs.

"The Hercules," declared an appreciative Philippine Air Force Lt. Col. Manuel R. Estrada, "is the greatest Lockheed invention of this generation for countries such as ours, that are developing. It is a big flying truck that has helped tremendously in bringing together our country of 7,000 islands."

The French-speaking Republic of Gabon, population 500,000—on Africa's west coast—has found the Hercules to be a Godsend.

"Gabon is just starting to boom and build," declared an official in Libreville. "It could be compared to the U.S. 30 years ago. The country has abundant natural resources. However, we have no national highways or railroads to connect the towns of our nation. The Hercules serves as our aerial railroad, enabling us to leap over the dense rain forests with heavy equipment and supplies." In 1976, an entire supermarket was hauled by Hercules from Libreville to Franceville, deep in the interior. In a major leap forward, modern telephone systems are being installed in Gabon and Nigeria, and most of the components are being airlifted to outlying communities by Hercules.

*   *   *

Nowhere has the nation-building muscle of the Lockheed propjet been better illustrated than across the northern reaches of Canada, including the High Arctic.

Canadian soldiers load building supplies into boxcar-size cargo compartment of Hercules during airlift from Thule, Greenland, to Ellesmere Island weather station. Lower photo, New Zealand crewmen and Nepalese offload roll of copper wiring at Katmandu, Nepal. New Zealand sent 30,000 pounds of equipment to Nepal for a joint Nepal-New Zealand government dairy factory. (CF, RNZAF)

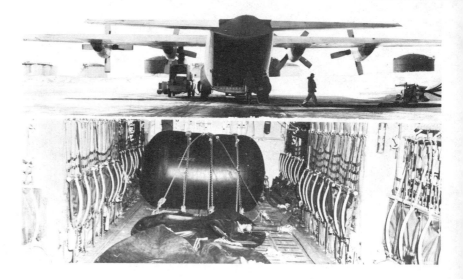

Hauling bulk fuel to remote construction and radar sites in northern Alaska, northern Canada and Greenland is a major role for the Hercules. In top two photos, Canadian Forces Hercules fitted its Hercules with collapsible fuel tanks to resupply Arctic weather stations near top of the world. The Canadians installed five 800-gallon butyl rubber "blubber bags" measuring seven feet long and four feet across. The tanks enabled Herks to airlift 1,120 gallons more fuel each trip than when fuel was carried in drums. Top photo, fuel is pumped into tanks. Another method of hauling bulk fuel is shown in Hercules at bottom—the installation of four 1800-gallon steel tanks set up on special platforms. (Lockheed)

In northern Quebec, 600 miles north of Montreal, an L-100 "flying truck" supports construction of the 16 billion dollar James Bay hydroelectric project in a spectacular fashion.

La Societe d'Energie de la Baie James purchased a Hercules in 1973 to provide an aerial bridge into the vast wilderness. The James Bay complex of reservoirs, dikes, dams and powerhouses—stretching 400 miles from Caniapiscau to Fort George—is expected to double Quebec's hydroelectric production capacity by the time it is completed around 1985.

In the first year, the single Lockheed airfreighter logged more than 5,000 rugged hours of night and day "bush country" flying, hauling equipment and supplies into remote gravel strips. Flare pots alongside the strips guided pilots making night landings. In February, 1974, the plane made its first landing on an ice runway, the 42-inch thick La Grand-3 camp.

Workers manning the construction camps across the spectacular territory look to the Hercules as their link with the world. Some 1,100 laborers at a dam site on the Caniapiscau River, for instance, consume 15,000 pounds of foodstuffs a day, burn 17,000 gallons of fuel and use up to 40,000 pounds of explosives. All of these items—plus the camp's monthly supply of beer, 3,000 gallons of it—go into Caniapiscau by Hercules.

Manned by two crews flying 12 hour shifts around the clock, the "Energie" aircraft makes 12 round trips a day to the camps from Schefferville. Turnaround time for loading and unloading averages only 23 minutes.

In a one-week period in July, 1977, the James Bay Herk—designated CF-DFX—made 51 flights from Schefferville to Caniapiscau, bearing 1.7 million pounds of diversified cargo—feed, fuel, pipes, motorboats, explosives and firefighting equipment.

The swift buildup of construction activity in 1977 on Caniapiscau, La Grand and Eastman Rivers (totaling 17,000 workers) resulted in the call for cargo haul contract help from Pacific Western Airlines and Canadian Forces. Both organizations carried out the job with—what else?—Hercules airfreighters!

"There is no doubt," *Canadian Aviation* magazine reported, "that the Hercules is earning its keep" in northern Quebec.

On the other side of Canada—in the nation's vast Northwest Territories stretching up to and including the High Arctic—Pacific

Western Airlines is making airfreight history with its three L-100-20 Hercules and its new L-100-30 Super Hercules, which are dedicated to supporting Canada's oil and gas industry. When the Arctic runways turn mushy during summer months, PWA diverts its L-100s on the world market as tramp freighters, hauling oil rigs into exploration sites in Africa and the Middle East.

* * *

PWA's director of Hercules and resupply operations, Bill Howie, described the "portability" of the C-130 in the Arctic in an interview with Cathay Pacific's "Cargo Clan" magazine:

"We send in a small plane—usually an Otter—to check the ice for a new strip. He literally drills through. The strip may be absolutely barren . . . . a flag on someone's map. The ice strip may be on land or on water. If the strip needs to be 'scarified' (roughed up to increase the friction), we may have to send some sort of a Cat in overland to even out the strip. But sometimes, if the ice checks out, the Herks can go right in. The first pathfinder Herk may carry a Cat to fix up the strip or a shack (trailer) for the new inhabitants to live in, plus navigational aids to help the rest of the planes land. Within a few plane trips, a camp emerges where there was nothing but barren ice previously. We run a 24-hour operation, so the build-up of a camp is very quick."

* * *

As mentioned earlier, the civic action role of the Hercules transport has been particularly noteworthy in South America, where eight nations operate the Lockheed propjet. Brazil utilizes its Hercules in numerous interior development programs, including the construction of the Trans-Amazon Highway and as the National Mail Service transport, linking hundreds of communities in its vast territory.

As in the other countries of South America, C-130 airlift was pioneered by the C-130 units serving with the U.S. Air Force's Southern Command at Howard AFB, Canal Zone. In the cooperative ventures, American Hercules and crews carried out government-requested civic airlifts with the nation paying for the fuel.

The airlifts by USAF Herks provided a tremendous eye-opener across South America and eight nations followed suit by buying and putting into operation their own Hercules fleets.

"With their Hercules," said Bill Campbell, Lockheed-Georgia export sales representative, "the air forces of South America are really the 'railroads of the interior.' Ninety percent of their missions are for country development, or long range logistics."

Campbell, who served as a Lockheed technical representative in Brazil, explained the rationale:

"The terrain in South America doesn't lend itself to highway construction or railroad construction. Once you get out of the major cities, the terrain is very inhospitable. Road building is tough. If you are lucky, you can make a quarter of a kilometer a week."

"Thus," said Lockheed sales representative Riq Vizurraga, a native of Peru, "until they get better roads and railroads—maybe 10 to 15 years from now—the Air Force does the job with its Hercules."

Campbell recalls weekly Brazilian Air Force Hercules flights into Indian communities in the jungles. "Take Xingu. Every week the BAF flies into Xingu—2,000 feet of dirt. There are no beacons, no navigational aids, just a dirt strip hacked out of the jungle. The Air Force has set up at Xingu a field hospital—a commissary— which they staff with BAF personnel. They re-supply it weekly with beans and rice and all commodities and medicines."

"They fly out of Rio—four hours and thirty minutes over the jungle. There are a few peaks and the navigators have to be exceptionally well qualified. They navigate by sextant and bearings from distant stations. Areas like Xingu have no distinguishing features. The first time I went to Xingu, I couldn't see that field at all until we turned on final. There were two or three hills there. The pilot picked the second hill and flew between it and the third one. When we got behind it and looked, there was the strip. You made a sharp bend on final and landed. It's just wide enough—60 feet—to turn around on. Of course, the Hercules is one of the few airplanes that easily ground maneuvers in reverse. From a parked position, you can back up."

Then there's Boavista, which is so far north in Brazil you are closer to Miami than to Rio. There is an outpost there, and to develop it, the BAF flew in a D-7 caterpillar weighing 35,000 pounds, also some additional road building and mining equipment. It has become a significant manganese area, and the entire development in that area was opened by BAF Hercules.

Campbell agrees with people who point to the Hercules as the ideal vehicle to develop the potentially rich interior of South America. "Hauling a 35,000 pound bulldozer to a remote site is a job for the C-130. There's no plane that can do it except the Hercules. And when you land, you don't need ground support. The Herk's got its own."

In some countries—trying to decide which is the most economical, building roads or buying aircraft to provide an aerial highway—the decision often has gone to aircraft.

In the Andean country of Colombia, for instance, studies carried out by the Colombian Air Force and Satena Airline, concluded that it was far more economical to acquire the C-130—taking into account its flexibility, capacity and speed—than to build highways through the treacherous mountains at a staggering cost. The landing strips for the C-130, it was concluded, would not be expensive, since they could operate into the same landing ports as the smaller C-47.

Following this study, Colombia acquired two used C-130Bs from Canada, when that nation stepped up to the "E" model (and later the H).

In making its decision to acquire C-130s, Colombia also considered the plane's potential in developing the cattle industry in the nation's Eastern Plains. Furthermore, the C-130 could be used, officials felt, to carry out total nation-wide aerial mapping—a task pioneered by the U.S. C-130s on loan.

In Peru, the coming of its own fleet of L-100-20 Hercules has been a big factor in interior oil exploration and the construction of an oil pipeline across the Andes to the Pacific. In another major accomplishment, the Hercules has helped Peru cut the price of fish in remote regions "over the mountains" from 50 cents per kilo to 18 cents. Flying for the Ministry of Fishery, the Herks airlift 20 ton loads of frozen fish from Lima to Aycucho in the interior. Leaping over the Andes in one hour, the Hercules is far superior to the truck, which requires a laborious, 22-hour trip, snaking through the high Andes with only a four-ton load. Thanks to the

Oil exploration and oilfield development are major roles for the Hercules. Top photo, Pacific Western Airlines L-100-20 pictured near oil well in Canada's far north. Lower photo, Southern Air Transport L-100-20 is seen at a remote base in Libya, on contract work for an oil company. (Lockheed)

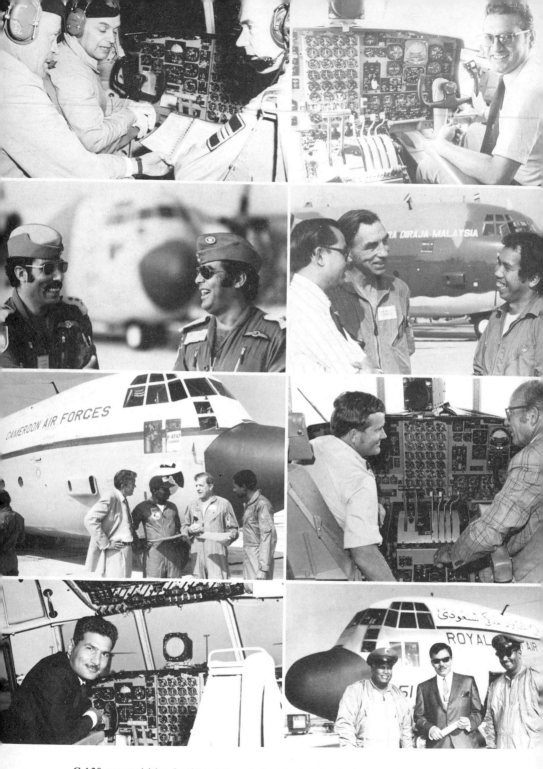

C-130 crews visiting Lockheed-Georgia to take training in the operation of their new aircraft afforded an opportunity to view the truly international flavor of the worldwide fleet of Hercules. Crewmen and officials representing eight nations are depicted above. Left column, top to bottom: Sweden, Abu Dhabi, Cameroon, Iran. Right column, top to bottom: Ecuador, Malaysia, Australia and Saudi Arabia. (Lockheed)

aerial fish lift, Peru is building freezer plants in mountainous Andes towns to improve the diets of the people.

In August of 1977, the commander of the Peruvian Air Force summed up the results of the seven years of Hercules operations. The fleet of L-100-20 Hercules had carried out, in the area of civic action, the following program between Lima, Trujillo, Tarapoto, Yurimaguas, Iquitos and Puerto Maldonada: 14,250,500 kilograms of cargo transported, plus approximately 6,000 passengers. In the area of commercial operations, mainly supporting petroleum exploration and development, the Air Force hauled 69,460,980 kilograms of cargo and 21,550 passengers with its L-100s. Disaster relief flights were carried out during this period to Guatemala and Romania.

In Peru—as in nearly all of the nations of South America—the importation of purebred livestock, mainly cattle, has been speeded up tremendously by the use of its Hercules. In one period, in the 1970s, 35,000 head of cattle were flown into Peru over a six months period to replenish breeding stock in its Amazon regions.

The C-130's role in the economic development of emerging nations was illustrated in a unique way in Ecuador. There, two U.S. Air Force Hercules, flying out of the Panama Canal Zone, airlifted heavy road graders into Sucua, home of the former headhunting Jivaro Indians. The Jivaros, who have taken up farming and cattle raising, put the graders to cutting roads, enabling them to move their cattle and produce to market.

After the C-130s had delivered their final loads into the dirt strip in the Andes, the former headhunters presented the two crews with 10-foot blowguns and feathered head-dresses.

Summing up the impact of the airlift, one of Ecuador's newspapers declared: "The town of Sucua appreciated the Hercules crewmen's effort in transporting the road equipment . . . . They have demonstrated the greatness of their country."

V

VIETNAM, THE SUPREME TEST

The C-130 is literally
priceless (in Vietnam)
    Senator Stuart Symington

It can land on those short
strips, take a lot of
firepower and it still
keeps going!

    —Vice-President Hubert Humphrey

VIGNETTES FROM VIETNAM: THE C-130's FINEST HOUR

> One of the American heroes of the Vietnam war is not a man but a machine—a snub-nosed whale-tailed airplane that looks as if it would be lucky to get off the ground . . . .
>
> —TIME

> I fought the Vietnam war in the C-130 . . . best flying in the world.
>
> —Lt. Col. Tim Brady

> The troops and crews liked the C-130s . . . with one exception. The C-130A was a whing ding whistler, noisy as hell. But for an operating aircraft, you couldn't beat it.
>
> —Lt. Col. Joseph Bilotta

It was December of 1965 and the conflict in Vietnam had escalated into a major shooting war. U.S. Marine Corps Captain George A. Baker III—taking pen in hand with artillery rounds booming all around his front line post—dashed off a letter to his cousin in Marietta, Georgia, Ann Fetner:

"Please tell everyone there at Lockheed thanks for the C-130 Hercules! Several times in the past year, we would have been in serious trouble without that aircraft. During the monsoon, when the ships couldn't get in, the C-130s came in. When the VC blew bridges on both sides of our artillery unit, the C-130s flew in ammo and chow. They are also used exclusively for mail (both ways), and a wonderful ticket out of this hell hole for recuperation in Bangkok, Okinawa and Japan. The possessor of a wonderful safety record, she is somewhat our guardian angel."

During the Vietnam war, the C-130 and its aircrews really came into their own, writing an incredible "can do" chapter of logistic heroism. By the end of 1967, just two and a half years after the heavy fighting began, the U.S. Air Force's tactical airlift fleet in Vietnam—led by its indominable workhorse Hercules—broke the world record for sustained airlift, two and one-third million tons set in the Berlin lift of 1948-49. Six months before, in July of 1966, the 315th Air Division's C-130/C-123 fleet had hauled more than 697,000 tons of materiel and personnel, surpassing the Korean War airlift which up to then was the greatest *combat* airlift in history.

In carrying out the Southeast Asia mission, the growing fleet of camouflaged C-130s, sneering at the short, rough strips and defying the elements—became *the* lifeline of the entire American effort. The 463rd Tactical Airlift Wing's deputy commander for operations, Col. David R. Lewis, put the war in perspective when he wrote in August of 1966: "Airlift is indispensable to our efforts. Without it we would surely be defeated . . . .The C-130 fleet lifts a good two-thirds of all the tonnage moved by air within RVN. It operates in all types of airfields, in all types of weather both day and night. It has provided such mobility to Army units (including the First Air Cav Division) that I understand the 'Big Red One' is considering changing its name to 'First Air Infantry Division.' "

Paul Hemphill, a columnist for the *Atlanta Journal*, hitched Herk rides all over Southeast Asia and returned to Atlanta singing the praises of the transport. "People would shudder to see what they do with that plane in Vietnam. They're working it to death. They fly those Herks into places where you woudn't imagine they could and it seems they fly them almost until the wings fall off. *It's one helluva airplane.*" Lt. Col. Carl E. Stone agreed. "Never before in the history of airlift has an aircraft been pushed so far," he said.

While airlift was its major role, the Herk quickly found many other outlets for its many splendored capabilities. Within time,

Troops grouped to board C-130 for flight to new battle zone. (USAF)

The C-130's ability to land and take off from short, unprepared strips made it a valuable airlift transport in Vietnam. As Lt. Col. Joseph Bilotta said, "We landed on 2700-foot runways of PSP with full loads of howitzer shells, mortar shells, ammunition and supplies. We went in at a steep angle with just a' little power off but at minimum air speed. We tried to hit near the end of the runway and then put on brakes and reverse props." (USAF)

dozens of ancillary roles were added to its primary job . . . such missions as med-evac, airborne command and control, reconnaissance, and rescue and recovery, including the air-to-air refueling of helicopters with the new HC-130Ps then moving into the USAF inventory.

It launched reconnaissance and electronic counter measure (ECM) drones, nursed entire Marine (and Navy) fighter wings across the Pacific with air-to-air refueling and became the world's champion "litterbug"—delivering over a billion psychological warfare leaflets over North Vietnam by the end of 1967. As a flare launcher, the C-130 was assigned "hunter-killer" missions—selecting enemy targets, dropping flares to illuminate the target area, then serving as forward air controller to direct fighter-bomber strikes. The development of the gunship role for the C-47 and C-119 led naturally to the C-130 and it became a night-time terror for convoys of Communist trucks venturing down the Ho Chi Minh trail.

But as never before in history, tactical airlift as performed by the C-130—"trash hauling" as the crews proudly boasted—was the make-or-break factor in the Vietnam war. "In my opinion," stated Col. Lewis, "it's the only airplane; if it had been grounded, the war would have ended. The Army couldn't have gotten where they were going. Nobody could have gotten where they were going. You could have grounded the F-4 and the war would have kept going, but if you grounded the C-130, the war would have had to end. People couldn't have gotten around. We hauled people ten miles, from one airfield to another, because they couldn't get there by land."

Senator Stuart Symington put it another way after a tour in 1966: "The C-130 is literally priceless in a country with practically no railroad capacity and so many at least periodically interdicted roads."

The key C-130 commander in the Far East, the 315th Air Division's Col. Charles Howe, was confident from the beginning that his fleet of Lockheeds would get the job done in Vietnam. An old hand in Hercules-flying from his days as c.o. of the 322nd Air Division in Europe, Howe personally led the first C-130s into the rough strips in India's high Himalayas in late 1962. The square-jawed colonel did the same thing in Vietnam. He took fully-loaded Herks into 2,500-foot strips in emergency situations. But he negotiated with the 7th Air Force people, the operational bosses in Vietnam, to give his C-130 flyers another 500 feet of runway. "I told them it would be a little easier if they'd put another 500 feet so long as they were blowing up the jungle anyway, and not push the airplane against the maximum wall of its performance capabilities all the time. I told them, 'Give us another 500 feet and we can do it with ease.'"

Colonel Howe would put a C-130 down into a Vietnam strip at a descent rate of 300 feet a minute, flying it right into the ground, then go into reverse. Virtually a controlled crash.

The C-130's role in Vietnam was indeed its finest hour. As H.G. Maxwell reported, the airplane "was subjected to overweight takeoffs, fighter type flying down in amongst the hills, thumped onto anything even remotely like a runway, dropped heavy equipment from any altitude starting about five feet and on up, was shot full of holes—in general, pushed right to her limit—and then some. The difference between disaster and success was so often the ability of the C-130 and her crews to deliver, despite the odds stacked against them."

*   *   *

The story of the Hercules in Vietnam is one that can best be told in the words of the people who were there. Here follow verbatim accounts of the various missions, situations and activities. In most cases, the people are identified with the ranks and positions they held in Vietnam. In some cases, interviews conducted at bases in the U.S. list their present location and current ranks:

C-130 DUTY IN VIETNAM: "BEST FLYING EVER"

**Lt. Col. Tim Brady, Squadron Commander,
32nd Tactical Airlift Squadron, Little Rock AFB, Arkansas**

Vietnam was the first big test of tactical airlift and the C-130 in particular. Many of us were based at CCK (in Taiwan). We'd go in-country (in Vietnam) and spend 15 days based at Cam Rahn Bay or Tuy Hoa, then come back to CCK for two/three days and

Preparing to take off on the biggest paratroop drop of the Vietnam War, C-130s of the 315the Air Division line up on a taxi strip at Tan Son Nhut AB, Republic of Vietnam (top photo). Vietnamese paratroopers (inset) float down over drop zone, lower photo. (USAF)

Army infantryman watches as rations cascade into drop zone at A Loui airstrip in A Shau Valley. The 1st Cavalry Division (Airmobile) needed food after several days of fighting, so C-130s were called in. Lower photo, USAF C-130 makes a PLADS (Parachute Low Altitude Delivery System) drop of a bundle of supplies at An Khe. (USAF) then go back in-country. There was a lot of minor complaining at the time, but in retrospect, it was the best flying I've ever done in my life.

In any synopsis of the American efforts in Vietnam, about the only success story you're going to find is in tactical airlift. C-130s were really the lifeline of Vietnam, particularly in places such as Khe Sanh and Kantum. They brought in the bullets and food and everything else that the forward locations needed. If they couldn't land it, they'd airdrop it. If they couldn't LAPES* it in, they'd CDS* it in from high altitude.

Col. Bruce Mosley,
Commander, Altus AFB, Oklahoma

Flying the C-130 in Vietnam was just absolutely super. We'd go in those 2,500 foot strips. And we felt like we were doing some good work, mostly carrying supplies, food and mail and a lot of ammo. The troops were always happy to see the C-130s come in. Usually the men would take us to the chow hall. You could trade for anything. We'd take them beer, some special kind of food. We'd be coming out of the Philippines and we'd take them tangerines, pineapples and the like.

We hauled doughnut-shaped bladders full of gas, JP4 fuel. If there was no ground handling equipment, they'd just roll them off the ramp, hook a chain to them and haul them off with a jeep.

We hauled refugees back and forth. I've carried as many as 250 people on one flight . . . 18 to 20 people in the cockpit. Sometimes in evacuating areas, RVN troops came aboard with their entire families. We didn't try to split them up.

The C-130 really showed it could do its stuff in Vietnam. The guys that flew it loved it because it was a forgiving airplane and took good care of us. The guys got to know it so well, you could go into some little short field and have a problem with it and they'd go out and jerry rig it so it would work well enough to get started again. Some cases we had to do what was called "buddy starts"—have another C-130 pull up in front of you. His prop blast

---

*LAPES stands for low altitude parachute extraction system. CDS stands for container delivery system in which cargo is paradropped from higher altitudes.

would start your engine. Or wind-mill taxi starts . . . run down the runway and start the engine if the runway was long enough. There was always something you could do . . . .

FLYING INTO THE SOFT FIELDS OF VIETNAM

T/Sgt. William E. Collins,
Loadmaster, 41st Military Airlift Squadron, Charleston AFB, S.C.

The most beautiful thing about the 130 was it was so beautifully overpowered. You could leave some place that was bad and just hang it right on its props and be gone . . . .

One of the greatest experiences of life, though, is takeoff down a real short runway where you're not sure you're going to make it and about halfway down the runway you look over in front of you and there is an Army chopper crossing in front of you. The "pucker factor" goes *very* high *very* fast. Pull back on the stick and pray a bunch.

Lt. Col. Tim Brady

We had C-130s go into 2,200 foot fields. Shortest I ever landed on was 2,500 feet. 3,500 was the average short field we went into. You could go into a 3,500-foot strip with a good load . . . 130,000 pounds gross weight, or so.

It was a challenge. That's what made flying so good over there, because you were flying the airplane to its maximum capability and you were flying yourself to your maximum capability. When you put those two together, it's a combination you'll remember for the rest of your life. Just beautiful.

Maj. Billy Morrell,
USAF C-130 Pilot

I had one B-4 bag that I lived out of for nine months. I lived where the airplane was and that was all over Southeast Asia. It wouldn't be unusual to leave early in the morning from CCK, (Ching Chuan Kang) Taiwan, have an "early bird" breakfast in Okinawa, eat lunch in the Philippines, drink a Coke in Da Nang, South Vietnam, and enjoy a steak dinner in Bangkok, Thailand.

The HH-3E helicopter, the "Jolly Green Giant," comes up for a feeding of fuel from HC-130P rescue/refueling Hercules version during Vietnam mission. With air-to-air refueling by the Hercules, helicopters during the Vietnam conflict were able to fly into North Vietnam from orbit positions to pick up downed pilots. (USAF)

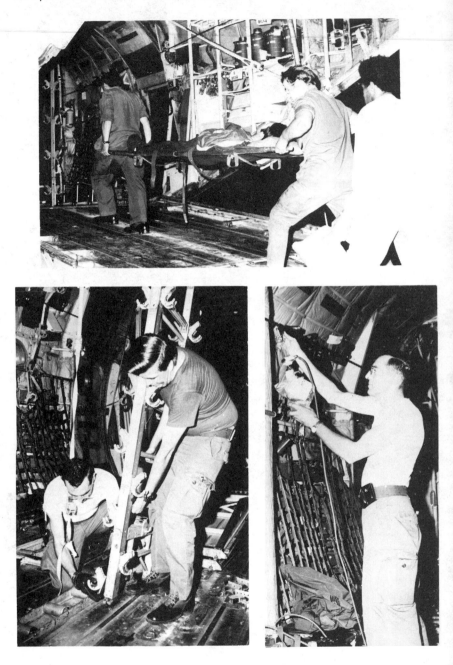

Army medical technicians rush a litter patient aboard C-130 at Pleiku Air Base. The Hercules was diverted from a cargo mission to the evacuation assignment, and reconfigured in flight (photos below) by medical technicians. Lower left, technicians set up stanchions for stretchers, and right, set up breathing apparatus of an in-flight liquid-to-gaseous oxygen converter. (USAF)

S/Sgt. William E. Collins

You never knew what the day held for you, day to day in Vietnam. You might end up with a combat essential move, where you'd shuttle between two places all day. Or you might just get a general garbage run. But the day could change character at any point with a call from the 315th Air Division Headquarters, which we called "mother." The official name was "Hilda." We called it "mother" over the air, which is interesting because my mother's name is Hilda.

Lt. Col. Joseph Bilotta, former MAC squadron commander and former assistant deputy for operations, 315th Air Division

We had a 130 down, needed two engines. We loaded up at Saigon and put in two engines. We flew in about 50 miles and they said, "Get in as close as you can to the field. We have North Viet machinegunners on the outer perimeter." The field was still open. They said, "We'll cut the lights on when you get close." So we went on in. I was driving and I took a look . . . those rockets . . . 50 caliber machine gun bullets right in front of us . . . beautiful. Didn't bother me. They weren't hitting us. But you could see those tracers coming at you like Roman candles. I said to the crew, "Hey, come take a look."

We came in at about 500 feet and we came right in to the end of the airfield power off, almost dead power and with minimum light. Instead of a thousand feet, we came in low. The lower you came, the safer you were; the further off, they could see you. They shot the hell at us, but they never did hit us.

Lt. Col. Tim Brady

We went into a Vietnam airfield on the southern coast where there was a huge crown in the runway; the airfield was shaped like a half moon almost.

There was absolutely no control facility at the field. We landed and taxied off the runway and kicked off our load. The taxiway that joined the runway was about in the center and below the crown. We checked the approach and as we taxied out, didn't see

C-130s take off at 15-second intervals from Rhein-Main Air Base, Germany. (USAF/SSGT. L. Emmett Lewis, Jr.)

anything. Just started to pull on the runway when . . . WHOOOO . . . here came another 130 right over the rise. He had landed and we couldn't see him because he was below the crown. Another couple of seconds we would've taxied out on the runway and would have bought the farm for sure.

**Lt. Col. Elmer H. Cryer, Commander,
774th Squadron, 463rd Troop Carrier Wing**

Some of the remote bases are so small that the C-130 is required to circle while another is being unloaded. Runways often are not much more than smoothed-over fields obscured by thick dust in the dry season and filled mud in the monsoon. Many of the airfields with runways of 4,000 feet must be approached depending on the navigator's knowledge of the terrain and skill with his radar set.

**Capt. Robert Bieber, USAF Combat Control Team Leader,
Howard AFB, Panama Canal Zone**

We were coming back from a battle zone. I had a MOD team with me, and a CCT. We loaded the forklift and whole mess of pallets and a jeep. We were pretty well loaded to the walls. The strip was short . . . 2,900 feet . . . and the procedure was to use all the runway you had and then take off. When we went to lift off, we went through quite a few bushes and branches and stuff. We got a few scrapes and a few little hits. We all realized the undercarriage had been scraped. It definitely got our attention. But it flew away, though!

I've watched 'em literally spank those C-130s into the ground in Vietnam, land 'em fully loaded in 2,000 feet, and yet they would fly away with no problem whatsoever. They can handle, as advertised, 60-foot widths with no problems, 3,000-foot runway with no problems.

**M/Sgt. Dwight Wilkenson,
C-130 loadmaster, Dyess AFB, Texas**

I was flying a C-130B out of Tan Son Nhut. Making a short final approach, we picked up six hits. Only problem, they were right across the wing and they hit five or six of our fuel tanks. We ended up defueling and transferring what we could. On the main tanks, we just put wooden plugs on the bottom of the wing and left the fuel in it. We had wooden plugs made up like a big old screw and you just screwed them up as tight as you could. Good enough to get you out of there.

'COMMANDO VAULT': THE HERCULES 'JUNGLE BUSTER'

Col. Bruce Mosley

The Americans had problems creating helicopter launching pads because the jungle was so thick. They had a bunch of these 10,000-pound B-36 bombs left over from World War II. Somebody came up with the idea, "Why not extract those bombs out of the back of a C-130 like you do an air-drop load and put a probe on it so it will explode four or five feet off the ground, to clear a helicopter pad." It worked so well, the Army had some 15,000 pound bombs made specifically for that.

Radar sites would track us down the line and tell us where we were to release. On the 30-second warning, we'd put this big drogue chute out. When you got over the site, you'd hit your green light. We had some tremendous scores. It really cleared the trees out. Army really liked it. They tried to use it to close some of the VC paths on the side of a hill to cause a landslide. But it was not too successful.

THE LOADS: AMMO TO K RATIONS
AND FAST TURNAROUNDS

T/Sgt. William E. Collins

We did 15-day shuttles in-country in Vietnam, while stationed at Clark Air Base (in the Philippines). We'd do a 15-day shuttle in country, go back to Clark for four/five days and go back to RVN for another 15 days in-country. At one time I had a buddy flying C-7 Caribous stationed at Cam Ranh Bay and I was doing more in-country flying than he was!

I look at a transport from the viewpoint of what it will do with a load. I skip over all the unimportant garbage like how big the engines are and how fast does it fly, and how many snap rolls it does on final, and I get down to the important points . . . how much will it carry? And how do you get it on?

Speed-off-load was a big thing in Nam with the 130s. There was never anything written that I know of. You had to work your own system to do this. My own personal plan went this way.

You come in, land, and the pilot would position the aircraft wherever the customer wanted the stuff. I'd go back and open the ramp and door and I personally would adjust the ramp so that the tail of the ramp was six inches lower than the front . . . just a little incline. I'd go up front and get on the head-set, open the locks on the right hand side. We had a "simil" Open Handle for the left hand locks. The pilot would rev up the engines and have on the brakes. I'd go on the head-set and say, "Ready?"

"Ready."

"Now."

He'd pop the brakes and I'd pop simultaneous handle and unlock the pallets. What happened, the pallets fell loose and you taxied out from underneath them. From the inside, they looked like they were rolling out the back. The pallets inside the airplane were two inches apart. If you did it right, they'd hit the ground perfectly aligned and two inches apart. If the area was hot, you'd do this on the end of the runway, and when he popped the brakes, that was the beginning of his takeoff roll. You'd run back and hit the ramp switch and it'd start coming up. You had to have it up before the pilot rotated. We didn't have a whole bunch about sittin' down with seat belts and being pretty. I made my standard takeoff and landing standing in the left troop door, hanging on, and that was it. We didn't have a whole bunch of "sittin' pretties."

Maj. Joel Thomas, USAF C-130 Navigator, Retired

"The Herk held up beautifully. There wasn't any place on that whole (Vietnam) peninsula that we couldn't go with that bird if we damn well wanted to. I wouldn't hesitate a moment going back to it. We have 'em out here at Davis Monthan (Arizona) with our drone birds. They smell good and they sound good and all that nostalgia comes up and my blood runs a little bit faster."

Sgt. Robert H. Miller,
News dispatch in 315th Air Division Airlifter

NGA TRANG AB, RVN—"What did you do in the war, Daddy?"

"Well, son, one day we hauled two elephants in our C-130 . . . ."

*   *   *

An Army Special Forces team at the isolated Vietnamese village of Tra Bong, offered to help 400 Montagnard and Vietnamese families start their own industry. Because of the dense forest, a sawmill appeared to be the logical answer to Tra Bong's plight.

After a few weeks, Tra Bong had a burgeoning business going, but soon all the timber close enough to haul by hand had been felled. Distant trees posed a problem. The terrain was rough, so conventional machinery was out of the question.

Village elders concluded an elephant or two was the only hope to keep the sawmill in operation. The elephants were located at Ban Don—170 miles away—but transporting them by land was too dangerous; sea transportation would take too long, and the animals might get seasick.

Lt. Col. Stanley J. Boren and crew were assigned the job of airlifting the two pachyderms, Bonnie and Clyde, in what came to be known as "Operation Bahroooom!"

Col. Boren landed the Hercules on a dirt strip at Ban Don that was "little more than a wide spot in the road." Clyde was "shot" first with a dart containing a sedative and lifted into the Hercules by fork lift. On board the Hercules, Clyde was fitted with a self-opening parachute in the event he awoke from his slumber and threatened the safety of the aircraft and his crew.

"We treated Clyde as an 'air evac' and gave him every consideration of cabin pressure, air conditioning, ventilation, and the smoothest ride possible," said 1st Lt. James J. Fortar, navigator.

After arriving at Chu Lai, the net-enclosed elephant was transferred to a forklift and then suspended under a Marine CH-53 helicopter for the remaining 15-minute journey to Tra Bong.

On the second trip to Chu Lai, Bonnie was transported without a hitch.

At Tra Bong, both elephants were met by a cheering and giggling crowd of several hundred villagers. "Operation Bahroooom" was a success.

CWO/4 Henry Wildfang, KC-130 Pilot, United States Marine Corps

I always had confidence in the C-130. The loads (in Vietnam) were always suspect. You were in hopes you were well within the weight limits and that they were accurate. But sometimes you had your doubts. But with the 130, that was never a great worry, at least not to me. I always felt comfortable with it and I thought, "Well, hell, if they've missed it by 10,000 pounds, it's not a big thing."

Capt. James Warner, Little Rock AFB, Ark.

John Roach was on his first night assault take-off (in Vietnam) loaded with two army trucks. Dark black out. Rolling down the runway . . . rolling . . . rolling . . . end of runway coming up . . . pulls it up and staggers into the air at stall speed, clipping tree tops, wallowing along. About that time, the loadmaster pipes up:

"Boss, I screwed up."

"How's that?"

"Those trucks aren't empty. They're each half full of Claymore mines. We have an extra 8,000 pounds."

They made it, but just barely.

Capt. Ted Lawson, 315th Air Division (PACAF)

The 776th Troop Carrier Squadron crews are among the highest paid "paper boys" in the world. Every night at 7:30 p.m., a crew from the 776th picks up a load of Pacific Stars and Stripes and begins a 2,400-mile journey to deliver papers to the U.S. fighting men in Vietnam . . . from Tokyo via Ching Chuan Kang, Taiwan (CCK), Da Nang Air Base, Nha Trang and Tan Son Nhut AB.

Capt. James F. Eberwine,
8th Aerial Port Squadron, Bein Hao AB

You name it and we've hauled it (in the 130). From 57,000 pound bulldozers to huge communications vans, we've loaded and off-loaded them right here. Even had livestock march through the port . . . live chickens and pigs and cows are air-dropped to Army special forces compounds in remote areas.

Maj. Billy Morrell

It wouldn't be unusual at all for one C-130 to haul 225,000 pounds in a nine hour day, making 16 landings. And loads! We hauled everything. In a matter of minutes we could off-load our cargo, rig our plane for passengers or litter patients, or ambulatory patients, or we could rig it for a combination of all these, including cargo. About the most unusual load we took was a group of 40 Viet Cong prisoners. I found that old Hercules to be an extremely reliable aircraft.

T/Sgt. William E. Collins

We hauled a couple of cows one day in Nam. You put pallets on the floor and then you spread plastic on that to catch the droppings. Then you walk the cow in and loop a tie-down strap around his horns. You hook it in the floor and pull it tight until his nose is touching the floor, and ratchet it in. Then you sit there with your 38 and tell whoever is shipping the cow that if the cow even looks at you wrong, all he's gonna get on the other end is horse meat.

It's the funniest thing in the world to watch a cow try to keep his footing as you take off. Lot of places that's the only way you could get meat in; you took it live so they could slaughter it there, in the Vietnamese village—for troops or whatever.

Air Force Times
Feb. 19, 1969

Vietnam's "flying cows" jumped over a milestone recently when Sgt. Brian C. Tuenage gushed the 10,000,000th gallon of fuel from a C-130 aircraft bladder.

C-130 transport aircraft that haul the petrol udders were dubbed "flying cows" by troops in the field. The bladder birds have flown as many as 6,000 gallons of fuel in one mission.

T/Sgt. William E. Collins

We called them the Carry-Everybody-You-Can emergency airlifts. You put the ramp down and run all the people you could as far front as you could, just as hard-packed as possible . . . close the ramp and door. Then come around to the crew entrance door, run them all the way back up the ramp door on the back. Run a new batch in from the front. Step in and scream, "SIT DOWN!" They couldn't hurt themselves if they tried—they couldn't fall down. There were too many of 'em!

The record for hauling Vietnamese was in excess of 300 . . . something atrocious. 'Course it's impossible to gross out the plane with bodies.

'YOU NAME IT, THE HERK DID IT'

Lt. Col. Joseph Bilotta

Some of the brainpower figured, with the rainy season coming on, if we'd put soap in the narrow passageways (of the Ho Chi Minh Trail), there'd be no way they could rebuild it because there'd be no cohesive agent. This was supposed to make a quagmire to where you couldn't even ride bicycles, couldn't get animals, pack-horse, *anything* through it.

We got the CCK people to handle it. They got down at a low level and dropped soap chips and detergent. They dropped it along the critical passes.

For the first one or two missions, we didn't have too much trouble, but after that they really shot hell out of us and some of the aircraft sustained quite a bit of damage.

*   *   *

(This was similar to a rainmaking mission involving C-130s and F-4s over a six-year period. The object was to muddy unpaved supply routes into Vietnam, but mostly on the Ho Chi Minh Trail in the Laotian panhandle. The Herks and Phantoms seeded clouds with silver and lead iodine, but the rainfall was increased only from 21 inches to 23 inches and the Air Force abandoned the project.)

**Lt. Col. Charles Simons,
U.S. Embassy, La Paz, Bolivia**

During our Vietnam missions, crewmen loved riding the ramp. We'd come back from a mission and the aircraft commander would put the ramp down and a crew member would put the safety (restraint) harness on. He'd get his heels out on the end of the ramp and lean out about 30 degrees (with the strap holding him). We'd fly over lakes (in Thailand) and he'd wave at the people in the sampans down there. It would blow their minds.

T/Sgt. William E. Collins

Turnaround time in Vietnam? At a full base with full facilities, the normal time was 30 minutes on the ground from touchdown to takeoff.

Now Bami-Tuiet, if you landed there at night, the C-130 was such a "mortar magnet" that they wanted to get rid of us. Turnaround was *fast*. The normal operating procedure was on landing. I was standing in the left troop door. That put me right there to open the ramp and door. So on rollout I'd start opening the ramp and door.

There was a fork lift chasing me. He would have the "milk stool" in the tongs. As soon as I stopped, I'd have the ramp just a little bit up; he'd run up underneath me with the milk stool, set it down (under the ramp). I'd put the ramp down on the milk stool . . . he'd back out and was ready for the first pallet. A forklift behind him was ready for the second pallet. It made for some *fast* ground times.

THE 'HEAD SHED' HERCULES: AB TRIPLE C

**From The Atlanta Journal, Nov. 17, 1965,
By Betty Halstead, UPI**

The U.S. Air Force's newest weapon in the Vietnam war is a bulky Hercules nicknamed the "head shed." As the name implies, it is a plane full of brain. The squat, full-bellied C-130 is loaded with electronic gear—an even dozen radio systems and five television circuits—and operates as an aerial command post to direct both ground and air operations. It proved its worth in the battle of Plei Me, when its specially-trained crew of 15 hovered 8,000 feet above the Central Vietnamese country-side calling the air strikes that routed Viet Cong battalions attacking the Special Forces camp with heavy losses.

315th Air Division Airlifter,
June 4, 1968

At regular intervals throughout the day and night, a C-130E, bristling with antennae, takes off from Udorn. This is the AB Triple C (Airborne Command and Control Center), code-named Hillsboro, one of which orbits over a central location where it can keep in contact with all U.S. military aircraft and helicopters in the air. Hillsboro performs many functions, summoning Forward Air Controllers (FACs) and fighter planes when ground forces need immediate support, coordinating rendezvous between tankers and thirsty fighters, logging fighters in as they head over the North and checking them off as they come out, overseeing search and rescue efforts, and in other ways acting as an extension of General Momyer's operations staff.

THE AC-130 GUNSHIPS:
TERROR ON THE HO CHI MINH TRAIL

Col Stanley Bramwell,
Former AC-130 Aircraft Commander in Vietnam

I arrived at Ubon, Thailand, just prior to Christmas of 1971 to join the 16th Special Operations (Gunship) squadron.

The first flight was an orientation. You could move around the airplane, seeing how the sensor operators worked and how the gunner worked. There's a fellow who hangs out the back of the airplane, called the I.O. (Illuminator operator). Some call him the "vertical observer." He spots ground fire. Of course, he's strapped in, and he wears a helmet and survival gear. His head protrudes over the ramp and, hanging there upside down, he can see all around. He has a restraint harness around his shoulders which holds him in. He's trained so he can tell how accurate the enemy ground fire is and then he can tell the aircraft commander to "break right" or "break left" when he sees some trouble coming.

I wanted the experience so I obtained a harness and I leaned over also. I saw red tracers arcing after us. They aim by tracers. They have one tracer and four rounds you can't see. If it had not been a wartime situation, it would have been a very beautiful sight. Suddenly, I heard this tremendous noise behind us (in the cargo compartment.) I thought we had been hit. What it was, our gunners on the airplane had begun to shoot and that was the first time I had heard the noise which startled me. They were 40 mike-mikes. We had two of 'em on the back.

T/Sgt. David Carr, AC-130 Aerial Gunner,
16th Special Operations Squadron

The greatest thing about the gunship job is knowing your guns have scored against the trucks. After a while, it's easy to tell what they were carrying by the way they burn. Thirty-seven millimeter ammunition is really something to watch. It's like a fireworks display. Tracers wriggle up in the air and all through the woods. It's a big relief to know that no one's ever going to fire any of that stuff at you.

A1C John Dubose,
16th Special Operations Squadron

We were having a fantastic night. The pilot just couldn't do anything wrong. We had several trucks lined up and the pilot fired a clip at the target. However, after several shots, the gun would no longer fire on the pilot's electrical command. Since we still had the objective in sight, I requested permission to fire the remaining round by hand. Right after it went off, one of the officers on board reported, "Score one for the gunner."

Troops relax inside C-130 while being airlifted by C-130 to another front. (USAF)

Col. Stanley Bramwell

I flew 134 AC-130 gunship missions mostly along the Ho Chi Minh Trail. One night, I destroyed or damaged 27 trucks. We had sensors on the airplane which detected trucks or other targets. Once you get the target in your sights, you circle. The gunsight was up front by the aircraft commander. He would look in the gunsight and there would be two pips. One would indicate the target. The sensors would acquire a target and the pip would show on the gunsight screen. The second pip indicated the gunsight. We had to fly the airplane a specific angle of bank, speed and altitude, to match up these two pips. When they matched up, we'd press the trigger and shoot.

Once you got a truck in your sights you'd first fire a couple rounds of Misch that would sparkle. The driver usually would stop his truck, jump out and run. Then we would circle until we destroyed it.

As far as I know, the AC-130 was probably the most effective truck destroyer in our arsenal at that time (1971-1972).

When those trucks first began to travel the Ho Chi Minh Trail, they'd go in convoys. That was before my time. I was told that they would destroy the first and last trucks which would block the road. Then it was just a matter of destroying the trucks in between.

Atlanta Constitution,
May 15, 1975

"The old C-130 has been used for a lot of things we never dreamed it could be used for, much less sinking part of the Cambodian navy."

The Lockheed spokesman was referring to the AC-130 aircraft that aided Wednesday in destroying three Cambodian gunships and damaging four others in defense of the U.S. freighter Mayaguez.

Lt. Col. Joseph Bilotta

In my opinion, the one-thirty gunship was more destructive than any fighter, bomber or anything, because with the gunsights and the firepower he packed, there was nothing safe. The gunships probably destroyed more enemy materiel than fighters and bombers because we worked at night. Some of the explosions they set up were tremendous. Just rock the damn aircraft.

Compared to fighters and fighter-bombers, number one, we had more firepower; number two, we could stay up three, four, five times more than a fighter, especially at low altitude. Plus we had six, seven people all looking for targets of opportunity. The jet fighter would look around at 400, 500 miles an hour when the one-thirty could do it at 150, 160 miles per hour. We had the advantage. But don't get me wrong. The fighter was needed, because if we hadn't had fighters, the enemy would have shot us down.

M/Sgt. Claude Ferrand,
C-130 Loadmaster, Dyess AFB, Texas

I had three tours of Vietnam and the C-130 got me out of trouble many times down there. If I had been in a 124, 141, or a

C-5, I wouldn't be here to talk about it. One day, operating an "E" model out of the Philippines (773rd squadron from Langley), we went into RVN to airdrop JP4 fuel mounted on eight-foot platforms to an Army helicopter unit.

Charlie had the word we were coming and opened up on us. When we got back to Clark, Colonel Hamilton counted 87 hits from the paratrooper doors to the tail section. We were lucky they were small arms hits. I don't think another airplane could have gotten us out of there. Somebody was looking over us.

TROOP PARADROP: A ONE AND A HALF MINUTE MIRACLE

1st Lt. John Duemmel, USAF combat correspondent
Tan Son Nhut Airfield, Vietnam

It came from the south—an armada of 15 C-130s carrying 1,200 Vietnamese paratroopers. In the more than two mile long in-trail formation were aircraft from three TAC wings. Their mission— drop assault troops on a 2,700 by 800-yard drop zone 20 miles north of Saigon. The paratroopers were to attack Viet Cong insurgents reported in the area.

The C-130s, each of which carried 80 fully-equipped paratroopers, climbed to 3,000 feet and slipped smoothly into formation. One minute from the drop zone, all aircraft were on the drop heading and at drop speed. The seconds ticked by. When the navigator gave the "green-light," two 40-man sticks of paratroopers stepped into each aircraft's slipstream. Within a brief 90 seconds, 1,100 troops left the C-130s and began to float to earth. Their exit was none too soon because they were enveloped almost immediately in a rain shower.

The jumpers immediately deployed seeking the Viet Cong. Days of preparation had been perfectly executed in a fleeting minute and a half.

THE RESCUE BIRDS: HUMAN DRAMA OF SAVING LIVES

Lt. Col. John McClure, Marietta, Ga.
Former HC-130H Pilot in Vietnam

The (crown bird) Hercules was just fantastic as far as mission capability (in Vietnam). Anything anybody called on it to do, it did.

If you wore a rescue patch you were proud. All the fighter people respected the crown people. It was a camaraderie there that you didn't find in many operations. What a great feeling to hear over the radio the Jolly Green pilot report, "He's onboard and we're coming out."

SHORT STRIP SPRINGER

SHORT STRIP SPRINGER—(Hercules Liftus Maximus) The short strip springer is, by far, the most famous of all Asian birds. A creature of many habits, the springer is represented by many sub-species. A few of the sub-species, and their habits follow, for it is impossible to write of the springer without including them. The first and most prominent sub-species to be encountered is the Hercules packa passengerous. In this variety, it is not uncommon to observe one hundred or more para-sitic creatures, known as pack the terminals, crowding the body feathers in attempts to gain the safety of their home grounds. Another species worth mentioning is the Hercules Droppa Chutist. The Droppa Chutist is often seen gorging on fierce creatures known as paratroopus horridius. Once filled with the paratroopus creatures, the Droppa Chutist takes wing, flies to an enemy's territory and expels the terrible paratroopae which then glide to the enemy and devour them. Thus proving the already well established fact that many earth-bound creatures maintain a working symbionic relationship with the aborials. The final species to be mentioned in this work is the H. Liftus Maximus. The Liftus creature is typical of the Merculid fowl. It is large, having a powerful body and sturdy wings. These two characteristics are what gives the springer the ability to "leap" into the air, hence his common name. The H. Liftus Maximus is capable of lifting a weight equal to its own. It is known and loved by all friendly jungle creatures as a result of its habit of carrying huge stores of vitally needed items to creatures in trouble, seeming to arrive just at the right moment with the item most suited for each particular need.

(Courtesy 7th AF News)

7th Air Force News Release, Aug. 19, 1966

Maj. Henry A. Barkalow and his C-130 crew were waiting for clearance to take off when a distress call from an Air Force F-4C Phantom pilot crackled over the radio. The Phantom pilot had ridden his F-4C down to a jungle crash. He was too injured to leave his cockpit. A rescue helicopter took to the skies immediately, but a malfunction in the chopper pilot's survival radio reduced his effectiveness.

Major Barkalow and his crew volunteered to carry on the search and skimmed the tree-tops for three hours in a blinding rain, trying to track the weak beeper signals coming from the downed pilot's emergency radio. A combination voice-beeper system, the radio was transmitting beeps and receiving voice communications, but the pilot was unable to transmit his own voice.

Marjor Barkalow radioed the pilot, "If you can hear me, shut off your beeper for a moment." Steady tone of the beeper suddenly quit, and the C-130 crew knew they had made contact. Using the same system, Barkalow was able to determine the pilot's condition, and, by flying back and forth over the general area, pin-pointed the downed pilot's location by the same method. A doctor was rushed to the crash scene in a helicopter and the pilot was taken to the hospital.

The F-4C co-pilot was still missing, however. The Hercules crew, assisted by a C-130 flare ship, continued the search into the night, and after another two and one half hours of flying, located the flyer's body.

MED EVAC C-130: SAVING THE LIFE OF A WOUNDED MARINE

Sgt. M.L. Ray, Information Writer, 315th Air Division

An Air Force C-130 Hercules of the 463rd Tactical Airlift Wing was flying near Da Nang with a load of cargo destined for Marines in Vietnam's northern provinces.

"Checker 54, this is DaNang ALICE," a radio burped into the aircraft commander's headphones.

"54, go," replied the AC.

"Checker 54, you are being diverted from your assigned mission. You are directed to rig for air evac after a rapid offload at this station. A representative of air evac will brief you on the ground."

"54, understand rapid offload at your house, rig for air evac. 54 out."

A new mission, a mercy mission and a new destination were in store for Captain Charles D. Kirkpatrick and his crew from the 29th Tactical Airlift Squadron. A wounded U.S. Marine lay in the hospital in Da Nang after an encounter with a North Vietnamese artillery shell. He was in critical condition and in need of a kidney machine to take the place of his own organ until it could recover enough to function normally.

A representative of the 903rd Aeromedical Evacuation Squadron met the aircraft. He shouted above the roar of the aircraft's ground turbine compressor. "We have a patient you have to get to Tan Son Nhut in a hurry. He needs a kidney machine and the only one in Vietnam is at Tan Son Nhut. This guy has got to have it and fast if he's going to pull through. It's up to you."

Minutes later the aircraft was airborne. The patient was strapped to a litter in the center of the cargo compartment. He was accompanied by a medical team consisting of a male nurse and two aeromedical evacuation technicians.

Meanwhile, Tan Son Nhut airfield was under attack with fire fights going on, on both ends of the runway. "We called the field from about 20 miles out and they told us we could land at our own risk," Captain Kirkpatrick related later. "If we didn't land at Tan Son Nhut, that Marine wasn't going to make it. But I was responsible not only for that Marine, but for the other four crewmembers and the medical team. It was a rough decision."

Captain Kirkpatrick made a descent as steep as possible to make a safe landing and provide maximum comfort for the patient. A minimum amount of space was used for the landing. A long roll would have sent the aircraft into ground fire on the far end of the runway.

It worked. Or at any rate, it almost worked. It was close though, as was made quite clear when the crew began to hear the sounds of small arms bullets striking the aircraft right before touchdown.

The Marine was saved.

Lt. Col. Joseph Bilotta

My closest call in Vietnam came when we were going in to pull out a bunch of wounded men from one of the bases that had been in a firefight. The weather closed in and we kept going lower and lower and we were down at about 300 feet, which was highly illegal, but we wanted to get in there. We finally found the air base and it was completely socked in. We were making 360-degree circles, trying to line up with the runway, because we wanted to get in to get those men. On the sixth pass, I saw enough of it that enabled us to land. A number of people on the ground didn't believe we were going to make it; so did a bunch of people upstairs. We stayed only a half hour, but we got the wounded out.

George Odgers, Australia
Department of Defense (Air Office)

The largest number of (Australian) casualties, 52, to be flown to Australia in one aircraft were flown home in one of the new C-130E Hercules then coming into service with RAAF's Number 37 Squadron at Richmond. The flight left Vung Tau for Australia on 27 February, 1967 . . . . In addition to the nine air crew the aircraft carried four medical officers, five sisters and four medical orderlies to attend the needs of patients, together with all necessary medical equipment . . . . The last four patients, all of whom were seriously ill, were retained in an air conditioned mobile operating room and carried into the Hercules shortly before the aircraft was ready for takeoff . . . . Every patient in that historic flight was handed over in as good a condition and in some cases better condition than when they entered the Hercules in Vietnam. It was a fine example of the devotion and dedicated effort the RAAF medical service provided.

THE BOB HOPE SHOW: 8,000 MILES BY HERCULES

Lt. Col. William H. Copp,
Co-Pilot, 1966 Road King Bravo

If you can, imagine Phyllis Diller on the flight deck of a 100,000-pound combat transport. It became a bedlam of laughter. No routine she has ever done could match her hilarious comments about our airplane.

Bill Faith, Hope's public relations man, brought members of the cast up to the flight deck and introduced them to the crew:

Vic Damone, Anita Bryant, Joey Heatherton and Les Brown and His Band of Renown.

Bob Hope's 1966 tour of military bases in Southeast Asia received 'round the clock airlift support from two 314th Troop Carrier Wing C-130Es. The C-130 was chosen because of its ability to get into and out of the short unprepared airfields. Aircraft commanders were Lt. Col. Clyde W. Huether and Capt. Frank C. Alberts. The itinerary included flights to Takhli, Korat, Udorn and Nakhon Phanom, Thailand, flying out of Bangkok. We also flew the troupe to Pleiku, Cam Ranh Bay, Tan Son Nhut, An Khe and Qui Nhon in the Republic of Vietnam.

Both C-130s performed magnificently. An additional aircraft was dispatched as backup for each mission, but it was never used. Upon arrival in Vietnam, the aircraft were specially fitted with seat pallets in the aft portion of the cargo area. The lower bunk on the flight deck served as unofficial command post. Hope would go over items about the show with various experts in his group. In the cabin area, set between the dual loading rails, were two GI cans full of ice and cold drinks. That, along with coffee and doughnuts, represented the "champagne flight service" of our combat zone C-130E.

There was an evening when "Road King Bravo" was transformed into a real old-fashioned Christmas home. Flying at 19,000 feet over the war area, members of the troupe, including the Hope family themselves, decorated a homespun Christmas tree. It was quite a moment with all the wonderful people aboard our airplane; there was a certain magic about this never-to-be-forgotten Christmas.

It was difficult to believe that only a few days before, this same aircraft had been carrying supplies, rations, ammunition and troops in the very same cargo compartment.

A/2C M.L. Ray, Writer,
315th Air Division

I was in Vietnam to write a story on the 315th Air Division's C-130s operating the Vietnam shuttle out of Cam Ranh Bay. I was ready to head home to Tokyo when I received word to stand by and await the arrival of the (Bob Hope) show.

A C-130 taxied onto the parking ramp and a large blue flag popped from the overhead escape hatch, announcing the arrival of the USO-sponsored show. As the Hercules rolled to a final stop and the crew door opened, there stood the man of the hour—Bob Hope . . . .

Hope walked on stage, complete with golf club, to ridicule himself, those around him, and everything the military holds holy. "This crew that brought me in here—I mean to tell you they're a happy-go-lucky bunch. You know, happy they got it off the ground and lucky they got it down again.

"Really though, they're a professional group and our flight in was without incident. The only thing that really bothered me was when the navigator couldn't find the cockpit."

Bob Hope in a familiar pose. This was his 1966 Christmas Special tour of troop units in Vietnam. His troupe was taken on the tour in a C-130 that only a short time before had been rigged for combat action. (USAF)

Lt. Col. Clovis T. Lightsey,
U.S. Air Force, Retired

There is an adage among airlifters that the rest of the Air Force, as well as the other services, neither knows nor cares about airlift until they don't have any. The exception to this was the time from the cease fire until all U.S. personnel departed South Vietnam. The C-130 provided the necessary airlift to evacuate Americans and South Koreans to the major aerial ports for further airlift to the U.S. and Korea. While this massive drawdown airlift was going on, the C-130 also provided the airlift to repatriate the North Vietnamese and Viet Cong prisoners of war. Of considerably more significance was the fact that a C-130E transported the Four Party Joint Military Commission team to Hanoi to supervise each release of American Prisoners of War during Operation Homecoming. This was a case when airlift in general and the C-130 in particular were in the limelight. The Hercules performed flawlessly. Perhaps the Hercules should plagiarize from an old VW advertisement: "Ugly is only skin deep."

C-130E Hercules crew demonstrates quick, on-the-spot, delivery of cargo with high degree of accuracy. The system is called PLADS (parachute low altitude delivery system) and was used extensively in Vietnam. Hercules discharges cargo from 200-foot altitude. Descent of cargo from aircraft to ground requires only six seconds. (USAF)

COURAGE IN THE C-130 COCKPIT

For the first time, airlift people are getting the recognition they deserve.

—General Lucius D. Clay,
Commander, Pacific Air Forces

When the final story of the Vietnam war is written, the role of airlifters, particularly C-130 airlifters, will doubtless receive their just desserts.

As Colonel Ray L. Bowers has noted, the airlift job in Vietnam was hard and dirty, and C-130 crews carried out their vital tasks without expecting glory or gain. Even so, they relished their duties, discovering satisfactions seldom known in peacetime. The airlifters called themselves *Trash Haulers*, "an unbitter reflection on their own unexalted status."

But the "Trash Haulers" came into their own in 1969, when the Air Force honored one of their C-130 colleagues, Major Daryl D. Cole, by naming him winner of the prestigious Mackay Trophy for the most meritorious Air Force flight of 1968.

Cole was aircraft commander of a C-130 which brought 200 passengers out of besieged Kham Duc airfield on May 12, 1968.

Cole aborted a takeoff roll when shrapnel struck his Herky's right rear tire, sending fuel streaming from five holes in the left wing fuel tanks. The AC tried to cut off the damaged tire but, with mortar rounds impacting close to the aircraft, decided to try to take off with most of the tire still on the rim. While aligning the Hercules with the runway, another mortar shell hit, puncturing the left outboard fuel tank and shattered two windows on the pilot's

373

side. Despite seemingly overwhelming odds, Major Cole got the Hercules into the air and was able to take his 200 passengers to a safe landing on a foam-covered runway at Cam Ranh Air Base without a single injury. Inspectors going over the airplane found 104 hits from hostile fire!

In this final chapter, we continue the Hercules saga in Vietnam with some accounts of courage in the C-130 cockpit.

MISSION TO AN LOC

On April 14, 1972, U.S. Headquarters in Vietnam directed USAF C-130 participation in the An Loc resupply missions. Five daylight container delivery system (CDS) drops were initially planned for the C-130s—on April 15th, 16th, and the 18th. The usual CDS method used a highspeed low-level route (250 knots and below 100 feet) to an initial point. The aircraft then climbed to 600 feet above the ground and set up for the drop which required slowing to 130 knots and opening the cargo door and ramp. Then, with the cargo door and ramp closed, the aircraft descended to treetop height and accelerated for its escape from the area. Sixteen tons of supplies in 16 individual containers could be delivered in one pass. Spare 617's airdrop on April 15 demonstrated the hazards facing C-130 crews on the daylight low level drop mission. Loaded with 27,000 pounds of 155-mm howitzer and 81-mm mortar ammunition, Spare 617 took off from Tan Son Nhut Air Base just after sunup and headed for An Loc. Here is the story of Spare 617 as told by the aircraft commander, Captain Bill Caldwell in the *TAC ATTACK*.

Captain Bill Caldwell

During my SEA tour, I flew C-130s out of CCK Air Base, Taiwan. Normally, we would go in-country for a 15-day shuttle, hauling cargo and people to the major bases of RVN, then back to CCK for a week or so flying other logistic missions, training, etc. I had just gotten back from stateside leave and was anxious to get in-country before my landing currency ran out. So, as soon as the scheduling shop and I saw eye-to-eye, I was deadheading to Tan Son Nhut. The guys coming out of RVN had told me about

"Charlie's" big play for 1972 and that things were a little grim up around Hue and the DMZ. I had convinced myself that this was no big deal—that's why you get combat pay—and really looked forward to renewing my associations with the detachment weenies at TSN (Tan Son Nhut) . . . .

I headed for the BOQ (bachelor officers' quarters). The "Q" was quieter than normal. Guessing that everyone was at the club, I headed there . . . . One healthy gulp of a gin and tonic focused my attention on two words: "An Loc" and "airdrop." There were phrases floating around too; "NVA's got 'em surrounded," "running out of ammo," "trucks can't get through." I turned to the guy I had elbowed to get to the bar and asked, "Hey! What the hell is going on?"

The previous three weeks came at me in a slightly slurred but understandable verbal barrage. The North had completely surrounded An Loc. Some 8,000 defenders, mostly RVN troops and a few American advisors, were caught. Anti-aircraft guns were all around the place. It looked like we were going to airdrop supplies and ammo to them soon but no one was saying when, just yet.

Always the image of the American fighting man, I muttered something cool like, "That's what we get paid for," while thinking privately . . . "How do I get out of here?" Then other thoughts started to creep in . . . "Who would they pick for a mission like that? Probably the most experienced. Who has the most airdrop experience around? But I've just gotten back. Surely they'll give me a little time to get back in step. But will they?" The gin started to taste funny.

When I got back to the "Q" a note on my door said to call the detachment. The call put me into crew rest for a 1500 show. The mission? "Can't tell you yet—get some sleep." It wasn't one of my best nights.

At 1500, the briefing started. "This evening you are going to drop 30,000 pounds of ammo to An Loc. The weather is good. You've got the best crew you can get. Your route of flight is from here to there."

"What's Intel got?"

"Don't know too much yet. We think you've got two 37mm's here and here, but we're not sure. Lots of small arms and 50 cal. stuff."

"What's the range on the 37mm?"

"Above you."

"Oh."

"Any other questions? Well . . . good luck."

When I got to the airplane, the loading had just started. Problems kept popping up and finally we ran out of daylight. The decision was to finish up and go into crew rest. We would launch first thing in the morning. It was a bad night. So many things to think about.

"Our mission is to fly and fight." When you hear this, visions of an F-4 rolling onto the target bounce around your brain. One seldom asks the question, "But where does that ugly '130 fit into the picture?" If you are a C-130 crew member, you ask that question over and over. Likewise, when you think about that F-4, you intrinsically know that it's armed to the teeth—bombs, rockets, a cannon, and a few CBU pods thrown in for color. A '130 crew member knows that he has a personal, stubnosed, 38 cal. revolver and it's been a long time since his last small arms training. Looking at the mission, you know that the F-4 starts high, does his trick, and lights the scat power to get out of there. A '130 troop does his act low and slow and wishes he had "just a little" scat power. Finally, if things aren't going right that day, the F-4 guy pulls his curtain and waits for the seat to kick him out into the blue. The '130 guy has to unbuckle, get out of the seat, run (walk if you still think you've got fighter pilot potential) about 50 feet to the cargo ramp, and then decide if a PLF (parachute landing fall) is better than riding this beast into the ground. Incidentally, it seems like a long time since you had PLF training too. I think you can readily see that the "fight" part of being an airlifter gives a guy a lot to think about. You think about it pretty damned hard when you hear about "Charlie" surrounding some place called An Loc and realize that you are the only way to get "shooting stuff" to our troops.

Somehow the night passes and 0530 hours found us in the briefing room. "Your mission is the same. The weather people say you'll be dropping under a scattered deck at 1,000 feet. Intel has pinpointed the Triple A. There are three 37's—here, here, and here—and one 23 here, about 3,000 yards from the drop zone. Everything else is the same. Oh! If you have to put it down or bailout, break out toward the east."

Using the Low Altitude Parachute Extraction System (LAPES), C-130 delivers a load of supplies to U.S. Army 1st Cavalry Division at An Khe (top photo). With LAPES, platform mounted loads are pulled from the rear of the aircraft at an altitude of five to ten feet. The landing gear remains down during the LAPES drop. Lower photo shows LAPES test at Pope AFB, N.C. (USAF)

"If you have to bailout." Those words brought all the thoughts and fears of the past 36 hours crashing through to reality. Suddenly, it was really possible that I, the infallible I, wouldn't come back. It took four cigarettes and as many cups of coffee to get the shakes out enough to walk. This just couldn't be happening to me! But it was.

Back at the aircraft, I found the crew making final checks and completing the rigging. Everything looked good. I got the crew together and laid down the facts. They were all volunteers and really pros. We were ready to go. Just before engine start, the commander stopped by to wish us luck. In 1900 hours of flying, this was the first time the leader had personally wished me well before a mission. The shakes started again.

We were late starting engines because of all the ceremony and "extra checks." Pressed for time, we made several silly blunders and almost missed a whole checklist. We got off on time. I still think the aircraft flew itself off the runway. I don't remember pulling back on the yoke.

We were No. 3 of a three-ship flight. Once airborne, we headed for a common orbit point. The profile called for each of us to make a solo pass. We were all pretty shaky. There was no chatter —just the running of the checklists.

Number one began his run-in. After his "two minutes out" call, all was quiet for an eternity. Finally, the UHF crackled his success. "Limited ground fire. Think I took one hit in the tail. Recommend a different approach."

When Number two called off the perch, we were sure that "Charlie" was awake and all ears were glued to the radio. The only sounds in the aircraft were the radio and the engines. On his slowdown, No. 2 had trouble. "Can't get the ramp down! Going to pull off and come back to the orbit. Three, you want it?"

My first reaction was NO! I'll wait. But fuel would not allow much waiting and the shakes were getting worse all the time. I looked at the "co" and then back at the engineer and nav. Their silent reply was go! "Tell 'em we'll take it," I said.

On the first pass, we missed the initial point and came back for another try. The second time around, everything fell into place. We made the two minute call and finished up the checklist. One minute out, we descended to drop altitude, 600 feet AGL. Thirty seconds out, the checkpoints started to come in right on the money. Fifteen seconds, ten seconds, "Got the timing point!? the nav yelled: "Five second warning!"

Suddenly the aircraft was a blast furnace. I heard a loud blast and the whole world pressed in on me. I glanced out the left side. The windows were shattered but holding. I glanced back at the engineer. He was slumped against his straps and bleeding badly. We were in a super hot hurricane. The noise was deafening. "We've had it!" I said, but nobody could hear me.

A voice far in the distance, the loadmaster's words cut through the intercom, "Jettison the load! Jettison the load! The load's on fire!" Each time he said jettison, I reached over and hit the button but the load didn't go. He finally released the load manually and watched two of the bundles blow up just as they cleared the aircraft. Now 30,000 pounds of class "A" ammo lighter, the airplane literally jumped through the scattered clouds above, and the airspeed was dropping through 115 knots.

"Fire on No 1! Fire on No. 1!" I snapped my attention to the T-handles.

"Number one engine fire control handle pull!" I shouted, but the copilot could not hear me for the noise. I reached over and did it myself. "Feather No. 1!" Again the action myself. The light stayed on. "Fire extinguisher agent—discharge number one bottle!" . . . Still the light . . . The prop had stopped . . . close the left isolation valve . . . got to get out of here . . . what's my airspeed . . . Damn! 110! . . . get the nose down . . . turn right, that will get you away from the ground fire . . . fire the No. 2 bottle . . . still got a light! I turned eastward. The copilot was all over the radios. Surely everyone knew our trouble. Help must be on the way.

"Fire on No. 2!" Just the T-handle displayed the trouble. I thought to myself . . . the whole wing's on fire! We shut down No. 2, but the fire lights stayed on!

"Nav! find us a spot to set this thing down!" We turned south. The loadmaster's voice came through again. "Fire in the left wheel well!! Can't get it out!" . . . wheel well—that's the GTC area (gas turbine compressor—Ed) . . . we've been hit in the GTC bleed duct . . . isolate it!

GTC fire control handle—pull! . . . Close the other wing isolation valve—closed . . . damn, it's hot in here . . . no place to land . . . bailout? . . . engineer's hurt bad—so's the loadmaster . . . airspeed? . . . 125! . . . it flies!

As soon as I closed the right wing bleed air valves and isolation valve, the noise began to subside. The temperature was still tremendous and the loadmaster was fighting the fire above the left wheel well, but we were flying. From this point, we managed to limp back to Tan Son Nhut.

The key to the problem we faced that day was the fire above the GTC compartment. A one foot chunk of bleed air ducting had been blown out, spewing 625 degree (F) bleed air into the cargo compartment. This was the cause of our scorching hurricane inside the aircraft and the reason the two pallets had caught fire. To make a long story short—the loadmasters cranked the gear down and, except for losing a third engine dropping to 80% RPM in the traffic pattern, we landed safely at Tan Son Nhut.

(Appreciation is expressed to Captain Caldwell and to the editors of *TAC ATTACK* which originally published this account in September, 1974).

FIRST NIGHT ASSAULT MISSION FOR THE C-130

T/Sgt. John M. Glass
7th Air Force News, November 18, 1966

NHA TRANG—This reporter accompanied a C-130 belonging to the 50th Troop Carrier Squadron of the 314th Troop Carrier Wing on a night assault mission to deliver ammunition to a Special Forces Camp near the Cambodian border.

The Special Forces had been under attack since dusk and by 10 p.m. were almost out of ammunition. Following a plea for help, the C-130 began loading 29,000 pounds of small ammunition onto aluminum pallets.

Takeoff was accomplished shortly after midnight and the small Special Forces dirt runway was sighted one hour later. A C-123 was dropping flares, lighting up the area for landing. This was the first time a C-130 had made a night assault landing in Vietnam using flares for runway illumination. In addition to the flares, one jeep was lined up at the approach end of the runway. The small dirt field had been carved out of a rubber plantation and still had 50-foot rubber trees growing on three sides.

Major Jack B. Shaw and his crew had never seen the im-

Airlift proved to be a vital factor in the survival of the Marine base at Khe Sanh, ten miles south of the DMZ. Shortly after the initial mortar attack on the base, USAF and USMC C-130s began landing large loads of combat-essential supplies (top photo). When enemy fire became too intense, the C-130s went to LAPES and GPES, then, eventually, to higher altitude drops (bottom). In the 30-day sustained airdrop in the spring of 1968, 90 percent of the missions were under "blind" conditions. Of 68 airdrops during one week, only two missed the mark, due to chute malfunctions. (USAF)

382/HERK: HERO OF THE SKIES

C-130 keeps watchful eye on Vietnamese refugees moving south from battle zone. (USAF)

provised field before, but had studied photographs. For these professionals, this was enough. Coming in low and fast, Shaw had to pull up to miss a jeep, maximum power was used to bring the big bird back into the sky, just clearing the trees on the far end of the field.

After clearing the trees, landing lights were blacked out since the Viet Cong were then within several hundred yards of the runway and trying to pinpoint the plane with heavy small arms fire.

Staying low and taking a 360 degree circle, Major Shaw dropped the Hercules over the jeep, touched down, and reversed the props—bringing the giant bird to a rib-busting halt.

Taxiing to the far end of the runway and while the C-130 was still moving, the loadmaster opened the rear ramp and door and with four men to a pallet, started pushing ammo out onto the ground. During this fast action, a truck loaded with Special Forces troops drove up and hurriedly began loading the life saving ammunition.

With full power, and engines roaring, the mighty Hercules thundered off of the strip and headed into the starlit sky. The crew and this reporter sighed with relief; however, the night was not complete. Yet to come was a flight to Bien Hoa for more cargo, an intermediate stop, and then back to our home station.

Eight hours after initial takeoff, the weary crew touched down. Following operations debriefing and a "warm beer," Major Shaw and his crew headed for their billets for a much desired and deserving rest. Tomorrow is another day!

Major Gen. John J. Tolson
Commanding General 1st Air Cavalry Division,
(In a letter to Col. Charles W. Howe)

On 26 and 27 April (1968) in the A Shau Valley, I witnessed your C-130 crews in one of the most magnificent displays of courage and airmanship I have ever seen. The low ceilings, mountainous terrain, lack of terminal navigation facilities and enemy antiaircraft fire all combined to create an exceedingly hazardous environment for the planned resupply airdrops.

To the crews who accomplished all of the scheduled airdrops on those days go the sincere thanks and admiration of all the skytroopers of the first team.

I strongly recommend that suitable awards for valor be presented to each member of the crews involved. It was just a fantastic and inspiring demonstration of real cooperation in getting the job done.

THE LIFELINE TO KHE SANH

Lt. Col. Joesph Bilotta

We went into Khe Sanh one aircraft at a time. As soon as we landed, we had the back doors open while we were taxiing and we threw all the stuff out and took off. The field was under fire. We were completely ringed and they were dropping mortar shells on us and they had our radios in the tower. They were sending rockets after us. One aircraft at a time would land, open doors, push it out, and take off. The first piece of cargo to go out would pull the other (sections) out and we wouldn't stop. We'd pull the doors up and take off . . . no checks, no nothing, and we took off in 2,000 feet, at mid-runway.

We lost a few aircraft there. They had machine gunners off the end of the runway. They moved in one night and the first plane that came in, they butchered him and took off. Some of my friends were in the crew.

CWO-4 Henry Wildfang

I should have stayed home that day—February 10, 1968, right during the Tet offensive. We had aboard five or six 500-gallon bladders of JP fuel for the choppers of Khe Sanh. It was high noon and it was my 13th landing at Khe Sanh. We never had been hit on approach there before. Normally when we went in there, either the weather was worse than that or they didn't get a shot at us and we went straight on in. This time, there were known enemy gunners set up on the east end of the runway so we were advised not to go in that way. We thought we had a better chance entering downwind and then coming down from the west and landing downhill a little bit.

We made a TACAN approach and broke out of the base of the clouds at about 1,100 feet. We hugged the ceiling as long as possible and made a steep descent approach. On the downwind we were hit repeatedly with Quad 50s. We experienced two or three explosions and then another just as we touched down. It blew out the right side of the aircraft. Number three engine was blazing merrily. I had no idea we were going to be able to make it. But we had nothing better to do at the time so we hung right in there. The plane was full of smoke and fire, coming through the vents. I was afraid of running off the end. There was a thousand foot drop. We pulled off to the side 300 or 400 feet from the end. The other pilot and I exited through the swing windows. Raw fuel was running out on the runway three or four inches deep at the crew entry door. The navigator came out that door after we opened it. The first mech and a passenger also got out. But they both died. The navigator and the two pilots were all who survived.

I went out the left swing window and Major White, the other pilot, went out the other swing window. I got painful burns on my nose and hands and Major White got burned worse. We lost seven lives. The first mech died on March 5 and another crew member died on March 17.

Lt. Col. Tim Brady

As long as there was a piece of runway big enough to land the 130 on, we kept going in to Khe Sanh. When there was no longer a runway big enough, then we put the stuff in there by LAPES (low altitude parachute extraction system) or by GPES (ground proximity extraction system). It's similar to LAPES, but a cable was installed across the touchdown area and there was a hook hanging out of the back of the airplane with a mike on the end of it. That fed through the pilot's head-set so he could tell when the hook was dragging along the gound; he'd know he was at the right altitude. The hook would engage the cable and jerk the load out of the airplane.

When we first started into Khe Sanh, we'd taxi off the runway to the off-load area, shut off all but one engine and off-load very nonchalantly. Then as it progressively grew more under attack, the perimeter of the airfield kept shrinking. Charlie would lob in mortars and destroy chunks of the airfield. The off-load area kept getting smaller and smaller, and our off-load methods kept getting faster and faster. Right at the last, we were landing, taxiing down to the end of the runway, turning around and kicking the load off (combat off-loading it) while we were moving, closing the ramp and (clap of the hand) we were airborne. Three minutes and we were gone again. Later, when we could no longer land, we'd airdrop the stuff in."

Raymond R. Coffee
The Philadelphia Inquirer

Major Joel J. Thomas, the navigator, sat hunched over his radar scope and kept one eye cocked on a stopwatch as the fat-bellied C-130 churned through the thick gray clouds.

"Mark . . . mark . . . mark . . ." over the earphone in the cockpit came the voice of the radar controller on the ground as the plane leveled off and roared over the runway below at only 500 feet altitude.

"Green light," Thomas snapped. The aircraft commander, Maj. Emmett Musser, punched a button that released a load of artillery and mortar ammunition, which slid out the rear ramp of the plane and dropped to the ground under great billowing parachutes. As the load cleared the ramp, which took only four seconds, the C-130's nose shot up sharply. Capt. Kent Davidson threw the plane into a sharp turn to get out of range of the enemy gunners on the surrounding hills. Within seconds, the ground controller in the drop zone passed the good word by radio: "All chutes opened and all cargo within 75 yards of the bull's eye."

"Not bad," said Thomas with a satisfied grin as he lit the long cigar he had been chewing and sat back to relax. Hitting the bull's eye is like "hitting a home run," he explained. Coming within 75 yards "is a double or maybe a triple."

According to Thomas, the whole business—plotting approach, speed, nose-up angle, timing—is "something like trying to make a science out of witchcraft."

Still the crews have remarkable accuracy in getting the supplies into the 300-yard wide drop zone.

Total time at Khe Sanh was 20 seconds.

The ammunition dropped by the plane to the besieged marines at Khe Sanh—more than 30,000 pounds of it in this load alone—is part of what has become the biggest single parachute airdrop operation in U.S. military history.

THE AC-130s: ELUDING THE SAMS AND MIGS

Col. Stanley Bramwell

During 1972, three of our AC-130s were shot down and other aircraft were hit. We flew mostly at night. We were one of the first, I guess, to be shot at by the Strella, a Russian-built heat-seeking surface to air (SAM) missile. It occurred north of Da Nang, just south of the DMZ. We were shooting at a truck and all of a sudden, the IO said, "Sir, there's something coming at us." He never had seen the likes of it before. It turned out to be a Strella. It came right at the right wing. We broke to the left, but it followed us. For some reason it exploded about twenty feet behind the aircraft, and made quite a large white flash. The right scanner said we had been hit. I gave a quick check of the instruments and everything appeared normal and the airplane flew well. We flew back to Udorn. I had not been hit.

To combat the Strella, our people devised a flare-launch decoy. The flares on the back of the ramp, which we used for illumination primarily, became a dandy decoy. We'd cut the fuse time down to about two seconds. The flare would illuminate almost immediately after leaving the airplane and the Strella would turn and follow the flare.

I was shot at by Strellas eight to ten times and each time the flares worked very effectively. Otherwise I probably would not be here right now.

Lt. Col. Tim Brady

The AC-130 gunships were much more effective than the F-4s, the F-100s or anything else in terms of the kinds of targets they were going after . . . the trucks, the sampans. But air superiority was necessary because of the slow speed, lack of defenses from fighter aircraft and an orbit firing pattern.

Col. Stanley Bramwell

It was about 3 or 4 o'clock in the morning. We were flying in Northern Laos in the Plain of Jars area, shooting at trucks. There

C-130s modified as Spectre gunships proved to be highly effective in Vietnam, particularly against truck traffic on the Ho Chi Minh Trail. The early AC-130s utilized the older A model Hercules (top photo). Later, C-130Es were utilized. They were equipped with a number of intriguing sensor devices—Pave Spot . . . Pave Nail . . . Igloo White—all wrapped in "Surprise Package" equipment. The "E" model proved to have greater survivability due to added armor plate for the crew, longer loiter time and greater ammunition payload. Lower photo, Col. Stan Bramwell (center kneeling) and crew posed with their 16th SOS AC-130 crew in Vietnam. (USAF)

is an area called "The fish's mouth." Comes out of North Vietnam and protrudes into Laos. That's the corridor. Brigham, the ground radar in Thailand, called "Bandits coming out of the fish's mouth going due west." That was quite a bit north of where we were; we weren't too concerned. When (the MIG) got north of us, he turned south directly toward us. Brigham advised us to evacuate the area. We headed south toward Thailand. Brigham kept saying he was gaining on us. Our only hope was to put the plane in a dive.

So, we put it into a pretty steep dive, exceeding the red line on the airspeed indicator. It was dark. There's a mountain range between Laos and Thailand and I was hoping to get into ground clutter. We finally leveled off and looking outside we saw mountains around us. We were concerned about the mountains but more concerned about the MIG. After returning to Ubon, Brigham Radar called and said the MIG had been about 18 miles behind us before losing us. I figured with what he had, in another three minutes, he would have downed us.

We popped a few rivets on that C-130 when we went into that dive. We kept power on and went about straight down. Other than a few popped rivets, the plane performed very well.

*   *   *

One night my I.O. was flying with another crew and they got hit by a Russian Strella. There was a tremendous fire in the back of the airplane. Two people were able to get out. One of them said he saw my I.O. pinned against the aircraft by centrifugal force as it went into a spin and he went down with the airplane. One of the gun mechanics on board, who had done some sport parachuting, was able to claw his way to the end of the ramp. He carried his chest pack and he jumped out of the airplane. He was able to hook up one side of his chest pack to his harness and he pulled the rip cord and made about one oscillation before landing. He was very fortunate. If it hadn't been for his nearness to the ramp and his presence of mind, he would have gone down, too. That year, three of our C-130s were shot down. A lot more took hits.

Lt. Col. Joseph Bilotta

We landed in an area that was in danger of being overrun. We

AC-130, being loaded in Ubon (top). Next aircrew prepares to taxi out. Bottom view, fisheye lens in booth of AC-130, with personnel monitoring the four television screens. In a peacetime environment, the highly sophisticated AC-130 has been used extensively for night search and rescue missions employing the aircraft's unique infrared and low-light-level television detection systems. When an airliner crashed in the Everglades in 1973, a gunship orbited the area for hours, using its two-kilowatt searchlight to locate and direct rescue workers to individual victims. (USAF photos by Ken Hackman)

had word that the Viet Cong were going to attack and it was easier to pull them out than to supply and fight. I was made project officer and given a fleet of C-130s to remove the troops from the outlying base. I went in expecting to remove x numbers of troops. I landed in the first one-thirty and saw several thousand troops, women, kids, goats, chickens, dogs and even pigs. The troops expected us to airlift everybody and everything. They wouldn't leave without their families and possessions. I said to hell with it and loaded everybody aboard . . . 200, 250 people per plane. We opened the rear ramps and jammed them all the way up to the flight station. I mean hundreds . . . kids, dogs, goats, you name it. People were on the ramp when we raised and locked it. The pilots didn't say a word and the one-thirties completed the job without incident. You had to do what you had to do.

Major Bobby Burd, HC-130H Navigator
Charleston AFB (formerly with 39th AR Squadron—Tuy Hua)

I had 54 saves. Got 32 saves on one mission. I was in a "king" airborne command post. They first called them the "crown bird," but changed it to "king." We'd go out and fly an orbit mission for 12 hours. We would be listening to battle frequencies. If we heard someone take a hit, we would start marshalling forces . . . calling choppers and A-4Es and get the location of the downed crew. We'd see if the area was hot . . . plan the route of flight in and direct the run in, flying overhead, watching.

You flew the King as high as you could get because you kept seeing little puffs of smoke under you. If you had to refuel (a helicopter), you picked a safe area to go down to refuel HH 53 large Jolly or HH3 small Jolly. You'd fly higher and faster for the 53 and lower and slower for the HH3. During refueling, C-130s flew right on the edge of stall. "Sandy" (A-4E) would go in and try to draw fire. If he didn't draw fire, he would lead the helicopter in, make a path in by smoke screen, if necessary, then circle the area and protect the chopper. We monitored them from above to make sure they had enough fuel. As soon as the new Sandys came on-scene, my job, as navigator, was to keep track of how much fuel they had until bingo time. I would recycle Sandys or we would refuel the helicopters, depending on the mission.

CWO-4 "Gunner" Wildfang

We were deeply involved in flare dropping for night operations and (rescue) extractions. That was at least half our job. We had at least one plane and sometimes two up from dark to daylight. We would provide the illumination on call from the helicopters that went in to extract people. We went in when anyone was down or when the ground troops were bothered by attack. We'd light up the area so they'd have a chance to see what the hell was going on and repulse it.

Most of our drops were about 7,000 to 8,000 feet which cleared the hills there nicely. They would give the flare time enough to expend its light so it would be of some use. Quite often we were in the soup and we dropped on radials and distance.

THE LAST HERK OUT OF VIETNAM

(The story below was obtained by Wayne Pryor in an interview with Col. Doan Van De at the Camp Pendleton, California, refugee camp, on May 28, 1975. Col. De was commanding officer of the Republic of Vietnam Air Force's 50th Maintenance and Supply Wing based at Tan Son Nhut—in charge of all RVN multi-engine maintenance in South Vietnam.)

On Tuesday morning, April 29, 1975, the fall of Tan Son Nhut Air Base was imminent. The Viet Cong were already marching into Saigon. Three days earlier, Colonel De had sent his wife and family out on a C-130 flight to the Philippines. Now the crump of mortars and the hammering of machine guns outside the main gate where the air base garrison was fighting a delaying action told the approaching end.

De ("don't call me colonel—that is all gone in past") was supervising loading of his last two flyable C-130s. Two C-130s were burning on the ramp, one Vietnamese, one USAF. People were rushing to the flight line, hoping to get aboard.

One C-130 started to taxi out, then stopped, its props whining in front of De. A familiar face was in the cockpit window, Major Phuong, an instructor pilot and friend of De. The major waved him aboard with an insistent gesture. De hesitated for a second.

He could see he had no more to do. More than 100 airplanes on the base had been destroyed. Of his force of 29 C-130s, this

C-130A pictured in flight at night in 1968 with battlefield illumination system (BIAS) lights on. (USAF)

South Vietnamese evacuees board C-130 at Cubi Naval Air Station, Philippines, for the U.S. (UPI)

As these two photos attest, Old Hercules don't die—and they don't fade away, either. Top photo was made at An Khe, Vietnam, where it served as "the Fanciest BOQ (bachelor officers quarters) in An Khe, complete with shower stall on the back side . . . enter through the left paratroop door." Notice water heater and tank on top of fuselage. Just another improvising twist for the "go-anywhere, do-anything" Herky Bird. Lower photo, fire-damaged C-130 at Naha AB, Okinawa, was towed to Camp Sukiran where it was subsequently utilized to train Army paratroopers how to jump from a C-130. (Lockheed)

Old Hercules Never Die

HERKY LIVES ON

OLD HERCULES DON'T DIE, and they don't fade away, either. Field rep L. W. Chunn forwarded this photo from Okinawa. It shows the remains of a C-130A aircraft (LAC 3082) which was damaged beyond repair by fire during refueling in 1963 at Naha AB. The aircraft was then towed to Camp Sukiran where it is now being utilized to train Army people in the correct way to jump from a C-130. Photo was made from access door of chopper tail.

was the next to last flyable one and the one far down the ramp was already starting engines. It was time to go. He ran for the plane.

But De was taken aback at what he found on the airplane. It was packed with people—all standing. He made his way to the flight deck and found he was one of 32 people crowded into the Hercules cockpit. Major Phuong, flying the airplane by himself without copilot or flight engineer, yelled at De to find him a copilot of some kind.

"I made a careful count," De said. "We had 452 people on the airplane, children, dependents of airmen, helicopter pilots, all kinds of people, and I am sure we are too heavy to get off the ground. I called for a multi-engine copilot. Finally, at the back of the airplane, there is a pilot—he is a C-7 pilot (small 2-engine airplane) and he starts to push our way but by this time Major Phuong is already on his takeoff run."

Major Phuong had approximately 10,000 feet of runway available. At the 9,000 foot mark, he tried to rotate the overloaded Hercules.

"I could feel it," De said. "It would not lift."

A full fuel load aboard, also?

"Oh, no," De said with an expert's preciseness. "We carry only 20,000 pounds. Normal full fuel is 28,000 pounds for C-130A."

De had had his last 14 flyable C-130s fueled to 20,000 pounds each the night before. He knew the fuel load exactly. Then a sortie by some 8 to 12 A-37 bombers, captured at Da Nang and flown by North Vietnamese fighter pilots, had wiped out six of his airplanes later in the evening of April 28.

"We went off the end of the runway and onto the overrun. It is only 1,000 feet. We must lift now, we know. Major Phuong rotated at the end of the overrun. We flew. Not much—in ground effect—but the airplane kept accelerating and then we began to climb."

The ordeal was still not over. In his haste to move the C-130 out, Major Phuong had not obtained a map. He took a general heading toward Utapao, Thailand. It is normally an hour and 20 minute flight. An hour and a half later, out over the Gulf of Siam, it was apparent that the heading was wrong.

Then the C-7 pilot who had finally struggled through the press of people up to the cockpit and the co-pilot's seat, remembered that he had a map in the knee pocket of his flight suit. He began to navigate, starting with a 180 degree turn. They found Utapao. Total time enroute: 3½ hours.

Major Phuong made a perfect landing, very soft and smooth because of heavy weight, but no sweat. "And I counted the people again as we disembarked," De said. "It is true—452 people. Hercules is a very fine airplane—I once visited the factory in Georgia in 1964—but I really did not believe it will carry this much load."

Major Robert Kenny, who was at Utapao keeping track of arriving Vietnamese refugees, saw the heavily overloaded Hercules arrive. "When the doors opened, we could hardly believe what we saw. The people stacked in there looked like a scene from a World War II newsfilm, like pictures of the old Nazi concentration camps. If that flight had been much longer, some of those people probably would have died."

A little simple mathematics shows just what an overload the doughty Hercules had aboard. Rated gross weight of the C-130A aircraft is 124,000 pounds. Airplane weight of 70,000 pounds with 20,000 pounds of fuel leaves 24,000 pounds for payload. Estimating a low average weight of 100 pounds per person— 45,200 pounds—means the Hercules took off with an overload of 20,200 pounds.

This feat ranks the Hercules with other great lifesavers among airplanes—the fabled 707 flown by Sabena that carried 300 people to safety from the Congo and the 747 in Australia that carried more than 600 hurricane survivors from Melbourne to Sydney.

De had complimentary words for the help supplied by his Lockheed-Georgia field service representatives:

"Dave Valley was with me for many months. Very good man for quality control. Worked hard—out on the flight line day and night. Then, only a few weeks before the end, Bob Helmuth came. He was best parts chaser I ever saw. He found things we didn't know we had. We had highest in-commission rate we'd ever had with Helmuth—we flew 1300 hours in three weeks when he helped us with parts. He knew where to put doublers without blueprints . . . very good man. He stayed longer than any other of Americans.

"Then one day he come and say he would like to stay and help me but DAO (Defense Assistance Organization) tell him to leave. We shake hands and we are both very sad . . . ."

A FOND FAREWELL

By Lt. Col. Mack Secord
U.S. Air Force Retired

Last week I said goodbye to one of my most trusted friends.

It was one of those farewells that have meaning only if you've been through some hard times and anxious moments together . . . not the innocuous kind when you wish 'em a pleasant journey and a "maybe we'll see each other again one of these days."

No, this farewell took place without a word being spoken between the two who were parting company. After all, the fastest way I know to get an appointment with the psychiatrist is to get caught talking to an airplane on an almost deserted flight line.

My friend and almost constant companion for the past 3½ years has been a Hercules . . . a Lockheed-built C-130E. Like a true friend, she was always there when I needed her, through the good times and the bad. Sure, she had her temperamental moments along the way, just like any girl . . . a balky starter here, a wobbly prop there, but those are the little things that merely draw friends closer together.

For more than 1700 hours, we've been airborne together, my friend and I, and for countless other hours we've waited on scorching ramps or frigid parking spots together for fuel, repairs or a load of cargo.

Some days, we'd be together for only an hour or two; just long enough to load some troopers in the back, drop them from 1200 feet over a clearing and touch down again on the runway before the chutes had been gathered from the drop zone.

Other days, that cozy compartment officially referred to as the flight station was our home for what seemed like an eternity, but which was really only ten or twelve hours. Most of those long flights were the kind where the only scenery was sky and water, interspersed with an occasional thunderstorm to be dodged or a sunset to be gazed at while colors ran rampant across an evening sky.

I've often wondered whether or not my friend got the same sense of well-being I did when first spotting a tiny dot of sand and coral like Wake Island after one of those long overwater legs. Or did she ever mentally give herself a pat on the back after a particularly feathery touchdown?

We went a long way together, my friend and I. Each day's mission was almost like a geography lesson that the teacher illustrates with a swift turn of the globe. We saw Tennessee first, then expanded our world to include Arkansas, Mississippi and Georgia. Then, we moved to the Carolinas and got to know them like a farmer knows his little patch of earth.

Soon our confidence grew as we came to know and understand each other better, and late one autumn afternoon my friend and I headed for Europe together. We soon learned that low clouds and poor visibility were the trademarks of a European winter, demanding instrument flying skills honed to a fine edge.

Just about the time we began to feel at home on the Continent, we had a hurry-up call from the Congo, so off we went together, proud that we could take part in a rescue mission in that distant land of sharp contrasts. When our opportunity came to utilize everything we'd trained for, a pair of Simbas aimed their loaded guns at us. Firing desperately, they missed me but struck my companion. This seemed to anger her, and she leaped into the air with her precious cargo of refugees as if to show those on the ground at Stanleyville that it would take more than a few lucky hits to keep her from her mission.

Later, when spring had come to the Carolinas and brought the greenery that marks another change of seasons, my friend and I hurried to a Caribbean isle that knows no winter with load after load of peace-keeping equipment . . . jeeps, trucks, weapons and the men to operate them. After a week or two, it almost seemed as if we belonged at San Isidro and Pope was just a place to rest and refuel before heading southeast again.

Still later, half a world away, Okinawa became home base and Southeast Asia became our backyard as we moved bombs and bullets, food and supplies to the war-torn land of Vietnam. There, our destination might be an almost endless ribbon of concrete stretching into the jungle or a wavy pitted mat of steel plates crowned by continuous clouds that seemed to tie earth and sky.

Maybe you understand now what my friend and I have been through together and why our parting brings a twinge of nostalgia. Those were demanding, yet rewarding days we spent together. Although I am sad at the separation, our parting is made easier by my knowledge that she makes friends easily. Right now, I'll bet she's soaring high above some far-off land with another companion, just doing the job she was made for in that same splendid manner she showed me.

Princess Margaret prepares to board a Royal New Zealand C-130 at Tuvalu on her way to Sydney, Australia. This was in October, 1978. (RNZAF)

AN AIRCRAFT FOR THE WORLD

"The Hercules has been the epitome of humanitarian relief. . . We are very proud to mark the anniversary of one of the world's greatest international aircraft. . ."

Sir Douglas Bader, President of International Air Tattoo '79

In June 1979, the International Air Tattoo — "Europe's largest military spectacular" — threw a birthday party marking the 25th anniversary of the C-130's first flight. It was a grand silver jubilee and 200,000 people joined in to celebrate the occasion.

Staged at Greenham Common in the rolling green hills west of London, the celebration attracted 27 Hercules aircraft of various versions, hues and forms from 15 nations.

Although the languages spoken were as varied as the paint schemes — the Herks came from nations ranging from Australia to Venezuela — crews felt an unusually warm camaraderie and many commented, "We have a common language. . . Hercules."

It was a historic event, perhaps the largest powwow of a large transport aircraft ever held. Tattoo Air Marshal Sir Denis Crowley-Milling saluted "the wonderful workhorse" and hailed its contributions to international goodwill. Lockheed-Georgia Company's President, Robert B. Ormsby (now president of the Lockheed Aeronautical Systems Group), took the occasion at the final banquet to toast the Hercules Industry Team "and the greatest team of all. . . the people who operate the C-130."

400

Twenty-seven C-130's from 15 nations converted on Greenham Common, England in 1979 at a silver jubilee salute to the doughty airlifter. Heading up the lineup in the honor first position was the "City of Ardmore", first USAF operational C-130A, now on Air Force Reserve duty in Chicago. The "C-130 Convention" came at International Air Tattoo west of London. Air Marshall Sir Denis Crowley-Milling, Tattoo chairman, hailed "the wonderful workhorse," praising its contribution to international goodwill in its role as a mercy bird and country-builder. Winner of the "Concourse D'Elegance" Trophy for the best turned out Hercules aircraft at Air Tattoo 79 was the C-130H entered by the Royal New Zealand Air Force. Lower photo, RNZAF crew from Whenuapai, headed by Squadron Leader Trevor Keith Butler poses with their trophy in front of the aircraft along with the then president of the Lockheed-Georgia Company, Robert B. Ormsby.

The event symbolized the fact that today the Hercules aircraft is truly an international instrument of goodwill. Being flown by operators in more than 50 countries worldwide — the last count was 57 — serves to underscore the saying that "the sun never sets on the world of Hercules."

In this additional chapter being added to the new 1986 edition of *Herk*, I'd like to give some attention to the International C-130/L-100 operators.

SAUDIA ARABIA'S FLYING HOSPITAL

Saudia Arabia's C-130 "flying hospital" — an aircraft dedicated totally as a medical vehicle — has proven to be a very efficient vehicle for quick delivery of modern medical treatment to citizens in that nation. The airborne hospital, during its first year of operation, airlifted over 90 persons from remote sites to central medical centers. In addition, numerous emergency operations were conducted in the plane at distant spots.

In one outstanding case, General Rida Khalifa, director of the Saudi Arabian Armed Forces Medical Services, headed a surgical team from Riyadh Medical Hospital which carried out two emergency cardiac operations at Solayel, 700 miles south of Riyadh. The airplane flew to Solayel, arriving within two hours following the emergency call, landing on a short gravel strip.

Dr. Alister Duff, a team member, found "medical care and equipment on the C-130 equal to those of any ground fixed hospital."

Built by Lockheed-Georgia and modified to the hospital configuration by Lockheed Aircraft Service Company, the flying hospital has four special hospital rooms. Patients enter through a ramp at the rear where they are processed to the other compartments: examination room/laboratory; operating theater, and intensive care unit.

Each room is outfitted with an X-ray/fluoroscope machine, incubator/neonatal transporter, computerized blood/gas analyzer, cardioscope-defibrillator; blood bank and autoclave. Five critical-care beds have patient monitors and life support systems. Telemetry capability on the aircraft enables doctors to transmit data to a base hospital for computer diagnosis. Three radio systems ensure communication with the base hospital while on the ground or in the air.

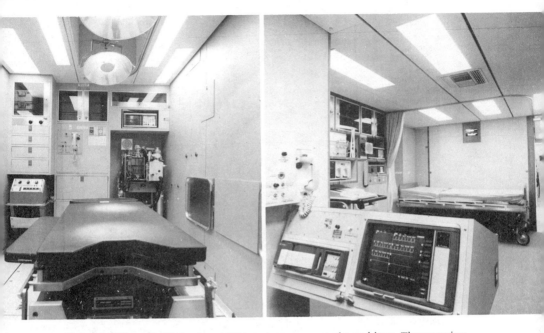

Saudi Arabian Hercules "flying hospital" interior rooms are pictured here. The operating room *(l)* is situated in the center wheel well area of the C-130 for stability. It features a hydraulically-operated surgical table, an anethesia machine and patient monitor. An electrosurgery unit allows the surgeon to cut and cauterize. The intensive care room *(r)* is one of four main compartments on the Emergency Hospital Aircraft. A radio-telemetry capability allows doctors to communicate with a base hospital and have vital medical data transmitted and analyzed. Four intensive-care beds can accommodate other patients, with full patient monitors as well as oxygen, aspiration and ventilating equipment, I.V. hangers and infusion pumps. A physician's station, foreground, monitors all beds and records cardiac and other conditions. Saudi Arabia has a fleet of the Lockheed "flying hospitals".

Saudi 1st Lt. Khaled Al-Hamdad recalled airlifting a seriously ill heart patient to England, during which the aircraft kept in touch with the Riyadh hospital until minutes before landing in London.

Dr. Duff foresees a continuing life-saving role for Saudia Arabia's flying hospital in the future.

"In a country like Saudia Arabia," he said, "where emergencies can occur in remote areas sometimes inaccessible by road, the hospital airplane can be crucial. By road, it would have taken us 15 hours to reach Solayel, whereas from takeoff preparation in Riyadh to the start of surgery on the strip at Solayel took only two hours in the C-130. That time difference speaks for itself." Saudia Arabia now has nine Lockheed Hercules "flying hospitals," of various configurations, including stretched versions.

A Royal Australian Air Force C-130H, outfitted with a modular airborne firefighting system (MAFFS) unit, swoops over a forest in Australia to drop fire retardant. The C-130 is also used as a firefighter by the U.S. Air Reserve Forces and by the Italian Air Force. In photo at bottom, six RAAF C-130's sweep past a RAAF C-130H parked on the ramp at Base Richmond as the Australians celebrated 25 years of Lockheed C-130 Hercules Operations on Nov. 6, 1983. Over the years, the RAAF has had a total of 36 C-130's — 12 "A" models (now decommissioned), 12 C-130E's and 12 C-130H's — and has accumulated more than 400,000 accident-free flight hours in operations worldwide.

AUSTRALIA'S FLYING FIRE TRUCK

Australia is the latest nation to use the C-130 as an "aerial firefighter." For years, Australia's Forests Commission had used only light aircraft to combat fire outbreaks, but they had proven inadequate.

The commission obtained a MAAFS unit from the U.S. Forestry Service and, using a RAAF C-130H manned by crews from No. 36 Squadron, ran trial programs during the 1981-82 and 1982-83 bushfire seasons.

In one instance, the RAAF "flying fire truck" roared to the scene of a raging bushfire and saved two houses in the fire's path. The fire in Australia's Mt. Macedon region had destroyed 18 houses. When the flames were about 300 feet from the home of Mr. and Mrs. Roggero Gregory, the 30 battling firemen on the ground were withdrawn and the Hercules was summoned from its base at Mangalore. The RAAF C-130 swooped in just above treetop level and squirted fire retardant onto a large area between the flames and the house. The fire was turned back.

FRANCE'S SFAIR AIRLINE

Although SFAIR is one of the world's youngest and smallest cargo airlines, the French carrier is proving to be one of the most innovative. With its two L-100-30s, the airline is getting attention in Europe, Africa and the Middle East with its slogan, "Airlifting le difficile freight to les difficiles destinations."

SFAIR Director General, Pierre Bodin, hails his airline's Super Herks, which can haul all types of cargo from small regional airports to destinations around the world, even to "carved out" strips. One of Bodin's L-100-30s, based in Bordeaux, easily hauled vital electronic equipment to an oil drilling field in the middle of the Mali desert in 1982. Until the arrival of the big Hercules turboprop, the strip had been utilized only for lightweight Cessna 404s.

With the help of SFAIR's engineer, the strip near the oil derrick was graded and lengthened to 3,940 feet (1200 meters). The L-100, packed with special electronic equipment, made an easy landing.

NIGER C-130s AIRLIFT SHEEP

The Niger Air Force utilizes its Lockheed C-130H Hercules transports for a variety of airlift missions, hauling such manifests as satellite dish-antennas, oil drilling equipment, automobiles and Hadj pilgrims.

In late 1984, a Niger propjet aircraft took on a new and unusual task — the transporting of sheep. In 21 round trips between the Niger capital city of Niamey, and Lagos, Nigeria, two Niger C-130Hs hauled 7,000 sheep. The animals were obtained for sacrifice during the Moslem holy holiday of Tabaski, celebrating the covenant between God and Abraham.

In order to airlift the large number of sheep efficiently, Niger workmen constructed two-level steel cages. Approximately 25 sheep were placed in each cage. The compartments were inserted into the aircraft's cargo compartment with a forklift.

The sheep lift was only the latest of a wide variety of airlift missions carried out by the Niger Air Force and its C-130 fleet. In flights to the Nigerienne city of Agadez, one C-130H airlifted 50,000 pounds of satellite dish-antenna equipment, replacing similar equipment damaged in a windstorm.

During September 1984, three C-130H flights carried Hadj pilgrims from the Nigerienne cities of Maradi and Zinder to Niamey where they boarded special flights to Mecca.

Niger is one of many African countries that operate the Lockheed Hercules aircraft. Other African nations operating the C-130/L-100 are Angola, Cameroon, Gabon, Nigeria, South Africa, Sudan, Uganda, Zaire, Morocco, Algeria, Tunisia, Libya, and Egypt.

PERUVIAN L-100 AIRLIFT SAVES ANDEAN DAM

A ten-million-ton rock slide was threatening the Tablachaca Dam high up in the Central Andes. The dam, located on the Mantaro river, a tributary of the Amazon River, supplies a large proportion of the electric energy for Peru's capital city of Lima.

The situation was declared an emergency by the Peruvian government. The slide had to be stabilized before the rainy season, which could have provoked a disaster.

Nigerian President Shehu Shagari steps down from Nigerian Air Force Hercules aircraft *(left photo)* on arrival back at Lagos following a C-130 flight to Sokoto. He is greeted by the Vice President, Dr. Alex Ekwueme. Nigeria operates a fleet of advanced model C-130H and C-130-30 Super Hercules on nation-building airlift and as military logistic tasks. Neighboring nations in West and Central Africa operating the versatile Hercules aircraft are Niger, Cameroon, Gabon, Zaire and Angola. *(Photo courtesy National Concord, Ikeja-Lagos).* In picture on right, Gabon's President Omar Bongo admires 1/25th scale model of his nation's Lockheed L-100-30 "quick change" convertible transport. Making the presentation was Major Oliver Omouala *(l),* Deputy Chief, Gabon Air Force. Immediately afterward, President Bongo and members of his cabinet were taken on a presidential inaugural flight. The chief executive said he would probably start using the aircraft for in-country transportation. The L-100-30 convertible aircraft can be used either as an all passenger airliner, as a cargo airfreighter, or as a "combi" aircraft. Conversion from all-freight to all passenger can be accomplished in less than an hour. Lockheed-Georgia Company technical respresentative Curt G. Harvey *(r)* and flight instructor (now Lockheed-Georgia Chief Pilot) Dick Clinton *(rear)* took part in the inaugural flight event.

Group Captain U.S. Abbas *(left photo),* Defence and Armed Forces Attache from the Nigerian Embassy, Washington, D.C. accepted his nation's third C-130H-30 "Super Hercules" transport in ceremonies at the Lockheed-Georgia Company, in March, 1984. Here he checks out the flight station of one of the airplanes. Altogether, the Nigerian Air Force has a fleet of nine Hercules aircraft — six C-130H's and three C-130H-30's. In right photo, Captain Paul Yakana, commander of the Cameroon Air Force, sits in the spacious flight station of one of his country's C-130H's. The Republic of Cameroon is using its new aircraft for various civic development projects in addition to its basic role of military transport. Cameroon thus joins its neighboring African countries of Nigeria, Gabon, Niger and Zaire in selecting the Hercules to perform a dual role of development assistance and military capability.

The story of the successful race against time was told by John D. Kelly, technical manager of Geotechnica, a Rio de Janeiro geotechnical consultant firm.

Through an arrangement with Fuerza Aerea Peruana (Peruvian Air Force), which operates a fleet of Lockheed L-100s, Geotechnica contracted for 15 L-100 flights to aiflift the necessary heavy equipment from Sao Paulo, Brazil, to Lima.

"Thanks to the Hercules airlift," stated Kelly, "We completed the emergency works in a very short time." Among the equipment airlifted were three 60-ton piling rigs with 70-foot leaders to stabilize soft material in the reservoir. The base of each piling rig alone weighed over 34,000 pounds. Measuring 26 feet long, six and one-half feet high, and six and one-half feet wide, the units were easily accommodated in the large Hercules cargo compartment with its aft-end loading ramp. Other equipment hauled in included air compressors.

With the heavy equipment, the contractors were able to build a rock-fill counterfort, as well as rock anchor rigs. An additional L-100 flight took equipment into a 3,000-foot strip at Huancayo Airport near the dam site, when a road from Lima was blocked. Said Kelly: "The emergency airlift was possible only by using the Hercules aircraft. To have utilized surface transportation of the equipment from Brazil would have required 30 days. The L-100s made the flights in a matter of hours."

INDONESIAN TRANSMIGRATION AIRLIFT

In early 1983, Pelita Air Service of Indonesia recorded 20,000 accident-free flight hours with its relatively new fleet of L-100-30 "transmigration" transports. Some 17,400 hours of the total were accumulated by only three of the Hercules propjets which were delivered in July and August of 1979.

Committed to the nation's vast transmigration airlift, the six aircraft flew more than 4,000 sorties over a 40-month period. During this time, more than 430,000 people and hundreds of tons of cargo were moved.

The transmigrants are being moved from the heavily populated islands of Java, Bali and Lombok to sparsely settled regions of Sumatra, Kalimantan (Borneo), Sulawesi (Celebese) and Iran Jaya.

Six Lockheed L-100-30 Super Hercules transports are flown by Pelita Air Services out of Jakarta on a unique Indonesian "transmigration" program. Entire families are being airlifted from heavily populated cities of Indonesia to virgin farmland on outlying islands. The Indonesian L-100-30's can carry 128 passengers and their personal belongings.

Accommodating a load of 128 migrants and their personal belongings, the L-100s airlift the families to their destinations of speeds of more than 300 miles per hour, then slow down and land at remote landing strips, near their new homes.

This capability was demonstrated dramatically in Irian Jaya (western New Guinea). Special permission was given for two heavily loaded Pelita L-100-30s to land at a short strip at Manokwari. Normally restricted to light aircraft no larger than the two-engine DC-3 or C-47, the remote Manokwari strip is only 1,341 meters long (4,400 feet), 30.5 meters wide (100 feet) and has only a light aircraft strength rating. Despite this, the L-100s, thanks to their high flotation landing gear, landed, taxied and took off at Manokwari without difficulty. Inspection of the runaway afterward revealed no damage to the strip surface.

While the main objective is to airlift families and their possessions, Pelita Air Service often gets the opportunity to demonstrate the airplane's cargo-hauling talents, also, transporting medical supplies, seeds, food, and sheep to outlying communities.

The Lockheed Hercules transport is no newcomer to Indonesia, A large fleet of military version C-130s is operated by the Indonesian Air Force. These include C-130Bs, KC-130B refueler/transports, advanced model C-130Hs, the long fuselage C-130H-30, and the Maritime Patrol Version C-130H-MP.

AUSTRALIANS SET SAFETY MARK

Twenty-five accident-free years of Lockheed C-130 Hercules operations were celebrated by the Royal Australian Air Force in late 1983.

Flying throughout Australia and around the world in supply, transportation and mercy missions, the RAAF has flown a total of 36 C-130s — 12 C-130As (now decommissioned), 12 C-130Es and 12 C-130Hs – and has accumulated over 400,000 accident-free flight hours and over 96 million nautical miles, equivalent to 200 round trips to the moon.

Australia was the first nation outside the U.S. to put the Lockheed C-130 into service, in 1958. During the 25th anniversary celebrations, Air Commodore S.S.N. Watson, Officer Commanding the RAAF base at Richmond, praised the role of the aircraft and the outstanding performance by the crews of Number 36 and 37 Squadrons:

"The C-130 Hercules is a valued aircraft in our RAAF inventory. It provides a capability and mobility to the Australian Defense Force which would be difficult to achieve without this fine aircraft.

"Number 36 and 37 Squadrons, ably supported by 486 Maintenance Squadron, have operated in the Vietnam conflict, flood relief, cyclone relief, and resupply/airdrop operations within Australia, Papua New Guinea, New Zealand, Indonesia, Malaysia and Singapore.

"Both squadrons have flown scores of missions with complete medical crews to places such as Fiji and Papua New Guinea and provided an all-year search and rescue cover for all Australian waters.

"Number 37 Squadron, carrying out the strategic airlift role, has flown resupply and support missions to Australian United Nations forces in Pakistan and Egypt and presently conducts scheduled courier for the Australian contingent of the multinational force observers group at El Gorah."

Number 36 Squadron is the RAAF's primary tactical transport unit. The squadron has flown resupply missions to Antarctica and regularly conducts airdrop missions to such places as Macquarie Island. The squadron also has provided firefighting support during the summer bushfire season.

The excellence achieved by individual units was reflected by the

RAAF Base Richmond team, which won the Best Allied Team trophy at Volant Rodeo competition 1983 held at Pope AFB, North Carolina.

UGANDA AIR CARGO: ONE-HERK AIRLINE

Uganda Air Cargo operates only one airplane — a Lockheed L-100-30 "Super Hercules" airfreighter — but the line experiences a profitable performance in hauling mine shafts, foodgrains and goats, among other items across the continents of Africa and Europe. Based in the Uganda city of Entebbe, the airline operates with two full crews and keeps its L-100 busy for the government and for commercial hire. Said Capt. John Kassami, flight operations manager:

"Our air machine, the Hercules, is a peach. She operates like a sewing machine. All you have to do is turn on the ignition and she goes. The only downtime we have had has been for periodic maintenance."

Certified as a civil freighter by the nation's Directorate of Civil Aviation/Transport Board, the Uganda L-100 has filled an important niche in hauling oversize cargo, particularly into short and unpaved runways that are inaccessible to Uganda Airlines' 707s and F-27s. Said Capt. Kassami:

"We've been into a lot of unpaved runways with our Hercules, and we've had no problems whatsoever."

"One of our biggest projects is transporting medicines, food-stuffs, tents, and other vital supplies into southern Sudan where there are 500,000 refugees," Kassami added. The flights were commissioned by the International Red Cross and the United Nations Refugee Commission. Many were staged out of Nairobi, Kenya, terminating in Juba, Sudan.

Since going operational in 1982, the Uganda Air Cargo L-100 has hauled mining and construction equipment from Europe to Africa (including a mine shaft to N'Dola, Zambia), 800 goats from Entebbe to Dubai (in five flights) and numerous refugee relief flights.

On an airlift into the famine region of Chad, in west central Africa, the Ugandan L-100 found itself in a joint airlift with other Hercules aircraft flown by Air Botswana, SFAIR (France) and

Transamerica (U.S.). In that mission, the grain was flown from the capital city to short strips in remote interior communities.

While cargo-hauling is the airline's primary mission, officials have installed a six-passenger seat pallet into the L-100's cargo compartment. "Airlift of passengers is allowed by Uganda for people in an emergency situation," Capt. Kassami said.

INDONESIA'S C-130H-MP

The Republic of Indonesia put its first new long-range Lockheed C-130H-MP maritime patrol aircraft on duty in 1982 patrolling the shorelines of its vast 13,000 island archipelago.

Operated by the Indonesian Air Force, the propjet aircraft gives the populous nation a versatile new tool for patrolling its 200-mile Exclusive Economic Zone (EEZ). With its specialized maritime mission equipment, the C-130H-MP provides Indonesia with a capability for dectecting, identifying, and intercepting intruding surface vessels; enforcing fishing laws and treaties; protecting the marine environment; and conducting humanitarian missions involving search and rescue.

The Indonesian Air Force Chief of Staff, Air Chief Marshal Ashadi, accompanied crews on the initial demonstration flights encompassing all Indonesian islands. The Indonesian C-130H-MP is similar in many respects to the U.S. Coast Guard maritime patrol fleet of 25 C-130s, which meet all International Civil Aviation Organization (ICAO) requirements for maritime surveillance and search and rescue.

Featuring fuel-efficient Allison propjet engines, long range and a comfortable cabin environment, the C-130H-MP has a highly accurate sea search radar and advanced computerized inertial and omega navigation systems.

Special maritime patrol equipment in the Indonesian aircraft includes a rest module for crews, a ramp pallet that holds rescue kits, flare launcher, loud speaker and a rear-looking observer station, and a specially modified telephoto camera linked electronically to the airplane's computerized navigation systems. The on-board computer provides a printout superimposed over photos of surface targets, giving precise latitude and longitude as well as date and time. Equipped with a galley, two lavatories, and five bunks, the module can be inserted easily into the plane's cargo compartment and latched down. When the airplane is needed for other purposes, the module can be removed readily.

An advantage of the C-130H-MP is that it can use four-engine speed to get its patrol station and then cut back to two engines to gain additional on-duty loiter time.

DEMONSTRATION TOURS

Lockheed-Georgia took a C-130H on a demonstration tour in the People's Republic of China. Touring with the approval of the United States government, the aircraft was displayed in Shanghai, Beijing and Canton.

Demonstrations included aerial drops, takeoff and landing performance capabilities, cargo loading and unloading and quick conversion of the aircraft for medical evacuation use.

The highlight was the aerial drop display before more than 600 spectators in Beijing. The demonstration started with a container delivery system drop of two bundles weighing 2,200 pounds each, from an altitude of 600 feet. The Hercules is capable of dropping 16 such containers weighing up to a metric ton each. The container delivery system is used to drop items such as medical supplies and food to remote locations.

Next to be parachuted from the aircraft into the 1,200-foot long, 150-foot wide drop zone was an 8,000-pound heavy equipment load dropped from an altitude of 1,100 feet. Light road building and construction equipment can be delivered to remote sites using this system.

Most impressive of the demostrations was a low-altitude parachute extraction system (LAPES) drop that drew heavy applause.

Carrying a 10,340-pound truck, the Hercules flew five feet above the drop area and released the vehicle directly in front of the viewing stand.

Another demonstration aircraft, a C-130H-30, was taken on a month-long, 30,000-statute-mile tour to India, Egypt, and Saudia Arabia.

"Our objective was to show off the increased capabilities of this new longer-fuselage Hercules transport," stated tour leader Bob Parker of Lockheed-Georgia's marketing organization. "The aircraft performed beautifully in every mission demonstrated — personnel and cargo airlift, container, personnel and heavy equipment drops and low-altitude parachute extraction (LAPES)." Flights in all three countries were made in 100 degree (F) plus temperatures.

The C-130H-30's aerodynamic handling qualities were praised by officials of the respective air forces, who stated that the responsiveness and ease of handling were equal to if not better than those of the standard short-fuselage C-130H. Egyptian Air Force officials were reported "very pleased" with the plane's capabilities following a series of short field takeoffs and landings. On a typical personnel airlift mission from Cairo to Aswan, the C-130H-30 carried over 70 people and 4,000 pounds of cargo, and on return flight airlifted over 70 passengers.

In Saudi Arabia, the aircraft was put on static display in Jeddah and Riyadh, and made local demonstration flights for Royal Saudi Arabian Air Force officials. Carrying a ballast load of 20,000 pounds, the airplane landed at a remote site in the Saudi desert — a dirt strip that had just been leveled by a bulldozer.

The India portion of the tour included a static display in New Delhi and a series of performance flights for Indian Air Force officials. Among missions performed by demonstration pilot Bob Hill was a simulated three-engine takeoff and climb-out carrying a 25,000-pound payload, at a high temperature.

The newspaper *India Today* declared that the Indian Government was interested in the Super Hercules. "The aircraft made by Lockheed and one of the most successful freighters built, was in India for trails and evaluation. The Hercules is being evaluated as a replacement for AN-12s and Fairchild (C-119) Packets that are well past their prime."

CANADA'S GOLD MINE HERCULES

Echo Bay Mines, Ltd, carried out a "Herculean airlift" of an entire $110 million gold mine/industrial complex to an otherwise inaccessible site at Contwoyto Lake near the Arctic Circle. The company used its Lockheed L-100-20 airfreighter as a "flying railroad" to establish the "new town" gold mining complex in Canada's Northwest Territories. During its first 12-month period of operation, the company's L-100, flying out of Yellowknife, hauled more than 47,000,000 pounds of freight, fuel and cargo, much of it heavy, oversize equipment, while logging 1,988 flight hours and 2,083 landings. Fuel, the lifeblood of the construction project, was airlifted to the site in special tanks carrying up to 6,500 imperial gallons.

The project started when the company's Hercules aircraft landed on the frozen Lake Contwoyto with earth-moving equipment which was used to carve out a 5,000-foot landing strip nearby.

Some 100 worker dormitories — "Herk Trailers" — were hauled in by the Hercules. Built to fit into the airplane's 9x10x48-foot cargo compartment, most modules have two rooms and a bath, and need only to be set up and plugged in.

"We started up there with nothing but staked out land in the tundra," said John Zigarlick, Echo Bay president. "Now we have living and eating accomodations for 500 people, a thousand-ton a day mill, a smeltering unit, a 700-foot deep mine shaft, garages and power plant. All of the structures are closed in. It is a factory surrounded by a small city, and everything has been hauled in and out with this one Hercules aircraft."

ITALIAN C-130 WINS VOLANT RODEO

In June 1984, for the second time in three years, the Italian Air Force — flying a Lockheed C-130H airlifter — flew away with the top award in the international airlift competition at Pope AFB, N.C., known as "Volant Rodeo." For the Italians, the victory was especially sweet, since they repeated their 1982 achievement as the top winner, taking the big trophy home to Pisa. Other 1984 winners included Australia for the best short field assault landing (C-130); West Germany, best in maintenance; New Zealand, first in the C-130 aircrew competition; and the British Royal Air Force in the security police event. All of the winning Allied units, except West Germany, flew Lockheed Hercules transports in the competition. In the overall competition, the Royal New Zealand Air Force won third place. The second spot was taken by the 437th Military Airlift Wing, a USAF C-141 unit from Charleston AFB, S.C.

Winners were determined by the highest scores in a series of events including airdrops, air and land navigation, aircraft maintenance, and combat endurance.

Altogether, 34 USAF, Air National Guard and Air Force Reserve wings flying C-130s and C-141s competed in the Rodeo event along with Allied entries from Australia, Brazil, Canada, West Germany, Italy, New Zealand, Saudi Arabia and the United Kingdom.

Calling it "the airlift summer olympics," that attracts "the best of the best," Brig. Gen. Robert B. Patterson, rodeo commander, declared:

"If we ever have to go to war, I would feel good knowing that the Allies we're fighting beside are qualified."

AIR GABON L-100-30 IS 1800th HERCULES SOLD

In late 1985, Air Gabon, the national airline of the West African nation of Gabon, purchased an L-100-30 airfreighter. The airplane was the 1800th to be ordered in the C-130/L-100 series.

To replace a VC-9 Vanguard aircraft that the airline has been using over the past few years, Air Gabon plans to log 1800 L-100 flight hours during the first year of Hercules operation, more than twice the VC-9 utilization.

Fabien Owono-Essono, director-general of Air Gabon, on a visit to Lockheed-Georgia Company, hailed the acquisition of the Lockheed propjet.

"This versatile airfreighter," he said, "is going to give Air Gabon a valuable new capability in helping us as a nation to continue to grow economically, and will be a tool to develop east-west trade links within Africa."

The L-100-30 will be used to interline with Air Gabon's 747-200C freighter in distributing goods within Gabon and to points in West and Central Africa.

Air Gabon's L-100-30 has been equipped with a specially modified PEMCO cargo-handling system that will enable the aircraft to take aboard 747-size, 20-foot-long M-2 containers as well as 96x125-inch commercial pallets. The system also will handle 96x125-inch "double pallets" measuring 238.5 inches in length.

Air Gabon became the eighth commercial carrier in Africa to operate the commercial version of the Hercules aircraft. Other African airlines operating the L-100-30 are Angola Airlines, Air Botswana, Air Algerie, SCIBE-Zaire, Uganda Air Cargo, United African Airlines and Zaire Cargo.

Indonesian Air Force officials inspect their C-130H-MP maritime patrol version aircraft on a visit to the Lockheed-Georgia Company prior to its ferry flight to Jakarta. Top left, Air First Marshall Hamsana of Hq. IAF, looks over spacious flight station from the left hand captain's seat. In photo at lower right, IAF officers check out the relief crew compartment, a palletized module which is easily inserted into the airplane's 9x10x41-foot cargo compartment, along with then Lockheed-Georgia Vice President Robert Roche, second from right. L-R: Air First Marshall Hamsana, Lt. Col. Soejitno, Mr. Roche and Colonel Dasiyo. Top right, the C-130H-MP is pictured on a demonstration flight as it drops a rescue packet from rear ramp. Lower left, special camera is operated from glass observation doors located on each side of cargo compartment. The camera is linked to the airplane's navigation systems, providing documentary photos of surface targets, giving precise latitude and longitude as well as date and time.

"I'm falling for you" could easily be the cry of these members of the famed Royal Air Force "Falcon" paradrop team (*left photo*). Framed against the backdrop of their Lockheed C-130K, the smiles on the jumpers' faces are probably more from the thought that their photographer can't order them about with "Just one more, please" or "Stand more to the left" rather than the traditional plea of "Say cheese." In photo on right, Royal Australian Air Force drops the M38A1 vehicle on a modular platform from the C-130 aircraft. This vehicle was continually dropped during airdrop training of pilots for number 36 squadron at RAAF Base Richmond.

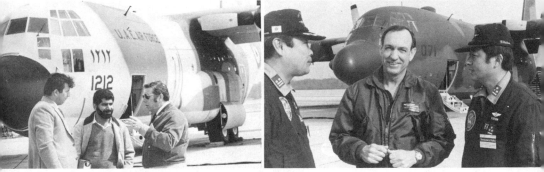

Flight crewmen from the United Arab Emirates Air Force (*left photo*) discuss the merits of their nation's newly-acquired C-130H aircraft with Lockheed-Georgia Company flight engineer instructor John Brown (*r*). The UAE took delivery of two of the new advanced model Lockheed propjects in 1984. Twelve nations in the Middle East region operate the C-130 and L-100 transport aircraft on airlift missions ranging from civic action "nation building" tasks to military logistic support. In photo on right, Japan Air Self Defence Force pilots Lt. Col. Tetson Kawada (*l*) and Capt. Kazuo Kudo confer at Lockheed-Georgia with their Lockheed instructor pilot, Billy Morell. In the background is one of the two advanced model C-130H's ferried to Japan in mid-March, 1984. Two more were delivered to Japan in late 1984. Stationed at Komaki Airbase west of Tokyo, the new airplanes are used to handle heavy transport missions. Japan has more C-130H's on order.

Billows of dust rise as Transamerica Airlines L-100-30 lands on dirt runway in Papua, New Guinea (*top photo*). Lower photo, local chiefs posed with Transamerica officials in front of the Hercules aircraft. Many of the local people helped the airline loadmasters in offloading oil drilling equipment.

Air Algerie pilot, in left position, is all smiles as he looks over flight station of his airline's L-100-30 Super Hercules. Right photo, pallet containing galley and lavatory is rolled aboard the Air Algeria convertible.

Air Algerie, Algeria's government airline, operates this "quick change" convertible version of the Lockheed L-100-30 "Super Hercules" transport. Based in Algiers, the airline took delivery of three L-100-30's in 1981. Thanks to the convertible feature, the airline can switch from the cargo mode to passenger mode in less than an hour, or fly with varied combinations of passengers and cargo. Conversion is accomplished by the use of seven pallets, which contain seating for 91 passengers, plus a galley/lavatory pallet. The pallets can be inserted into the aircraft's cargo compartment, using its floor rollers. When the airplane is needed for cargo-hauling missions, the pallets can be removed quickly. The Governments of Gabon and Kuwait also have bought similar "quick change" cargo/passenger conversion kits from Lockheed. As these photos will attest, the switch from cargo mode to passenger mode goes quickly. Top to bottom: Seat pallets are brought to airplane on trailer truck. . . inserted on rollers into cargo compartment. . . presto, you have an airliner with five-abreast seating and stewardesses serving coffee and tea. . . then the airplane makes takeoff and away we go! (The galley and lavatory also are inserted into the cargo compartment on pallets to provide total passenger comfort. The plane, of course, is fully heated and air conditioned.)

When the Swedish Air Force marked the 20th anniversary of operating the Lockheed C-130 Hercules in early 1985, Lockheed-Georgia Company paid special tribute to the Scandinavian operator. Lockheed-Georgia Company's Director of Manufacturing, Herb Brady, led a delegation in visiting Stockholm and Base Satenas to honor the occasion. Here Col. Bjorn Amelim *(r)*, Satenas Base Commander, accepts a silver salver from the Lockheed group. L-R: Hoyt Vaughn, Lockheed technical representative for Europe and Scandinavia; Eddie Gustafson, regional sales manager-Europe; Mr. Brady; and Col. Amelim. In the background is the first C-130 that was delivered to Sweden in 1965 and which is still in operation along with the fleet of seven other C-130's. The Swedish Air Force is noted for its outstanding worldwide humanitarian airlift work with its Hercules fleet.

The President of Colombia, Dr. Belisario Betancur *(center)*, along with cabinet members, inspects his nation's new Lockheed C-130H Hercules aircraft. This followed a ceremony at Bogota's El Dorado International Airport in 1984 introducing the two new aircraft into the Colombian Air Force inventory. Accompanying the President at the ceremony were, *(l-r)*: Chief of the Colombian Armed Forces, General Miguel Vega; Minister of Defense, General Gustavo Matamoros; and, at right, the Minister of Foreign Relations, Dr. Augusto Ramirez Ocampo. Colombia is using the advanced model Lockheed-Georgia built propjet for nation-building airlift and military logistic support. This marked the third Hercules buy for the Colombian Air Force. The popular Hercules is known familiarly as "The Little Horse of the Andes."

EPILOGUE

The Hercules story is far from over. While present aircraft rolling off Lockheed's assembly line will be flying well into the twenty-first century, technical developments now under way could give the persevering bird an even longer life and greater usefulness to its operators and beneficiaries.

Major breakthroughs in engine and propeller technology, plus significant new Lockheed airframe derivative designs, are bringing renewed excitement to Herk buffs worldwide.

Part of the exuberance is due to the renewed acceptance of the propeller, which is staging a dramatic comeback on the wings of the energy crisis.

As Lockheed-Georgia's former Director of Engineering Carroll Dallas likes to declare, "The propeller is the most efficient propulsive mechanism yet known to man for generation of takeoff thrust."

Moreover, the modern propjet burns on takeoff about half as much fuel per pound of thrust as a high-bypass fanjet engine. Once the airplane reaches altitude, the propjet engine also shows remarkable efficiency.

But the real excitement on the propeller is the pioneering energy efficiency research now under way, sponsored by the National Aeronautics and Space Administration.

In the meantime, in continuing the Lockheed C-130 engineering philosophy of continually improving and updating the airplane, latest improvements include the installation of modernized, easy-to-maintain fuel gauging systems, improved crew seats, ventral strakes that improve range, speed and fuel performance, and additional emergency exits.

New versions of the airplane are continually being studied. The latest military version is the C-130H-30 "Super Hercules." Featuring a 55-foot long cargo compartment, such as the commercial L-100-30, the new version has a near 40 percent increase in cargo volume, permitting the loading of two additional cargo pallets. The C-130H-30 carries 92 paratroops, compared to 64 on the standard C-130. The aircraft's infantry troop capacity is 128 fully equipped soldiers. Nations operating the C-130H-30 include Algeria, Cameroon, Dubai, Indonesia, Nigeria, Saudi Arabia and Thailand. Britain's Royal Air Force operates an extended-fuselage version that is designated the C Mark 3.

Another new version actively being studied by Lockheed and GEC Avionics Ltd. (GAv) of Great Britain is a C-130 Airborne Early Warning (AEW) system. In a joint announcement at the 1985 Paris Air Show, the two firms confirmed that with the receipt of sufficient orders, Lockheed and GAv are prepared to launch a production program in 1986. Lockheed conducted an independent radar investigation and determined that the GAv system "has great growth potential and can meet all of its targeted requirements." Flying at a 27,000-foot altitude, the C-130 AEW would provide a 360-degree surveillance coverage to the 200-nautical mile radar horizon and beyond. The high-power, long- range radar would scan the skies with space stabilized antennas, allowing continuous target tracking during normal aircraft manuevers.

The heart of the radar installation would be contained on modular units installed in the aircraft's cargo compartment through the full-width rear ramp opening.

With the use of the modular equipment units, the plane could be converted from the AEW system to a basic multi-mission aircraft without any appreciable loss in operational flexibility.

Another recent development at Lockheed-Georgia with bearing on the C-130's future is the company's acquisition of an L-100-20 that it has converted into its "High Technology Test Bed" aircraft. Supported by more than 40 suppliers, the HTTB is enabling Lockheed's engineers to integrate into a large cargo/support aircraft advanced technologies such as high lift systems, advanced flight controls, cockpit displays, navigation, guidance and en route survivability.

Although the airplane is being used to test out a wide spectrum of aviation technologies, its impact on the Hercules could be significant. In early 1985, the airplane, with only a few external modifications such as addition of horsal and dorsal fins, set three STOL time-to-climb world records. With additional modifications upcoming — included a full-span dropped high camber leading edge and new double-slotted aft flaps — the HTTB is expected to become an even greater STOL performer. Flight station improvements also may lead the way for similar improvements in future Hercules production aircraft.

A C-130 Airborne Early Warning system has been proposed by Lockheed-Georgia Company and GEC Avionics, Ltd. (GAv) of England. They announced at the 1985 Paris Air Show that with sufficient orders, they were prepared to launch a C-130 AEW system in 1986. The system, with radar in the nose and tail as shown in this artist's concept, provides a 360-degree coverage to the radar horizon. The cutaway drawing shows the layout proposed. Forward pallet would contain radar processing equipment. An enclosed insulated module provides space for six AEW control stations. A rear pallet contains communications equipment.

Where will it all end?

The basic Hercules itself indubitably will find still additional roles to play in the years ahead. Don't be surprised if you read that the C-130 has become a pesticide spray vehicle, and/or an environmental patroller (particularly to monitor oil spills and waterway pollution). One of its major new roles may be that of "typhoon moderator" (cloud seeder). Other potential new missions could be that of an earth resources observation platform, mine layer aircraft, cruise missile tactical aircraft, and an improved TACAMO platform (serving as a communications link with Poseidon/Trident submarines).

Thus goes the seemingly endless saga of the Lockheed Hercules.

Pilot Ralph Evans, who took Lockheed's demonstrator Hercules to Alaska in 1965, brought back a beautiful word picture of the plane's performance in the Arctic wilds. It might well serve as a memorial to the spirit of the indomitable bird. Here is Ralph's report to his fellow employee's, as published in the Lockheed *Southern Star:*

If only that bird could talk . . . that fabulous Hercules, N-1130, that is. It would puff up with pride in its accomplishment during the Alaskan lease.

It would speak of being stuffed with all degrees of bulk and weight that man could imagine, yet lifting lightly and gracefully into the air.

It would tell of flights through the dance of the Northern Lights, or high above snowy mountains that defy description, or yet through the Arctic "whiteout," when the horizon completely disappears.

It would describe landings on a frozen lake, or on a gravel river bed, and through drifting snow a foot or more deep. It would talk of storied places like Nome and Point Barrow, Fairbanks, Anchorage and many more.

It would brag of doing it all, day and night, never missing a flight for maintenance.

You (Lockheed people) designed and built it to do such good work. You may be justly proud.

The 1700th Lockheed C-130 Hercules transport was delivered at the Lockheed-Georgia Company flight line Dec. 12, 1983. Recipient of the milestone aircraft — an advanced model C-130H — was the Air Self Defense Force of Japan, which took delivery of two of the propjets in the Marietta, Ga., turnover ceremony. Alex Lorch, then executive vice president of Lockheed-Georgia, turned over the symbolic key to U.S. Air Force Col. Ronald D. Patchett, who in turn officially presented the aircraft to Maj. Masamichi Shishido of the Japan Air Self Defense Force, Air Transport Wing. Japan becomes the 55th nation to operate the Lockheed propjet.

The 1800th Hercules aircraft sold by the Lockheed-Georgia Company was also delivered in December, 1985, to Air Gabon, the state-owned Gabonaise national airline. In photo, officials of the airline, headed by its deputy technical director, B.A. Ntoma-Mengome (on right), accept the airplane from Lockheed-Georgia Vice President-Marketing, Charles Ray, to the left of the American flag. Air Gabon is using the L-100-30 "Super Hercules" for "flying railroad" duty, interlining with Air Gabon's 747-200C freighter in distributing goods within Gabon and to points in West and Central Africa.

Fleet of Many Flags. Composite photo shows the variety of paint schemes and markings on Hercules from various countries. Left column, top to bottom: Egypt, Bolivia, Cameroon, Nigeria. Right column, top to bottom: Argentina, Sudan, Gabon and Norway. Operators in fifty-seven nations have taken delivery of C-130's and L-100's from Lockheed-Georgia. In addition, Angola, Singapore and Uganda have bought Hercules from original operators. (Lockheed)

Thanks to Safair Airfreighters and its Hercules, the rare Roan Antelope in Africa was saved from extinction in 1971. Top photo, Hercules lands in a dry river bed in the barren Bushmanland of South West Africa. Quietly waiting for a ride was an antelope *(below left),* one which had been tranquilized by a dart gun fired earlier from a helicopter. Altogether 71 roans were placed aboard the Herk and flown to Etosha National Park, world's largest game reserve. Two years later, the herd had more than doubled.

Hercules from Scandinavia can be found on duty around the world. Left, a Norwegian C-130 offloads foods in the new nation of Bangladesh, a project of the Norwegian Church Relief. Right, a Royal Danish Air Force C-130H makes a midnight mail drop at Daneborg, Greenland, on its way to Thule. The Danish Hercules fleet carries out iceberg and fish patrol and reconnaissance and scientific research missions. To supply patrol units in northern Greenland, the Danish Herks land on frozen fiords in the winter and dry lake beds in the summer. The Danish C-130's also fly numerous Red Cross mercy flights into Africa and Asia. (Lockheed)

Lockheed-Georgia's High Technology Test Bed (HTTB) aircraft — a modified L-100-20 — comes in for landing after setting three STOL "time-to-climb" world records. Lockheed Staff Engineers John Barker and Carl Hughes measure the wind velocity as part of the record verification. Results of the record-breaking flight were announced at the 1985 Paris Air Show. In setting the records, the HTTB took off in an estimated 427 meters, climbed to 3,000 meters in three minutes 57.4 seconds; to 6,000 meters in nine minutes .35 seconds, and to 9,000 meters (around 31,000 feet) in 17 minutes 41.71 seconds. Gross weight at takeoff was 98,600 pounds (44,724 kilograms). The landing roll was 335 meters at a gross weight of 95,000 pounds (43,091 kilograms). Pilot on the record-breaking flight was Lockheed-Georgia Company's Chief Engineering Test Pilot, Frank Hadden.

Taking delivery of 12 new C-130Hs in 1978, the Royal Australian Air Force achieved the distinction of flying three basic models of the C-130—the "A," the "E," and the "H." The new C-130Hs took over the role of 12 C-130As which were phased out of duty after 20 years of outstanding RAAF service and more than 150,000 flight hours. Australia's squadron of C-130Es have accumulated around 200,000 hours. In honor of twenty years of Hercules, the RAAF put aloft the three planes in right photo (flying over the Blue Mountains). From front to back, they are the C-130A, the C-130E and the C-130H. Left photo, first two C-130Hs fly over Sydney Harbor on way to Base Richmond. (RAAF)

HERCULES PRODUCTION MILESTONES

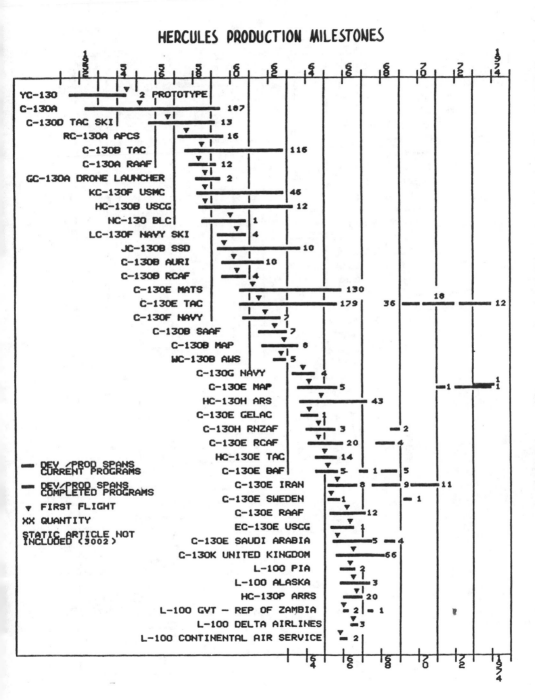

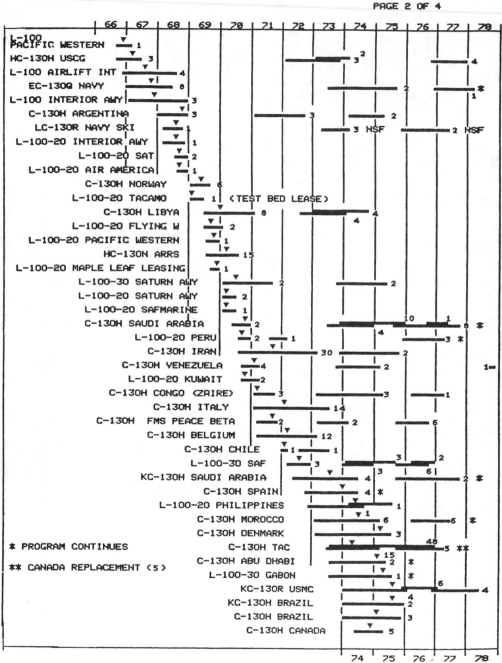

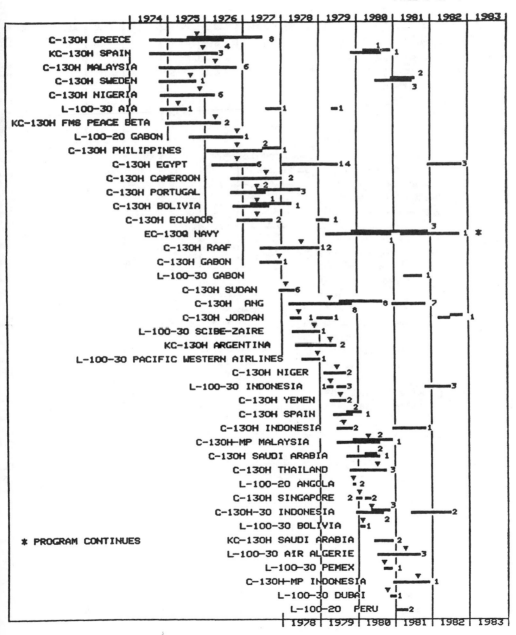

* PROGRAM CONTINUES

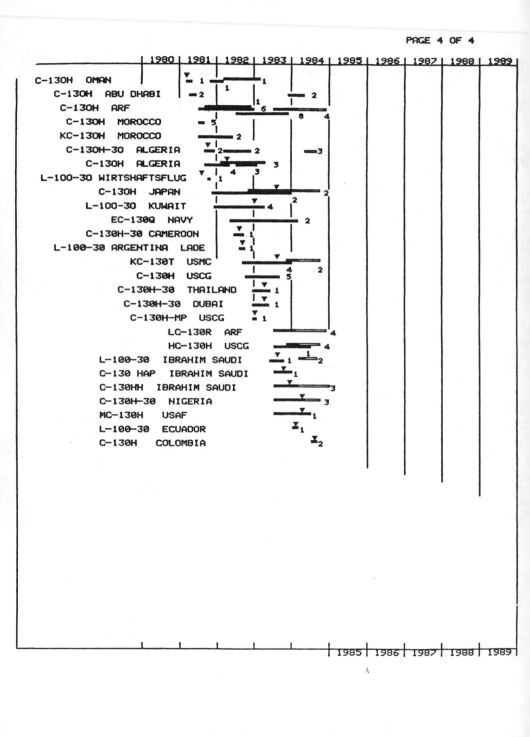

C-130 PERTINENT DATA – USAF AIRLIFT MODELS

		C-130A	C-130B	C-130E	C-130H
Maximum Ramp Weight (2.5g)	lb	124,200	135,000	155,000	155,000
Maximum Landing Weight – 5 fps	lb	124,200	135,000	155,000	155,000
Design Landing Weight – 9 fps	lb	96,000	118,000	130,000	130,000
Operating Weight	lb	61,842	69,376	73,563	80,606*
Maximum Payload (2.5g)	lb	35,000	34,840	45,579	38,536*
Fuel Capacity @ 6.5 lb/gal	lb	39,975	45,240	62,920	60,112*
Internal Tanks	gal	5,250	6,960	6,960	6,652*
External Tanks	gal	900	–	2,720	2,596*
Total Fuel Volume	gal	6,150	6,960	9,680	9,248*
Engine Model	–	T56-A-9	T56-A-7	T56-A-7	T56-A-15
Engine Takeoff Power, S.L., Std. Temp.	eshp	3,750	4,050	4,050	4,508
No. of Propeller Blades	–	3/4	4	4	4
Propeller Diameter	ft	15/13.5	13.5	13.5	13.5
Outboard Propeller/Ground Clearance	in	68/79	79.0	79.0	79.0
Inboard Propeller/Ground Clearance	in	60.6/69.6	69.6	69.6	69.6
Inboard Propeller/Fuselage Clearance	in	28.8/37.8	37.8	37.8	37.8
Wing Area	sq ft	1,745	1,745	1,745	1,745
Wing Loading	lb/sq ft	71.2	77.4	88.8	88.8
Wing Aspect Ratio	–	10.09	10.09	10.09	10.09
Cargo Compartment Floor Length	ft	41.0	41.0	41.0	41.0
Cargo Compartment Width	in	120.0	120.0	120.0	120.0
Cargo Compartment Height	in	108.0	108.0	108.0	108.0
Cargo Compartment Floor Area	sq ft	533	533	533	533
Cargo Compartment Usable Volume	cu ft	4,500	4,500	4,500	4,500
Wing Tip Turning Radius	ft	85.0	85.0	85.0	85.0
Nose Gear Turning Radius	ft	37.0	37.0	37.0	37.0
Wheel Base	ft	32.1	32.1	32.1	32.1
Main Gear Tire Size	–	20:00-20	20:00-20	20:00-20	20:00-20
Nose Gear Tire Size	–	12:50-16	12:50-16	12:50-16	39 x 13

Notes: Operating weights include external fuel tanks for C-130A, E, and H models.
Cargo compartment floor areas and usable volumes include ramp space.
T56-A-15 engine can produce 4910 eshp but is flat-rated to 4508 eshp for takeoff
in order not to exceed nacelle/wing structural capability.

*The FY84 and FY85 Air Reserve Forces versions include blue foam for fire suppression
in fuel tanks.
International versions do not include blue foam.

HERCULES CUSTOMER LIST
(Operators in 57 Countries)

C-130 Operators

Abu Dhabi Defense Force — C-130H's
Algerian Air Force — C-130H's, C-130H-30's
Argentine Air Force — C-130H's
Royal Australian Air Force — C-130A's, C-130E's, C-130H's
Belgian Air Force — C-130H's
Bolivian Air Force — C-130H's
Brazilian Air Force — C-130E's, C-130H's, KC-130H

Cameroon Air Force — C-130H's, C-130H-30
Canadian Forces — C-130B's, C-130E's, C-130H's
Chadian Air Force — C-130A's
Chilean Air Force — C-130H's
Colombian Air Force — C-130B's
Royal Danish Air Force — C-130H's
Dubai Air Force — (see commercial listing)
Ecuadorian Air Force — C-130H's
Egyptian Air Force — C-130H's
Gabonaise Air Force — C-130H (see commercial listing)
Hellenic Air Force (Greece) — C-130H's
Indonesian Air Force — C-130B's, C-130H's, C-130H-30's
    (see commercial listing)
Iranian Air Force — C-130E's, C-130H's
Israeli Air Force — C-130E's, C-130H's
Italian Air Force — C-130H's
Japan Air Self Defense Force — C-130H's (first delivery in late
    1983)
Jordanian Air Force — C-130B's, C-130H's
Kuwait Air Force — (see commercial listing)
Libyan Arab Air Force — C-130E's
Sultanate of Oman Air Force — C-130H
Royal Malaysian Air Force — C-130H's
Royal Moroccan Air Force — C-130H's
Royal New Zealand Air Force — C-130H's
Niger Air Force — C-130H's
Nigerian Air Force — C-130H's
Royal Norwegian Air Force — C-130B's, C-130E (see com-
    mercial listing)
Pakistan Air Force — C-130H's
Peruvian Air Force — (see commercial listing)
Philippine Air Force — C-130H's
Portuguese Air Force — C-130H's
Royal Saudi Air Force — C-130E's, C-130H's
Singapore Air Force — C-130B's, C-130H's
South African Air Force — C-130B's
Spanish Air Force — C-130H's
Sudanese Air Force — C-130H's
Royal Swedish Air Force — C-130E's, C-130H's
Royal Thai Air Force — C-130H's
Tunisian Air Force — C-130H's
Turkish Air Force — C-130E's
Royal Air Force — C-130K (designated C Mark 1, C Mark 2,
    C Mark 3)

U.S. Services:
- U.S. Air Force — C-130A's, C-130B's, C-130E's, C-130H's
- U.S. Air Reserve Forces — C-130A's, C-130B's, C-130E's, C-130H's
- U.S. Navy — C-130B's, C-130E's, C-130H's
- U.S. Marines — C-130B's, C-130H's
- U.S. Coast Guard — C-130B's, C-130E, C-130H's
- NASA — C-130B
- NOAA — C-130B

Venezuelan Air Force — C-130H's
Yemen Air Force — C-130H's
Zairian Air Force — C-130H's

Commercial Hercules Operators

Air Algerie — L-100-30's
Air Botswana — L-100-30's
Air Gabon — L-100-30
Angola Airlines (TAAG) — L-100-20's
Bolivian Air Transport (TAB) — L-100-30
Dubai Air Force — L-100-30
Echo Bay Mines, Ltd. — L-100-20
Ecuadorian Air Force — L-100-30
Gabonaise Air Force — L-100-20, L-100-30's
IKS Guernsey, Ltd. (Ireland) — L-100-30
Indonesian Air Force — L-100-30
Kuwait Air Force — L-100-20, L-100-30's
LADE, Lineas Aereas Del Estado — L-100-30
Mark Air — L-100-30
Northwest Territorial Airways — L-100-30
Pakistan Air Force — L-100
Pelita Air Services (Indonesia) — L-100-30's
Peruvian Air Force — L-100-20's
Petroleus Mexicanos (PEMEX) — L-100-30
Philippine Aerospace Development — L-100-20's
Safair Freighters — L-100-20, L-100-30's
Saudi Arabia — L-100-30's
SCIBE/Zaire — L-100-30
SFAIR (France) — L-100-30
Southern Air Transport — L-100-20, L-100-30's
St. Lucia Airways — L-100-20
Transamerica Airlines — L-100-30's
Uganda Air Cargo — L-100-30
United African Airlines — L-100-20's, L-100-30
Zaire Cargo — L-100-30

436/HERK: HERO OF THE SKIES

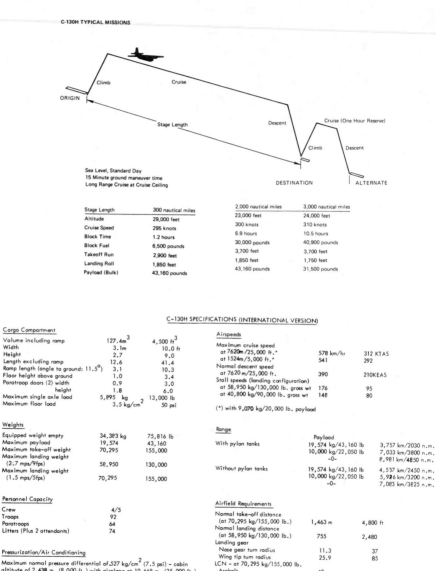

C-130H TYPICAL MISSIONS

Climb — Cruise
ORIGIN
Stage Length — Descent — Cruise (One Hour Reserve)
Climb — Descent
DESTINATION — ALTERNATE

Sea Level, Standard Day
15 Minute ground maneuver time
Long Range Cruise at Cruise Ceiling

		2,000 nautical miles	3,000 nautical miles
Stage Length	300 nautical miles		
Altitude	29,000 feet	23,000 feet	24,000 feet
Cruise Speed	295 knots	300 knots	310 knots
Block Time	1.2 hours	6.9 hours	10.5 hours
Block Fuel	6,500 pounds	30,000 pounds	40,900 pounds
Takeoff Run	2,900 feet	3,700 feet	3,700 feet
Landing Roll	1,850 feet	1,850 feet	1,750 feet
Payload (Bulk)	43,160 pounds	43,160 pounds	31,500 pounds

C-130H SPECIFICATIONS (INTERNATIONAL VERSION)

Cargo Compartment

Volume including ramp	127.4m³	4,500 ft³
Width	3.1m	10.0 ft
Height	2.7	9.0
Length excluding ramp	12.6	41.4
Ramp length (angle to ground: 11.5°)	3.1	10.3
Floor height above ground	1.0	3.4
Paratroop doors (2) width	0.9	3.0
height	1.8	6.0
Maximum single axle load	5,895 kg	13,000 lb
Maximum floor load	3.5 kg/cm²	50 psi

Weights

Equipped weight empty	34,383 kg	75,816 lb
Maximum payload	19,574	43,160
Maximum take-off weight	70,295	155,000
Maximum landing weight (2.7 mps/9fps)	58,950	130,000
Maximum landing weight (1.5 mps/5fps)	70,295	155,000

Personnel Capacity

Crew	4/5
Troops	92
Paratroops	64
Litters (Plus 2 attendants)	74

Pressurization/Air Conditioning

Maximum normal pressure differential of .527 kg/cm² (7.5 psi) - cabin altitude of 2,438 m. (8,000 ft.) with airplane at 10,668 m. (35,000 ft.)

Powerplants

Engines – Four Allison T56-A-15, 4,508 ESHP each
Propellers – Four-blade Hamilton Standard 54H60-117 hydromatic
Auxiliary Power Unit – supplies air for engine starting, ground air conditioning and ground AC power

Fuel

Internal capacity	26,344	6,960 U. S. gals.
Pylon tank capacity	10,295	2,720
Total fuel capacity	36,639	9,680
Single point refuel rate	2,270 lpm	600 U.S. gpm
Single point defuel rate	1,458	385
Jettison rate	2,060	550

Airspeeds

Maximum cruise speed		
at 7620m /25,000 ft.*	578 km/hr	312 KTAS
at 1524m/5,000 ft.*	541	292
Normal descent speed		
at 7620 m/25,000 ft.	390	210KEAS
Stall speeds (landing configuration)		
at 58,950 kg/130,000 lb. gross wt	176	95
at 40,800 kg/90,000 lb. gross wt	148	80

(*) with 9,070 kg/20,000 lb. payload

Range

	Payload	
With pylon tanks	19,574 kg/43,160 lb	3,757 km/2030 n.m.
	10,000 kg/22,050 lb	7,033 km/3800 n.m.
	-0-	8,981 km/4850 n.m.
Without pylon tanks	19,574 kg/43,160 lb	4,537 km/2450 n.m.
	10,000 kg/22,050 lb	5,926 km/3200 n.m.
	-0-	7,083 km/3825 n.m.

Airfield Requirements

Normal take-off distance (at 70,295 kg/155,000 lb.)	1,463 m	4,800 ft
Normal landing distance (at 58,950 kg/130,000 lb.)	755	2,480
Landing gear		
Nose gear turn radius	11.3	37
Wing tip turn radius	25.9	85
LCN – at 70,295 kg/155,000 lb.		
Asphalt	42	
Concrete	36	

Typical Assault Mission

Radius	926 km	500 n.m.
Payload	9,070 kg	20,000 lb
Take-off weight	52,203 kg	115,109 lb
Take-off distance	856 m	2,810 ft
Midpoint landing weight	47,949 kg	105,729 lb
Midpoint landing distance	680 m	2,230 ft

HERCULES PROGRAM MILESTONES

January, 1951	– USAF Tactical Air Command develops requirements for new tactical transport; conceptual studies initiated
February 2, 1951	– USAF Air Materiel Command issues Request for Proposals (RFP) to Boeing, Douglas, Fairchild, Lockheed
April, 1951	– Preliminary designs submitted by Lockheed to Air Force
July 2, 1951	– Lockheed named winner of competition, awarded contract for two YC-130A prototype aircraft
August, 1951	– Work started at Burbank on prototypes
September 19, 1952	– Air Force issues letter contract to Lockheed for seven C-130A aircraft
September 22, 1952	– First Georgia Company engineering personnel transferred to Lockheed-California to work on C-130
September 3, 1953	– Full scale wooden mockup arrives at Marietta after trip by ship from LA via Panama Canal to Savannah
April 21, 1954	– Definitive contract issued by USAF for 20 C-130As
August 23, 1954	– YC-130A No. 1002 makes first flight at Burbank
September 15, 1954	– Air Force issues letter contract for 48 C-130As
January 12, 1955	– Static test program started with number 3002
March 10, 1955	– First production C-130 (LAC No. 3001) rolls out at Marietta
April 7, 1955	– First production aircraft (No. 3001) makes first flight at Marietta
April 14, 1955	– On third flight of first production C-130A, fire erupts on wing after plane touches down at Dobbins AFB
August 10, 1955	– Air Force issues letter contract to Lockheed for 84 C-130As
November 26, 1955	– First flight of C-130A equipped with Aeroproducts propellers accompished on No. 3006
January 6, 1956	– C-130A No. 3005 delivered to USAF and flown to Eglin AFB, Fla., for Phase V, flight testing
February 6, 1956	– First flight of No. 3001 following fire
July 6, 1956	– Flight testing completed of Aeroproducts propellers on No. 3006
July 28, 1956	– C-130A No. 3003 delivered to Edwards AFB, Calif., for Phase IV testing
October 25, 1956	– C-130A No. 3005 delivered to TAC at Dayton. (First USAF fleet delivery.)
November 8, 1956	– Simulated TAC mission of 2026 miles flown utilizing No. 3011. Duration, 7:08 hours
December 9, 1956	– First C-130As delivered to TAC operational squadron at Ardmore AFB, Okla. (463rd Tactical Airlift Wing)
January 12, 1957	– First ski-equipped C-130–No. 3048–makes first flight
February 17, 1957	– The ski-equipped No. 3048 delivered to Air Force for snow evaluation testing at Bemidji, Minn.
November 8, 1957	– First flight recorded for Air Photo and Charting Service test bed airplane (No. 3019)
February 10, 1958	– New world record for ski-equipped airplane–124,000 pounds lift, established by C-130A at Bemidji Lake, Minnesota
November 20, 1958	– First C-130B (No. 3501) makes first flight

December 19, 1958   —   First C-130B delivered to Air Force

August 15, 1961   —   First flight of C-130E (No. 3609)

June 1, 1961   —   Delivery of first C-130E (No. 3609) to USAF

April 27, 1962   —   First fleet delivery of C-130E to USAF (No. 3651)

April 20-21, 1964   —   Longest first flight by a commercial aircraft—25 hours and one minute achieved by Lockheed-Georgia's L-382B commercial demonstrator Hercules (No. 3946)

November 19, 1964   —   First flight of C-130H (No. 4052 for New Zealand)

December, 1964   —   Maximum delivery rate of 18 C-130s per month

February 28, 1965   —   Delivery of first HC-130H to (No. 4037) to USAF ARRS

February 16, 1965   —   FAA certification of Commerical Hercules (Model 382 No. 3946)

March 24, 1965   —   Delivery of first C-130H to New Zealand

September 17, 1965   —   First flight of L-100 commercial Hercules (No. 4101)

September 30, 1965   —   Delivery of first L-100 (No. 4101) to Continental Air Services

May 1, 1968   —   1000th Hercules delivered (No. 4260) to U.S. Coast Guard

October 4, 1968   —   First flight of L-100-20 (No. 4300)

October 10, 1968   —   Delivery of first L-100-20 to Interior Airways

August 14, 1970   —   First flight of L-100-30 Super Hercules (No. 4388)

December 10, 1970   —   Delivery of first L-100-30 (No. 4388) to Saturn Airways

October 23, 1973   —   Delivery of first LC-130R ski Hercules (No. 4508) to the National Science Foundation/U.S. Navy

March 31, 1975   —   Delivery of first Advanced C-130H Hercules (FY '74 aircraft) to USAF (No. 4579)

May 28, 1976   —   1400th Hercules delivered (No. 4666) to USAF Military Airlift Command

April 6, 1978   —   1500th Hercules (No. 4771) delivered to Republic of Sudan

June 23, 1979   —   Air National Guard takes delivery of first C-130H model direct-from-factory (Oklahoma ANG)

September 15, 1980   —   First C-130H-30 delivered to Indonesian Air Force

December 12, 1980   —   1600th Hercules delivered to Indonesia

October 2, 1982   —   First C-130H delivered to Air Force Reserve (94th Tactical Airlift Wing, Dobbins AFB, Ga.)

October 23, 1983   —   Delivery of first KC-130T aerial refueler transport to U.S. Marine Corps Reserve

December 12, 1983   —   1700th C-130H Hercules delivered to Japan, 55th nation to operate the aircraft

December 20, 1984   —   First LC-130H ski Hercules delivered to New York Air National Guard (109th Tactical Airlift Group, Schenectady, New York)

March 29, 1985   —   Tunisia takes delivery of two C-130H's, 56th nation to operate the Hercules aircraft

October 15, 1985   —   1800th Hercules aircraft sale recorded. Purchaser of L-100-30, Air Gabon

June 20, 1986   —   First C-130H for Republic of China Air Force (Taiwan) — title transferred to USAF. (Taiwan 57th nation to operate Hercules)

(Accumulated flight time for Hercules fleet: More than 17,800,000)

FAREWELL to the HERK

by Maj Joe Tillman

Last month TAC lost its airlift force. Airlift aircraft and crews have been turned over to MAC, and especially in the case of the Hercules, we lost quite a workhorse.

The C-130, designed in 1951 to TAC specs, has been subdesignated the A, B, E, F, H, J, K, P and R — an indication of its versatility. The Herk has trash-hauled, air-dropped, flare-dropped, bombed, machine gunned, fire-suppressed, drone-launched, photo-mapped, missile-tracked, air evac'ed, Fulton-rescued, capsule-recovered and air-refueled. It has landed on dirt, mud, sand, snow, PSP and the USS Forrestal.

How about the trash-haulers themselves? Probably the most versatile aircrews anywhere, they have all the traits of fighter pilots with one exception — they're literate. What have they hauled? They have hauled (and air-dropped), food, Class 'A', guns, toilet paper, jeeps, tanks and paratroopers. They have extracted, ejected and kicked out loads of every size and description in every fashion imaginable. They have CDS'ed, LAPES'ed, GPES'ed and PLADS'ed — but most of all they have hauled. On notice so short most aircrews would still be standing in their jocks, Herky Haulers have lifted off with portable bridges

for the Dominican Republic, food and water for Peruvian earthquake victims, and hay bales for starving cattle in North Dakota. They have supplied the Marines with ammo at Khe Sanh (remember, "mortar-magnets"?), Africans with wheat in Mali and fighter pilots with beer at Phu Cat. Their spirits were lifted by the delivery of overdue mail to grateful grunts at Kham Duc, then suddenly saddened with the discovery that the outbound load would consist in part, of ugly seven-foot rubberized bags.

Trash-haulers have the thickest skins in the business. They have been cursed by the locals for being overpaid, oversexed and "over here." They have been overscheduled, poorly scheduled and unscheduled. They have been subjected to prop leaks, prop fluxes, and dual-rail rollers that don't. They invariably brief at 0330, have a cigarette and a coke for breakfast (if the machine isn't broken), then sit under the wing and wait to be loaded/unloaded/fixed/fueled/fragged/refragged — or cancelled.

Their departure is our loss. TAC won't be quite the same without them.

To hell with the rest of 'em, Herky — keep on haulin'. ➤

Reprinted from the TAC ATTACK of January, 1975, with permission.

INDEX

NOTE: Page numbers in italics indicate photographs.

hydrostatic testing, *122*, 131-132